WHO OWNS PSYCHOANALYSIS?

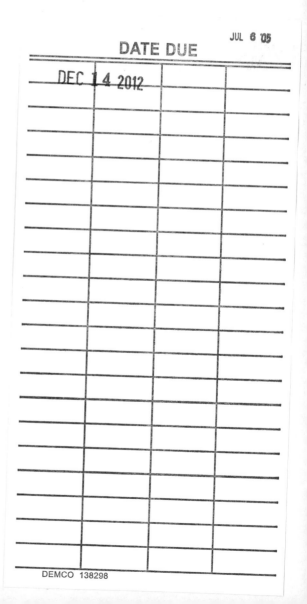

WHO OWNS PSYCHOANALYSIS?

Editor

ANN CASEMENT

KARNAC
LONDON   NEW YORK

First published in 2004 by
H. Karnac (Books) Ltd.
6 Pembroke Buildings, London NW10 6RE

British Library Cataloguing in Publication Data

A C.I.P. for this book is available from the British Library

   ISBN 1 85575 370 7

Edited, typeset and produced by The Studio Publishing Services Ltd,
Exeter EX4 8JN

Printed in Great Britain

10 9 8 7 6 5 4 3 2 1

www.karnacbooks.com

CONTENTS

EDITOR AND CONTRIBUTORS

Jorge Ahumada graduated with honours from the School of Medicine, University of Buenos Aires, Argentina in 1962. He is a Member of the Argentine Psychoanalytical Association, an Honorary Member of the British Psycho-Analytical Society, and was the Editor for Latin-America 1983–1988 of the *International Journal of Psychoanalysis*. He received the Mary S. Sigourney Award, New York, in 1996, and is the author of papers published in six languages and the book *The Logics of the Mind. A Clinical View* (Karnac, 2001).

Pearl Appel, PhD, has a BS in Chemistry, an MS in Biology, a PhD in Nutritional Sciences, and is a graduate of the National Psychological Association for Psychoanalysis (NPAP), where she is a senior member, a training and supervising analyst, and is on the Board of Trustees. She is legislative representative for psychoanalysis on the Joint Council for Mental Health Services Coalition, is currently President of the National Association for the Advancement of Psychoanalysis (NAAP), and is in private practice in New York City.

Bernard Burgoyne is a psychoanalyst, a founder of the Centre for Freudian Analysis and Research, a member of the London Society of the New Lacanian School, and a member of the European School of Psychoanalysis and the World Association of Psychoanalysis. He was educated at the University of Cambridge, the London School of Economics, and the University of Paris. He is Professor of Psychoanalysis and Head of the Centre for Psychoanalysis in the Institute for Health and Social Science Research at Middlesex University. He has published many articles on psychoanalysis, amongst which are "Autism and topology", in B. Burgoyne (Ed.), *Drawing the Soul*, Rebus, 2000; "What causes structure to find a place in love?, in Glynos & Stavrakakis (Eds.), *Lacan and Science*, Karnac, 2003; and "From the letter to the Matheme: Lacan's scientific methods", in Rabate (Ed.), *The Cambridge Companion to Jacques Lacan*, Cambridge University Press, 2003.

Ann Casement BSc, FRAI, is a Training Analyst at the Association of Jungian Analysts which she represents on the Executive Committee of the International Association for Analytical Psychology (IAAP). She is also on the Programme Committee for the 2004 IAAP International Congress in Barcelona. She is a member of the British Psychological Society, the National Association for the Advancement of Psychoanalysis, and a founding member of The International Neuro-Psychoanalysis Society. She is currently conducting research into statutory regulation at London University and writes for *The Economist* and professional journals. Her last book *Carl Gustav Jung* was published by Sage in 2001.

Frank Cioffi is Honorary Research Professor of Philosophy at the University of Kent. He was born and raised in the United States but received his University education in England. He has taught at the Universities of Singapore, Kent, Berkeley and Essex, and is the author of *Wittgenstein on Freud and Frazer* (1998) and *Freud and the Question of Pseudo-Science* (1998).

Morris Eagle is a Professor at the Derner Institute of Advance Psychological Studies at Adelphi University. He is on the faculty of the NYU Postdoctoral Program in Psychotherapy and Psychoanalysis, Toronto Institute for Contemporary Psychoanalysis, and the NYU Psychoanalytic Institute of the New York University School of Medicine. He is a Diplomate in Psychoanalysis and has a part-time practice. He is the author of more than 150 journal articles and has authored *Recent Developments in Psychoanalysis: A Critical Evaluation*, and co-edited *The Interface Between Psychology and Psychoanalysis and Psychoanalysis as Health Care*. His most recent journal articles are: (with D. L. Wolitzky and J. Wakefield in 2001) "Knowledge and authority in the psychoanalytic situation: A critique of the 'new view' in psychoanalysis". *Journal of the American Psychoanalytic Situation*; (with M. Parrish in 2003) "Attachment to the therapist". *Psychoanalytic Psychology*, 20(2): 271–286; "Clinical implications of attachment theory" (2003). *Psychoanalytic Inquiry*, 23(1): 27–53; and, in press, "The postmodern turn in psychoanalysis: A critique". *Psychoanalytic Psychology*.

Peter Fonagy, PhD, FBA is Freud Memorial Professor of Psychoanalysis and Director of the Sub-Department of Clinical Health Psychology at University College, London. He is Chief Executive of the Anna Freud Centre, London. He is Consultant to the Child and Family Programme at the Menninger Department of Psychiatry at Baylor College of Medicine. He is a clinical psychologist and a training and supervising analyst in the British Psycho-Analytical Society in child and adult analysis. His clinical interests centre around issues of borderline psychopathology, violence and early attachment relationships. His work attempts to integrate empirical research with psychoanalytic theory. He holds a number of important positions, which include chairing the Research Committee of the International Psychoanalytical Association, and Fellowship of the British Academy. He has published over 200 chapters and articles and has authored or edited several books. His most recent books include *Attachment Theory and Psychoanalysis* (published 2001 by Other Press), *What Works For Whom? A Critical Review of Treatments for Children and Adolescents* (with M. Target, D. Cottrell, J. Phillips, & Z. Kurtz—published 2002 by Guilford), *Affect Regulation, Mentalization, Attachment and the Development of the Self* (with G. Gergely, E. Jurist, and M. Target—published 2002 by Other Press), *Psychoanalytic Theories: Perspectives from Developmental Psychopathology* (with M. Target—published 2003 by Whurr Publications) and *Psychotherapy for Borderline Personality Disorder: Mentalization Based Treatment* (with A. Bateman—Oxford University Press, 2004).

Adolf Grünbaum is the Andrew Mellon Professor of Philosophy of Science, Chairman of the Center for Philosophy of Science, and Research Professor of Psychiatry at the University of Pittsburgh (Pennsylvania, USA). His books and many articles deal with the philosophy of physics, the theory of scientific rationality, the philosophy of psychiatry, and the critique of theism. Professor Grünbaum's offices include the presidency of the American Philosophical Association (Eastern Division), and of the Philosophy of Science Association (two terms). He is a Fellow of the American Academy of Arts & Sciences and a Laureate of the international Academy of Humanism. In 1985, he delivered the Gifford Lectures at the University of St Andrews in Scotland, as well as the Werner Heisenberg Lecture to the Bavarian Academy of Sciences in Munich. In June 2003, he delivered the three Leibniz Lectures at the University of Hannover, Germany. He is the recipient of a 1985 "Senior US Scientist" Humboldt Prize, and of Italy's 1989 "Fregene Prize" for science (Rome, Italy). All four prior recipients of this Prize, which is awarded by the Italian Parliament, were Nobel laureates in one of the natural sciences. In May 1990, Yale University awarded him the Wilbur Lucius Cross Medal for outstanding achievement.

R. D. Hinshelwood is a Member of the British Psycho-Analytical Society, and a Fellow of the Royal College of Psychiatrists. He was previously Clinical Director of The Cassel Hospital and is currently Professor, Centre for Psychoanalytic Studies, University of Essex. He authored *A Dictionary of Kleinian Thought* (1989), and *Clinical Klein* (1995). He has written widely on therapeutic communities, and the psychoanalysis of organizations (*Thinking about Institutions* (2001)); and published a book on psychoanalytic ethics, *Therapy or Coercion* (1997).

Pearl King, MSc. (Psych.) is an Honorary Member, Training and Supervising Psychoanalyst, former President of the British Psycho-Analytical Society and Honorary Secretary of the International Psychoanalytical Association. She served as Secretary to the Sponsoring Committee of the Finnish Study Group with Donald Winnicott as Chairman and is an Honorary Member of the Finnish Psychoanalytical Society. She co-edited, with Riccardo Steiner, *The Freud/Klein Controversies 1941–1945* and is the editor and compiler of *No Ordinary Psychoanalyst: The Exceptional Contributions of John Rickman* (Karnac 2003). Pearl King received the Sigourney award 1992 for her contributions to psychoanalysis.

Darian Leader is a psychoanalyst practising in London. He is a member of the Centre for Freudian Analysis and Research and the author of numerous publications on psychoanalysis. His books include: *Why Do Women Write More Letters Than They Post?*; *Freud's Footnotes*; *Stealing the Mona Lisa, What Art Stops Us from Seeing*, all of which are published by Faber & Faber. His most recent publication is a contribution to the *Cambridge Companion to Lacan*, edited by Jean-Michel Rabaté (Cambridge, 2003).

Dany Nobus is a Senior Lecturer in Psychology and Psychoanalytic Studies at Brunel University, where he directs the MA Programme in Psychoanalysis and Contemporary Society. He is also an Adjunct Professor of Sociology at the University of Massachusetts-Boston and a Faculty Member in the Department of Psychiatry at Creighton University Medical School in Omaha. Apart from being the editor-in-chief of *Journal for Lacanian Studies*, he is the author of *Jacques Lacan and the Freudian Practice of Psychoanalysis*, as well as numerous papers on the history, theory, and practice of psychoanalysis.

Michael Pokorny is a psychiatrist, psychoanalyst, and psychotherapist who was in private practice in London for thirty-one years. He led the formation of the UK Council for Psychotherapy and the launch of the National Register of Psychotherapists. He has published on a number of psychotherapy topics, including theoretical, political, and ethical papers. He has been an editorial adviser to the *British Journal of Psychotherapy* since it began in 1985, and acts as external examiner for the Gestalt Psychotherapy Training Institute. He was co-editor of *The Handbook of Psychotherapy* (London, Routledge, 1993). His special interests are couple psychoanalytic psychotherapy and holocaust studies.

Paul Roazen was educated in political philosophy at Harvard College (class of 1958), University of Chicago, and Magdalen College, Oxford. After receiving his Ph.D. in Government from Harvard in 1965, he continued teaching there until moving in 1971 to York University in Toronto, Canada; in 1995 he became Professor Emeritus in Political and Social Science. He has published seventeen books that have been translated into more than half a dozen languages. His titles include *Freud and His Followers, Helene Deutsch*, and *Oedipus in Britain: Edward Glover and the Struggle Over Klein*. Most recently he authored *The Historiography of Psychoanalysis, Political Theory and the Psychology of the Unconscious, On the Freud Watch: Public Memoirs*, and *Oedipus in Italy: Edoardo Weiss and the House that Freud Built*.

Elisabeth Roudinesco is a writer, historian and psychoanalyst, whose work has been translated into 20 languages. Member of the *Ecole Freudienne de Paris* from 1969 to 1981, she has a PhD in literature and a *Doctorat d'Etat* in History. She has taught a longstanding post-graduate seminar in the history of psychoanalysis at the Ecoles des Hautes Etudes en Sciences Sociales and at Paris VII, where she currently teaches. She is vice president of the International Society for the History of Psychiatry and Psychoanalysis, and a regular contributor to *Le Monde*. Her principal publications in English include: *Jacques Lacan and Co. A History of Psychoanalysis in France*. (Jeffrey Mehlman, trans.), (London: Free Associations, 1990); *Théroigne de Méricourt: A Melancholic Woman during the French Revolution* (Martin Thom, trans.), (London: Verso, 1991); *Jacques Lacan: Outline of a Life, History of a System of Thought* (Barbara Bray, trans.), (New York: Columbia University Press, 1997); *Why Psychoanalysis?* (Rachel Bowlby, trans.), (New York: Columbia University Press, 2001); and, with Jacques Derrida, *De quoi demain . . . Dialogue* (Paris: Fayard, 2002) (translation forthcoming with Stanford University Press).

Sonu Shamdasani is a historian of psychology and a Research Associate of the Wellcome Trust Centre for the History of Medicine at University College London. He is the author of a number of works, most recently *Jung and the Making of Modern Psychology: The Dream of a Science*, (Cambridge University Press, 2003).

Mark Solms is the Hon. Lecturer in Neurosurgery at St Bartholomew's and the Royal London School of Medicine, director of the Neuro-Psychoanalysis Centre, Lecturer in Psychology at University College London, Professor of Neuropsychology at the University of

Cape Town, and Director of the Neuro-Psychoanalysis Center of the New York Psychoanalytic Institute. He is an Associate Member of the British Psycho-Analytical Society, Honorary Member of the New York Psychoanalytic Society and Member of the British Neuropsychological Society. He has published widely in both neuroscientific and psychoanalytic journals. His book *The Neuropsychology of Dreams* (1997) was a landmark contribution to both fields. He is co-editor of the journal *Neuro-Psychoanalysis,* and co-chairperson of the International Neuro-Psychoanalysis Society. He received the "International Psychiatrist" award from the American Psychiatric Association in 2001, and his book *Clinical Studies in Neuro-Psychoanalysis* (with Karen Kaplan-Solms) won the NAAP's Gradiva Award (Best Book, Science Category) in 2001. He has recently published *The Brain and the Inner World: An Introduction to the Neurosciences of Subjective Experience* with Oliver Turnbull.

Thomas Szasz A.B., M.D., D.Sc. (Hon.), L.H.D. (Hon.), is Professor of psychiatry emeritus, State University of New York. He is the author of thirty books, among them *The Myth of Mental Illness* (1961) and, most recently, *Liberation By Oppression: A Comparative Study of Slavery and Psychiatry* (New Brunswick, NJ: Transactions, 2002). Dr Szasz is widely recognized as the world's foremost critic of psychiatric coercions and excuses. He maintains that just as we reject using theological assertions about people's religious states (heresy) as justification for according them special treatment, we ought to reject using medical–psychiatric–psychological assertions about people's mental states (mental illness) as justification for according them special legal treatment. Dr Szasz has received many awards for his defence of individual liberty and responsibility threatened by this modern form of totalitarianism masquerading as medicine. A frequent and popular lecturer, he has addressed professional and lay groups, and has appeared on radio and television in North, Central, and South America, as well as in Australia, Europe, Japan, and South Africa. His books have been translated into every major language.

Mary Target, PhD is a Senior Lecturer in Psychoanalysis at University College, London, and an Associate Member of the British Psycho-Analytical Society. She is Professional Director of the Anna Freud Centre, Member of the Curriculum and Scientific Commitees,

Chairman of the Research Committee of the British Psychoanalytic Society, and Chairman of the Working Party on Psychoanalytic Education of the European Psychoanalytic Federation. She is Course Organizer of the UCL MSc in Psychoanalytic Theory, and Academic Course Organizer of the UCL/Anna Freud Centre Doctorate in Child and Adolescent Psychotherapy. She is on the editorial board of several journals including the *International Journal of Psycho-Analysis*, and she is Joint Series Editor for psychoanalytic books, Whurr Publishers, and an Associate Editor for the New Library of Psychoanalysis, Routledge. She has active research collaborations in many countries in the areas of developmental psychopathology and psychotherapy outcome. Her most recent books include *Evidence-Based Child Mental Health: A Comprehensive Review of Treatment Interventions* (with P. Fonagy, D. Cottrell, J. Phillips, & Z. Kurtz—published 2002 by Guilford), *Psychoanalytic Theories: Perspectives from Developmental Psychopathology* (with P. Fonagy—published 2003 by Whurr Publications) and *Affect Regulation, Mentalization and the Development of the Self* (with P. Fonagy, G. Gergely, & E. Jurist—published 2002 by Other Press), which received the Gradiva Prize of the American Psychology and Psychotherapy Institute for Best Theoretical and Clinical Contribution of 2003.

Jerome C. Wakefield (Ph.D., University College, Berkeley, 2001; D.S.W., University College, Berkeley, 1984) is Professor, School of Social Work; Core Faculty Member, Institute for Health, Health Care Policy and Aging Research; and Affiliate Research Faculty, Center for Cognitive Studies, all at Rutgers University, and Lecturer in Psychiatry at the Columbia University College of Physicians and Surgeons. He holds the MSW in clinical social work, MA in Mathematics with a speciality in Logic and Methodology of Science, the DSW in social work, and he has recently completed a second doctorate in Philosophy with a speciality in philosophy of mind, all from Berkeley. His writing focuses on the conceptual foundations of the mental health field as well as other conceptual topics in the philosophy of psychiatry, psychology, social work, and psychoanalysis. A major area of recent work has been clarification of the concept of mental disorder (versus non-disordered problems of living) and using that analysis to identify invalidities in the *DSM-IV*'s criteria for diagnosing disorder.

INTRODUCTION

The idea for this book was first suggested to me in 2000 by Oliver Rathbone, the Managing Director of Karnac, after the United Kingdom Council for Psychotherapy's (UKCP) AGM of that year. As Chair of the UKCP, I had to steer the AGM through lengthy debates to do with the proposed designation of "psychoanalyst" in its Register of sixty-three UKCP registrants from one of its Sections. This title, or "label" as it is termed at that organization, had not previously appeared in its Register. It was clear to me that it would be worthwhile producing a book on entitlement, particularly with the statutory regulation of psychotherapy in the air, but, although I was interested in the idea of working on a book of this kind, I did not have the time to do so then. Oliver again mentioned the idea at the end of 2002 and, as I still thought it would be an interesting project to work on, I agreed to be the editor.

The book has been divided up into four sections: academic, history, politics, and science, and each of the eighteen chapters has been allocated to the most appropriate section. Many of them would fit into more than one and the choice as to which was most fitting was done on the basis of the predominant theme of each chapter. As the content of some of the chapters is critical of the

International Psychoanalytic Association (IPA) and the British Psycho-Analytical Society (BP-AS), I made several efforts to invite prominent officials of those organizations to be their spokespersons. It eventually became clear that, as it was put to me, there was "no-one, unfortunately, willing to do it". The writer of the e-mail informing me of this went on to say that they had checked with those who are particularly interested in these issues. Apparently, there is much thinking going on about them but my respondent suggested "that the timing of the invitation may not be right".

Although an "official" response from the IPA or the BP-AS was not forthcoming, the book includes contributions from several eminent members of both organizations. In any case, the scope of this book incorporates not only political issues but also other contributions that give some idea of where psycho-analysis fits into the history of ideas.

It is important to note here that the contributions to the book are concentrated in certain geographical areas, i.e. Western Europe, the United States of America, and Latin America. This does not indicate a lack of awareness of the importance of other parts of the world where psycho-analysis is a thriving concern, for instance, Africa, Australia, India, Israel, Japan, Korea, and Russia. I myself originate in India, and have worked in several of the countries that are not represented here. The only reason for their omission is the pressing one of lack of space.

I would like to express my gratitude to all the contributors who have taken part in this project and to say that it has been a great pleasure working with them. They are: Jorge Ahumada, Pearl Appel, Bernard Burgoyne, Frank Cioffi, Morris Eagle, Peter Fonagy, Adolf Grünbaum, Robert Hinshelwood, Pearl King, Darian Leader, Dany Nobus, Michael Pokorny, Paul Roazen, Elisabeth Roudinesco, Sonu Shamadasani, Mark Solms, Thomas Szasz, Mary Target, and Jerome Wakefield.

Finally, a special thank you to Oliver Rathbone.

Ann Casement, Editor
April 2004

PART I
ACADEMIC

CHAPTER ONE

Pathways for psychoanalysis

Bernard Burgoyne

Introduction

N o one today seriously asks: "Who owns physics?" Claims about patent rights in science exist—thankfully—only around its edges. Any claims for "ownership" or privilege in the field of psychoanalysis needs to be supported by—at least—a serious consideration of the place of science within the psychoanalytic field. Minimal desiderata for groupings of psychoanalysts would equally include that they have a view of their own history, a critical distance from their own theories, an engagement with questions of scientific method, and an awareness of the consequentiality of their own work. These considerations would seem not to be optional, but forced by the place that Freud gave to psychoanalysis. And any agency completely outside of psychoanalysis would lack these desiderata, by definition. Any orthodoxy or standardization goes against the grain, in psychoanalysis as in science.

Psychoanalysis has drawn on a particular environment for the formulation of its concepts and its techniques, and it needs in some ways a similar environment to provide the conditions for its development. There seem to be at least three elements involved in the construction of such a facilitating environment. The first is quite complex: it arises from the nature of psychoanalytic work, and originates in Freud's concern to find a response to human suffering in traditions that valued listening and speech—in the nineteenth century reception of certain research programmes in social philosophy, those that he found for instance in his reading of Hume, and of Socrates. The second is allied to this, but focused more directly on questions of technique: it concerns the way in which certain effects of what was initially hypnotic, and later, psychoanalytic, clinical practice display a causation by complexes of words. The third is what in some respects could be seen as the most straightforward: it involves the construction of desiderata for the institutional organization of psychoanalysis. A plausible formulation for this last condition would be this: a school or institute responsible for training psychoanalysts needs to have within it a range of experienced analysts who, together with more junior members, provide theoretical and clinical seminars and the access to supervision and personal analysis that such training requires.

There are a number of aspects of these dependencies that are quite straightforward. In many other ways, however, the theme is made up of difficult issues that are of some degree of obscurity. Moreover, little agreement exists in the field as to how to distinguish and differentiate the simpler aspects of this question from the more intricate ones. The relation between theory and technique has never been crystal clear in psychoanalysis; the internal structure that an analytical school might best equip itself with is not evident; and the central question of the position of the analyst—and the subsequent conditions under which the analyst directs the work—are all subjects of a great amount of dispute. In these circumstances, everyday questions of the organization of teaching, or of the gaining of clinical experience, or of recommendations to the analyst in training as regards his or her personal analysis, all of these issues become surrounded and influenced by problems that have been only partially formulated. Problems that have been insufficiently addressed then come to hinder the clear formulation of what psychoanalysis is, what its consequences are, and how it relates to other fields, particularly those of public health and the sciences.

Complex questions conjoined to inadequate formulations of simpler ones: this is a formulation that can describe much of the contemporary questioning of psychoanalysis. There are in this field many difficult questions that require much research—such as what it is that the analyst needs to know, and how this relates to the more fundamental question of what it is that the subject in analysis knows, but as yet only unconsciously. At the same time there are formulations and proposals put forward about the nature of psychoanalysis that would be ridiculed in any other field: that the length of a session should be fixed at fifty minutes, or forty-five, or thirty, or twenty—and that five minutes above or below such a norm changes the nature of the work; that five sessions a week is to be demanded, or three, or one, or six, or ten—and that any divergence from such a norm changes the nature of the work. There are many serious themes—the nature of transference, the relation between transference and interpretation, the question of the structure of phantasy—whose formulation is obscured and weakened by giving such comparative prominence to relatively minor questions of the details of the analytical setting.

There are questions here of knowledge—of theoretical knowledge and clinical knowledge and their relation; of the knowledge of the analyst and the knowledge of the patient, and the different places that they occupy in the analytical work. This theme of knowledge naturally raises a further question: that of the relation that psychoanalysis has to science. One might have expected that all the various schools included in the domain of psychoanalysis would have worked within a frame that appeals to the structure and functioning of the sciences. In psychoanalysis, however, it has been more frequently the case that critical analysis—the formulation and testing of research hypotheses throughout the field—has been given second place, while the focusing on contentious issues has allowed argumentation to replace an interest in science. There have been some moments in the history of the psychoanalytic movement when this has not been the case—where the relation between knowledge and clinical work has been given some serious consideration—and these high points constitute the strength of the analytical tradition. It would throw considerable light on a range of current claims for ownership and authority in the field of psychoanalysis if some of these crucial moments and periods could be revisited.

The tension between science and controversy has sometimes led to scientific advance; it has also sometimes led to the imposition of dogma and the perpetuation of dispute. In the light of such contro-versies, let us try to construct a thought experiment so as to see what might be involved in some of these disputatious issues. Consider a class of psychoanalysts—with or without trainees—that is engaged in a series of discussions about the foundations of their work. Given that any psychoanalytic school is called upon to formulate and maintain the methods and conceptual structures of psychoanalysis—as well as to train new psychoanalysts—it would seem that such discussion would be a necessary element of the workings of any such institute. Or at least it would seem so if psychoanalysis makes any claim to having the structure of a sci-ence. Such a claim needs to be considered by psychoanalysts, and having been discussed, it then deserves rejection or support, reasons being given in either case. If scientific knowledge is consti-tuted by, among other things, an engagement in critical discussion, then an institution that maintains some relation to science needs to have arrangements that guarantee that such criticism is not swept away by the vagaries of what usually presents itself as orthodox opinion. This internal discussion, then, is the first step in the consti-tution of an ethics that can relate psychoanalysis to science, and such an ethics is to be expressed as a series of demands as to the desired structure for such an institute.

In this kind of school, then, the discussion might proceed as fol-lows. In order to distinguish the speakers I have allocated as names a series of Greek letters. The discussion starts in a lively way—with an appeal to the functioning of creative imagination in science.

Epsilon: "A student who is going to be a valid technician will discover anew for himself by scientific method what Freud discov-ered."

The very best students in any domain might well be expected to do this. However, such an expectation calls into question the nature of scientific explanation and its relation to empirical work; in partic-ular, it raises some questions about Freud's view of the methods of science, and his recommendations for the use of the procedures of science in psychoanalysis. Within this context of such a series of debates it would seem that almost any discussion of psychoanalytic practice would lead—immediately or via mediate steps—to an investigation of the nature of science. The actual development of science, however, is not uniform, not untroubled, not guaranteed in advance. Accordingly, this class, as well as containing optimists, puts forward some pessimistic views about the functioning of any current of scientific investigation in the domain of psychoanalysis.

Delta: "For some years past, there have occurred transference eruptions so powerful that they not only make scientific discussion impossible, but reduce analytical training to an unscientific level."

If the current structure of clinical discussion were to have been affected in this way, the question arises as to whether that is the end of the matter—and the end of the consideration of psychoanalysis as a science—or whether rescue procedures need to be introduced that might re-establish the required engagements with science. But perhaps such kinds of change are beyond the realistic resources of the organization: perhaps a scientific organization of things is beyond the ability of this kind of institute.

Beta: "Scientific procedures are not counsels of perfection, they are only special developments of reality testing".

Advice of this kind seems to recommend focusing on down-to-earth practical problems. And of course there are difficulties, even with such advice: there may be differences between what one person perceives as the reality of the situation and a series of judgements made by someone else. In particular, there may be differences even in the most central areas of what it is that constitutes appropriate and effective forms of analytical technique. But, as regards the question of proper or variant forms of technique, a dispute about such issues cannot be settled by either the imposition of standards or a dictation of ethics.

Gamma: "For who is to decide whether a particular extension is justifiable or a particular correction necessary? Only if we had an omniscient leader who could impose his opinion on us, or if by some miracle we all of us always arrived at the same conclusion, could this difficulty be avoided. And neither of these ways out seems likely to be offered us."

The inability of decisions made by a nominated authority to solve problems of this kind leaves open the possible alternative of a wide ranging series of discussions operating within a specially commissioned forum. This structure might even be extended so as to compose the basic training format of the institute.

Alpha: "Gamma has put forward the suggestion that the analytic institute might form an open forum where current analytical theories and techniques are taught without giving preference to any one among them."

However, the existence of delicate training formats—of supervision and of theoretical and clinical references to an individual's analysis—raises a range of difficulties, and even the practice of psychoanalysis can well be a hindrance to the development of psychoanalytical theory in this way.

Alpha continues: "Such a change of programme, far from diminishing the present difficulties, presents the institute with a whole series of new problems."

Problems however, are not a disincentive to theoretical work—quite the contrary. New problems, provided that they resolve some old ones, are often welcome within a scientific project. It may even be that some of the new problems are superior to the old; but Alpha doubts that this is the case. Assuming the impossibility of including absolutely every orientation to analytical work—and in a field as small as psychoanalysis, this is actually by no means impossible—raises some grounds for pessimism here too.

Alpha: "Where would the line be drawn between current theories to be included in the teaching programme and others that are disregarded?"

In the situation as Alpha presents it, there seems to be a lack of appropriate or scientific methods of choice. Scientists, on the other hand, make such choices every day: the choices are made by the theories, when they are put in relation to empirical results. In this context clinical results would have to be assessed in some way, in relation to the theoretical presuppositions of the analyst who is directing the work. This assessment would also involve the consideration of alternative ways of conducting the work. For this reason alone not only the methodology of the sciences, but also the details of analytical technique would, it seems, need to be explicitly structured into the programme of the institute.

Beta: "Gamma noted that the details of individual technique 'continue to be wrapped in unholy mystery'. Unless this mystery is substantially reduced I do not see how we are to find out what the limits are within which technique may vary and yet retain validity."

One of the discussions that a school of psychoanalysts needs to hold within it is that of the relation of psychoanalytic theory to psychoanalytic technique. It could follow from such a discussion that certain proposals for variations in technique are assessed as well-founded, and others as more speculative. Variations of technique have actually been proposed at certain periods of the history of psychoanalysis, and any assessment of technique relies on some solution being to hand as regards this difficult problem of the relation of theory and technique. The problems of analytical practice, in this perspective, demand an appraisal of a range of alternative formulations of psychoanalytic concepts, and a study of their corresponding implications for forms of technique.

Gamma: "One of the main causes of our trouble is a confusion over the relation between findings and theories on the one hand and technical procedure on the other. I have already remarked that people are inclined to say of their opponents: 'His views are wrong so his technique must be wrong'.".

Criticism of views, in psychoanalysis as in any science, is widespread, but this is not always true within a training institute. The central importance of psychoanalytic concepts is often lost sight of—sometimes discarded—in favour of a supposed standardizing of analytic practice.

Delta: "Many young analysts are quite frankly afraid to admit an interest in theory lest it should be construed as a sign of lack of conviction."

Any toleration given to divergent views and to critical commentaries is often done only under the aegis of a claim to sound clinical technique.

Gamma: "If his technique is valid, then any gaps in his knowledge (and there are sure to be many) and any mistakes in his deductions (and they are not likely to be few) will have only what I may call a *local* effect, they will not lead to any *generalized* distortion of the analytical picture."

Such a proposal moves the stress away from questions of the validity of a body of knowledge, and on to the question of the validity of technique. Unfortunately, the two cannot be separated as easily as this. Any claim for the soundness of technique needs to be related to the question of the aims and end of psychoanalysis, as well as to the whole body of its conceptualization. As for the residual scientific problems, Gamma hopes that they can be addressed.

Gamma: "It will moreover always be possible for the gaps to be filled in and the mistakes corrected."

Is this good scientific methodology—this filling in of gaps? A question of this kind presupposes quite a lot of investigation of the structure of scientific theory: it would seem that, yet again, the nature of science is being appealed to, even in the midst of a discussion focused on technique. Assuming that the rudiments of such a discussion are seen to be lacking, what kind of account of proposals would remain? What kind of hypotheses would be used in Gamma's proposal for a technique-based construction of knowledge? And what kinds of hypotheses should be allowed in the process?

Kappa: "Alpha's hypothesis implies an arbitrary division between the intellectual and emotional development in young children."

Often it is not clear in such commentaries what kind of criticism is being made, whether it is one based on theoretical consequences, on some notion of clinical validity, on inconsistency of theory, or on a conflict with facts. Kappa, in continuing, makes this clear.

Kappa: "This is scientifically untenable and in contradiction of all the observable facts and to the understanding of the data which analysis has given us."

Three criticisms are made here in the same phrase. They all presuppose much about the nature of science, about the relation of theory to technique, and about the place of understanding in science. All of them seem to presume some notion of how one gains access to truth. Although they are not presented explicitly, claims are being made here as to the nature of science and research.

Correspondingly, much is being demanded of the individual analyst.

Delta: "All analysts should regard themselves as research workers."

I should explain that a German sense of research is being invoked here; that is, what is being referred to in this context is foundational, as well as empirical, research. The resources needed for this work should be provided by a school—but still, even individual analysts can find themselves confronted with a demand.

Delta: "In no other branch of science is it more vital for the individual worker to retain his independence of mind, to prove and re-prove for himself and to form his judgements on the results within his own experience."

So, then, here we are again with a challenge and with the theme from the beginning. Psychoanalysis needs somehow to be involved with scientific method, with proof and scientific deduction. Some familiarity with the works of Karl Popper, of Thomas Kuhn, and of the much lamented Imre Lakatos—who is probably already blushing at the development of this dialogue—could well be asked for. What is demanded here, in fact, is a reopening of Freud's pathway towards psychoanalysis as a science.

This discussion actually took place: the discussion is a collage of contributions from members of one analytical school, the British Psycho-Analytical Society. When the coding of the contributors is taken away one has the following: *Alpha*: Anna Freud; *Beta*: Marjorie Brierley; *Gamma*: James Strachey; *Delta*: Edward Glover; *Epsilon*: Ella Sharpe; *Kappa*: Melanie Klein. Most of the interventions are taken from the "Memoranda on Technique" that were contributed between February and November in 1943 as part of the resolution of the theoretical and clinical disputes current within the British Psycho-Analytical Society at that time. The intervention by Melanie Klein came somewhat later, in March 1944, but was still prepared as part of this series of discussions (for all these interventions see King & Steiner, 1991). And Glover's second intervention is taken from his comments on his investigation of problems of technique in Britain in the 1930s (published at the beginning of the following decade as Glover, 1940), as are his final contributions to this dialogue.

One of the most productive periods in the history of the British Psycho-Analytical Society generated these critical discussions. Such a mixture of problems, consisting of ranges of clarity together with regions of obscurity, is encountered in any developing science. Whether or not psychoanalysis is, by this indication, something that can bear the hallmark of a science is a question that still needs to be answered. Despite formulations put forward, initially by Freud, concerning this question of the relations of psychoanalysis to science—and despite further work done after Freud, most notably by Hermann, by Bion, and by Lacan—the idea that the consideration of these issues is a forced step, and not optional for psychoanalysis, is looked on by most psychoanalysts in the Anglo-Saxon world as a proposal that is both far-fetched and inappropriate. But some of the most central—and unsolved—problems in the field require that this step be taken.

At the Congress of the International Psychoanalytical Association in Berlin in 1922, Freud set a Prize Essay on a topic that he took to be central to psychoanalysis. It was on the relation of theory to practice. More specifically, its title was "The relation of psychoanalytical technique to psychoanalytical theory", and Freud wanted contestants to stress especially the ways in which technique and theory "are furthering or hindering each other at the present time". The prize was 20,000 Marks; no one won that prize—it was far too difficult a topic for the psychoanalytic movement at the time.

It might seem that an adequate investigation of the nature of scientific thinking has been absent from the field of psychoanalysis. Nothing could be further from the truth. Freud's own account of the relations between psychoanalysis and science can be found in his response to the American psychiatrist and psychoanalyst James Putnam, who had contacted Freud in November 1909 with a particular clinical problem about the end of analysis. Putnam and the small group of analysts working with him in New England were relatively confident about the nature of analytical work in its early and middle phases. However, with respect to the end of the analytical work, Putnam thought that the good of the patient could only be aimed at if the psychoanalyst were to function in this phase as a moral philosopher. He thought that the direction of the work should in this end period of technique be brought about by directing the patient towards some moral good. This proposal effectively subordinated the methods and orientation of psychoanalysis to those of philosophy, and Freud's response to this suggestion was unambiguous. Psychoanalysis has no need to adopt the world-view of a philosophy, he claimed, and so has no need to make a choice amongst the many philosophical programmes that might suggest themselves for such a role. The reason that he gave for this is crucial. Psychoanalysis has no need of a philosophical world-view, said Freud, because it already has an orienting principle which guides its researches: this principle he described as that of "the methods of the sciences" (Freud, 1933a). In his time, this would have been taken to refer to the methods of mathematical physics. Moreover, in his view, psychoanalysis, once constituted in this way, would change the basic outline of the sciences.

Freud's claim would already explain why any psychoanalytic institute ought to concern itself with the nature and methods of the sciences. Actually the British Society, after this period of discussion in the years of the Second World War, -devoted considerable energy to opening up serious investigation of the nature of science, and of its bearing on clinical practice. Marjorie Brierley and John Rickman—and after them Wilfred Bion—in particular tried to bring an explicit consideration of the methods of the sciences into psychoanalysis in Britain. Whether or not this succeeded in establishing a series of relations that were sufficiently able to distinguish the field of psychoanalysis and science from that of philosophy is subject to disagreement: for one view see my Introduction to Burgoyne, 2000. Whatever the valuation one gives to these investigations, little attention has subsequently been given to these relations between psychoanalysis and science and philosophy. Freud was aware that there exists a large common ground between philosophy and science: that there are processes and constructions in the development of the sciences that depend on programmes of philosophy. The details of his argument are to be found in Hale 1971 and in Freud 1933a, and they constitute a programme for the inter-relation of clinical work and what Freud perceived as the deductive structure of science. However, there are a number of differences in his view between philosophy and science: the one that Freud accentuates is the intolerance of incompleteness that he takes to be characteristic of philosophy. It is to the credit of the sciences, claimed Freud, that they are able to tolerate incompleteness in their results. Rather than glossing over such gaps with ideal—and illusory—constructions, Freud recommends that a science take stock of its incompleteness. It was in the context of constructing such a scientific framework for psychoanalysis that Glover constructed his survey.

Glover's survey, together with his commentary on its results, was published in 1940, and reprinted in 1953. His questionnaire research was based on results submitted by twenty-four of the thirty to forty analysts who were then Full Members of the British Society. In his analysis of his survey, Glover found that there was within the Society considerable divergence of clinical technique: he had wanted to find out how large this was, and what were the reasons for it. Glover complained that discussions about the nature of technique tended to go on "in small private groups" (Glover, 1940); by this he meant small private groups of psychoanalysts. Any wider setting for critical enquiry in this area is something, he claimed, that is organized and encountered "less frequently". So, in this formulation of things, there were already some grounds for concern. This lack of a scientific setting for the development and articulation of psychoanalytic theory led, claimed Glover, to a situation where clinicians settled for a variety of orthodoxies around which they could still their anxieties and their doubts about the direction of their work. The outcome of this was that institutional groupings "combine to foster powerful and not always unobtrusive traditions". Given that the conditions for unhindered discussion seemed lacking at this time in the Society, the best that could be hoped for was that individuals would escape from these shackles by a range of techniques—not always the most adequate: "analysts whose training was acquired before the existence of training institutions, who in fact trained themselves by the system of trial and error, are likely to be more sensitive" (ibid.). This incitement to scientific research that stemmed from Glover's investigation went some way to create the climate for the "controversial" discussions within the Society that were to so much advance the situation of psychoanalysis in the 1940s.

Discussions organized around the theme of variations in classical technique were widespread within the psychoanalytical movement in the early 1950s. The strongest of these post-war proposals to vary classical technique came from two different centres within the International Psychoanalytical Association: France and the

USA. Sacha Nacht in France put forward the first of these, Kurt Eissler in the USA the second. Nacht's idea was to replace the classical neutrality of the analyst—the "absent" analyst who is there only to listen—by a replacement "presence" of the analyst (see, for instance, Nacht, 1950). According to Nacht, there often emerges a need to detach the patient from the transference relation, to "push the patient out" of the analytical situation and into the real world. Nacht's assumption was that the transference relation was a world of illusion, and his conclusion was that it is necessary in these circumstances to "upset the ritual". What he meant by this was that the analyst departs from neutrality by altering the regularity of the hours and the number of sessions, the frequency and length of interpretations, the system of payment, and by directing the patient off the couch on to a chair, and so on. These variations on classical recommendations for technique were supposed to lead to an analytical relation which is that of "adult to adult, equal to equal". His aim was to put the patient back into contact with reality, taking a direction that led them more and more away from what he took to be the relative fictions of the transference and into the grounded realities of the everyday world. He recommended introducing into the work "a clear, tangible, durable, unambiguous form of ourselves and of our interest (for the patient)". In this way the patient could detach themselves progressively from the analysis, and move towards "a happy liquidation of the transference".

The fictional, unreal plane Nacht opposed to a direction that led to true contact with objects. He started from the problem of "a world dominated by the imaginary" and proposed a solution that allowed the patient—like the analyst—to become "anchored in living reality". There are many problems with this. His colleague Jacques Lacan gave a much more adequate formulation of the problems that Nacht was trying to address, and proposed variations in technique that were minor by comparison with those put forward by Nacht. Lacan, however, after the split in the French Psychoanalytic Society, was the one who was notoriously expelled—for "improper" variations of technique. Leave it to posterity to judge whether Lacan's solutions were the more appropriate, and the more fruitful.

Eissler, on the other hand, devised a notion that left classical technique as a merely residual notion. A senior member of the

International Psychoanalytical Association, he devised a series of indices or "parameters" that measured the distance away from classical technique: parameters have to be zero for classical technique to be able to be maintained. The burgeoning development of such proposals led Anna Freud in the mid-1950s to the following comments on classical technique:

> Logical as these regulations appear in the light of the definition of analytic technique given above, not one of them has remained unchallenged. I name as examples—probably well-known ones—a few only: the denouncing of the rule of free association in a recent Congress paper by Burke (1949); the break with regular hourly work advocated by Lacan (1953–1955); the distrust of the unlimited development of transference by members of the Chicago Institute (Alexander & French, 1946); the sole use of transference interpretations by part of the English school of analysts. [A. Freud, 1954].

She took the discussion of such proposals to be "fruitful and interesting when it includes their theoretical background". The value of serious conceptual considerations of questions of technique was widely recognized at this time: no orthodoxy was appealed to in order to close down the discussion.

Debate on these issues became so widespread that an entire Panel was devoted to them at the Congress of the IPA held in Paris in 1957. Nacht and Eissler were joined there by Rudolph Loewenstein, Annie Reich, Maurice Bouvet, Herbert Rosenfeld, and Ralph Greenson. Greenson (1958) and others attempted to relate these questions of divergenge and deviation, modification and variation in classical technique to functions of the ego. The centrality given to the ego in this period when psychoanalysis was dominated by the programme of ego-psychology led many contributions to this panel into a series of perplexities from which there seemed few exits. Of all the interventions in these proceedings, Loewenstein's are the most subtle, and the most articulate. His, however, was the only contribution to recognize the important role played in this problem by the functioning of language. He had posed the aim of an interpretive intervention as being the generation of insight, and not everyone in his audience would have been aware of the way in which he perceived this as being dependent on structures of language. In his final summary he gave one brief indication that the "expressive and cognitive functions of speech" were "essential for analytical insight" (Loewenstein, 1958a). However, tensions arising from his attempt to rely on the dual themes of language structure and ego-psychology appear throughout his work: his formulations move, sometimes emphasizing the one, sometimes the other (see Lowenstein, 1957, 1958b).

Loewenstein had already developed a theory of technique that relied fundamentally on assumptions about the functioning of language. An interpretation is effective, he claimed, when it produces insight that the patient had previously been lacking. The question as to what it is that brings about such new insight Loewenstein answered as follows: it is the generation of new vocabulary, introduced by the interpretation. Where the patient had previously been unable to translate unconscious material into consciousness, this new vocabulary is able to bring about the movement into consciousness of what had previously been only unconscious. In Loewenstein (1956), he looked at the theories of language put forward by Ferdinand de Saussure, Karl Bühler, Roman Jakobson, and Emile Benveniste. In effect, his whole programme for assessing the effectiveness of psychoanalysis rested on hypotheses concerning the functioning of language and speech.

Loewenstein stressed the processes of translation and retranslation that are involved both in the production of analytic material and in its interpretation. Insight, as well as being a bringing into consciousness, was a process of the re-establishing of connection. In the material produced by the patient there are overt messages that have certain allusions and certain existing connections: there are, however, also hidden messages—there is, says Loewenstein, a "kind of coded message" (Loewenstein, 1956). How it is that an interpretation can suddenly give this coded message access to a direct expression is his main problem of linguistics. There are, he claimed, two kinds of vocabulary involved in human speech. There is an everyday vocabulary, which is a vehicle for ordinary conscious representations of the world, but there is also a second, hidden, vocabulary that is more "limited in scope". It is this further vocabulary, "less definite, usually unconscious, and unintelligible" which is utilized as the coding apparatus for the production of symptoms. Analytical work, says Loewenstein, "elicits expressions of this unconscious vocabulary" (*ibid.*), and interpretation then permits the translation of thoughts expressed in this language into words of ordinary language. By this means the patient gains gradual insight into previously repressed material. In all of this he—and other psychoanalysts investigating these themes—needed access to a research community investigating the structures of language. He did not have it at the time, and little work on the nature of language has been done since in Anglo-Saxon schools of psychoanalysis. It is, however, not only the structure of language that would bear investigation—the field of research opened up by these clinical problems extends widely into the domain of science.

Other psychoanalysts have faced such problems. Among the marginal annotations that Paula Heimann made in her copy of Freud's "Project" (Freud, 1950a) there is one that she had added to the section that Freud had called "Thinking and reality". Her addition reads as follows: "Cf my technical rule 1) verbalization of actual transference elements, 2) definition of characters of analyst and patient, 3) release of memories". The passage in Freud's text that this addition comments on is concerned with the distinction between judging forms of thinking on the one hand, and what Freud calls reproductive thinking on the other. Freud's passage is the following: "Judging thought operates in advance of reproductive thought by furnishing it with ready-made facilitations for further associative travelling". Paula Heimann, in referring to her "technical rule" is attempting to base her formulation of countertransference technique on the claims made here in Freud's "Project". You can find her tripartite rule described explicitly in the paper that she gave to the 1955 Congress of the IPA in Geneva (Heimann, 1956). First, she claims, the analyst makes a judgement: "The question the analyst has to ask himself constantly is 'Why is the patient now doing what to whom?'. The answer to this question constitutes the transference interpretation". Second, this answer "defines the character of the analyst and the character of the patient at the actual moment". And third, as a result of these reflections, "some picture of his earlier object-relations emerges, to which the patient responds with . . . direct and specific recollections". The reason Heimann assumes that such a technique will work lies in her reading of Freud's claims about forms of judgement. The act of judgement that she describes precedes the facilitating of new associative connections, and leads to the production of new childhood memories. The "rules" that she generated, and the way that she found them, would have been formulated better, and tested better, if they had been subjected to critical development within a school of analysts. A research community would have better formulated a context for her work, and would have allowed the working through of its consequences to extend to a wider public, and to a wider discussion.

The counter-transference technique that she proposed is in fact a development of the technique of interpretation of the transference, introduced by James Strachey in 1933, but in none of her explanations of this does she explicitly introduce the theory of the ego that she would have found in the text of Freud's "Project". In the "Project" there is also a certain development of the theory of word representations, but she does not develop this either. The technique she proposes is a part of the spectrum of techniques that Lacan, in 1958, proposed to call ego-to-ego techniques, opposing them by this to his own alternative proposal: that of the technique of reconstruction of the subjective history of the analysand. Elsewhere in her presentation she asserts the importance of words: "his parents, who first gave him words and ideas"—only to lose this a few lines later when the phrase is repeated as "(his parents) . . . whom he internalised together with the ideas and the activity of thinking" (Heimann, 1956). Much needs sorting out here; much of her text demands a more scientific discussion. The problem of the inadequate treatment of words is one of which she is only half aware. There are other problems that seem not to strike her: for instance, these two acts of thought in Freud take place in one person, while in Heimann's version of counter-transference, they take place in two. In the last phrases of this paper she briefly describes a linguistic mechanism—that of parabole. But this kind of barely sporadic development of the theory of language is not good enough; it is done better in Loewenstein, but even there it is still not good enough. What is needed in all of this is a psychoanalytical society that is seriously able to claim a relation to science. Only if this were to be the case could such a society claim some propriety rights over psychoanalysis.

Freud, in his discussion in 1919 of what it is that the psychoanalyst needs for his training points out two fairly simple components:

What he needs in the matter of theory can be obtained from the literature of the subject, and, going more deeply, at the scientific meetings of the psychoanalytic societies, as well as by personal contacts with their more experienced members. [Freud, 1919j]

The second thread Freud describes as follows:

as regards practical experience, apart from what he gains from his own personal analysis, he can acquire it by carrying out treatments, provided that he can get supervision and guidance from recognised psychoanalysts. [Freud, 1919]

But as we have seen, these two threads span further, and more complex, questions. Fifteen years after she presented her paper, Paula Heimann was still struggling with questions of language. In 1970 she wrote, "The 'word' is not only a designation of something which is there, it also creates new mental entities". The claim she makes here is no doubt true, and it is to her credit that she has given it a clear formulation; but the problems that it raises are immense.

In the face of such a complexity of problems it is not surprising that many Psychoanalytical Societies have taken refuge in simpler ones. Often they have tried to do this by focusing on the supposed uniformity of clinical practice, on a supposed standard practice which does not exist. In 1982—fifty years after Glover's previous survey—Anne-Marie Sandler surveyed the results of her own open-minded survey of training formats within IPA Societies in Europe, and recapitulated something of Glover's experience, as she expressed an "initial shock at how large the differences" were in these trainings. Such differences exist, they are large, and they demand consideration within a context that can address them: that of science.

The relation of language to clinical problems has been a recurrent theme in psychoanalysis since its first formulation by Freud. There are arguments that claim this to be the central problem of psychoanalysis; of psychoanalytic theory and of psychoanalytic practice. Other arguments oppose this view. Any organization that claims to be a legitimate inheritor of Freud's work needs to be able to address this question, and to resolve it—one way or the other. It was in order to be able to resolve such a question that Freud asked psychoanalysis to take into itself the "methods of the sciences". This situation has not changed since Freud's time: the only way in which legitimate claims can be made concerning psychoanalysis is to formulate them within the context of the relations of psychoanalysis to science.

References

Alexander, F., & French, T. (1946). *Psychoanalytic Therapy*. New York: Ronald Press.

Brierley, M. (1991). Memorandum on her technique. In P. King & R. Steiner (Eds.), *The Freud–Klein Controversies, 1941–1945* (pp. 617–628). London: Brunner-Routledge.

Burke, M (1949). The fundamantal rule of psycho-analysis. Abstract in *The International Journal of Psycho-Analysis*, 30: 200.

Burgoyne, B. (2000). Introduction. In: B. Burgoyne (Ed.), *Drawing the Soul*. London: Rebus.

Eissler, K. (1958). Remarks on some variations in psycho-analytical technique. *International Jounral of Psycho-Analysis*, XXXIX: 222–229.

Freud, A. (1954) [1998]. Problems of technique in adult analysis. In: R. Ekins & R. Freeman (Eds.), *Selected Writings by Anna Freud* (pp. 244–265), London: Penguin.

Freud, A. (1991). Memorandum. In: P. King & R. Steiner (Eds.), *The Freud–Klein Controversies, 1941–1945* (pp. 629–634). London: Brunner-Routledge.

Freud, S. (1950a) [1895]. Entwurf einer Psychologie. In: *Aus den Anfängen der Psychoanalyse*. London: Imago.

Freud, S. (1919j). On the teaching of psychoanalysis in universities. *S.E.*, XVII. London: Hogarth, 1955.

Freud, S (1933a). On the question of a Weltanschauung. New intrductory lectures on psychoanalysis, Lecture XXXV. *S.E.*, XXII. London: Hogarth, 1964.

Glover, E. (1940). *An Investigation of the Technique of Psychoanalysis, Research Supplement to the International Journal of Psycho-analysis*. London: Baillière, Tyndall and Cox.

Glover, E. (1991). Edward Glover's Response to Memorandum by James Strachey. In P. King & R. Steiner (Eds.), *The Freud–Klein Controversies, 1941–1945* (pp. 611–616). London: Brunner-Routledge.

Greenson, R. (1958). Variations in Classical Psycho-Analytic Technique: an Introduction. *International Journal of Psychoanalysis*, XXXIX: 200–201

Hale, N. G. (Ed.) (1971). *James Jackson Putnam and Psychoanalysis: Letters between Putnam, Sigmund Freud, Ernest Jones, William James, Sandor Ferenczi, and Morton Prince, 1877–1917.* Cambridge, MA: Harvard University Press.

Heimann, P. (1956). The dynamics of transference interpretations. *International Journal of Psychoanalysis, 37*: 303–310.

Heimann, P. (1970). The nature and function of interpretation. In: M. Tonnesmann (Ed.), *About Children and Children-No-Longer: Collected Papers, 1942–1980 Paula Heimann* (pp. 267–275). London and New York: Tavistock/Routledge, 1989.

King, P., & Steiner, R. (Eds.) (1991). *The Freud–Klein Controversies, 1941–1945.* London: Brunner-Routledge.

Klein, M. (1991). Fourth paper for discussion of the scientific differences. In: P. King & R. Steiner (Eds.) *The Freud–Klein Controversies, 1941-1945* (pp. 752-878). London: Brunner-Routledge.

Lacan, J. (1953–1955). Commentaires sur des textes de Freud. In: Psychanalyse, I, pp. 17-28.

Lacan, J. (1958) [1977]. The direction of the treatment and the principles of its power. In: J. Lacan (Ed.), *Ecrits, A Selection.* London: Tavistock.

Loewenstein, R. (1956) [1982]. Some remarks on the role of speech in psychoanalytic technique. In: R. Loewenstein (Ed.), *Practice and Precept in Psychoanalytic Technique: Selected Papers of Rudolph M. Loewenstein,* (pp. 52–67). New Haven and London: Yale University Press.

Loewenstein, R. (1957) [1982]. Some thoughts on interpretation in the theory and practice of psychoanalysis. In: R. Loewenstein, (Ed.), *Practice and Precept in Psychoanalytic Technique: Selected Papers of Rudolph M. Loewenstein* (pp. 123–146). New Haven and London: Yale University Press.

Loewenstein, R. (1958a). Remarks on some variations in psycho-analytic technique. *International Journal of Psychoanalysis, XXXIX*: 202–209.

Loewenstein, R (1958b): Variations in classical technique: concluding remarks. *International Journal of Psychoanalysis, XXXIX*: 240–242.

Loewenstein, R. (1982). *Practice and Precept in Psychoanalytic Technique: Selected Papers of Rudolph M. Loewenstein.* New Haven and London: Yale University Press.

Nacht, S. (1950). *De la Pratique à la Théorie Psychanalytique.* Paris: Presses Universitaires de France.

Nacht, S. (1958). Variations in technique. *International Journal of Psychoanalysis, XXXIX*: 235–237.

Sandler, A.-M. (1982). The selection and function of the training analyst in Europe. *The International Review of Psycho-Analysis*, 9: 386–397.

Sharpe, E. (1991). Memorandum on her technique. In: P. King & R. Steiner (Eds.), *The Freud–Klein Controversies, 1941–1945* (pp. 639–647). London: Brunner-Routledge.

Strachey, J. (1991). Discussion Memorandum. In: P. King & R. Steiner (Eds.), *The Freud–Klein Controversies, 1941–1945*) (pp. 602–610). London: Brunner-Routledge.

CHAPTER TWO

What is psychoanalysis?

Thomas Szasz

Introduction

Freud identified psychoanalysis in contradictory ways. I suggest that modern organized psychoanalysis is morally bankrupt, intellectually corrupt, and professionally dead. Viewed as a method or type of treatment for disease, it is time to bury it. Only after burying "medical" psychoanalysis can we try to resurrect it as a secular cure for souls.

I. Who owns psychoanalysis

I consider the question "Who owns psychoanalysis?" rhetorical, intended to stimulate discussion about the meaning of the term and the identity of the discipline it ostensibly names. Ownership, a legal concept, requires that at least two elements be present: it must be possible to clearly define and objectively identify the "thing" owned and the state must recognize "it" as property subject to ownership. Psychoanalysis does not qualify on either count.

Psychoanalysis is a word, invented by Sigmund Freud. It began life as a neologism and is now part of the English language and of other languages. Words are common property. No one owns the English language or other languages. To be sure, certain terms, called "trademarks", can be patented and owned. *Webster's* defines *trademark* as "a device (as a word) pointing distinctly to the origin or ownership of merchandise to which it is applied and legally reserved to the exclusive use of the owner as maker or seller." For example, the Coca-Cola Company owns the term "Coca-Cola." Would-be competitors cannot make a drink and sell it under that name. Trademarks refer to material objects. Psychoanalysis is not a material object.

Psychoanalysis may also be said to be the name of a particular method of medical treatment and/or psychological treatment (psychotherapy). Even if that statement were valid, or were generally recognized as valid, psychoanalysis would still not be subject to ownership. No form of medical treatment—say, analgesic therapy or antibiotic therapy—is subject to ownership. To be sure, *the practice of medicine* —like the practice of many other professions and skills, including the practice of psychology and, potentially, of psychoanalysis— may be subject to licensure. That term denotes a political–economic arrangement whereby the state guarantees monopolistic protection to a group, in return for which it exercises power over qualifications for membership in it.

Familiarity with the history of psychoanalysis and the habits of "important" psychoanalysts can leave the scholar in no doubt that the term psychoanalysis is not subject to precise definition. In addition to the inconsistencies in Freud's use of the term, which I shall consider presently, I refer here to the habit of "senior analysts"—in the days when I was a young analyst—of dismissing colleagues of whom they were jealous by caustically observing that what they were doing was not "real analysis". "Real analysis" was (only) what they were doing.

However, there is something we can say regarding this matter, albeit it is not very interesting: namely, that medical treatment, in so far as it forms a part of *medical practice*, may be said to be the property of the medical profession. That means that the state may prohibit the practice of medicine by persons not trained in medicine or not licensed by the state as physicians, and can prosecute and punish persons who violate this prohibition.

I propose to reframe the question, Who owns psychoanalysis? by asking, What is psychoanalysis? John Selden, a seventeenth-century English jurist and scholar, warned

> The reason of a thing is not to be inquired after, till you are sure the thing itself be so. We commonly are at, *what's the reason for it?* before we are sure of the thing. [Thomas, 1971, p. 435]

We know what physics is: the study of matter and energy. We know what biology is: the study of living things. But what is psychoanalysis? The one thing—I dare say the only thing—on which everyone who addressed this question might agree is that psychoanalysis was the invention of Sigmund Freud.

A rose, the poet tells us, is a rose by any other name. Psychoanalysis, said Freud, was any activity that he said, in one place or another, was psychoanalysis. To illustrate this point, I have constructed a catalogue of the various descriptions and definitions of psychoanalysis that Freud himself has offered. I list these without internal comment and then offer some of my own reflections on Freud's views concerning the "neuroses" and their "treatment".

II

The psychoanalytic situation

> With the neurotics, then, we make our pact: complete candour on one side and strict discretion on the other. This looks as though we were only aiming at the post of a secular father confessor. [Freud, 1940a, p. 174]

> [T]he "analytic situation" allows of the presence of no third person. [Freud, 1926e, p. 185]

> I make use of his [the patient's] communication without asking his consent, since I cannot allow that psychoanalytic technique has any right to claim the protection of medical discretion. [Freud, 1914d, p. 64]

> For practical reasons, this [training] analysis can only be short and incomplete. Its main object is to enable his teacher to make a

judgment as to whether the candidate can be accepted for further training. [Freud, 1937c, p.248]

The patient must be an independent adult

[I try to follow the rule] of not taking on a patient for treatment unless he was *sui juris,* not dependent on anyone else in the essential relations of his life. [Freud, 1916–1917, p. 460]

Analysis . . . presupposes the consent of the person who is being analysed . . . [Freud, 1914d, p. 49]

Psychoanalysis is a medical procedure (as well as a science)

Psychoanalysis is really a method of treatment like others. . . . It is in fact technique that necessitates the specialization in medical practice. [Freud, 1933a, p. 152]

[W]hen we have carried out all the improvements in technique to which deeper observation of our patients is bound to lead us, our medical procedure will reach a degree of precision and certainty of success which is not to be found in every specialized field of medicine. [Freud, 1910d, p. 146]

As a method of treatment it [psychoanalysis] is one among many, though, to be sure, *primus inter pares* [first among equals]. If it was without therapeutic value it would not have been discovered, as it was, in connection with sick people and would not have gone on ·developing for more than thirty years. [Freud, 1933a, p. 157]

Psychoanalysis is a medical procedure which aims at the cure of certain form of nervous disease (the neuroses) by a psychological technique. . . . Psychoanalysis has no therapeutic effect on the severer forms of mental disorder properly so-called. [Freud, 1913j, p. 165]

The theory of the neuroses belongs to psychiatry . . . [Freud, 1925d, p. 60]

The neuroses are a particular kind of illness and analysis is a particular method of treating them—a specialized branch of medicine. [Freud, 1926a, p. 229]

The first piece of reality with which the patient must deal is his illness. [Freud, 1914d, p. 66]

I have attempted to give some idea of the still incalculable wealth of connections which have come to light between medical psycho-analysis and other fields of science. [*ibid.*, p. 38]

I allow—no, I insist—that in every case which is under considera-tion for analysis the diagnosis shall be established first by a doctor. Far the greater number of neuroses which occupy us are fortunately of a psychogenic nature and give no grounds for pathological suspicions. Once the doctor has established this, he can confidently hand over the treatment to a lay analyst. [Freud, 1926e, p. 243]

I have always felt it as a gross injustice that people have refused to treat psychoanalysis like any other science. [Freud, 1925d, p. 58]

While it [psychoanalysis] was originally the name of a particular therapeutic method, it has now also become the name of a science—the science of unconscious mental processes. [*ibid.*, p. 70]

Psychoanalysis is not a medical procedure

I have assumed, that is to say, that psychoanalysis is not a special-ized branch of medicine. I cannot see how it is possible to dispute this. [Freud, 1926e, p. 252]

It may perhaps turn out that in this instance [psychoanalysis] the patients are not like other patients, that the laymen are not really laymen, and that the doctors have not exactly the qualities which one has a right to expect of doctors and on which their claims should be based. [*ibid.*, p. 184]

[T]he relation in the transference may make it inadvisable for the analyst to examine the patient physically. [*ibid.*, p. 244]

You want to show me what kind of knowledge is needed in order to practise analysis, so that I may be able to judge whether only doctors should have a right to do so. Well, so far very little to do with medicine has turned up: a great deal of psychology and a little biology or sexual science. [*ibid.*, p. 218]

For we do not consider it all desirable for psychoanalysis to be swallowed up by medicine and to find its last resting-place in a textbook of psychiatry under the heading "Methods of Treatment," alongside of procedures such as hypnotic suggestion, autosuggestion, and persuasion . . . [*ibid.*, p. 248]

I only want to feel assured that the therapy will not destroy the science. [*ibid.*, p. 254]

[I]n his medical school a doctor receives a training which is more or less the opposite of what he would need as a preparation for psychoanalysis. [*ibid.*, 1927, p. 230]

[I] wish to protect analysis from the doctors (and the priests) [1928]. [Freud, 1963, p. 126]

We [analysts] serve the patient . . . as a teacher and educator. [Freud, 1940a, p. 77]

Such activity as this is pastoral work in the best sense of the word. [*ibid.*, p. 256]

It is not without satisfaction that I have learnt that the majority of my audience are not members of the medical profession. You have no need to be afraid that any special medical knowledge will be required for following what I have to say. [Freud, 1909, p. 9]

Psychoanalysis is a type of dialogue

Nothing takes place between them [analyst and analysand] except that they talk to each other. The analyst makes use of no instruments—not even for examining the patient—nor does he prescribe any medicines. [Freud, 1926e, p. 187]

The course of an analysis is most inconspicuous, it employs neither medicines nor instruments and consists only in talking and an exchange of information; it will not be easy to prove that a layman is practicing "analysis," if he asserts that he is merely giving encouragement and explanations and trying to establish a healthy human influence on people who are in search of mental assistance. [*ibid.*, p. 236]

Each patient is allotted a particular hour of my available working day; it belongs to him and he is liable for it, even if he does not make use of it. This arrangement, which is usually taken as a matter of course for teachers of music or languages in good society, may perhaps seem too rigorous in a doctor, or even unworthy of his profession. [Freud, 1913, p. 126]

"I understand," says our Impartial Person. "You assume that every neurotic has something oppressing him, some secret. And by getting him to tell you about it you relieve his oppression and do him good. That, of course, is the principle of Confession, which the Catholic Church has used from time immemorial in order to make sure its dominance over people's minds."

We must reply: "Yes and no!" Confession no doubt plays a role in analysis . . . But it is very far from constituting the essence of analysis or from explaining its effects. In Confession the sinner tells what he knows; in analysis the neurotic has to tell more. Nor have we heard that Confession has ever developed enough power to get rid of actual pathological symptoms. . . . It would certainly be strange if it were possible by such means to control purely physical phenomena as well, such as vomiting, diarrhea, convulsions; but I know that influence like that is in fact quite possible if a person is put into a state of hypnosis. [Freud, 1926e, p. 189]

The role of the fee in psychoanalytic treatment

The absence of the regulating effect offered by the payment of a fee to the doctor makes itself very painfully felt; the whole relationship is removed from the real world, and the patient is deprived of a strong motive for endeavoring to bring the treatment to an end. [Freud, 1913, p. 132]

There can no longer be any doubt that it [psychoanalysis] will continue . . . Out of their own funds these local [psychoanalytic] societies support (or are in the process of forming) training institutes, in which instruction in the practice of psychoanalysis is given according to a uniform plan, as well as students give free treatment to patients of limited means. [Freud, 1925d, p. 73]

Mental illness is brain disease

I was thus led into regarding the neuroses as being without exception disturbances of the sexual function, the so-called "*actual neuroses*" being the direct toxic expression of such disturbances, and the *psychoneuroses* their mental expression. My medical conscience felt pleased at my having arrived at this conclusion. . . . The medical aspect of the matter was, moreover, supported by the fact that sexuality was not something purely mental. It had a somatic side as well, and it was possible to assign special chemical processes to it and to attribute sexual excitation to the presence of some particular, though at present unknown, substances. [Freud, 1925d, p. 25]

All that I am asserting is that the symptoms of these patients [suffering from neurasthenia] are not mentally determined or removable by analysis, but that they must be regarded as direct toxic consequences of disturbed sexual chemical processes. [*ibid.*, p. 26]

It would nevertheless be a serious mistake to suppose that analysis favors or aims at a purely psychological view of mental disorders. It cannot overlook the fact that the other half of the problems of psychiatry [the psychoses] are concerned with the influence of organic factors (whether mechanical, toxic, or infective) on the mental apparatus. Even in the case of the mildest of these disorders, the neuroses, it makes no claim that their origin is purely psychogenic but traces their etiology to the influence upon mental life of an unquestionably organic factor to which I shall refer later. [Freud, 1913, p. 175]

But here we are concerned with therapy only in so far as it works by psychological means; and for the time being we have no other. The future may teach us to exercise a direct influence, by means of particular chemical substances, on the amounts of energy and their distribution in the mental apparatus. [Freud, 1938, 1940, p. 182]

It is here, indeed, that hope for the future lies: the possibility that our knowledge of the operation of the hormones (you know what they are) may give us the means of successfully combating. [Freud, 1932–1936, p. 154]

Whereas in fact they [the neuroses] are severe, constitutionally fixed illnesses, which rarely restrict themselves to only a few attacks but persist as a rule over long periods or throughout life. [Freud, 1933a, p. 153]

Determinism and polemics in psychoanalysis

> If the distinction between conscious and unconscious motivation is taken into account, our feeling of conviction informs us that conscious motivation does not extend to all our motor decisions. ... what is thus left free by the one side receives its motivation from the other side, from the unconscious; and in this way determination in the psychical sphere is still carried out without any gap. [Freud, 1901b, p. 254]

> Analysis is not suited, however, for polemical use; it presupposes the consent of the person who is being analysed and a situation in which there is a superior and a subordinate. [Freud, 1914, p. 49]

III

Freud was right when he told his friend, Wilhelm Fliess, that "I am not at all a man of science, not an observer, not an experimenter, not a thinker. I am by temperament nothing but a conquistador." (Masson, 1985, p. 398). He did not define or identify psychoanalysis. "It" was whatever he said it was. Had he not been famously averse ("phobic") to using the telephone, he himself might have suggested that analysis may be conducted without the analyst's being in the presence of the patient. The June 2003 issue of *Insight*, an official publication of the International Psychoanalytical Association, is devoted largely to a discussion about psychoanalysis by telephone (*Insight*, 2003, Issue 1).

Instead of identifying psychoanalysis, Freud used the term to create and legitimize a scientistic ideology. In this enterprise, he succeeded only too well. The result is that instead of being a system of critical inquiry, psychoanalysis became a servant of society—specifically, of the modern therapeutic state. Consider how and what today's official leaders of psychoanalysis say about psychoanalysis.

Richard Fox, President of the American Psychoanalytic Association (2001):

> Psychoanalysis today is a far cry from what it was thirty to forty years ago ... We lobby in Washington ... We work with other groups such as the ACLU to further our goals. [Fox, 2001, p.1]

Inter alia, the ACLU formulates commitment laws, the better to justify incarcerating innocent Americans accused of mental illness.

Glenn Gabbard, M.D., editor of the *International Journal of Psycho-Analysis*:

> [B]ehavior therapy and drug therapy [are] affecting the same brain areas and in the same manner. . . . Psychotherapy seems capable of favorably influencing the minds and bodies of persons with bodily diseases and perhaps is even capable of countering those diseases. . . . [It is important] to get scientific results that lend credibility to psychotherapy as a *real treatment*. [Arehart-Treichel, 2001, p. 33]

Daniel Widlocher, president of the International Psychoanalytical Association (2003):

> When we refer to the presence of psychoanalysis . . . in the world of mental health care, we are actually talking about the achievement of a therapeutic consensus accruing from an in-depth knowledge of the differences between our therapeutic targets. This joint purpose calls for the active participation of psychoanalysts in mental health care institutions and the establishment of interdisciplinary research programmes. (Widlocher, 2003, pp. 8 & 47]

Sverre Varvin, member of the International Psychoanalytical Association's "Working group on terror and terrorism", reports:

> We believe that psychoanalysis has important insights into processes related to war and terror, and we believe we have a duty to let these be known and put to use by politicians, planners, and all those dealing with prevention and social violence and with the consequences. [Varvin, 2003, p. 41]

These declarations, typical of leading contemporary psychoanalysts, clearly and proudly place psychoanalysis at the service of the therapeutic state and enlist its powers against individuals in conflict with it.

Many years ago, I ceased to identify myself as a psychoanalyst. Why? Because I wanted to be faithful to my belief, which I have held ever since I knew anything about psychoanalysis, that *psychoanalysis is a moral, not a medical, activity*. Psychoanalysis has nothing whatsoever to do with illness or health, medicine or treatment, or any other idea that places "professional" listening and talk-ing within the purview of the state's licensing authority. (Szasz, 1965). Accordingly, wherever possible, I refer to the recipient of the service as a client, not a patient. I continue to use the word "thera-pist" because we lack an appropriate term to identify his role and function as secular, moral counsellor.

Few contemporary psychoanalysts share these views. Most analysts equate psychoanalysis with psychotherapy, consider psychotherapy a part of psychiatry, and believe that problems in living are diseases and that verbal and non-verbal communications are treatments.

Elsewhere, I have written about the profound and pervasive confusion regarding the boundaries between disease and non-disease that characterizes our age. (Szasz, 1961). A good deal of the blame for this may be laid on Freud's shoulders; or, perhaps, he only glimpsed the dawning of a new *Zeitgeist* and made the best of it by becoming one of its prophets. In either case, psychoanalysis is, among other things, one of the emblems of the celebration of the medicalization of (mis)behaviour and therapeutization of dialogue ("talk therapy").

Perhaps nothing illustrates better the transformation of habits into diseases—and, more generally, the conflation of morals and medicine—than Freud's unyielding belief that masturbation caused disease. Once again, a catalogue of some of his pertinent statements speaks for itself.

IV

Self-punishment is the final substitute for self-gratification, which comes from masturbation. This key opens many doors. [Freud, 1898; Masson, 1985, p. 345]

Neurasthenia in males is acquired at the age of puberty . . . Its source is masturbation . . . [Freud, 1893; *ibid.*, p. 40]

This second noxa is *onanismus conjugalis*—incomplete intercourse in order to prevent conception. [Freud, 1893; *ibid.*, p. 41]

Undoubtedly there exist cases of juvenile neurasthenia *without* masturbation, but *not* without the usual preliminaries of overabundant pollutions—that is, precisely as though there had been masturbation. [Freud, 1893; *ibid.*, p. 50]

The use of a condom is evidence of weak potency, being something analogous to masturbation, it is the continuous cause of his melancholia. [Freud, 1894; *ibid.*, p. 94]

Melancholia develops as an intensification of neurasthenia through masturbation. [Freud, 1894; *ibid.*, p. 98]

The insight has dawned on me that masturbation is the one major habit, the "primary addiction," and it is only as a substitute and replacement for it that the other addictions—to alcohol, morphine, tobacco, and the like—come into existence. [Freud, 1897; *ibid.*, p. 287]

What would you say if masturbation were to reduce itself to homosexuality . . .? [Freud, 1895; *ibid.*, p. 380]

V

Having said all this, I nevertheless wish, to paraphrase Shakespeare's Mark Antony, not to rebuke Freud but to bury the leading (mis)interpretation of his legacy. Sadly, it is all too true that "The evil that men do lives after them; The good is oft interred with their bones." The good that Freud did and thought appears to have died with him or predeceased him.

Freud tried hard—and both succeeded and failed—to understand the predicaments that plagued his fellow Viennese and the wealthy people who came from abroad to seek the help of this twentieth-century miracle healer. Healing the non-sick has always been, and always will be, absurdly easy and maddeningly impossible.

Freud neither inherited nor married money. He had to make a living. He made a living the only way he knew how, creating and curing non-diseases. When I say "creating", I do not, of course, mean, crudely, that he "made his patients sick". I mean only that he colluded, and more, with them in defining and legitimizing their human problems—their problems in living—as bona fide medical maladies. I have devoted much of my professional life to an effort to demolish this misinterpretation.

To repeat my introductory remarks, psychoanalysis, *qua* psychoanalysis, is morally bankrupt, intellectually corrupt, and professionally dead. Viewed as a method or type of treatment for disease, it is time to bury it. Only after burying "medical" psychoanalysis, can we try to resurrect it as a secular cure for souls.

As I have stated elsewhere, I believe psychoanalysis possesses a valuable moral core that has never been properly identified and is now virtually unrecognized: *it is, or ought to be, a wholly voluntary and reliably confidential human service, initiated and largely controlled by the client who pays for it.* Freud himself compared the psychoanalytic relationship with the Catholic confessional (Freud, 1926e, p. 189). If psychoanalysis is to have a future—which, in our disease- and treatment-obsessed culture seems doubtful—it lies in adapting that model to the needs of modern secular man, increasingly isolated from his fellow man and community, and betrayed by the therapeutic state in which he mistakenly seeks protection from the vicissitudes of life.

The psychoanalyst must re-embrace his commitment to serve his client and no one else. He must earn the client's confidence and trust by entering into a clear contract with him and by conscientiously adhering to its terms. The Bill of Rights limits the powers of the state *vis-à-vis* the citizen, not the citizen's *vis-à-vis* the state. Similarly, the analytic contract limits the powers of the therapist *vis-à-vis* the client, not vice versa. The analyst's overriding obligation to the client is to protect his confidences. This obligation permits no exceptions. If the analyst morally abhors what his client tells him, he has the option, like a defence attorney, of discontinuing the relationship. Under no circumstances does the psychoanalyst have the option to betray his client's confidence and use the information he has acquired, especially against what the client considers his own interest.

We often speak of empowering this or that politically weak or disfranchised individual or group. But people cannot be empowered directly. They can be empowered only indirectly, by taking power away from, or not giving power to, individuals or institutions that have actual or potential control over them. This is a lesson every parent must learn if he wants his child to become an independent adult. It is a lesson that all forms of psychiatrized psychotherapy violate, indeed indignantly reject—by assuming responsibility for the client's health, safety, and general well-being.

References

Arehart-Treichel, J. (2001). Evidence is in: psychotherapy changes the brain. *Psychiatric News*, 6 July.

Fox, R. (2001). Will the real psychoanalyst please stand up? *The American Psychoanalyst*, 35: 1.

Freud, S. (1901b). The psychopatholgy of everyday life. *S.E.*, 6: 254.

Freud, S. (19010a). Five lectures on psychoanalysis. *S.E.*, 11: 9.

Freud, S. (1910b). Future prospects of psychoanalytic therapy. *S.E.*, 11: 46.

Freud, S. (1913c). On beginning the treatment. *S.E.*, 12.

Freud, S. (1913j). The claims of psychoanalysis to scientific interest. *S.E.*, 13.

Freud, S. (1914d). On the history of the psychoanalytic movement. *S.E.*, 14.

Freud, S. (1916–1917). Introductory lectures on psychoanalysis. *S.E.*, 16: 460.

Freud, S. (1925d). An autobiographical study. *S.E.*, 20.

Freud, S. (1926e). The question of lay analysis. *S.E.*, 20.

Freud, S. (1933a). New introductory lectures on psychoanalysis. *S.E.*, 22.

Freud, S. (1937c). Analysis terminable and interminable. *S.E.*, 23.

Freud, S. (1940a). An outline of psychoanalysis. *S.E.*, 23.

Masson, J. M. (Ed.) (1985). *The Complete Letters of Sigmund Freud to Wilhelm Fliess, 1887–1904*. Cambridge, MA: Harvard University Press.

Szasz, T. (1961). *The Myth of Mental Illness: Foundations of a Theory of Personal Conduct*. New York: Harper Collins.

Szasz, T. (1965). *The Ethics of Psychoanalysis: The Theory and Method of Autonomous Psychotherapy*. Syracuse: Syracuse University Press.

Thomas, K. (1971). *Religion and the Decline of Magic*. London: Weidenfeld & Nicholson.

Varvin, S. (2003). The IPA working group on terror and terrorism. *International Psychoanalysis*, 12(1): 41.

Widlocher, D. (2003). The President's column. *International Psycho-analysis*, 12(1): 8 & 47.

CHAPTER THREE

Reflections on psychic ownership and psychoanalytic studies

R. D. Hinshelwood

"When I use a word," Humpty Dumpty said, in rather a
scornful tone, "it means just what I choose it to mean—
neither more nor less."

"The question is," said Alice, "whether you can make
words mean so many different things."

"The question is," said Humpty Dumpty, "which is to be
master—that's all."

Lewis Carroll, *Alice Through the Looking Glass*, Chapter 6

Introduction

This chapter approaches the question of who owns psychoanalysis by seeking to understand the nature of ownership
from a psychoanalytic point of view. Owning and using
psychoanalytic ideas is not like owning and using physical objects,
though in our current consumer culture there is a pressure to
reduce "intellectual knowledge" to the status and nature of a physical possession. The possession of ideas is better understood in
terms of identification, about which psychoanalysis has a lot to say.

These considerations lead to views about training and professional qualification which could supplement the criteria we already use.

Owning psychoanalysis means something different from owning a Picasso painting. For instance, to own the idea of the Oedipus complex means to be in agreement with the idea as plausible or probable. D. H. Lawrence recognized its relevance as a means to understand his book, *Sons and Lovers*—probably in 1913, just before his final draft. Did he then become an owner of psychoanalysis? Not really. May Sinclair probably discovered psychoanalytic ideas a little earlier when she collaborated in opening the Medico-Psychological Clinic, also in 1913. Her novel *Mary Oliver: A Life* (1919) seems influenced by Freudian ideas on personal development. Lytton Strachey certainly informed his biography, *Elizabeth and Essex* (1928), with Freudian ideas, and even sent a copy to Freud for comment. A segment of literary intellectuals in Britain in the first quarter of the twentieth century found psychoanalytic ideas useful. They did not have to pay for their use. Their use of Freud's ideas is different from, say, buying a car manufactured by BMW.

Havelock Ellis was central to the late nineteenth-century movement for sexual freedom. He knew of Freud's views and accepted them as conforming to his own—on sexuality, its repression, oral and anal gratifications, autoerotism, and narcissism and the whole of childhood sexual development (Sulloway, 1979). After Ellis published the first volume of his work in Germany (*Studies in the Psychology of Sex, Vol. 1*) in 1896, he triumphantly sent a reprint of his paper on autoerotism to Freud (in 1898, actually). From this Freud took that term as well as "narcissism". There was some correspondence between the two (Jones, 1957); and Freud acknowledged his debt to Ellis's work in the "Three essays on the theory of sexuality" (1905a). Ellis then regarded Freud as a follower (Grosskurth, 1980). Later, Freud's fame grew beyond Ellis's, who was then perplexed that Freud had taken over his own place as campaigner and visionary for the sexual revolution Ellis's particular project had led him to appropriate Freud as one of his disciples. Freud would have none of it, and appropriated Havelock Ellis's ideas. Who owned these ideas—Havelock Ellis, or Freud? It is hard to answer one way or the other.

This quarrel over the provenance of ideas is different from the quarrel over the rights to physical property. Authors can, and publishers do, claim "intellectual property" as if they were pieces of physical property—like a piece of land, say. And in law, copyright has a monetary value. A legal formula has developed similar to that of patents for inventions. The first person to have an idea, and to publish it, has the right to claim it as "his", and thus make it analogous to physical property, with monetary value. But that is not what is meant by owning an idea, and not what is inferred in the title of this book. The kind of owning we want to consider is much more interesting: why these meanings have converged.

Owning clearly has interesting, and perhaps quite complicated, and obviously diverse, meanings. Do these meanings matter? And, does it matter who owns psychoanalysis, whatever we mean by that? Would it not be more straightforward to ask, "Who uses psychoanalysis?" We might then avoid tedious semantic discussions, or legal niceties that turn ideas into money. However, it does seem to me that there should be some interest in the question. First, Freud and others *did* want to own psychoanalytic ideas in the sense of having a control over what was done with them, how they were used, and developed. The early dissidents from Freud departed from him on the grounds of his possessiveness in this respect. It is as if this kind of possessiveness has promoted the profligate variety of species of psychoanalysis that now exist. Second, in my view, "owning" an idea does have interesting meanings, which can throw light on quite important social processes, both within the psychoanalytic world and outside it.

Matter, energy and information

Lytton Strachey's brother, James, found psychoanalytic ideas more than useful. He became a psychoanalyst, and then he "belonged" to the Psychoanalytical Society. Owning and belonging are clearly complex things when it comes to ideas and people.

The circulation of ideas is different to the circulation of money or of physical goods. It is also different from the circulation of energy in an electrical circuit. Ideas, like information, do not obey the "law of conservation of matter and energy". They are, like life, infinitely reproducible. So, one can barely control who takes ideas into their own possession—as Freud found out with Adler, Jung, Rank, and the other dissidents. In fact, Freud did conflate the circulation of energy with the circulation of ideas. His economic model was aimed at doing just that. He wanted to give an account of psychology in terms of physical processes and a mythical law of "the conservation of psychic energy".

In such a physical account there is a constancy of energy—or of matter (and therefore of physical goods). However, when we make a photocopy of a letter, the information, the symbols are infinitely reproducible. The same with downloading a computer file. The physical matter (paper), energy (electricity) or disc space are limited. They can be used up in a way that information is not. Information, as symbols and representations, can multiply without being consumed, even though the physical matter and energy can.

Freud, when inventing his economic model, was probably wrong in equating the existence of representations (as memories, dreams, fantasies, etc.) with the consumption of energy. The economics of representations is simply *not* the same as the economics of matter and energy. Freud erred in explaining mind in terms of quantities of physical energy. Jung put his money on the immaterial world; he then descended into a world of mysticism and mystery. Without properly clarifying this, Jung took his leave of Freud in 1913; and they both thought it was to do with mythology.

However, there is a perfectly materialist way of conceptualizing the demise of the economic model. Norbert Weiner (1948) was one of the first prophets of the information age, and saw the difference between what he called energy and information. It is the contrast between what flows in an electrical power cable, and what flows in a telephone cable. One exists to transmit quantities, and the other to transmit differences.[1]

Products of the mind are radically different from products of the body. Mental products are representations and they are not identical with that which they represent. If they are equated with bodily products and parts, then that is psychosis.[2] If mental products, parts and contents that inhabit our thoughts are representations, what is their "nature"? And how can they be "owned"?

Identification

Psychotic and primitive mental functioning operate as if thoughts are physical objects that can be relocated from one place to another,[3] but more mature mental functioning uses representations which, though movable, are infinitely reproducible.[4] So, representations do not comply with the rules that govern physical bodies, and can therefore be moved from mind to mind without obeying any law of conservation, or even conforming to post-Newtonian physics. The rules that govern representations are different. Ownership of representations is very different from the concrete ownership of body parts and primitive mental objects.

Some schools of psychoanalysis might regard the specific laws governing the communication of representation as those of semiotics and language. However, in this chapter, I explore the ownership and belonging of representations and ideas as a matter of identification.[5] For instance, I have a view of England; that is my mental representation. It is truly *my* view; but it is true, too, that I have gained my view of "England" from others—other English people. Indeed, it is *because* of others that I have a view of England. *We* share a view, a representation of England. The trade in representations is governed by the rules of group dynamics, to which we need to turn.

My starting point is Freud's "Group psychology and the analysis of the ego" (Freud, 1921c).[6] Psychodynamically, a group is formed by a negotiation between individuals at an unconscious level. So, a group exists when the individuals have successfully agreed on the same "ego-ideal". This means that each individual internalizes the same representation of the group and its purpose. We can be said to "identify" with the ideal of our group. This is then a defining feature of the group, its "group ideal", in which each individual possesses, or owns, the same internal representation. Central to Freud's theory is this common internalization. His example is the congregation of a Christian church where all have "Christ in their heart". "Christ" is owned and all the members of that church group give internal allegiance to him. It also creates a bond between all the individuals with the same allegiance. The key is that trade in a representation proliferates until all members possess it—or, to put it differently, the group exists when all members have this internal representation, whoever else is in the geographical vicinity.[7] The collective group-ideal defines the group for as long as the allegiance to the ideal lasts. So a group is formed, and defined, by who internalizes and pays allegiance to a particular ego-ideal. There is a belonging to the group, as well as a deep kind of *ownership* of it. Ownership, in this important sense, is an allegiance to the defining group ideal—and that ownership is an internal state.

When we come to groups of analysts, we can give this meaning to the idea of "owning psychoanalysis". Owning psychoanalysis means allegiance to a collective internal representation of psycho-analysis—the group ideal of psychoanalysts. It is a process of identifying with the group ideal. Our group is bound together by our allegiance to the collective representation of psychoanalysis—or perhaps, more personally, bound together by allegiance to the collective representation of Freud himself.

Motives. What makes for an allegiance like this, one that constitutes ownership of the ideal? Allegiance to psychoanalysis is motivated by something personal that leads to the internalization of its representation. That internalization may come simply from reading a psychoanalytic text, for instance Freud's popular joke book (Freud, 1905c). However, it is not so simple; it is not simply an intellectual absorption of the ideas. I remember, in my case, discovering Freud's "Three essays on sexuality" (Freud, 1905d), soon after going to medical school as a late adolescent. There was more to my motivation than a pure wish for intellectual learning. I was emotionally motivated, as a puzzled adolescent, by sexual matters. I could say this was the beginning of my allegiance to psychoanalysis—I began to possess an internal representation. Later, I remember as a young psychiatrist reading a Penguin book called *The Psychotic; Understanding Madness* (Crowcroft, 1967), where the dynamic theories of psychosis evolved by various psychoanalysts and psychiatrists were systematically presented. It spoke to my own sense of obligation towards patients with whom I felt helpless and bemused. My angst when trying to work with them, as well as probably an unconsciously need to help, gave another root to my motives. The section of that book on Melanie Klein was so intricate and mind-numbing, it struck me that this might really be the key to the equally mind-numbing mind of the schizophrenic patient. So, I decided her theory might be worth looking into further.

For myself, troubled feelings of a personal and a professional kind drove me to an internalization and allegiance of some kind to my psychoanalytic reading. Personal anxieties prompted my internalization of psychoanalytic ideas as an ego-ideal. Subsequent allegiance could be called an "ownership; and the ego-ideal developed under the influence of a psychoanalytic group I decided to join. First, as a confused adolescent, I was emotionally drawn to reading Freud because of the wish to know more about my own, and others', sexuality; then in the second place, I needed some purchase on my professional ambitions to help the intractable patients I found in the wards when I was a psychiatric trainee; and third, I joined a group with whom I shared a group-ideal.

This explanation of my motivation may not be very deep psychoanalytically; those insights were considerably deepened when I eventually started my own analysis. The point is that the process of ownership is a compound process starting emotionally with an internalization resulting in a mental representation—the representation may be intellectual, but the motive is more personal; and, then, a subsequent allegiance to the ideal as a group one.[8] Not only did I give an allegiance to psychoanalysis, but increasingly training involved developing an allegiance specifically to the Klein group ideal (or perhaps "sub-group" ideal would be the correct term).[9] Training is therefore partly an exercise in internalizing and stabilizing the group ideal of a particular school of psychoanalysis. It is *both* intellectual learning *and* personal identifying.[10]

In summary, the process of ownership is a mixture of external and internal processes involved in developing an allegiance to a group ideal.

Part-identification

Since Freud died in 1939, the allegiance to psychoanalysis has multiplied with an increasingly diverse set of group ideals (or sub-group ideals), promoted by the diverging set of psychoanalytic schools. A large number of specific constellations of psychoanalytic ideas exist which can be adopted as ego-ideals. Therefore what is internalized now has to be chosen from a wide variety of sub-group ideals.

So, a contemporary representation of psychoanalysis has many variants. Clearly, the psychoanalytic group ideal is capable of considerable mutation. Because this plurality of psychoanalysis is often cited to the discredit of psychoanalysis, and against the scientific status of psychoanalysis, it is worth seeing whether this view of "owning" based on identification with a group ideal has anything to say about the alarming mutability of the psychoanalytic group-ideal.

Speculatively, it is possible to give a brief sketch of the factors which are involved, for the purpose of further enquiry. The factors would include:

(i) *Personal biography*. Illustrating with my own case, motivation was initially of a very personal kind. I absorbed my representation of psychoanalysis into the space that my personal needs and anxieties occupied. It is well known that Freud's own childhood background had intergenerational confusions in which his older half-brother was roughly the same age as his mother. Therefore, it might not be surprising that his psychological theories orbited around the intergenerational problems of Oedipus. Melanie Klein had post-natal depression following the birth of all three of her children. Hence, she was personally "primed" to describe the depressive position.

Thus, the constellation of psychoanalytic ideas which compose a person's internal representation may partly be an individual response on the basis of their own life pre-occupations. There is a degree of personal selection and distortion that can creep into each person's ownership.

(ii) *Social history*. The *zeitgeist* can contribute to the way psychoanalytic theory develops at any particular phase of history over the last century. For instance, in the later 1940s, after the Second World War, there was a significant push in British politics towards a collaborative caring society—the welfare state. It is not surprising that issues of motherhood and infancy became at the same time articulated in psychoanalysis, particularly with Bowlby and Winnicott (as well as Melanie Klein). The ownership of the ideas arising from an allegiance to those of the social context may therefore have a selective influence on the way psychoanalytic ideas developed in Britain at the time. In short, did the representation of society as a caring mother influence the allegiance of psychoanalysts to representations of motherhood?[11]

(iii) *Group anxiety and conflict.* The division of psychoanalysis into separate groups, with distinct "group ideals", has led to pressures that are placed by one sub-group upon another. Each of the psychoanalytic groups can represent, not only psychoanalysis to themselves, but also the errors of another group's representation. The records of the "Controversial Discussions" in British psychoanalysis in the early 1940s (King & Steiner, 1991) are scrupulously documented, and give us an insight into the way psychoanalytic groups separated from each other, gaining their own specific group-ideals. They exemplify the inter-group dynamics involved in the formation of a sub-group, and of sub-group ideals.

For instance, in those discussions the Viennese analysts and the Klein group polarized over the question of mental activity at birth—the first group said it did not occur, the second that it did. Entrenched positions were taken up partly through allegiance to an ego-ideal and at the same time a sort of counter-allegiance *against* the ideal of the opposing group. The groups did not split apart completely but remained sub-groups of the British Psycho-Analytic Society.[12] As a result, the British Society did not deal with the Kleinian dissidents by disowning them; nor did the Viennese withdraw in disgust. Instead, the Society remained one, but split between two group ideals. At the time, and enduringly since, the sub-groups have tended towards polarities, partly defined by each other (Hinshelwood, 1997).

(iv) *Scientific challenges.* In parallel with the emotional and group dynamic influences on psychoanalytic representations, psychoanalytic practice has always been challenged by new and difficult patients. When Freud was defeated by Dora, he did not give up his allegiance to psychoanalysis, as he represented it to himself in 1900. Instead, he evolved his ideas on transference, and especially negative transference. He did not change his allegiance, he changed his ideal, to which he continued to give the old allegiance.

New kinds of patients lead to new ideas—for instance, the Kleinian interest in psychosis in the 1940s and 1950s led to developments in technique (part-object interpretations) and to theories (especially of projective identification). Also, new kinds of techniques lead to new kinds of patients amenable to psychoanalytic influence—for instance, the development of techniques with toys led to the possibility of the psychoanalytic treatment of children (as opposed to mere observation of them). All these developments of new patients, conceptual developments, and technical innovations interlock and give rise to modifications in the representation of psychoanalysis within psychoanalysts. If these influences are not consistent amongst all psychoanalysts, then some will be influenced by these challenges, and others not, leading again to divergence in group ideals, and thus matter for inter-group dynamics.

These factors are some of the influences on how the internal representation of psychoanalysis mutates. The psychoanalytic group ideal is a plastic mental structure. Its plasticity is an advantage in allowing realistic and scientific advance; but has proved disadvantageous in allowing emotional factors to give rise to fraught schisms within the movement. Owning rigid group ideals, within polarizing inter-group dynamics, leads to an internal incoherence that fuels emotional contests within psychoanalysis and disrespect from without.

Constructing and selecting representations. Outside the world of trained psychoanalysts, the internal representations of psychoanalysis are also very variable. Those ideals to which non-analysts ally themselves can be composed of quite erratic selections of ideas. The take-up within a culture is influenced by factors extraneous to psychoanalysis. In Britain between 1893 and 1918, at least seven different cultural locations took ownership of psychoanalysis.[13] I mentioned one of these cultural groups earlier, in connection with Havelock Ellis: the sexual liberation movement. Their interest in Freud was his understanding of the pernicious effects of sexual repression. Another was the group of literary intellectuals, Lawrence, Sinclair, and Lytton Strachey, who used the Oedipus complex as the means to deepen understanding of the characters in their writing.

There was also the medical profession. They noted Freud for his method of treating hysteria—Bernard Hart, Ernest Jones, and Wilfred Trotter. Educationists, such as Homer Lane and, later, Susan Isaacs and A. S. Neill, were interested in another aspect of psychoanalytic theory, that of child development. Also, at the turn of the century, the Society for Psychical Research, an élitist international group of intellectuals in the latter half of the nineteenth century, applied the new methods of natural science to conquer religious questions, particularly to find evidence of life after death. Frederick Myers (1904), chief researcher of the Society, directed the research towards the altered states of consciousness found in hysteria and in psychic mediums. Hence, he particularly focused on Freud's conception of the unconscious as the element in psychoanalysis to which he and the Society could give an allegiance.[14] In 1900 the British Psychological Society was founded, to pursue the newly established discipline of experimental psychology, and turned in part to psychoanalysis and, therefore, to Freud's claim to an experimental approach corresponding to the experimental method of natural science. So, psychoanalysis captured their allegiance for its experimental method. Philosophers became interested in psychoanalysis, for their own specific reasons too—their interest in the "nature of mind". For instance, Karen Stephen, a niece of Bertrand Russell (and eventually a psychoanalyst herself) originally studied Bergson (Stephen, 1922). Bergson's (1919) philosophy was based on his idea of a life force, the *"élan vital"*, and hence Freud's theory of psychic energy was her representation of psychoanalysis.

There are thus seven cultural sites that took an interest in Freud through seven specific aspects of psychoanalysis, which they isolated. The representation of psychoanalysis that they owned was highly constructed from psychoanalytic ideas pertinent to the crucial issues in their own fields. Their allegiances to psychoanalysis involved seven different representations which they composed for themselves. They "owned" psychoanalysis, but in very different forms. Their various allegiances to psychoanalytic ideas came from their pre-existing interests, anxieties or preoccupations. Thus, owning psychoanalysis involved incorporating some aspect of psychoanalysis into the group ideals of their own discipline. The plasticity amongst psychoanalytic group ideals arose from the particular requirements of the owning group; it comes from the very motive the group had for owning the ideas as theirs. If the motive prompts a variation, it makes grave difficulties for controlling what psychoanalysis is owned, and for restricting the owners to the group that accepts psychoanalysis just as Freud required.

Indicative identity

Until he died in 1939, Freud did try to control ownership of psychoanalytic ideas by his paternalistic act of indicating who was in and
who was out of the psychoanalytic fold.

Owning and belonging. Freud's favoured method of dealing with
dissidents, after conducting debate with them, was to push them
out of the psychoanalytic movement. They no longer "belonged".
That is, psychoanalysis no longer owned them. There is an implicit
symmetry between owning and belonging; you can be owned by
the group whose ideas you own. Does psychoanalysis belong to
me, or do I belong to psychoanalysis? Such a question is confusing,
if we use the ordinary everyday meaning of the words. Owning and
belonging as applied to physical goods, have a clear reciprocal relation—I own my car, which belongs to me. In the physical world,
owning and belonging come from a relation of possession.

However, when it comes to the symbolic, representational
world, ideas in the mind are different. What happens to the relation
of possession when I talk of "my" train journey or "my" accoun-
tant, "my" preference or "my" stalker. These point to a clear distinction from physical possessions, which has a philosophical depth
that needs greater investigation. Maybe philosophers have made
that investigation, though I do not propose to pursue it here. It is
sufficient that we recognize that Freud (amongst others) felt that to
disown a certain follower dispossessed that person of ownership of
psychoanalysis. Essentially, this is group maintenance.

Professional identity. Enduring squabbles over who shall use the
word "psychoanalyst" became important after the First World War,
with the debate over lay analysis (Freud, 1926e). The dispute is
current today between the United Kingdom Council for Psychotherapy and the British Confederation of Psychotherapists. The use
of the terms "psychoanalyst", and "child psychotherapist" are
presently disputed. The International Psychoanalytical Association
and the American Psychoanalytic Association have been hauled
through the legal system for restrictive practices. The issue is both
enormously important and yet rather trivial. It is important because
it defines a professional practice with the intention that the public
should be protected. It is trivial in so far as it can become a battle-
ground for professional status and income protection.

Status, personal income and professional rigour should all go hand-in-hand, but there are many accusations that they do not. Psychoanalytic psychotherapists may accuse psychoanalysts of operating a closed shop; and psychoanalysts accuse psychoanalytic psychotherapists of wanting a status (and patients) not earned by rigorous training and professional practice. This professional jousting is tedious yet inflammatory; and the flames are stoked by the fact that there is no definitive boundary between the practice of psychoanalytic psychotherapy and psychoanalysis based on generally agreed principles or techniques (Frisch, Hinshelwood, & Gautier, 2001).

In Britain, the early stages in creating professional boundaries for the related field of psychotherapy, led to an indicative definition (Sieghart, 1978). This means we can tell who psychotherapists are by pointing to them, as opposed to functional definition, where the precise function is uniquely defined. Indicative definition is a basic and pragmatic form of definition—simply pointing to who has the identity. The definition is set just by usage within the language domain. However, when Humpty Dumpty decided a word means just what he wants it to—neither more nor less—then the arbitrariness of that method becomes obvious. It leads quickly to feelings of exclusion, rivalry, and resentment. Using a word, Humpty fashion, is the current mode of arguing out professional ownership.

The failure of definition is partly because the inclusion/exclusion criteria depend as much on group identities as on reasoned argument. The group formations seem, on the evidence of history to be uncontrollable—at least since 1939. And the purpose of this essay is to suggest that the psychoanalytic understanding of group dynamics and allegiances needs to be taken into account in discussions on the ownership of psychoanalysis.

Who belongs, owns.

Taking the identity. The rational arrangements for deciding who belongs is based on training. However, training in psychoanalysis, as in many fields, is more than instilling necessary knowledge and forms of practice. It is the process of offering the set of ideas that is the group ideal of psychoanalysis. The trainee identifies with his colleagues. He learns to belong as well as to practise. This gives psychoanalytic training a guild status; do we need something else? If training is to avoid being a recruitment drive for a particular group ideal, then what should it be? I believe there are a number of points to consider:

1. We should be more explicitly aware that training serves an important professional identity function, and that this can subvert the stated aims of training in favour of group recruitment. We need to be more explicit because the forces pushing in that direction are to do with the *unconscious* needs for a personal and professional identity. Identifying with professional ideas and practice are integral to personal identities.
2. Training needs to recognize the group identity and the group ideal; so, training should include a reflective element on those purposes which implicitly motivate trainers and trainees.
3. That reflection would necessarily recognize the unconscious history and pressures that have given rise to identifications and counter-identifications with the group ideals that are taught.

All these components of awareness and reflection involve the use of psychoanalytic understanding itself. Subjecting the trainees to such a process is compatible with the reflective nature of the subject they are learning. Eventually, as practising psychoanalysts, they will be expected to subject their analysing to reflection while they do it. There is no reason why such a reflective practice should not begin with their training itself.

4. A fourth element of training is really a process of "unlearning". If attitudes within society imply that professional learning is a product to be acquired like any material consumer item, we and our trainees may need to critique that; that is to say, we need to debate explicitly if ideas and identity are subject to the economics of consumer trade.

If the process of training might include a reflective syllabus with a critical eye on the nature of "ownership" of ideas (and the relation to belonging), then perhaps we could begin a project to discover what might constitute a training in which ownership and allegiance were disconnected.

Conclusions: psychoanalytic studies

I have tried to consider the manifold ways in which persons acquire identities, professional identities, and group identities. This inevitably requires a reflective practice that considers the relations between psychoanalysis and the cultural attitudes of the society in which it is practised. Neither the acquisition of ideas, nor of a professional identity, can be reified as "things" that a consumer society would normally trade. Ideas and belonging are not commodities; they are a matter of personal identity.

Over recent years, my allegiance to psychoanalysis has changed. I have become increasingly involved in the academic study and teaching of psychoanalytic ideas—where they come from, what can be done with them, how to compare them. In realizing that all kinds of academic disciplines use psychoanalytic ideas, I have had to consider the question to which this paper is addressed. In fact, the whole field of psychoanalytic studies appears to be a discipline that is focused around just this question: Who owns psychoanalysis? The question is adjacent to, and considerably overlaps with, the question: What can one do with the ideas? Various people adopt psychoanalytic ideas for certain purposes—for instance, surrealists believed they could adopt some of the techniques of the clinical practice of psychoanalysis in order to tap into the creativity of the primary process of their own unconscious. Do they "own" psychoanalysis? Freud did not espouse Dali, when they met. The surrealists did not identify with psychoanalysis in the way that psychoanalysts do in training.

In fact, Freud's own ambitions led him to a contradictory strategy. He constantly wished to make psychoanalysis relevant to other disciplines in the humanities. Just as the Society for Psychical Research thought that the powerful methods could be used to play upon religion and spirituality, so Freud thought that psychoanalysis could play upon issues in social science, and in aesthetics as well as in religion. But this led to frequent heartache when others took up his ideas, owned them as theirs, and then used them in their own way. For instance, Bronislav Malinowski, Professor of Anthropology at the London School of Economics, took Freud seriously and applied psychoanalytic ideas to his own field. Ultimately, he poured scorn on psychoanalysis for an ill-conceived attempt to illuminate anthropology with the Oedipus complex. However, he also fulsomely acknowledged

> But with all this, Freud's contribution to anthropology is of the greatest importance and seems to me to strike a very rich vein which must be followed up. For Freud has given us the first concrete theory about the relation between instinctive life and social institutions. [Malinowski, 1923, p. 650]

Malinowski was interested in Freud's theory of instincts, their material basis, and their manifestation in immaterial social structures. But, he dropped the Freudian Oedipus complex. He could be said to be giving Freud's psychoanalysis a fully anthropological perspective, though with a quite un-Freudian content. In fact, psychoanalysis rejected Malinowski (e.g. Jones, 1926).

As psychoanalysis directs itself towards influencing the whole field of the humanities as Freud believed it should, we also find it marching away in the opposite direction to close off a sealed world of knowledge against influence. The ironic result has been to create a fragmented world that lacks coherence in its world of knowledge and practice. If the proper field of psychoanalytic research is the clinical process, then the proper field of psychoanalytic studies is just the subject of this paper. It is a chance for a reflective moment on how psychoanalysis is doing in its project to influence the wider academic world. It can consider how psychoanalytic ideas are owned, how they are taken on as part of an identity—whether that is as a psychoanalyst or as a member of a discipline adjacent to psychoanalysis. We can consider out of the pressures of clinical strain, what sort of ideal is being internalized and given allegiance.

To this end, I have tried to create a space here to reconsider the nature of ownership, without it being closed off by possessive psychoanalysts; and without that space being immediately closed off by attitudes endemic in a consumer society, which places money and status on the same level of commodities as professional skills and material goods. In turn, psychoanalytic ideas themselves help us to understand the field of psychoanalytic studies, and to bring a psychoanalytic lens to bear on the idea of ownership.

The futility of legalizing ownership of ideas is apparent from the investigation in this chapter. The objects of a subjective mind do not conform to those of economic trade; and it is interesting how our cultural history has got us to a point where there is a serious argument that intellectual products should be considered like ordinary consumer goods. Unfortunately, the question of who owns psychoanalysis prompts a serious questioning of consumerist assumptions—and the need to examine the nature of trade in subjective goods—a project quite beyond Freud's own original one.

Notes

1. Although the contrast between quantities and differences does not quite capture that between energy and representations, we can see the direction that this should take. We need to somehow give "qualia" (in the sense of secondary qualities) a clearer conceptual distance from quantity. That clarification should perhaps be the central question for our contemporary neuroscience, rather then Freud's reductionist project.
2. We can remind ourselves of the patient described by Segal (1957) who when talking of a stool he had made in his occupational therapy session, blushed and became embarrassed as if the word/symbol "stool" had actually been a piece of faeces he had brought to the session with his analyst.
3. See Hinshelwood (1997) for a discussion of concrete internal objects in the psychoanalytic literature from the 1930s onwards.
4. Bion postulated a conversion process, which he called "alpha-function", that creates genuinely "'mental'" contents, representations ("conceptualizations", or "dream furniture" as he variously called them) out of raw sense data. Bion's alpha-function is a good enough representation of the maturation of sense data to mental contents, and serves as a marker of the boundary between material states and ideas.
5. As Segal (1957) argued, processes of identification are more fundamental than processes of symbolisation, and in fact underlie them.
6. A Jungian approach might perhaps start by considering the way the individual is inserted into the collective unconscious.
7. Even more complex are the *inter*-group dynamics, where the internal representation of one group includes a counter-representation of some other identified group—e.g. part of being a 1930s Nazi entailed being *not-Jewish*. It is perhaps an inevitable part of any

group identity (and thus the group ideal) that it involves a contrasting identification of the ideal of one or more other groups

8. This process is comparable to that which occurs in a successful analysis. The internalization is of a particularly personal kind. It is the analyst who is internalized as the representation of psychoanalytic ideas and functions. Perhaps one could say it is the analyst's own internal representation that is then reproduced as the analysand's representation. There is a strong link with Freud's "unconscious-to-unconscious communication", and, in fact, an internalization of the analyst's ego-ideal.

9. I have described the initial sub-group formation of Kleinians in a previous paper (Hinshelwood, 1997).

10. Some, such as Bion, would argue that there can be no process of learning without processes of identification (Bion, 1962).

11. See Zaretsky, 1999, for instance.

12. It was important for British psychoanalysts at the time that psychoanalysis should survive. It had been more or less wiped out by the Nazis on the continent of Europe. Small psychoanalytic societies did survive during the Nazi period in Switzerland and Sweden, but the British Psycho-Analytical Society was the only surviving "first division" group of psychoanalysts in Europe. And psychoanalysis in America was always regarded as very suspect by Freud and his most loyal followers at the time. Hence psychoanalysts in Britain, with whatever allegiances, were impelled to remain as solidly together as possible.

13. The numerous references to psychoanalytic users are available in Hinshelwood, 1995.

14. Freud wrote a paper called "The Unconscious" for the Society's journal, in 1910—a paper he wrote in English, it is claimed.

References

Bergson, H. (1919). L'Energie Spirituelle. Paris: Alcan.

Bion, W. R. (1962). Learning from Experience. London: Heinemann.

Crowcroft, A. (1967). The Psychotic: Understanding Madness. London: Penguin.

Ellis, H. (1896). Das Konträre Geschlechtsgefühl (Studies in the Psychology of Sex, Vol. 1). Leipzig: Wigands.

Freud, S. (1905d). Three essays on the theory of sexuality. *S.E.*, *7*. London: Hogarth.

Freud, S. (1905e). Jokes and their relation to the unconscious. *S.E.*, *8*. London: Hogarth.

Freud, S. (1921e). Group psychology and the analysis of the ego. *S.E.*, *12*. London: Hogarth.

Freud, S. (1926e). The question of lay analysis. *S.E.*, *20*. London: Hogarth.

Frisch, S., Hinshelwood, R. D., & Gautier, J.-M. (2001). *Psychoanalysis and Psychotherapy: The Controversies and the Future*. London: Karnac.

Grosskurth, P. (1980). *Havelock Ellis: A Biography*. London: Allen Lane.

Hinshelwood, R. D. (1995). Psycho-analysis in Britain: points of cultural access 1893-1918, *International Journal of Psycho-Analysis*, *76*: 135–151.

Hinshelwood, R. D. (1997). The elusive concept of "internal objects" and the origins of the Klein group 1934–1943. *International Journal of Psycho-Analysis 78*: 877–897.

Jones, E. (1926). The origin and structure of the super-ego. *International Journal of Psycho-Analysis*, *7*: 303–311.

Jones, E. (1957). *The Life and Work of Sigmund Freud. Volume III. The Last Phase 1919–1939*. London: Hogarth.

King, P. & Steiner, R. (1991). *The Freud–Klein Controversial Discussions 1941–1945*. London: Routledge.

Lawrence, D. H. (1913). *Sons and Lovers*. London: Duckworth.

Malinowski, B. (1923). Psychoanalysis and anthropology. *Nature*, *112*: 650–651.

Myers, F. W. H. (1904). *Human Personality and its Survival of Bodily Death*. London: Longmans.

Segal, H. (1957). Notes on symbol formation. *International Journal of Psychoanalysis*, 38: 391–397.

Sieghart, P. (1978). *A Report of a Professions Joint Working Party*. Rugby: Joint Professions Working Party.

Sinclair, M. (1919). *Mary Olivier: A Life*. London: Cassell.

Stephen, K. (1922). *The Misuse of Mind*. London: Kegan Paul, Trench and Trubner.

Strachey, L. (1928). *Elizabeth and Essex*. London: Chatto and Windus.

Sulloway, F. (1979). *Freud, Biologist of the Mind*. London: Basic Books.

Weiner, N. (1948). *Cybernetics: or Control and Communication in the Animal and the Machine*. Cambridge, MA: MIT Press.

Zaretsky, E. (1999). "One large secure, solid background": Melanie Klein and the origins of the welfare state. *Psychoanalysis and History*, *1*: 136–154.

CHAPTER FOUR

From insight to self-begetting:

On the post-modern vicissitudes of psychoanalytic ownership

Jorge L. Ahumada

Introduction

Though understood as a practice, psychoanalysis seems scarcely liable to ownership; it is argued that as soon as it is freed from its clinical anchors and responsibilities it starts to function at the service of new-fangled goals in the guise of "psychoanalytic discourses". In the wider frame of the current media-led Society of the Spectacle, those goals are commonly ruled by self-begetting in its Romantic emancipatory format, as illustrated in Fichte's dictum "I am solely my own creation". Thus it happens that on passing from private spaces into public ones the rhetorical goals of post-modern academic "psychoanalytic discourses", acknowledgedly fictive and celebratory, are on a different track from the evidences-led goals of insight on our up-to-then unknown psychic realities, as happened for Freud. Epistemically, post-modern "psychoanalytic discourses" rely on reductionistic, formalistic definitions of what science is, and thereupon declare all other realms, mind included, to be purely discursive and literary.

Who owns psychoanalysis? A quick response is: nobody. A second one might read: those who can benefit from it. A likely third response would be: those who master it. An unlikely fourth answer, everybody, is all too relevant.

1. That nobody owns psychoanalysis appears self-evident, because enquiry on one's own mind and on another person's mind cannot be possessed. Enquiry can only be pursued.
2. Those who may personally benefit hold legitimate rights. As clinical enquiry and therapy coincide, psychic evolutions are the guide for its exercise, technically and ethically. Besides, in order to be worthy, the conceptual scaffoldings that go by the name of "theory" need to derive from clinical evidences.
3. Those who actually master its exercise might appear closest to actual ownership. Actually, such an idea is at loggerheads with the post-modern tenet of the egalitarianism of knowledge and opinions, and would smack of elitism; besides, given that mastery quickly collapses to possessiveness, it rests on renouncing ownership pretences.
4. That everybody owns psychoanalysis admits a positive and a negative: Who owns psychoanalysis?, and: Who disowns psychoanalysis? Fields deemed *Seelisch*, relating to psyche, mind, soul, or spirit, readily co-opt psychoanalysis for their outlooks and purposes, or disown the relevance of its claims.

On private and public spaces

Although in the main psychoanalysis cannot be forthrightly owned, fights go on around and within it: the "Freud wars" are common parlance in the current "culture wars", and this book's title *Who Owns Psychoanalyis?* points to hassles over its place and nature. Freud may have anticipated such hassles when he stamped Virgil's phrase at the forefront of his "Traumdeutung" ("The interpretation of dreams") (1900a): *"Flectere si nequeo superos, Acheronta movebo"* ("As I cannot bend the heavens, I must shake the hells"). Anyway, psychoanalytic enquiry has sought its modest heavens while braving its way through various hells.

A path out of this morass would be to assume that the term "psychoanalysis" presently encompasses diverse activities, and varied hells, both private and public.

Public spaces are prone to lofty infighting in most if not all disciplines: should psychoanalysis be excepted? Freud knew it didn't immunize its offspring against the collegiate bickering and manoeuvering, fraternal and intergenerational, that plague the academy. That possessiveness, sibling rivalry, and the two-fold nature, up-down and down-up, of Oedipal rivalry, prove more enduring than the laborious insights gained on the couch puts the accent on all too human frailties of insight and attempts at maturity, most noticeable when issues are played out in public settings.

Private spaces and public spaces. This duality becomes a gap in what Guy Debord (1967) called the Society of the Spectacle, highlighting that psychoanalysis makes double duty, for clinical insight and for academic protagonism. In private spaces, the possessiveness analysand and analyst may display in session are part and parcel of what is being studied. This allows a chance to seek the evidences and deal with them from the twin Freudian vertices of *Deutungsarbeit*, the work of interpretation, and *Durcharbeitung*, working-through.

It is unclear what in public spaces might provide an evidential role similar to the personal evidences the analysand musters in order to pursue and monitor the work of interpretation and working-through. Moreover, that in public realms eloquence takes centre stage is powered by the fact that, unhooked from its Aristotelian subservience to logic, post-modern rhetoric furthers imaginative self-begetting.

The privacy requirements for psychoanalytic evidences-finding

In order to illustrate the double work on the clinical evidences, analysand and analyst each playing a distinct interpretive role, let me recall the initial process in the treatment of a rather disturbed young woman in her early thirties, who at that time considered internment in a psychiatric day-care hospital; she hadn't sought it yet because she feared being unable eventually to extract herself from it. Some three years before, her mother had died from breast cancer, with skin ulcerations all over her chest; my patient, an only daughter, undertook the harrowing nursing care. After mother's death she kept together until she had a fall after being accidentally pushed.

Thereafter she felt utterly alone and became seriously depressed, started psychotherapy, and was put on antidepressants by psychiatrists, to no avail. Overburdened by the demands of her two-year-old child to the point of being unable to care for him, she in turn overburdened those around her with demands for company and relief, which overflowed into phone calls to almost anyone, and frantic searches for faith-healers, making her question her sanity. Because of her emotional demands her friends avoided her, while her fed-up husband threatened divorce and to request judicial custody of the baby on account of her manifest incapacity to handle him.

The diagnostic interviews brought enacted evidence of what she voiced. Her narrative amounted to an unending scream, psychic survival being at stake on both sides: she as the screaming baby in search of a container—at the level, in Money-Kyrle's (1977) terms, of desperate projective identification—while I tried to contain the uncontainable and to attend to my psychic survival; spine-chilling memories of a case of hebephrenia treated long ago kept popping up. That on their symmetry her everyday universe and what went on with me seemed to be one and the same risked signalling the road to psychic oblivion.

It was unclear, then, whether the enmeshing, ongoing primitive emotional phenomena would be eventually contained and understood at psychic levels and dealt with by insight, or whether she had rightly assumed she belonged in a psychiatric day hospital. Said in terms of Matte-Blanco's (1975, 1988) understanding of the logic of the unconscious, consciously we think in terms of individuals while the unconscious does not acknowledge individuals, only unconscious classes. It could therefore be said that I found myself equated to a primordial all-containing mother, as calamitously happened to her friends and her husband.

While unable or unwilling to stop pressuring others or pressuring me, she was not unaware of the result, dimly acknowledging that (non)survival of the object, in Winnicott's (1971) terms, was crucial in her predicament. Additionally, she grasped that she was burdening herself with emotional tasks and anxieties beyond her capacities, as had happened with her trying to nurse her mother's ulcerations. Besides, humour flickered through at times, and sometimes she managed to hold herself to some measure. Fleeting awareness of evidences encouraged hope, and I felt confident enough to verbally map what went on in terms of her being the screaming infant forcing her ill-feelings into others, including myself, and that efforts to relieve malaise by shoving it into others backfired badly, which left her devastated.

This bare clinical sketch aims to show that the clinical situation is intensely personal and is loaded with issues of psychic survival, which must be patiently contained and resolved by way of discrimination of levels and step-by-step insights. Thus, although only later in treatment when survival was less to the fore, she came to recognize the veritable odium that—mainly on the occasions of her husband's at times enormous mindblindness—went together with her desperation. Here, what Money-Kyrle calls an error easy and terrible, to mistake a desperate projection for a destructive one, an error whereby "the beginnings of a constructive link between patient and analyst may be destroyed" (Money-Kyrle 1978, p. 463) shows itself as technical rather than substantive. Once contained in the analytic link and thereafter, through insight, at intra-psychic levels, desperate and destructive projective identifications often come out as steps in the same process.

Enquiry on issues of psychic survival is right at the core of the clinical situation, so much so that Bion affirms in one of his last works that

> An analyst is not doing his job if he investigates something because it is pleasurable or profitable. Patients do not come to him because they anticipate some agreeable imminent event; they come because they are ill at ease. The analyst must share the danger, and has, therefore, to share the "smell" of the danger. . . . It is your job to be curious about that danger—not cowardly, not irresponsible. . . . Anyone who is not afraid when he is engaged on psycho-analysis is either not doing his job, or is unfitted for it. [Bion, 1979, p. 83]

Enquiry on the anxieties and enactments pivots on starkly *de re* issues of personal psychic survival for analysand and analyst. Put in terms of Matte-Blanco's symmetrical and asymmetrical logics, it can be said that the interplay of the primitive levels of mind operating in terms of classes, and the evolved levels recognizing individuals, is crucially deployed in the analytic session in ways that mightily depend on the anxieties involved, which can thus be intuited and shown.

Detailed clinical enquiry aimed at accessing the interplay of primitive and evolved levels of mind amounts to a different universe from its celebratory and rhetorical uses in academia, flaunting psychoanalysis as a performing/literary art, or deriding it as an unworthy simile of the hallowed role of the literary.

The reader must judge whether either or both of these tasks—enquiry and rhetoric—is legitimate, and which, if any, amounts to misuse.

The literary disowning and re-owning of psychoanalysis

In a founding document of English Romanticism, his *Biographia Literaria*, Samuel Coleridge complained of how literary critics put their might at the service of disowning:

> With the pen out of their hands they are *honourable men*. They exert indeed power (which is to that of the injured party who should attempt to expose their glaring perversions and misstatements, as twenty to one) to write down, and (where the author's circumstances permit) to *impoverish* the man, whose learning and genius they themselves in private have repeatedly admitted. [Coleridge, 1817, pp. 290–291]

With the advent of the "linguistic turn" in philosophy during the second half of the twentieth century, language was hypostatized into an autonomous object, power or activity, as noted, among others, by Jameson (1981, p. 63); later (1983) he advances that pastiche having replaced parody, a new kind of academic writing called "theory" mounts a free-wheeling "theoretical discourse". More recently still, he points out that the post-modernist yearns for breaks, for the tell-tale instant after which it is no longer the same, for shifts and irrevocable changes in the representation of things and of the way they change: thereby the contents are dealt with as being just one more image, and what is titled "theoretical discourse" gets privileged place among the arts and genres (Jameson, 1990, p. xvi). As the Derridian critic Gregory Ulmer puts it, post-modern academic discourses are referential in the manner of "narrative allegory", exploring the literal—*letteral*—level of the language itself: narrative allegory no longer seeks an instance of truth but a consideration of effects—like a piece in a collage. These effects constitute a second language where the abstraction of concepts is diverted to fictive ends (Ulmer, 1983, pp. 95–96). On such fictive "theoretical discourses", Simpson explains in *The Academic Postmodern and the Rule of Literature*, the world outside the academy gets radically redefined "as a result of the exporting of literary–critical categories into disciplines that previously would have resisted them" (Simpson, 1995, p. 2), in a refiguring of boundaries that mostly abolishes the said disciplines.

The disowning of psychoanalysis and its literary reappropriation often, but not always, go hand in hand. Predictably, critical disowning aims at the pertinence of both its clinical method and its clinical evidences, under two distinct motives: as fake evidence in the case of physicalistic epistemologies, and as fake literature in the case of such literary luminaries as Foucault, Harold Bloom, Frederick Crews, and George Steiner. Derision and mock-dismissal in order to reappropriate it for the ludically literary has Jacques Derrida as its champion.

The stereotypical manoeuvre disqualifying the evidential value of the psychoanalytic method and of whatever comes out of it involves putting forward as prescriptive, and as the test for empiricity, a formalistic-mechanistic version of science. Having discussed elsewhere (Ahumada, 1997a,b) Grünbaum's and Popper's critiques of the evidential value of clinical psychoanalysis, I need add now that Popper (1994) finally acknowledged *in articulo mortis* that his steadfast demarcationism had no way to give Darwin's work proper entrance into the hallowed realm of science!

This sobering admission concerning Darwin's work is *a fortiori* valid on Freud's work: Popperian demarcationism is equally unfit in both cases, and for similar reasons. Because, as the Nobel Prize-winning immunologist and neurobiologist Gerald Edelman (1992) notes, the methods of doing science on inanimate objects (those brandished by Grünbaum and Popper) are not adequate for doing science with animals possessing intentionality (man included) and thus, where we want our ideas on mind to keep in line with physics, we should declare an embargo on all the psychological phenomena we are acquainted with in everyday life! The moot point is that people are unlike orbiting celestial bodies, which should suffice on why psychoanalysis cannot be like physics.

A strikingly formalistic–mechanistic definition of science presides over Michel Foucault's effort to sustain

"the experimental or formal criteria of scientificity . . . which are indispensable to the constitution of a science. . . . Only propositions that obey certain laws of construction belong to a domain of scientificity. [Foucault, 1969, pp. 182–183]

To such formally ruled *scientific domains* able to provide scientific knowledge (*connaissance*) he counterposes *archeological domains*— discursive realms where knowledge (*savoir*) is found in varied practices: fiction, reflection, narrative accounts, institutional regulations, and political decisions (*ibid.*, p. 183); from the point of view of archeology as a general theory of production all these belong at the same level (*ibid.*, p. 207). Soon after (Foucault, 1971), he avows that the evidential value of what emerges there is to be dealt with simply as enunciations, such domains being considered "not sciences, but 'disciplines'" (*ibid.*, p. 222). Thus, to Foucault, "sciences" are defined by their formal structure, while "disciplines" are just "discursive practices" unbound from evidences, understood as language-driven on the shaky grounds that "to speak is to do something" (*ibid.*, p. 209). Except for the formalized sciences, there are no evidential substrates to which statements should adhere. Similarly for Derrida, who in *The Postcard from Socrates to Freud and Beyond* (1980) defines science in equally formalistic terms, liberating the field of psychoanalysis for a playful literary *bricolage* assuming (*"il n'y a pas de hors-texte"*) that there is nothing outside of the text and no way to get outside language. A forthright Derrida admirer, the philosopher Richard Rorty describes this basic attitude thus: "he is concerned more and more with the beautiful, if fantastical, rearrangement of what he remembers" (Rorty, 1988, p. 136).

Now, arguing from decades in Continental academic circles where, he says, he found intolerable the political–philosophical terrorism starting in the 1960s, the French philosopher Jacques Bouveresse bewails "what happens when rhetoric, the power of words, and the cult of personality prevails over reason, logic and the rules of argumentation" (Bouveresse, 1991a, p. 140), adding that in the universes coming from the "poetic world-disclosers" like Hegel, Heidegger, and Derrida, philosophers generally don't believe that such a thing as error can exist in philosophy. Which, it must be said, allows no slot for the fine art of the nonsensical; - for what, as concerns Derrida's case, Ferry and Renaut (1985) call the pure play of meaning without end. Bouveresse reasons that presently "discussion is a narcissistic exercise, where each person takes turns showing off: quite soon, no one knows what they are talking about" (Bouveresse, 1991a, p. 142), and thus in those *letteral* realms philosophers just take turns inventing concepts.

One may then wonder why, when psychoanalysis is at issue, Bouveresse changes tack on the crucial theme of the evidential weights the philosopher's argument should respect for it to be taken as serious talk, as different from narcissistic exercises. In the case of psychoanalysis he puts forward a radical critique from the side of linguistic philosophy on its scientific character and the pertinence of the psychoanalytic method. His influential 1991 book, *Philosophie, mythologie et pseudo-science: Wittgenstein lecteur de Freud*, translated into English in 1995 under the title *Wittgenstein reads Freud. The Myth of the Unconscious*, steadily grants Wittgenstein the upper hand in what is at stake. Pointedly, Bouveresse here sustains that "what characterises the philosophical method is precisely the fact that there is nothing "hidden" to exhume, that everything is in principle immediately accessible to the surface, and that we already know, in a way, everything we need to know" (Bouveresse, 1991b, p. 9).

Such a straightforward idealistic manifesto holds that there are no evidences out there needing to be sorted and sifted: taken to be constraints to the philosopher's disquisitional liberty, evidences are blotted out as a matter of principle in a veritable demise of a need for evidences. That all that is relevant is supposed to be immediately available cuts evidential enquiry short.

This stance, though, is arguably true of Wittgenstein, who, at the root of the "linguistic turn" maintained in his *Philosophical Investigations* (1953):

> Not, however, as if to this end we had to hunt out new facts; it is, rather, of the essence of our investigation that we do not seek to learn anything *new* by it. We want to *understand* something that is already in plain view. For *this* is what we seem in some sense not to understand. [Wittgenstein 1953 p. 36e]

And he continues:

> We feel as if we had to *penetrate* phenomena: our investigation,
> however, is directed not towards phenomena but, as one might say,
> towards the *possibilities* of phenomena. We remind ourselves, that
> is to say, of the *kind of enouncement* that we make about phenomena
> ... Our examination is therefore grammatical in kind. [*ibid.*, 1953,
> pp. 36e–37e]

And then:

> This finds expression in questions as to the *essence* of language, of
> propositions, of thought ... *"The essence is hidden from us"*: this is the
> form our problem now assumes. We ask: *What is* language? *What is*
> a proposition? And the answer to these questions is to be given
> once for all; and independently of any future experience. [*ibid.*,
> 1953, p. 37e]

The later Wittgenstein's enquiry is "grammatical in kind"—that
is all there is to it. But then, as Max Black warns (1961), language
taken as universal metaphor becomes an ontology. Such approach
in no way limits its anti-evidential bias to Freud's method and
opus: a mighty issue that Bouveresse keeps silent on. A Wittgenstein note from 1931, published posthumously in *Culture and Value*
(1980) advises that "What a Copernicus or a Darwin really achieved
was not the discovery of a true theory but of a fertile point of view"
(Wittgenstein, 1980, p. 18e), and in his final notes, *On Certainty*
(1969), not even the obviousness of George Moore's argument "here
is one hand" (Wittgenstein, 1969, p. 2e) does fully or easily pass
muster, because no empirical statement can afford the certainty of
calculation: "calculation is treated as absolutely reliable, as certainly
correct" (*ibid.*, 1969, p. 7e), and then:

> Well, if everything speaks for an hypothesis and nothing against
> it—it is then certainly true. One may designate it as such. But does
> it certainly agree with reality, with the facts? With this question you
> are already going around in circles. To be sure there is justification,
> but justification comes to an end. [*ibid.*, 1969 p. 27e]

It is overall Wittgensteinian policy for the human realm that
empirical searches need not proceed—less than less clinical

enquiries on our feelings and minds. He therefore urged psycho-analysis to abandon evidential pretensions.

Thus, what to that pioneer in the study of the scientific method, John Stuart Mill (1852), was *the* main error, the *a priori* fallacy or fallacy of simple (un)inspection, is here policy. Demise of evidences in keeping with linguistic ones is hailed by Bouveresse, though Wittgenstein's emphasis, from the *Tractatus* onwards, on what can only be *shown* might well propel the need for ostensive knowledge. Pertinently, to Edelman our personal happenstances are experi-enced by us singly, so whatever aspires to work as a phenomenal psychology cannot be fully shared in the way in which physics can be shared (Edelman, 1992, p. 114).

That in the literary and philosophical post-modernist worlds the demise of evidences is both a fundamental right and a basic policy stands against what recently, adressing psychoanalysts, was deemed essential:

> Each area of specialized enquiry or activity has to develop its own procedures, and to create the taste by which the rest of the culture will judge it. [Rorty, 2000c, p. 823]

As sketched in my "The crisis of culture and the crisis of psycho-analysis" (Ahumada, 1997c), the gap between psychoanalysis's clinical procedures and methods, and creating the taste by which the rest of the culture judges it, does not get any easier in passing from a culture of reflection to a culture of protagonism. At the gap emerge the diverse claims to ownership or dismissal.

On the unbridled freedom accorded to language, post-modern theoreticisms harvest the emancipatory freedoms of a poeticized language placed beyond truth and falsity. For the literary critic George Steiner (Steiner, 1975, p. 245) such is its basic Promethean point:

> Man has "spoken himself free" of total organic constraint. Langu-age is a constant creation of alternative worlds. That thus "We speak, we dream ourselves free of the organic trap". [Steiner, 1975 p. 238]

driven on, as he puts it, by the mythologies of hope, of fantasy, of self-deception, reverts, however, the respective valuations of veracity and fallacy, and for so doing Steiner seeks crucial support by quoting Nietzsche's *The Will to Power*:

> "There is only *one* world, and that world is false, cruel, contradictory, misleading, senseless . . . We need lies to vanquish this reality, this 'truth', we need lies *in order to live.*" [Steiner, 1975, p. 238]

Therefore language, he holds, "is centrally fictive because the enemy is 'reality'" (Steiner, 1975, p. 237).

Where "reality" is felt as an enemy to be vanquished through the creation of alternative worlds, psychoanalysis turns fictive. A recent example is Carlo Strenger's *The Quest for Voice in Contemporary Psychoanalysis* (2002) counterposing a classical psychoanalysis centered on insight and on seeking psychic maturity, and a Romantic one having at its core the unfettered fulfilment of desire. Invoking Nietzsche and Foucault, Strenger frames psychoanalysis within an aesthetics of experience where, in the fight against the tyranny of identity, unconscious desires become the ultimate source of truth about human life. Fittingly, he puts at the core of the Oedipus complex the subject's unrenounceable humiliation at confronting his being born from his parents, instead of being his own begetter as *causa sui*.

This follows a Nietzschean thread: his first book, *The Birth of Tragedy from the Spirit of Music*, argued that the ancient Greeks made use of *"will"* as a transfiguring mirror in order to veil or withdraw from sight the vulturous Moira, the powers that nature exerts over our lives. Nietzsche found in contemporary man a similar longing, a primordial desire for "complete absorption in the beauty of appearance" (Nietzsche,1872, p. 964).

Coming back now to Bouveresse's claim that in academia discussion becomes a narcissistic exercise, each person taking turns showing off so that quite soon no one knows what they are talking about (1991a, p. 142), a suitable conceptual backcloth is provided by Baudrillard's (1990) avowal that currently the aseptic effusion of communication, the illusory contact and interchange arrive at a clone-ideal where the subject is thrown to an undecidable metastasis of himself, to a pure repetition: thus every act and every event refracts upon an image or screen, and turns eternally reproductible. While Baudrillard refers in the main to technical images or screens, the same applies to the mirroring, euphoric games of the infinitized instant in the academic scenes played out for mutual idolization.

Ownership in Latin America

What counts as particularities in the ownership of psychoanalyis in Latin America? In this huge and diverse region, local trends may arguably have as much if not more weight than unifying ones, and furthermore, in the context of globalization, erosion of differences between world regions is as quick in Latin America as elsewhere. Besides, de León de Bernardi (2000) points out, the waves of major influences (the Freudian pioneers such as Garma and Cárcamo in the early forties, then Melanie Klein and later the French influences of Lacan and thereafter André Green) were not digested fast enough for a unified Latin American school of thought to arise.

However, starting in the sixties, ownership shifted significantly from clinical enquiry as carried on in the work at the psychoanalytic societies, to academic, "theoretical" psychoanalyses anchored mainly in the universities. It applies there for "psychoanalytic discourses" what Jameson (1990, p. 42) asserts for post-modernist discourses generally: that, intensifying the auto-referentiality of present-day culture, these come to designate their own cultural production as their content.

Transcoding what psychoanalysis consists of, clinical enquiry is substituted by "psychoanalytic discourses", discourses of emancipation in future present tense (Habermas, 1985). This, and Jameson's characterization of magical realism as a major tendency of post-modern discourses, fits well a deep vein of Latin American culture reflected in its literature in the second part of the twentieth century by García Márquez, Vargas Llosa, Carpentier, and Cortázar. Vargas Llosa lucidly pointed out three decades ago that magical realism is the literary invention of a Latin American reality, aimed at frank competition with it by offering an alternative world as complex, wide, and deep as reality. The need for such radical transposition derives, he thought, from the felt instability of the social–historical circumstances (Armani, 1971).

The ongoing split between the clinically-based and the academic or journalistic, as it happens presently in Latin America, is given due place by Cláudio Eizirik (1997), who reviewed over a six-month period two of the most influential Brazilian newspapers. In one, 50% of the articles on psychoanalysis were written by journalists or literary men, 40% by Lacanians, and only 10% by members of IPA societies. In the other, 50% were authored—mostly ironically—by disgruntled IPA ex-members, 40% by Lacanians, and 10% by journalists. This should be no surprise, given the literary tinge and appeal of Lacanism, starting in the thirties as a result of Lacan's status as the new Mallarmé.

Signalling the current flight from the clinical and from in-depth exploration of feeling, Elias and Elisabeth Rocha Barros (2004) maintain that in our placebo civilization contact with what is real is substituted by a discourse on reality. May I add that in such free-wheeling discourses on reality both orator and audience can attain the performance equivalent of being *causa sui*.

The view that Jameson (1981, p. 67) holds of post-modernist discourses generally, that in a veritable rewriting of Freud's work these build an allegory where the master narrative is the story of desire itself, as it struggles against a repressive reality, fits the dominant academic discourses on psychoanalysis in Latin America. These academic discourses build, Jameson says, both a metaphysic and a myth, of which the great narrative events are repression and revolt.

Some final words

Lyotard (1986) argues that the abeyance of the difference between the here–now and the there–then, as a result of tele-relationships, produces a downturn in feeling to the benefit of strategies. Fragmentation replaces alienation while affect wanes because there is no longer a self present to do the feeling. What comes in its wake, in an ambiance where everyone seems less and less capable of fashioning representations of current experiences, turns free-floating and impersonal, identified by a peculiar sort of euphoria. "Texts" themselves become ephemeral fragments in flight, disposable works folding back into the accumulating detritus of historical time: the cultural paradigm of which, says Jameson (1990), is the drug-like experience of the present of the image in the videotape.

The waning of feelings and affects amid the flight into the euphoria of an infinitized present is in dire contrast with the need for observation and memory in the clinical process—personal memory being the framework for one's experiences, into which our successive ongoings can be inserted and thought out.

The clinical enquiry of psychoanalysis, seeking a grasp of our immediate personal realities past and present, extends our everyday emotive enquiries and our everyday informal logics to hitherto undisclosed areas: here *memory and experiential reference are at the core*. On their side, and as I stated elsewhere (Ahumada, 2001) those extensions of the literary bent on dissemination, the essentially anti-experiential "theoretical" psychoanalytic discourses, further a strategy of bricollating mock-emancipation in the frame of an infinitized present: witness the idea that the *après-Lacan* now opens the way for a Derridian psychoanalysis (Major, 1993).

Speaking from the academic left, Miyoshi (1998) underlines a huge turn toward "the university classroom as a talk show that promises to entertain rather than discuss" (Miyoshi, 1998, p. 267). Passage to entertainment ties in well with what, back in 1937, the philosopher of art Roger Collingwood adumbrated, an emptying of everyday reality by the rule of entertainment, which amounts to a sea-change in the university's role. How the familiar traps of rhetoric that, according to Foucault himself, "work to sway the reader without his being aware of the manipulation, and ultimately win him over against his will" (Foucault, 1972, p. xiv) are to be reined in is anybody's guess. Two French philosophers, Luc Ferry and Alain Renaut (1991, p. 106) urge for a distinction between the public space of argumentation and the media sphere of performance. However, that for literary criticism presently "reality" is meant to be vanquished does not seem to help matters.

So the question "Who owns psychoanalysis?" deserves different answers for diverse happenstances, clinical and public. Here Rorty's statements to the effect that truth and facts being nearly equivalent we must get rid of both (Rorty, 2000a, p. 184), and that there is no such thing as a search for truth as distinct from a search for happiness (Rorty, 2000b, p. 376), can contrarily trace the line between honest enquiry and theoreticist self-begetting.

Honest enquiry for both analysand and analyst is the *sine qua non* of clinical work. To state the obvious, theoreticist psychoanalytic discourses cannot take up the tasks of psychoanalysing, just as the concept of dog is not supposed to bark.

Nietzsche had maintained that philosophers "are commanders: they say 'Thus it shall be'" (1901, p. 510). Interestingly, Bouveresse, based on his long-standing experience in the post-modernist philosophical scenes working under the premise that "everything is political", concedes to Musil that

> Philosophers are violent and aggressive persons who, having no army at their disposal, bring the world into subjection to themselves by means of locking it up in a system. [Bouveresse, 1991a, p. 145].

Granted that a place must be made there for systems of protagonism, and that Musil's valuation need not be taken too literally; it would, however, be rash to underrate the way in which academic ownership games make right out of rhetorical might, begetting new worlds in a permanent recycling of the ephemeral.

Acknowledgements

My thanks to Drs R. Horacio Etchegoyen, Beatriz de León de Bernardi, Ricardo Bernardi, Roberto Doria Medina, Manuel J. Gálvez and Elias M. da Rocha Barros for their careful reading and comments on the manuscript.

References

Ahumada, J. L. (1997a). Towards the epistemology of clinical psychoanalysis. *Journal of the American Psychoanalytic Association*, 45: 507–530.

Ahumada, J. L. (1997b). Disclosures and refutations. Clinical psychoanalysis as a logic of inquiry. *International Journal of Psychoanalysis*, 78: 1105–1118.

Ahumada, J. L. (1997c). The crisis of culture and the crisis of psychoanalysis. In: *The Logics of the Mind. A Clinical View* (Transl.) (pp. 1–13). London, Karnac, 2001.

Ahumada, J. L. (2001). The rebirth of the idols. The Freudian unconscious and the Nietzschean unconscious. *International Journal of Psychoanalysis, 82*: 219–234.

Armani, H. (1971). Vargas Llosa: los estímulos de la realidad. *La Nación Suplemento Literario*, 1August, p. 2.

Baudrillard, J. (1990). *La transparence du mal. Essai sur les phénomènes extrêmes*. Paris: Gallilée.

Bion, W. R. (1979). *The Dawn of Oblivion*. Perthshire, Clunie Press.

Black, M. (1961). *Models and Metaphors*. Ithaca, NY: Cornell University Press.

Bouveresse, J. (1991a). Reading Rorty: Pragmatism and its consequences. In: R. B. Brandom (Ed.), *Rorty and his Critics* (Transl.) (pp. 129–146). Malden, MA & Oxford: Blackburn, 2000.

Bouveresse, J. (1991b). *Wittgenstein reads Freud. The Myth of the Unconscious*. Princeton NJ: Princeton University Press, 1995.

Coleridge, S. T. (1817) [1997]. *Biographia Literaria*. London: Everyman.

Collingwood, R. G. (1937) [1958]. *The Principles of Art*. London: Oxford University Press.

de León de Bernardi, B. (2000). The countertransference: a Latin American view. *International Journal of Psychoanalysis, 81*: 331–351.

Debord, G. (1967). *The Society of the Spectacle* (Transl.). New York: Zone Books, 1985.

Derrida, J. (1980). *La carte postale de Socrate à Freud et au delà*. Paris: Flammarion.

Edelman, G. M. (1992). *Bright Air, Brilliant Fire. On the Matter of the Mind*. New York: Basic Books.

Eizirik, C. (1997). Psychoanalysis and culture: some contemporary challenges. *International Journal of Psychoanalysis, 78*: 789–800.

Ferry, L., & Renaut, A. (1985). *French Philosophies of the Sixties. An Essay on Antihumanism* (Transl.). Amherst, MA: University of Massachussets Press, 1990.

Ferry, L., & Renaut, A. (1991). What must first be proved is worth little. In: L. Ferry & A. Renaut (Eds.), *Why We Are Not Nietzscheans* (Transl.) (pp. 92–109). Chicago ILL: University of Chicago Press, 1997.

Foucault, M. (1969). *The Archeology of Knowledge*. New York: Pantheon.

Foucault, M. (1971). The discourse on language. In: *The Archeology of Knowledge* (Transl.) (pp. 215–237). New York: Pantheon.

Foucault, M. (1972). Preface. In: G. Deleuze & F. Guattari (Eds.) *Anti-Oedipus. Capitalism and Schizophrenia* (pp. xi–xiv). Minneapolis MI: University of Minnesota Press, 1983.

Freud, S. (1900a). The interpretation of dreams. *S.E.*, *4*. London: Hogarth.

Habermas, J. (1985). *The Philosophical Discourse of Modernity* (Trans.). Cambridge, MA: MIT Press, 1990.

Jameson, F. (1981). *The Political Unconscious. Narrative as a Socially Symbolic Act*. Ithaca, NY: Cornell University Press.

Jameson, F. (1983). Postmodernism and consumer society. In: H. Foster (Ed.), *The Anti-Aesthetic. Essays on Postmodern Culture* (pp. 111–125). New York: The New Press.

Jameson, F. (1990). *Postmodernism, or the Cultural Logic of Late Capitalism*. Durham, NC: Duke University Press.

Lyotard, J.-F. (1986). *Le Posmoderne expliqué aux enfants*. Paris: Galilée.

Major, R. (1993). Depuis Lacan: ——— . In: The Collège Internationale de Philosophie (Ed.), *Lacan avec les philosophes* (pp. 373–390). Paris: Albin Michel.

Matte-Blanco, I. (1975). *The Unconscious as Infinite Sets*. London: Duckworth.

Matte-Blanco, I. (1988). *Thinking, Feeling and Being*. London: Routledge.

Mill, J. S. (1852). *A System of Logic, Ratiocinative and Inductive*. New York: Harper.

Miyoshi, M. (1998). "Globalization", cultures and the university. In: F. Jameson and M. Miyoshi (Eds.), *The Cultures of Globalization* (pp. 247–270). Durham, NC & London: Duke University Press.

Money-Kyrle, R. (1977). On being a psycho-analyst. In: D. Meltzer (Ed.), *The Collected Papers of Roger Money-Kyrle* (pp. 457–465). Perthshire, Clunie Press, 1978.

Nietzsche, F. (1872). *The Birth of Tragedy from the Spirit of Music*. In: *The Philosophy of Nietzsche* (Trans.) (pp. 947–1088). New York: Modern Library, 1927.

Nietzsche, F. (1901). *The Will to Power* (Trans.). W. Kaufmann (Ed.). New York NY, Vintage, 1968.

Popper, K. (1994). *The Myth of the Framework--In Defence of Science and Rationality*, M. A. Notturno (Ed.). London & New York: Routledge.

Rocha Barros, E. M., & Rocha Barros, E. L. (2004). Preformed transference: a response to the patient or to the culture? Panel: Frontiers on Psychopathology. New Culture, New Patients. IPA Congress, New Orleans.

Rorty, R. (1988). *Contingency, Irony and Solidarity*. Cambridge, Cambridge University Press.

Rorty, R. (2000a). Response to Robert Brandom. In: R. B. Brandom (Ed.), *Rorty and his Critics* (pp. 183–190). Malden, MA & Oxford: Blackburn.

Rorty, R. (2000b). Response to Bjørn Ramberg. In: R. B. Brandom (Ed.), *Rorty and his Critics* (pp. 370–377). Malden, MA & Oxford: Blackburn.

Rorty, R. (2000c). Pragmatism. *International Journal of Psychoanalysis, 81*: 819–823.

Simpson, D. (1995). *The Academic Postmodern and the Rule of Literature. A Report on Half-Knowledge*. Chicago: University of Chicago Press.

Steiner, G. (1975). *After Babel. Aspects of Language and Translation*. Oxford & New York: Oxford University Press, 1998.

Strenger, C. (2002). *The Quest for Voice in Contemporary Psychoanalysis*. Madison CT: International Universities Press.

Ulmer, G. L. (1983). The object of post-criticism. In: H. Foster (Ed.), *The Anti-Aesthetic. Essays in Postmodern Culture* (pp. 83–110). New York: The New Press.

Winnicott, D. W. (1971). *Playing and Reality*. London & New York: Routledge.

Wittgenstein, L. (1953) [2001]. *Philosophical Investigations*, 3rd edn, revised, G. E. M. Anscombe (Trans.). Malden, MA & Oxford: Blackburn.

Wittgenstein, L. (1969). *On Certainty*. G. E. M. Anscombe & G. H. von Wright (Eds.). New York: Harper & Row.

Wittgenstein, L. (1980). *Culture and Value*. G. H. von Wright (Ed.). Chicago: University of Chicago Press.

PART II
HISTORY

CHAPTER FIVE

Notes towards the genealogy of a word: "psychotherapy"

Sonu Shamdasani

"It is enough to create new names and estimations and probabilities in order to create in the long run new 'things'."

Friedrich Nietzsche, 1887[1]

The end of the nineteenth century witnessed a plethora of new therapeutics, as fads and fashions spread throughout the medical world. *Fin de siècle* nervous patients had an extensive menu of dietic treatments, medications, remedies, air cures, water cures, bath cures, rest cures, electric treatments, psychic treatments, mental healing, massage, gymnastics, spas, and private and public institutions to choose from. New terms and neologisms abounded. While electrotherapy, balneotherapy, climatotherapy, metallotherapy, mechanotherapy, and magnetotherapy did not survive, two which entered the vocabularies at this time and rapidly spread across Europe and America are still with us today. In this chapter, I explore the genealogies of the word, "psychotherapy" and trace how the manner in which it became taken up may serve as a window into the constitution of this discipline and finally, how this may enable Freud's nomination of psychoanalysis to be located.

It was in 1872 that the word "psycho-therapeutics" was coined by Daniel Hack Tuke in his work *Illustrations of the Influence of the Mind Upon the Body In Health and Disease Designed to Elucidate the Action of the Imagination*.[3] Tuke was a psychiatrist and the great grandson of William Tuke, the founder of the York Retreat. Tuke claimed that physicians had long known the healing power of the imagination, but that now it could be made rational. This would serve to distinguish them from quacks—the latter being individuals who healed without knowing how they did so. The penultimate chapter of his book was titled "Psycho-therapeutics—practical applications of the influence of the mind on the body to medical practice". While discussing animal magnetism, he argued:

> Assuming that the first French Commission on Animal Magnetism (1784) were correct in regarding the phenomena as fairly referable to Imagination and Imitation, we must agree with them that they constitute the groundwork of a NEW SCIENCE—that of the Moral over the Physical.[4]

The commissioners, who included Benjamin Franklin and Lavoisier, rejected the claims of animal magnetism to be scientific, and argued that the results of Mesmer and his disciples should be "ascribed solely to the influence of the imagination".[5] Tuke inverted their intention, and claimed that as their report showed that what animal magnetism "really" demonstrated was the physical effects of the imagination, a new science and therapeutics could be founded upon their apparent denunciation of animal magnetism. For Tuke, mesmerism thus displayed how "certain purely psychical agencies produce certain physical results".[6]

While boldly proclaiming the new science of psycho-therapeutics, Tuke appears not to have made further use of the term. The fourth edition of his *A Manual of Psychological Medicine* of 1879, written with John Bucknill, does not mention the term, and nor indeed do the numerous articles which he wrote in the *Journal of Mental Science*.[7] Thus the new science might well have been stillborn had it not been taken up by Hippolyte Bernheim.

It was through the work of Bernheim and the Nancy school that the therapeutic practice of hypnosis and suggestion rapidly spread throughout Europe and America. Bernheim, a professor of medicine at Nancy, had become interested in the work of Auguste

Ambroise Liébault, a country doctor who practised hypnosis. According to Bernheim, it was Liébault who established "the doctrine of therapeutic suggestion".[8] He claimed that suggestion was as "old as the world".[9] What was new was its systematic application to therapeutics. For Bernheim, the use of suggestion not only featured prominently in his practice, it formed the theoretical key to understanding hypnosis and a general psychology of the mind. Hypnosis was understood as a state of heightened suggestibility, akin to sleep. He defined suggestion widely, as the act by which an idea is accepted in the brain. For Bernheim and the Nancy school, suggestive therapeutics consisted in the deliberate manipulation of credence, belief, and expectation under the rubric of suggestion and autosuggestion in the treatment of a wide range of psychological and physical conditions. In addition to functional neuroses, Bernheim claimed that it was effective in cases of paralyses, contractures, insomnia, muscular pain, hemiplegia, paraplegia, rheumatism, anaesthesia, gastric disorders, neuralgia, and sciatica. For Bernheim, the common factor active in religious healing, as well as in many therapeutic practices, was suggestion:

> In the waking state credence is increased by religious faith (religious suggestion, miraculous cures), and by faith in medicines or medical practices (cure by fictitious medicines, magnets, metals, electricity, hydrotherapeutics, the tractors of Perkins, massage, the system of Mattei, &c.). The idea of cure suggested by these practices may cause the psychical organ to act and obtain from it the curative effect, not that the sum total of these practices is suggestion, but that suggestion is a factor in every one of them.[10]

Thus "suggestion" was presented as a modern rational scientific concept which both explained and unmasked prior and contemporary medical therapies and forms of religious healing. Individuals flocked to Nancy to visit Bernheim and Liébault and watch them at work, and gain instruction in hypnosis. Nancy became a "medical Mecca".[11] A hypnotic movement spread rapidly through Europe. A controversy raged between the Nancy school and the Salpêtrière school, under the neurologist Jean-Martin Charcot. For Charcot and his followers, hypnosis was a pathological condition, which was only found in cases of hysteria. What Charcot described as "grand hypnotisme" followed three stages, each of which had distinct physiological characteristics: catalepsy, lethargy, and somnambulism. At the Salpêtrière, Charcot used hypnosis to study the underlying architecture of hysteria; because he claimed it was a pathological state, he was not interested in its therapeutic applications.

In 1886, Hack Tuke's *Illustrations of the Influence of the Mind Upon the Body* appeared in French translation.[12] That year, the second expanded edition of Bernheim's work on suggestion appeared. Bernheim cited the French edition of Tuke's book and referred to what he termed the "psycho-therapeutic action." (L'action psycho-thérapeutique"). He wrote: "*to provoke this special psychic state by hypnotism and to exploit it with the aim of cure or of relief . . . this is the role of the hypnotic psycho-therapeutic* [psycho-thérapeutique hypno-tique]."[13] Thus Bernheim appropriated Tuke's terms as adjectival descriptions of his suggestive therapeutics. As the word was used as a synonym, there was no need for a separate definition of psycho-therapeutics. Tuke, meanwhile, took an active interest in the French developments which he reviewed and reported on in *The Journal of Mental Science*, but did not himself connect them with his new science of psycho-therapeutics.[14] One may conjecture that if Tuke had pursued his new science, the keyword would have been imagination, and not suggestion.

In 1889, the word was taken up by an English physician, Charles Lloyd Tuckey, who published an exposition of the work of the Nancy school. Tuckey titled his work, *Psycho-therapeutics, or Treatment by Hypnotism and Suggestion*. This appears to have been the first work employing this word in its title. Following Bernheim's usage, Psycho-therapeutics for Tuckey was a synonym for what was being practised by the Nancy school. Thus we find that no separate definition of "psycho-therapeutics" was offered. Tuckey claimed that it was Liébault who had "arrived at the truth of psycho-therapeutics".[15]

In 1887, two Dutch physicians, Frederik van Eeden and Albert Willem van Renterghem opened a clinic for suggestive therapy in Amsterdam.[16] Interest in hypnosis in the Netherlands had been sparked through a tour by the stage hypnotist Hans Donato in 1887. Van Eeden and van Renterghem had visited Bernheim in his clinic, and were impressed by what they had witnessed. In 1889, they named their clinic the "clinique de psycho-thérapeutique suggestive".[17] Their clinic appears to have been the first institution to employ the word "psycho-therapeutic". The term was contagious. By 1891, there was already a "clinique de psycho-thérapeutique suggestive" in Brussels.

Shortly after Tuckey's book appeared, Robert Felkin published a long article in the *Edinburgh Medical* Journal, which was republished as a book in 1890 under the title *Hypnotism, or Psycho-therapeutics*.[18] Psycho-therapeutics features here in a titular sense—Felkin did not discuss the word itself in his book.

In 1891, Bernheim himself took up the word as the title of his work, *Hypnotisme, suggestion, psychothérapie: études nouvelles* [*Hypnotism, Suggestion, Psychotherapy: New Studies*]. Here, "psycho-thérapie" was employed without a hyphen. One may conjecture that it was through translation that psychotherapists became unhyphenated. Bernheim argued that

> It is enough to recall the considerable action of the moral on the psychical, of the spirit on the body, of the psychic function of the brain on all the organic functions. It is this action which the doctor must utilise to obtain acts useful for the cure. To make the mind intervene to cure the body, this is the role of suggestion applied to the therapeutic, this is the aim of the psycho-therapeutic.[19]

By making psycho-therapeutics synonymous with hypnosis and suggestion, the word became widely disseminated. "Psycho-therapeutics" rode on the back of the burgeoning hypnotic movement. For Bernheim, the word "psychothérapie" took on the same rational, modern, scientific connotations as "suggestion".

Initially, there was no need to create a separate designation of "psychotherapist," as it was quite clear that psychotherapy was practised by physicians.

During this period, there was great controversy concerning the use of hypnosis by individuals who weren't physicians. Ironically, a great deal of the interest in hypnosis had been brought about by the tours of accomplished stage hypnotists such as Hansen and Donato.[20] At the 1889 International Congress for Experimental and Therapeutic Hypnotism in Paris, a motion was proposed to ban the use of hypnosis by non-medical practitioners. The rights of the latter were strongly defended by Joseph Delboeuf, a Belgian philosopher who practised hypnosis.[21] The interest in hypnosis was not restricted to the medical profession. Others who took it up included the psychical researchers Edmund Gurney and Frederick Myers in England. By helping to open a legitimate space for the practice of hypnosis and suggestion outside of the medical profession, such figures played an important role in the development of "lay" psychotherapy in Europe and the subsequent separation of psychotherapy from medicine.

In 1889, psychotherapy featured as the title of a work by a French author, Maurice Barrès. His work was titled *Trois stations de Psychothérapie*, [*Three Stations of Psychotherapy*] and consisted of three chapters: "A visit to Leonardo da Vinci (Homage to analysts of the self [moi])"; "A visit to Latour de Saint-Quentin (Homage to psychologists)"; "The legend of a cosmopolitan (Homage to Neo-catholics)". Barrès described his essays as "Treatises of the culture of the self (moi)." He wrote:

> these small essays, in my view, are for moderns, consolations in the manner in which the most precious of our masters, Seneca, addressed, with an extreme elegance, the refined people of his time who were so weary.[22]

Barrès utilized the word in a quite different sense than the psychologists here, and it did not refer to any particular practice. For him, psychotherapy was a form of literature, a "reading cure", which consisted in stoical consolations for weary, refined individuals.

Van Eeden and van Renterghem presented the work of their clinic at the Second Congress of Experimental Psychology in London, held in 1892, which created a great deal of interest. In retrospect, van Eeden credited himself with coining the term "psychotherapy".[23] In his presentation, van Eeden indicated the rationale behind the choice of the term:

> In 1889 we chose psychotherapy as a collective name to refer to this treatment, and we thus name all therapy which cures by the intermediary of the psychic functions of the patient. The priority of the term goes back to Hack Tuke.
>
> We add the word "suggestive" because suggestion—understood in the sense of Bernheim—plays the principal role in our therapy.

We avoid the words "hypnotism" or "hypnosis" deliberately. As for myself, I would prefer that one did not use these words concerning psychotherapy. The unreasonable use of these words has given rise to preconceptions, to confusion and misunderstandings.[24]

He claimed that the association of hypnosis with psychotherapy had done the latter much harm. Thus we see that for van Eeden, the use of the word psychotherapy offered a neat escape from the controversies concerning hypnosis. While the word came from Hack Tuke, the specific connotation with which it was being employed stemmed from Bernheim. But could the simple substitution of one word for another clear up the "preconceptions, confusions, and misunderstandings"? Van Eeden offered the following definition: "I call psychotherapy all curative methods which use psychic agents to combat illness through the intervention of psychic functions".[25] This was a pretty wide definition! What "psychic agents" were was left unspecified. Over the following years, the word became rapidly taken up and widely disseminated. Part of the reason for this was that in contrast to hypnosis or suggestion therapy, the word itself was not closely to tied to a particular practice or theoretical conception. As a prefix, "psycho-" presented itself as sufficiently vague to be filled in however one chose. In 1893, van Eeden himself vacated the field of psychotherapy. He continued with his literary activities, and later became a spiritualist.

In 1892, there was a debate concerning "Psycho-therapeutics" in *The Lancet*. George Robertson, a physician in Edinburgh, distinguished the rational and scientific use of psycho-therapeutics by figures such as Bernheim from the "unconscious and indirect" use on a daily basis by family physicians. He advocated its study, but noted that it was likely to have an uphill struggle to gain recognition, as it was "unconventional and different from orthodox practice".[26]

During this period, controversies raged concerning hypnosis, which contributed to its decline. The Salpêtrière school attacked the therapeutic pretensions of the Nancy school. In 1887, Gilles de la Tourette argued that while hypnosis had some therapeutic utility in treating the symptoms of hysteria, its use in other cases could develop symptoms far worse than those with which one was initially presented.[27] By contrast, Henrik Petersen claimed that the hypnotism of the Salpêtrière has been the greatest enemy of psycho-therapeutics by frightening both sick and well, and in this fact is to be found the only valid excuse for doctors making such remarks to patients as follows: "Do as you like, but never allow anyone to hypnotize you!" Or, whenever a patient has been successfully treated by psycho-therapeutics: "Well, well, the cure, as you call it, is only apparent, as you will find out at your cost later!"[28]

Bernheim and the Nancy school had stressed that hypnosis consisted in heightened suggestibility, and not in a separate state. In the early 1890s, Delboeuf drew the radical conclusion that hypnosis did not exist, or, in other words, that "the power of hypnotism consists above all in the very word of hypnotism, because [the subject] does not understand it well".[29] The dissolution of hypnosis had the effect of promoting the word "psychotherapy". Delbouef noted "from the point of view of scientific exactness, the term psychotherapy, or better still, of psychodynamic, is much preferable."[30] With the word "hypnosis" falling into disrepute, psychotherapy offered itself as a ready alternative. Unlike hypnosis, it was free of controversial connotations. Having come to prominence due to the rise of the hypnotic movement, the word "psychotherapy" now benefited from the decline of hypnosis, and through its capacity to be dissociated from it. But could one say that subjects understood the word "psychotherapy" any better? Was the power of psychotherapy similarly bound up with the suggestive effect of the word itself?

In 1896, the Zeitschrift für Hypnotismus, Suggestionstherapie, Suggestionslehre und verwandte psychologische Forschungen (journal for hypnotism, suggestion therapy, the theory of suggestion and related psychological researches) changed its name to Zeitschrift für Hypnotismus, Psychotherapie sowie andere psychophysiologische und psychopathologische Forschungen (journal for hypnotism, psychotherapy as well as other psychophysiological and psychopathological researches).[31] This appears to be the first journal to employ the term. "Psychotherapy" had taken the place of "Suggestion therapy" and the "theory of suggestion".[32] In the following year, Leopold Löwenfeld, an Austrian physician, published a Lehrbuch der Gesammten Psychotherapie (Textbook of General Psychotherapy). What he had been content to describe in 1894 as "psychic treatment (*psy-chische Behandlung*) in a wider sense" was now described as psycho-therapy.[33] Löwenfeld commenced by complaining that the works that had been put forward to the medical public under the title "Psychotherapy" had unfortunately been exclusively concerned with hypnosis and hypnotic treatment.[34] This gave the impression "that there was no other form of psychic treatment than the hypnotic".[35] He differentiated hypnosis, as one psychotherapeutic method, from psychotherapy in general. For Bernheim and his followers, as psychotherapy was identified with hypnotic and suggestive therapies, the history of psychotherapy was identical with that of the latter. In differentiating the two, it was time to give psychotherapy a history. Löwenfeld argued that

> Psychotherapy is no achievement of the modern age. If we look in history towards the first beginnings of our art, it is clear as an unmistakable fact that among the different methods of healing which were used at that time, psychotherapy is the oldest, and that it represents the first and original form in which the practical art of healing was exercised.[36]

He divided the history of psychotherapy into four periods: reli-gious psychotherapy, Greco-Roman psychic therapy in medicine, the rational and profane psychotherapy since the middle ages, and the era of hypnosis and suggestion, commencing in the 1880s with Liébault and Charcot. In his retroactive history of psychotherapy, what Löwenfeld classed as psychotherapy would previously simply be regarded as medicine. His long history of psychotherapy could be said to have taken its cue from the manner in which Bernheim reinterpreted prior medical and religious therapeutics in terms of suggestion.[37]

The question of the relation of psychotherapy to medicine—raised by its nomination as a distinct entity unto itself—was henceforth a subject of debate within medicine. In 1901, an editor-ial in *The Lancet* noted that a "London Psycho-therapeutic society" had been formed at the Frascati Restaurant. This was possibly the first society bearing this designation. The editorial expressed disap-proval:

> we cannot help thinking that the gentlemen responsible for the first meeting having been held on April 1st was singularly happy in his

choice of a date. The idea of medical men, or of any other body of men capable of exercising common sense, meeting on a common platform with the so-called Christian Scientists, with the exponents of the Viavi system, or with osteopathists is too ridiculous for words.[38]

Allowing that hypnotic treatment could have a value when carried out by medical practitioners, the editor contended that he saw no need for a separate "psycho-therapeutic" society, which would "open the door to fraud".[39]

The disidentification of psychotherapy from hypnosis and suggestion reached its apogee with the work of Paul Dubois, a physician in Berne. In 1904, he published *Les Psychonévroses et leur traitement moral* (*Psychoneuroses and Their Moral Treatment*), which was a very popular work. Dubois launched a critique of suggestion, claiming that it only increased the state of servitude of patients. Psychoneurotics needed to be immunized from suggestion, so that they would accept "nothing but the councils of reason".[40] Patients needed to regain their self-mastery. In place of suggestion, he spoke of moral persuasion. In his preface to the 1909 American edition of his book, he referred to "Suggestive therapeutics, erroneously termed psychotherapeutics".[41]

According to Dubois, it was Pinel who "first introduced psychotherapy in the treatment of mental diseases".[42] Liébault and Bernheim, and the whole magnetic and hypnotic tradition were displaced. The implications were clear: psychotherapy was simply the modern form of moral treatment.[43]

While Bernheim had stressed the application of suggestion— and hence psychotherapy—to physical and what would today be classed as psychosomatic disorders, the purview of psychotherapy became increasingly restricted to the "psychoneuroses". Dubois argued that

Having eliminated the neuroses where somatic origin is probable, I only conserve in this group of psychoneuroses the conditions where psychic influence predominates, those which are more or less under the jurisdiction of psychotherapy; these are neurasthenia, hysteria, hystero-neurasthenia, the light forms of hypochondria and melancholy; finally, one can include certain more serious states of disequilibrium, such as vesania.[44]

The conditions noted by Dubois do not feature in contemporary diagnostic manuals. Part of the longevity of psychotherapy as a profession has resided in its effectiveness in ever formulating and catering for new disorders.[45]

This differentiation of psychotherapy from hypnosis and suggestion was to prove extremely fortuitous for the fate of the word, as the latter went into a rapid decline. Psychotherapy narrowly avoided going down with the ship.

In 1895, Jules Déjerine had instituted a method of treatment based on isolation (the Weir Mitchell rest cure) and psychotherapy (understood as moral treatment) in his service at the Salpêtrière. In 1904, two of his students, Jean Camus and Philippe Pagniez, wrote up the results of this work. Significantly enough, they commenced with an eighty-page history of isolation and psychotherapy, which seems to be the lengthiest that had been undertaken up to this point. Concerning psychotherapy, they wrote that it was difficult to give a definition of a subject which "everyone understands but which seems indefinable by nature".[46] Nevertheless, they put forward the following definition: "one should consider psychotherapy (medicine of the mind), as the ensemble of means by which we act with the aim of cure on the sick mind or on the sick body through the intervention of the mind".[47] If psychotherapy was hard to define, they noted that it was harder to fix historically. Hence, they differentiated between the conscious manifestations of psychotherapy and its unconscious use. They argued that both modalities went back to antiquity, and arranged their history thematically under four headings: psychotherapy by remedies, by which they meant "suggestion by medicinal therapeutics", psychotherapy by "the marvellous" (understood as the intervention of supernatural beings), psychotherapy by hypnotism and suggestion, and psychotherapy by persuasion. If psychotherapy was nothing new, the value of the present was one of "determining its mechanism of action, of making its usage precise and of grouping together all the scattered rules and indications".[48]

In Camus' and Pagniez's work, the terms "psychotherapist" (psychothérapeute) and "psychotherapist doctor" (médecin psychothérapeute) featured prominently. They indicated the requirements necessary for being a psychotherapist. First of all, they argued that one had to be a doctor to make the necessary diagnostic discriminations. In addition, one needed to be patient, good, to love one's art, to be profoundly convinced of the efficacity of one's method, to be an observer, to know how to analyse a character, to have had a wide worldly experience, and to be a good judge of character.[49] As to the significance of this new figure of the psychotherapist, they wrote:

> Today, psychotherapy in going back to the methods employed by philosophers and by religious persons, speaks to reason and makes an appeal to the collaboration of the patient. It no longer demands that the doctor be a sort of priest of a science of initiates, but simply a gentleman (honnête homme), in the elevated sense which the eighteenth century gave to this word.[50]

Thus the new science was to be an art practised by gentlemen doctors possessing eighteenth century virtues.

These developments in Europe intersected with those in the United States, where certain specific parameters came into play. The second half of the nineteenth century saw the rise of the Mind-Cure movement in America. The instigator of this was Phineas Parkhurst Quimby. From 1838, Quimby took up the practice of mesmerism. From this, he developed his own conception that all diseases were mental delusions, and that they could be mentally healed. In the 1860s mental healing schools spread throughout New England. Quimby's most well-known pupil was Mary Baker Eddy, who elaborated the doctrine of Christian Science. In 1875, she published her bestselling work *Science and Health*. As Eric Caplan notes, while Christian Scientists stressed the necessity of adopting their doctrine for mental healing to be effective, proponents of New Thought rejected this, and drew instead on the work of Bernheim.[51] In the United States, the rise of psychotherapy was made possible through the Mind-Cure movement. Indications of this are given in James Mark Baldwin's *Dictionary of Philosophy and Psychology* from 1901: the entry on "Mind-Cure" gives "Psychotherapie" as the equivalent German term.[52]

In 1906, a collaboration of clergymen and doctors arose at the Emmanuel Church in Boston, which gave rise to the "Emmanuel Movement." As Caplan argues, this movement "was the primary agent responsible for the efflorescence of psychotherapy in the United States during the first decade of the twentieth century."[53] In 1908, W. B. Parker published a multi-volume work entitled *Psycho-*

therapy: A Course of Reading Combining Sound Psychology, Sound Medicine and Sound Religion.[54] The title implied that psychotherapy consisted of a combination of sound psychology, medicine, and religion. Richard Cabot, who played a prominent role in promoting psychotherapy, wrote an article on the "American type of psychotherapy." Cabot noted that "Mind cure is the English for psychotherapy", oblivious to the English origins of the word, and attesting to its prominence in the French- and German-speaking worlds.[55] For Cabot, it was the translation of Dubois' work which showed the American medical public that there was such as a thing as "scientific mind cure." He presented the following definition and justification of the term psychotherapy:

> Psychotherapy means the attempt to help the sick through mental, moral and spiritual methods. It is a most terrifying word, but we are forced to use it because there is no other which serves to distinguish us from the Christian Scientists, the New Thought people, the Faith Healers, and the thousand and one other schools and of all of the accumulative knowledge of the past.[56]

Cabot saw the linkage with religion as the specifically American form of psychotherapy.

By the beginning of the twentieth century, the word "psychotherapy" had become firmly established, but it was not the exclusive preserve of any one figure or school. It was viewed as ancient and resolutely modern. It was variously adopted to refer to a variety of procedures, ranging from mesmerism, hypnosis, suggestive therapy, moral therapy, Mind-Cure, mental healing, strengthening of the will, re-education, the cathartic method, rational persuasion, to general medical practice or the "art" of medicine. Through association with each of these, the word "psychotherapy" was able to gain circulation and prominence, and yet at the same time, it was able to be perceived increasingly as a distinct profession. This set the pattern for how it would come to be used in the twentieth century. The use of the word gave an appearance of novelty and innovation and brought a scientific aura—Tuke's new science—yet whether this actually reflected any far-going transformation in practice is another question.

To grasp the significance of Freud's nomination of psychoanalysis, it is important to set it in the wider context of the nomination of psychotherapy. Freud's word enabled the differentiation of his practice from a wider psychotherapeutic movement. Furthermore, through the elaboration of the Freudian legend, Freud was figured as the founder of modern psychotherapy: and much of what should be ascribed to the psychotherapeutic movement became solely ascribed to Freud. In the twentieth century, Freudian apologists rescripted the history of psychotherapy as if it began and ended with Freud.[57]

After a period practising electrotherapy as a neurologist in private practice, Freud took up the practice of suggestion and hypnosis. He initially utilized psychotherapy and psychic treatment to designate his activities. He translated the second edition of Bernheim's *De la Suggestion et de ses applications à la therapeutique* in 1888 and the first edition of Bernheim's *Hypnotisme, suggestion, psychothérapie; études nouvelles* in 1892. In so doing, he contributed to the dissemination of the word "Psychotherapie" in the German-speaking world. In 1893, Breuer and Freud announced a supposedly new psychotherapeutic procedure, the cathartic method. In 1895, Freud's theoretical contribution to their *Studien über Hysterie* ("Studies on hysteria") was titled "the psychotherapy of hysteria." It was in the following year that Freud first employed the word "psychoanalysis" in the course of his ill-fated papers on the seduction theory.

Contrary to general opinion, the word "psycho-analytical" had been employed prior to Freud. In 1979, Kathleen Coburn noted that the term had been used by Coleridge in his notebooks. He had written about the need for a "psycho-analytical understanding".[58] As Erling Eng noted, Coleridge understood this as what was "needed to recover the presence of Greek myth hidden with Renaissance epic verse, this for the sake of realizing a purified Christian Faith".[59] While Coleridge's diaries were not published until the twentieth century, the *OED* also notes a published use of the word in 1857 in *Russell's Magazine*: "[Poe] chose . . . the psycho-analytical. His heroes are monstrous reflections of his own heart in its despair, not in its peace". Whether the word may have been in wider circulation has not yet been established.

Freud's first use of word "psychoanalysis" was in a paper in the *Revue Neurologique*. His French neologism, "psychoanalyse", appears to have been directly modelled on the word "psychotherapy." He wrote:

I owe my results to a new method of psychoanalysis [*d'une nouvelle méthode de psychoanalyse*] , Josef Breuer's exploratory procedure. . . . By means of that procedure—this is not the place to describe it— hysterical symptoms are traced back to their origin, which is always found in some event of the subject's sexual life appropriate for the production of a distressing emotion.[60]

Curiously, Freud provides no definition, justification or extended description of the term, but simply applies it retroactively to what he had been content to describe in the previous year as a method of psychotherapy.

Pierre Janet was later to complain that Freud had simply appropriated his work and the name of his procedure:

They spoke of "psychoanalysis" where I had spoken of "psychological analysis". They invented the name "complex", whereas I had used the term "psychological system" . . . They spoke of "catharsis" where I had spoken of the "dissociation of fixed ideas" or of "moral disinfection". The names differed, but the essential ideas I had put forward . . . were accepted without modification.[61]

Thus, for Janet, "psychoanalysis" was nothing but a copycat name for his own "psychological analysis."

In 1894, Leopold Löwenfeld had noted that "a third hypnotherapeutic method was recommended in recent times by Breuer and Freud".[62] Rather than simply being a method of psychotherapy amongst others, or a "third hypnotherapeutic method", the simple stroke of a neologism served to differentiate Freud's procedure—at a linguistic level, if not on any other.

However, in calling his discipline "psychoanalyse" Freud had contravened German grammatical rules for forming compounds from Greek terms. The correct form would have been "psychanalyse". This grammatical howler was not lost on Freud's audience, and a number of figures such as Dumeng Bezzola, Eugen Bleuler, August Forel, Ludwig Frank, C. G. Jung, Oskar Pfister, and Herbert Silberer referred to "psychanalyse".[63] Others, such as Emil Kraepelin and Wilhelm Wundt, referred to "psychoanlayse" in quotation marks.[64] As Horst Gündlach notes, "Freud's contemporaries, friends and foes alike, perceived the extra 'o' in 'psychoanalysis' as a trademark of ignorance."[65] In 1910, Ludwig Frank titled his book *Die Psychanalyse*.[66] Bleuler published a work under the title: *Die Psychanalyse Freuds. Verteidigung und kritische Bemerkungen* [*Freud's Psychanalysis: Defence and Critical Remarks*].[67] In the 1912 edition of his *Hypnotismus*, Forel commenced his chapter on "Psychanalyse" by noting:

> I write "psychanalysis"(*psychanalyse*) like Bezzola, Frank and Bleuler, and not "psychoanalysis" (*psychoanalyse*) like Freud, because of the rational, euphonic derivation. Bezzola quite rightly draws attention to the fact that one also writes "psychiatry" (*psychiatrie*) and not "psychoiatry" (*psychoiatrie*).[68]

In the face of the linguistic correction by colleagues and critics, Freud obstinately stuck to his original formulation. The early history of the psychoanlaytic movement can in part be written in terms of how "psychoanalysis" triumphed over "psychanalysis."

In subsequent years, Freud would dissolve the initial linkage of psychoanalysis with Breuer's "exploratory procedure," and periodically resignify the term, "psychoanalysis." For Freud, psychoanalysis was a word to be defined and redefined as he alone saw fit. Its nomination preceded the determination of its essence. His polemical history of the psychoanalytic movement had the aim of policing the use of the word:

> Psycho-analysis is my creation . . . no one can know better than I do what psycho-analysis is, how it differs from other ways of investigating the life of the mind, and precisely what would better be described by some other name.[69]

As Freud saw it, the very survival of psychoanalysis depended upon maintaining this singular power of nomination. For him, it was essential that the word "psychoanalysis" did not circulate freely, like the word, "psychotherapy". Meanwhile, in 1917, Bernheim complained of the number of works that used the word "psychotherapy" without even mentioning his name.[70] Paradoxically, it was the very success of the psychotherapy movement and the open manner in which it developed that made psychoanalysis possible. The former opened up a practical, theoretical, social, and linguistic space without which the latter would not have arisen. One may conclude by asking, how much of the rise of the psychotherapeutic and psychoanalytic movements was actually due to the success of these neologisms?

Notes

1. Nietzsche, *The Gay Science*, tr. W. Kaufmann, (New York, Vintage, 1974), p. 58.
2. Jacqueline Carroy has presented interesting reflections on the adoption of the word "psychotherapy" in the French context and raised significant issues not pursued here, "L'invention du mot de psychothérapie et ses enjeux", *Les psychothérapies dans leurs histoires, Psychologie Clinique, 9,* 2000, pp. 11–30. The approach presented here is modelled after the linguistic trajectories traced by Jean Starobinski. Unless otherwise noted, translations are my own.
3. Prior to this, the *OED* notes one reference to "Psychotherapeia" in 1853.
4. Tuke, D. H. (1872). *Illustrations of the Influence of the Mind upon the Body in Health and Disease Designed to Elucidate the Action of the Imagination.* London: J. & A. Churchill, p. 405.
5. *Report of Dr. Benjamin Franklin and other commissioners charged by the King of France with the examination of the animal magnetism, as now practised at Paris,* W. Godwin (Trans.). London: J. Johnson, 1785, p. 69.
6. *Ibid.,* p. 5.
7. Bucknill, J. C., & Tuke, D. H. (1879). *A Manual of Psychological Medicine, Containing the Lunacy Laws: the Nosology, Aetiology, Statistics, Description, Diagnosis, Pathology, and Treatment of Insanity, with an Appendix of Cases.* London: J. A. Churchill.
8. Bernheim, H. (1980) *Bernheim's New Studies in Hypnotism (Hypnotisme, suggestion, psychothérapie: études nouvelles,* 1891). R. Sandor (Trans.), New York: International Universities Press, p. 16.
9. *Ibid.,* p. 18.
10. Bernheim, H. (1892). In: D. H. Tuke (Ed.), *A Dictionary of Psychological Medicine : Giving the Definition, Etymology and Synonyms of the Terms Used in Medical Psychology with the Symptoms, Treatment, and Pathology of Insanity and the Law of Lunacy in Great Britain and Ireland.* London: J. A. Churchill, p. 1214.
11. Petersen, H. (1897). Hypno-suggestion, etc., Medical letters. In: O. Wetterstrand (Ed.), *Hypnotism and its Application to Practical Medicine.* H. Petersen (Trans.), New York: G. P. Putnam, p. 126.

12. Tuke, D. H. (1886). *Le corps et l'esprit. Action du moral et de l'imagination sur le physique*. V. Parent (Trans.), Paris: J.-B. Ballière.

13. Bernheim, H. (1886). *De la suggestion et de ses applications à la thérapeutique*. Paris: Doin, p. 218. Alan Gauld notes that in Italy, Enrico Morselli referred in 1886 to the "efficacia psico-terapica" of hypnotism in his work, *Il magnetismo animale: la fascinazio e gli stati affini*. Turin: Roux e Favale. *The History of Hypnotism*. Cambridge: Cambridge University Press, 1995.

14. Tuke, D. H. (1880–1881). Hypnosis redivivus. *Journal of Mental Science*, 26: 531–551. Tuke reviewed the second edition of Bernheim's book in the *Journal of Mental Science* and did not comment on Bernheim's appropriation of his term.

15. Tuckey, C. L. (1889). *Psycho-therapeutics, or Treatment by Hypnotism and Suggestion*. London: Baillière, Tindall and Cox, 1889, p. xi. Tuckey's book was translated into German in 1895, losing the hyphen in the process: *Psychotherapie oder Behandlung mittelst Hypnotismus und Suggestion (Psychotherapy, or Treatment by Means of Hypnosis and Suggestion)*. In the fourth English edition of his book of 1900, psycho-therapeutics was relegated to the subtitle: *Treatment by Hypnotism and Suggestion, or Psycho-therapeutics*.

16. See Ilse Bulhof (1981). From psychotherapy to psychoanalysis: Frederik van Eeden and Albert Willem van Renterghem. *Journal of the History of the Behavioral Sciences*, 17: 209–221.

17. Van Eeden, F. (1893). Les principes de la psychothérapie. *Revue de l'hypnotisme*, 7: 97.

18. Edinburgh: Pentland, 1890.

19. *Hypnotisme, suggestion, psychothérapie, avec considérations nouvelles sur l'hystérie*, Paris: Octave Doin, 1903, (3rd edn), p. 50.

20. On the significance of Hansen for understanding the case of Anna O., see Borch-Jacobsen, M. (1996). *Remembering Anna O: A Century of Mystification*. New York: Routledge.

21. See Duyckaerts, F. (1990). "Delboeuf-Ladame: un conflit paradigmatique!" *Revue internationale d'histoire de la psychanalyse*, 3: 25–37 and my (1997) "Hypnose, médecine et droit: la correspondence entre Joseph Delboeuf et George Croom Robertson", *Corpus: Revue de philosophie*, 31: , 71–88.

22. Barrès, M. (1891). *Trois stations de psychothérapie*. Paris: Perrin, pp. xviii–xix. On Barrès' conception of psychotherapy, see Carroy, "L'invention du mot de psychothérapie et ses enjeux," pp. 20–23.

23. Noted in Ellenberger, H. (1970). *The Discovery of the Unconscious: The History and Evolution of the Dynamic Psychiatry*. New York: Basic Books, p. 330.
24. van Eeden, F.,"Les principes de la psychothérapie", pp. 97–98.
25. *Ibid.*, p. 99.
26. Robertson, G. (1892). Psycho-therapeutic: another fragment, *The Lancet*, 17 September, 1892, pp. 657-658. As late as the 1920s, the hyphenated form, "psycho-therapy", was in use in *The Lancet*. At the end of the nineteenth century, the practice of medicine was undergoing a transformation. See Bynum, W. F. (1994) *Science and the Practice of Medicine in the Nineteenth Century*. Cambridge: Cambridge University Press.
27. de la Tourette, G. (1887). *L'hypnotisme et les états analagues au point de vue médico-légal*. Paris: Plon, pp. 279–319.
28. Petersen, H. "Hypno-suggestion, etc., Medical letters", p. 142.
29. Delboeuf, J. (1893). Quelques considérations sur la psychologie de l'hypnotisme, à propos d'un cas de manie homicide guérie par suggestion, (reprinted in Delboeuf, J. *Le Sommeil et les rêves et autres textes*, Paris: Fayard, 1993, p. 421.
30. *Ibid.*
31. Noted by Tanner, T. (2003) in "Sigmund Freud and the Zeitschrift für Hypnotismus". *Arc de Cercle*, 1: 81.
32. In a similar manner in 1910, the *Revue de l'hypnotisme* changed its name in 1910 to the *Revue de psychothérapie et de psychologie appliquée* [*Review of Psychotherapy and Applied Psychology*].
33. Löwenfeld, L. (1894). *Pathologie und Therapie der Neurasthenie und Hysterie*. Wiesbaden: J. F. Bergmann.
34. *Lehrbuch der Gesammten Psychotherapie, mit einer einleitenden Darstellung der Hauptthatsachen der Medicinischen Psychologie*. Wiesbaden: J. F. Bergmann, 1897, p. ix.
35. *Ibid.*, p. 10.
36. *Ibid.*, p. 1.
37. In the twentieth century, there have been quite a number of such long histories of psychotherapy. On the problems with such an approach, see my (2003) review of Stanley Jackson's *A History of Psychological Healing*, in *Medical History*, 47(1): 115–117.
38. *The Lancet*, 4 May, 1901, p. 4292.
39. Collective organization seemed to be in the air: the same page bore the news of concerning the formation of a register for plumbers.

40. Dubois, P. (1909). *Psychic Treatment of Nervous Disorders* (*Les Psychonévroses et leur traitement moral*, 1904). S. E. Jeliffe and W. A. White (Trans.), New York: Funk & Wagnalls, p. 221.
41. *Ibid.*, p. xiii.
42. *Ibid.*, p. 96.
43. A similar perspective was presented by Déjerine, J., & Glaucker, E. (1911). *The Psychoneuroses and their Treatment by Psychotherapy* (*Les manifestations fonctionnelles des psychonévroses : leur traitement par la psychothérapie*). S. E. Jelliffe (Trans.), Philadelphia: J. B. Lippincott, 1918. On this question, see Gauchet, M., & Swain, G. (1994) "Du traitement moral aux psychothérapies: remarque sur la formation de l'idée contemporaine de psychothérapie". In: G. Swain (Ed.), *Dialogues avec l'insensé* (pp. 237–262). Paris: Gallimard.
44. Dubois, P. (1905) *Les psychonévroses et leur traitement moral.* (2nd edn). Paris: Masson, p. 19.
45. On this question, see Borch-Jacobsen, M. (2002) *Folies à plusieurs— de l'hystérie à la dépression.*, Paris: Les empêcheurs de penser en rond/Le seuil, and my (2001) "Claire, Lise, Jean, Nadia, and Gisèle: preliminary notes towards a characterisation of Pierre Janet's psychasthenia". In: M. Gijswijt-Hofstra & R. Porter (Eds.), *Cultures of Neurasthenia: From Beard to the First World War* (pp. 362–385). Amsterdam: Rodopi.
46. Camus, J. & Pagniez, P. (1904) *Isolement et psychothérapie: traitement de l'hystérie et de la neurasthénie, pratique de la rééducation morale et physique.* Paris: Alcan, p. 25.
47. *Ibid.*
48. *Ibid.*, p. 26.
49. *Ibid.*, pp. 177–180.
50. *Ibid.*, p. 82.
51. Caplan, E. (2001). *Mind Games: American Culture and the Birth of Psychotherapy.* Berkeley, CA: University of California Press, p. 80. See also Taylor, E. (1999). *Shadow Culture: Spirituality and Psychology in America.* New York: Counterpoint.
52. http://psychclassics.yorku.ca/Baldwin/Dictionary/defs/M3defs. htm#Mind%20Cure. In 1903, Richard Ebbard noted that "Thought-Cure" was also used as a synonym for "Psycho-Therapy." *How to Restore Life-Giving Energy to Sufferers from* Sexual Neurasthenia *and Kindred Brain and Nervous Disorders (Neurosis, Hysteria, etc.)* London: Medical Publishing Co., 1903. "Thought-Cure" evidently did not catch on.
53. Caplan, *Mind Games*, p. 199.

54. New York: Centre Publishing, 1908.
55. Cabot, The American Type of Psychotherapy: A general introduction, in Parker (Ed.), *op. cit.*, p. 1.
56. *Ibid.*
57. A recent example of this is Joseph Schwartz, *Cassandra's Daughter: A History of Psychoanalysis in Europe and America*. London: Allen Lane, 1999. On Schwartz, see Anthony Stadlen's review in *Arc de Cercle*, 1, 2003. On the constitution and maintenance of the Freud legend, see Borch-Jacobsen, M., & Shamdasani, S. (2001) "Une visite aux archives Freud". *Ethnopsy: Les mondes contemporains de la guérison. 3*, 2001, 141–188.
58. Cited in Eng, E. (1984). Coleridge's "psycho-analytical understanding" and Freud's psychoanalysis. *International Review of Psychoanalysis, 11*: 463.
59. *Ibid.*, p. 465.
60. Freud, S. Heredity and the aetiology of the neuroses. *S.E., 3*, 151.
61. Janet, P. (1925). *Psychological Healing: A Historical and Clinical Study*, 2 vols. E. & C. Paul (Trans.), London: George Allen & Unwin, pp. 601–602. Janet appears to have taken up the word "psychotherapy" relatively late: it does not feature in his *États mentales des hysteriques* (Paris: Rueff, 1892–1894), nor in his *Névroses et idées fixes*, (Paris: Alcan, 1898).
62. Löwenfeld, *Pathologie und Therapie der Neurasthenie und Hysterie*, p. 688.
63. The significance of this issue was brought to light by Gündlach, H. (2002) in "Psychoanalysis & the story of 'O': An Embarrassment". *The Semiotic Review of Books, 13*(1): 4–5.
64. Noted by Gündlach, *ibid.*, p. 4.
65. *Ibid.*, p. 5.
66. Munich: E. Reinhardt, 1910.
67. Vienna: Deuticke, 1911.
68. Forel, A. (1911). *Der Hypnotismus oder die Suggestion und die Psychotherapie* (6th edn). Stuttgart: Ferdinand Enke, p. 189.
69. Freud, S. On the history of the psycho-analytic movement. *S.E., 14*: 7. Psychoanalysis was hyphenated in translation by James Strachey.
70. Bernheim, H. (1917). *Automatisme et suggestion*. Paris: Alcan.

CHAPTER SIX

The British Medical Association: Report of the Psycho-Analysis Committee, 1929

Ann Casement

Introduction

The focus of this chapter is on a brief history of psycho-analysis in Britain with particular reference to the British Medical Association's Report of 1929. "Psycho-analysis" is spelt with a hyphen except when it appears in quotations as that is the way it is rendered in the Report. The first section of the chapter concentrates on the early beginnings of the discipline taken from the impressive book edited by Pearl King and Riccardo Steiner entitled *The Freud—Klein Controversies 1941–45*, published in 1991. I attended the weekend conference chaired by Joseph Sandler that launched the book, and subsequently reviewed it for *The Journal of Analytical Psychology*. The chapter ends with a brief look at the current situation in Britain with regard to who is entitled to be registered as a "psycho-analyst."

The early history of psycho-analysis in Great Britain

"The history of psychoanalysis in Great Britain is closely linked with Ernest Jones, the creator of the British Psycho-Analytical

Society." (King & Steiner, 1991, p. 9). Jones was a successful physician and neurologist when he became interested in problems of psychopathology and used the new therapy on his first psychoanalytic patient from 1905 to 1906. Through meeting Jung in 1907, he came to work at the Burghölzli in Zurich and took an active part in the First International Psychoanalytical Congress held in Salzburg the following year. It was there that he first met and began a personal and scientific association with Freud that lasted until Freud's death in London in 1939.

King states that Jones found it as difficult to be a pioneer of psycho-analysis in London as Freud had done in Vienna because medical colleagues in both places were suspicious of discussing sexual matters with patients. King suggests that this is an important reason for Jones's departure for Toronto to take up the post of Director of the Psychiatric Clinic there. While there, Jones was responsible for propagating psycho-analysis in Canada and the USA but he also made numerous visits to continental Europe, where he had a personal analysis with Sandor Ferenczi in Budapest.

On his return to England in 1913, Jones formed the London Psycho-Analytical Society, which was composed of a number of people interested in psycho-analysis but only four practitioners. He despaired of this group ever forming a satisfactory basis for the development of psycho-analysis in England and eventually disbanded it. In 1919 Jones, with some former members of the London Society, founded the British Psycho-Analytical Society (BP-AS). In the case of both Societies, Jones was confronted with decisions about who were appropriate members and what basic psycho-analytic theories should be held. These two issues continue to be debated in the wider psycho-analytic community in Britain and other parts of the world.

The BP-AS was the seventh society to be affiliated to the International Psychoanalytical Association (IPA). A library was formed and translations of psycho-analytic writings into English were undertaken by Jones, Joan Riviere, and James and Alix Strachey, who formed the Glossary Committee. In 1920 *The International Journal of Psychoanalysis* was founded—the first psychoanalytic journal in English.

The institutionalizing of psycho-analysis was now under way, with the establishing in 1924 of the Institute of Psycho-Analysis as a legally registered company that dealt with financial matters related to book publication. Premises were obtained at 96 Gloucester Place, which housed the BP-AS, the Institute, and the London Clinic of Psycho-Analysis until 1950 when the Institute moved to Mansfield House in New Cavendish Street, London. (There has been a further move of premises in recent times to Shirland Road in West London.) The Clinic was underwritten by the membership, who either contributed sessions to it without charging or performed an equivalent service, and during the first fifty years of its existence approximately 3,080 patients had free or low fee psychoanalysis.

By 1926 the British Society under Jones's guidance had come into being. The difficulties that it encountered in the 1920s centred on issues to do with medically qualified psycho-analysts referring patients to lay colleagues. This exposed the former to possible accusations of malpractice by the General Medical Council. There were also attacks on psycho-analysis in the press culminating in a letter to *The Times* from the Chairman of the National Council for Mental Hygiene, a lay body, that declared they were setting up a committee to investigate psycho-analysis. Jones complained to appropriate medical bodies that it was unacceptable for a lay organization to investigate members of the medical profession.

Report of the Psycho-Analysis Committee

Preliminary

At the instigation of the Annual Representative Meeting of the British Medical Association (BMA) held at Nottingham in July 1926, the Council of the BMA set up a Special Committee "to investigate the subject of Psycho-Analysis and report on the same" (BMA, 1929, p. 3). The meetings of this Committee extended over a period from March 1927 until May 1929. Its membership was made up of twenty-one members of the medical profession, including "Ernest Jones representing the Freudian School of Psycho-Analysis, and H. Godwin Baynes, representing the Jungian School of Analytical Psychology" (BMA, 1929, p. 4). These two members were added to the Committee in July 1927.

The main focus of the Committee's work was on psycho-analysis but it was decided to include a survey of the whole field of psychotherapy. Jones attended twenty-four of the twenty-eight meetings held by the Committee and worked hard with Edward Glover of the British Society to prepare evidence and comment on criticism against psychoanalysis. The findings of the Committee enabled psycho-analysis to be treated like any other specialism in medicine.

This was the first time an official national body of the medical profession from any country had recognized the distinction between "psycho-analysts" and " pseudo-analysts", as well as the qualifications established by membership of the International Psychoanalytical Association. (King & Steiner, 1991, p. 13).

Various documents were prepared for the assistance of the Committee in its work, which included a memorandum on psycho-therapy; a questionnaire on psychological analysis; a statement of Jung's conception of psychological therapy; memoranda on psycho-analysis, and on the psycho-analytic process. The Report starts with a brief historical survey of work done with mental disorder, stating that an analytic or exploratory approach only began in the 1880s. Prior to that there existed considerable activity which revolved around hypnotism or suggestion, but these practitioners did not evince any serious interest in the pathogenic aspects of mental disorder.

This investigation had at least one positive result: it enabled the Committee to get a clearer view of what psycho-analysis actually is, i.e., the technique and theory elaborated by Freud and his co-workers, and to approach some definition of the respects in which it differs from other methods of psycho-therapy (BMA, 1929, p. 4).

Historical Survey of Psycho-analysis

[Everything that follows is taken from the BMA Report except for comments by this author, which are presented in paranetheses as here.]

In the 1880s interest developed along exploratory lines and the Report cites in this connection Myers in England, Morton Prince in the United States, Binet and Janet in France, Breuer and Freud in

Austria. These researches were conducted with the aid of hypnotism, automatic writing, and other methods, and supported the
conclusion that it is possible for mental processes to exist and
produce effects without the subject being in any way conscious of
them. Divergence occurred along the lines put forward by Janet, for
instance, who inclined to think that dissociation was due to an
inherent incapacity to maintain the mind's unity heightened by
traumatic physical or mental experiences. The psycho-analytical
school stressed that dissociation is the result of forces actively at
work within the mind itself. The first approach concentrates on
what is commonly referred to as the "sub-conscious"; the second on
the "unconscious".

The Report concludes this brief history with a mention of Breuer
and Freud's collaboration on *Studies on Hysteria* in 1895, in which
they first distinguished between mental acts that were conscious
and those that were unconscious. Freud's abandoning of hypnotism
as an aid in favour of his new method of psycho-analysis is touched
on, as well as the fact that the new discipline had undergone a
continual evolution since its discovery.

This brief history is followed by a summary of psycho-analytical methodology and teaching, including the emotional relationship
to the physician referred to as "influence of the physician", "suggestive state", "transference", and the way that this can obstruct
emerging unconscious material unless dealt with "by the technical
devices peculiar to psycho-analysis" (BMA, 1929, p. 7). The Report
states that the essential feature of psycho-analysis that distin-
guishes it from other forms of psycho-therapy is the special technique whereby through the analysis of the "suggestive state" the
unconscious conflict is allowed to emerge fully into consciousness
and be resolved there. It concludes that "all forms of psychotherapy can be reduced in essence to (1) suggestion, (2) psychoanalysis, and (3) pseudo-analysis" (BMA, 1929, p. 8).

The central importance of resistance and repression are also
considered in relation to the strength of the forces maintaining the
unconsciousness of buried mental material. "Every psycho-analysis, therefore, comprises an arduous fight against the opposition
offered by the patient's unconscious mind . . ." (BMA, 1929, p. 8).
This part of the Report ends with a brief exposition of infantile
sexuality and the Oedipus complex.

The next section is entitled *Other Analytical Methods* and concentrates on four prominent names who had accepted some of Freud's conclusions but went on to inaugurate their own schools of analysis. The four—Adler, Jung, Rank, and Stekel—between them discounted many of Freud's theories, such as infantile sexuality, repression, resistance, and even the existence of an unconscious. The main ideas of each are mentioned, for instance, Adler's "will to power" [and "masculine protest"]; Jung's "psychic energy", "individuation", and the religious dimension; Stekel's criminal and religious conflicts; and Rank's "birth trauma".

Despite these differences between analytical schools, the Report concludes that one thing they hold in common was that psychopathology was not limited to treatment through medicine as the problems were seen to be far more social than medical. The result was that other sciences such as anthropology were invoked in the pursuit of analytical goals.

The next section of the Report deals with the conditions that have been treated by psychotherapy and psycho-analysis. These include the psychoses such as early dementia praecox, paranoia, manic-depressive insanity; the psycho-neuroses like anxiety states, phobias, obsessional neuroses, hysteria; personal and social maladjustments like marital difficulties, impotence, sexual perversions and inversions, anomalies of temperament or of character, delinquency; mental states associated with physical disease like asthma and Graves' disease.

Misconceptions concerning psycho-analysis

The Committee's Report now turns its attention to certain misconceptions that had been brought to its attention in the course of its sittings. It acknowledges that the term "Psycho-Analysis" is used loosely by the medical profession as well as the general public instead of being applied only to the method evolved by Freud and the theories related to it, and it sets out to rectify this with the following statement:

> A psycho-analyst is therefore a person who uses Freud's technique, and anyone who does not use this technique should not, whatever

other methods he may employ, be called a psycho-analyst. In accordance with this definition and for the purpose of avoiding confusion, the term "psycho-analyst" is properly reserved for members of the International Psycho-Analytical Association. [BMA, 1929, p. 12]

In this way, the Committee points to the fact that criticisms of psycho-analytical theory or practice should be confined to those who fall into the category delineated above. At that time the IPA consisted of four hundred members and the British Psycho-Analytical Society was one of its ten national societies. The following was a statement on the constitution, methods and objects of the IPA presented to the Committee:

The criterion for membership of the International Psycho-Analytical Association is an adequate knowledge of the subject. What is regarded as adequate depends on whether the candidate proposes or does not propose to practise psycho-analysis, a higher standard being imposed in the former case. Members of the Association may be defined as persons who have so dealt with the internal obstacles normally interposed between consciousness and the unconscious as to be able, in the opinion of their fellow members, to appreciate the functioning of unconscious mental processes. Psycho-analysts have been reproached for shutting themselves off from the rest of the medical profession by forming societies of their own, but they merely follow the custom of other special workers: that is, although they freely discuss their work in various other medical societies, they also further it by discussing the more advanced aspects of it with colleagues who have a common basis of understanding and knowledge of the problems concerned.

The higher standard for admission to membership, applicable to those who propose to engage in practice, depends on the fact that the activity of the internal "resistances" is apt to be intensified by personal contact with psycho-analytic work: this applies equally to the analyst and the person being analysed. It is, in the latter case, for instance, invariably more intensified during the first stages of a psycho-analysis, this incidentally explaining the apparent paradox that a person who breaks analysis during this stage is often in a less favourable position to discuss the subject objectively than he was before. The standard of insight demanded by the Association is therefore higher with those who propose to carry out psycho-analytic explorations, *e.g.*, for therapeutic purposes, than it is with those whose interest in the subject is, so to speak, an external one, *e.g.*, educationalists, anthropologists, and so on. This is because the former would otherwise expose themselves to the likelihood of their internal resistances being stimulated and mobilised, with correspondingly deleterious effects on their therapeutic work, *i.e.*, on the interests of their patients.

The degree of insight varies spontaneously among different people (and even at different times among the same people); it can be aided by appropriate measures, *i.e.*, by psycho-analysis. There are two forms of this, auto-analysis, and allo-analysis. The former was the only one available in the early days of the work and several of the leading psycho-analysts, including Abraham, Ferenczi, and of course Freud himself, had perforce to be content with it. Experience soon showed, however, that only very exceptional persons could proceed far by means of auto-analysis and that in any event it is inferior as a method to allo-analysis, so the latter is strongly recom-mended. In the interests of their patients future practitioners are expected to equip themselves as far as possible to avoid the dangers otherwise inevitable in analytic work.

Curricula have been devised by special Training Committees in various countries and they include courses of lectures, reading, personal analytic work and analyses of patients under the direction of experienced psycho-analytical physicians. The training takes at least three years. There are six training centres: in Berlin, Budapest, Frankfort, London, New York and Vienna; of these the most fully equipped are those in Berlin, London and Vienna.

To sum up, there are two objects of the Association to which the two standards of admission correspond. The first is the furthering of knowledge by the usual methods (Society discussions, publica-tions, etc.). The second is the safeguarding of the public by provid-ing adequate training of practitioners. Until this educational work is taken over by some other body full membership of the Association is the nearest existing approach to a Diploma in the practice of psycho-analysis. [BMA, 1929, p. 14]

The Report goes on to enumerate various misconceptions about psycho-analysis. These include the following: that harmful conse-quences and even insanity may result from its practice, which is counteracted by psycho-analysts claiming that this is a danger only when it is practised by those imperfectly equipped for the task.

Added to this are the polarized claims that psycho-analysis neglects the mind–body relationship or that it leaves out the more spiritual aspects of humankind. The response to the first is that psycho-analysis is a biological doctrine and that further advances in neuro-physiology would throw light on what then could only be described in psychological language. [In recent years this is what has happened through the work of psycho-analysts like Peter Fonagy and Mark Solms but there still remain a number of psycho-analytical practitioners who are resistant to the new insights it affords.] The response to the second point is that Freud postulates a conflict between the spiritual and more primitive side of human nature.

Other misconceptions include the claim that psycho-analysts see their treatment as a panacea for all mental disorders. The response to this is that practitioners make no such claims and recognize the limitations of psycho-analysis as a treatment. There is also the dread charge of suggestibility based on the claim that the personality of the practitioner is an important factor in successful treatment. This is denied by practitioners who state that treatment by any skilled analyst would have similar results. [In recent times it is acknowledged that the personality of the practitioner is indeed a hugely important factor in psycho-analysis or psycho-therapy.]

The response to the claim that the expense of psycho-analysis restricts it to a limited field of patients is countered by the following points from practitioners: they are willing to work for modified fees; these fees are subject to considerable variation; the cost is spread over a lengthy period; free treatment is available for some. [Taking all these counter-claims into account, however, it must be said that the popularity of other psychotherapies for many years now is due to a great extent to their being cheaper and shorter-term treatments than psycho-analysis.]

This section ends with an important point relating to suggestions that keeping written records of analysis would enable practitioners to present psycho-analysis in this form to the public. The Committee were satisfied with the response from psycho-analysts themselves that writing in the course of sessions would disturb the free train of thought necessary for analyst and patient; the presence of a device to keep such a record would interfere with the confidential relationship between patient and analyst; and what happens in sessions to do with body language and hesitations on the part of the patient are important elements in analytic interpretation that are impossible to describe in writing. [Keeping written records is still strongly resisted by many analysts because of the above and also because it makes it akin to quite different disciplines such as medicine and social work.]

Criticisms and replies

There follow the main criticisms aimed at psycho-analysis with replies by Ernest Jones, the President of the British Psycho-Analytical Society. The *first criticism* states that there is a difficulty cited by many critics of not having their criticisms listened to by psycho-analysts—"an attitude which they hold is itself deserving of criticism"(BMA 1929, p. 16). Further, the principle justification used by psycho-analysts for turning a deaf ear even to those who know something of the subject is that the critics have not overcome their personal resistances and are therefore not in a position to appreciate or fruitfully criticize psycho-analysis. In this way, critics claim that any criticisms are discounted beforehand and psycho-analysts can erect defences that are impervious to any attack or argument.

Ernest Jones's *response* is to say that there is plenty of evidence to show that psycho-analysts do listen to criticism and that the impression that they do not is susceptible of a different explanation. He asserts that it is necessary in the first instance to distinguish between objective criticism, which is appropriate in science—this presupposes that the critic understands the meaning of the conclusion he is criticizing; and that the criticism itself is more than an unsupported assertion.

According to Jones, the reason why psycho-analysts isolate themselves from other branches of science is that most criticism is of the uninformed kind and practitioners themselves deplore the paucity of informed criticism. This regret on their part has two obvious consequences—the first being that they have been untiring in dealing at length, both verbally and in their writings, with such criticisms that have any claim to objectivity.

Jones claims that it is impossible to point to any criticism made of psycho-analysis that has not been extensively considered in its literature.

A second result of the paucity of objective external criticism is to be seen in the vigorous use of internal criticism which is equal to that in any other branch of science. Jones says that it is "grotesque" to suggest that a psycho-analytical society consists only of uncritical agreement.

What Jones calls "uncritical opposition" soon leads to an impasse as the criticism being barren in its content does not lend itself to much discussion. He says that opponents of this kind can hardly win over practitioners who have ample personal experience of the things denied:

> For instance, to tell a psycho-analyst that the phenomena he is dealing with all day long do not exist leaves him as little impressed as a chemist would be by the argument that oxygen and hydrogen, being invisible, cannot exist."[BMA, 1929, p. 17]

Jones puts the responsibility on the opponents of psycho-analysis who fail to achieve any result from such tactics and says that they then turn to inventing the fiction that psycho-analysts are afraid of criticism. In their turn, psycho-analysts conclude that opposition of this kind is dictated by subjective and largely unconscious factors and leaves the former no alternative but to deny that their work is wrong.

[Whatever the reasons, it is still true today that psycho-analysis has not evolved into an interdisciplinary science and remains instead isolated from other scientific disciplines such as evolutionary biology, cognitive psychology, neuroscience and linguistics.]

The *second criticism* relates to the findings reported by psycho-analysts to do with symbols, particularly in relation to the interpretation of dreams. Critics claim that these have more to do with what is in the mind of the analyst rather than that of the patient. The gist of the criticism is that the same signification is attached to the same symbols produced by a variety of different people, which suggests a preconceived interpretation that is unrelated to particular cases. Suggestibility is pointed to here, owing to the special relationship that exists between analyst and patient. It is further contended that psycho-analysts are subject to suggestion from each other which leads to their being prone to holding the same views.

The *response* put forward to this is that the crux of the matter lies in whether psycho-analysts have discovered or invented the unconscious. Jones contends that this question can only be answered by investigation that will have to take into account two major considerations. The first is *intellectual*, whereby analysts claim to have had years of experience in the use of suggestion and to know the difference between that and the unexpected discoveries revealed by studying psycho-analytic data. The course of an analysis makes it clear which interpretations are correct and which are not and there are innumerable technical and clinical means that testify objectively to these.

Psycho-analytic conclusions may also be tested from sources outside the field such as the output of writers long dead; data to be found in anthropology and folklore; poetry and other products of the imagination, all of which reveal the same mechanisms, associations, and interpretations that feature in psycho-analysis. This applies above all to symbols, very few, if any, of which are peculiar to psycho-analysis. The charge of preconceived ideas relating to symbols can only be finally settled by examination of the evidence.

There is also an *affective* component to this issue. Jones says that the criticism about the suggestibility of the analytic relationship is vastly exaggerated and misconceives the nature of the emotional relationship on which it is based. One of the main tasks of psycho-analysis has been the investigation of the nature of this relationship, which in itself has thrown light on suggestion. The result of the latter has shown that treatment by suggestion can only be effective when the patient has a positive emotional attitude to the analyst, e.g. one of trust, respect, even affection. These influence the ideas that are already present in the patient's mind, which the latter has connected with an imaginary conception of the analyst. However, this condition is rarely present in psycho-analysis as the opposite feelings of mistrust, fear, suspicion, and hostility towards the analyst almost always predominate. "The picture of the docile patient meekly accepting the analyst's explanation is extremely remote from the truth"(BMA, 1929, p. 19). Where a patient has an exaggerated fear of the analyst's influence this can be shown to be based on a fear of certain buried mental processes and replaces fear of the unconscious mind.

The *third criticism* comes from those who assert that no unconscious mental processes can or do exist. The phenomena described by psycho-analysts are either seen to be neuro-physiological processes without any mental correlation; or their contents as described by psycho-analysts are rejected. The contents alluded to are infantile sexuality, particularly the Oedipus and castration complexes, that evoke in some critics feelings of incredulity and repugnance. Their universal validity is denied as the evidence for their existence is considered insufficient.

The *response* to these criticisms is that the existence of mental processes in the subject of which the latter may be unaware has been proved independently of psycho-analysis. The statement made above is reiterated that when the knowledge exists to render these processes in physiological language that will be welcomed. For the time being, only psychological vocabulary is available for the task.

However, the more serious charge is obviously to do with the alleged content of the unconscious mind. Critics of this are not convinced by the evidence that is put before them, which may be due to the fact that most have sampled only a small selection of the evidence that exists rather than made a study of it as a whole. Psycho-analysts can only point to the need to study more evidence so that the sheer weight of the confirmatory evidence may bring about acceptance. Psycho-analysts may also point to "resistance" on the part of critics, which is due to subjectively experienced unconscious bias that, it is claimed, is invariably operative in this area. A last resort may be to suggest that critics make a first-hand study of the material, which is the only way that a final judgement can be arrived at.

The *fourth criticism* maintains that people may be made neurotic through the introspection that is part of psycho-analysis.

The *response* to this is that morbid introspection is a characteristic symptom of neurosis which denotes someone who is unduly attached to personal thoughts and unable to free themselves to get on with life. It is release from this bondage that can be enabled by psycho-analysis through exploring the nature of the attachment and resolving it. An analysis would be considered a failure if morbid introspection persisted after it had ended. It is admitted that the tendency to introspection may increase in the course of an analysis, which is compared with the worsening of a patient's state immediately following an operation. However, as the analysis proceeds, it is claimed that the fruitless, circular kind of introspection is replaced by a healthy one that brings the morbid tendency to an end. It is only when the practitioner does not have the requisite training that there is a risk of stimulating the sense of guilt that is present in every case of neurosis and of worsening the underlying conflicts.

The *fifth criticism* is directed at moral health and the dangers inherent in directing a patient's thoughts to sexual matters. This is based on the stress laid on sexuality in psycho-analytic literature and is directed against a psychology that considers the sexual impulse as the strongest, if not the only, factor in the unconscious. This is the one that is seen to over-ride all the others in its effect on mental health and sees in most, if not all, abnormal conduct and pathology the influence of perverted sexuality. This approach is said to be a danger especially to the young, for instance, the unravelling of the sexual life in a sensitive, suggestible adolescent is thought to have a prejudicial effect on the outlook and life of a young person.

The *response* here is to state that this view is founded on a combination of ignorance and prejudice and is one-sided and misleading about psycho-analysis. It states unequivocally that the complex problems involved with the sexual instinct are a subject for dispassionate study.

> The policy of flight from these problems, together with the implied denunciation of those who try to face them objectively, is not only a confession of bankruptcy, but is the advocacy of an attitude which it is no longer possible to maintain now that the import and urgency of such problems are increasingly forced upon us. [BMA, 1929, p. 22]

It goes on to state that a vast amount of misery and mental ill health arises from abnormal development in the area of sexuality especially in the young. Ernest Jones goes on to say that he is confident that the medical profession, once enlightened, will incorporate psycho-analytic insights in this area into its therapeutic approach.

Otherwise it would be suggesting that only the psycho-sexual system in the whole of the mind–body complex should be excluded from the fields of pathology and therapeutics. He ends by saying that this criticism stems from the popular belief that psycho-analysis encourages socially forbidden impulses in patients, although evidence put before the Committee is devoid of any such instances. On the contrary, psycho-analysis aims to restore normality where abnormality has prevailed, which includes a higher standard of responsibility on the person's part than before. Far from any moral harm being done to patients by psycho-analysis there is ample evidence to suggest changes in exactly the opposite direction.

Conclusions

The conclusions of the Psycho-Analysis Committee state that the term "psycho-analysis" is used in two ways. Its popular extension is incapable of definition or description but there is also its strict sense denoting the theory and technique devised by Freud.

> It is accordingly recognized that in any scientific inquiry into the matter the claims of Freud and his followers to the use and definition of the term are just and must be respected. [BMA, 1929, p. 22]

The Committee also recognized that there are practitioners in the field of psychology and psycho-pathology who do not claim to be practising psycho-analysis but instead use such terms as analytical psychology, individual psychology, and deep mental analysis. Further, there are other methods of psycho-therapy that have little in common with analytical methods, and often the public wrongly applies the term psycho-analysts to the practitioners of these methods. The Committee recognized that psycho-analysts should be not held accountable for the opinions or actions of those who are not actually psycho-analysts.

The Committee also confirmed that it had dealt with various misconceptions in relation to psycho-analysis. It also found that even among many of those most hostile to psycho-analysis, there is a disposition to accept the hypothetical existence of the unconscious mind, though others would not do so.

The most important criticisms against psycho-analysis have been set forth by the Committee together with responses from a recognized psycho-analyst. However, the Committee is of the opinion that it cannot make any general pronouncement on these questions.

As the Committee had no means of testing psycho-analysis as a therapeutic method it felt that it was not in a position to express a collective opinion in its favour or against its practice. It ended its Report by stating:

> The claims of its advocates and the criticisms of those who oppose it must, as in other disputed issues, be tested by time, by experience, and by discussion. [BMA, 1929, p. 23]

Entitlement to be registered as a psycho-analyst

In February 1999, in my role as Chair of the United Kingdom Council for Psychotherapy (UKCP), I met with a Peer, Lord Alderdice, and his Special Adviser at the House of Lords. In the course of this meeting, Lord Alderdice offered to bring a Private Member's Bill to regulate psychotherapy. The thinking until then was that regulation was a long way off as there had been a failed attempt in 1981 and subsequent governments had made it clear that they were not prepared to take any action.

Lord Alderdice's was the beginning of a flurry of activity that included meetings with Ministers and other Peers, combined with a series of meetings with stakeholders in the field at the House of Lords. UKCP was one of the founder stakeholders at these meetings, as were member organizations of the British Confederation of Psychotherapists (BCP) that had been formed by a breakaway group from the UKCP in 1992. The BCP organizations included the British Psycho-Analytical Society (BP-AS) as well as other psycho-analytically orientated groups and two representing analytical psychology.

Shortly after the initial meeting at the House of Lords in February 1999, the Psychoanalytic and Psychodynamic Section of the UKCP applied to have the title "psychoanalyst" represented in that umbrella organization's register. [The non-hyphenated spelling of the title "psychoanalyst" or "psychoanalytic" is used when referring to its usage at the UKCP as that is how it is spelt at that organ-ization.] Initially, this went through on the nod at the Registration Board's meeting in April 1999. This was then repeated at the Governing Board's meeting in May 1999. No one on either of these Boards had any idea of the implications of this event, as there already were psychoanalysts included in the UKCP Register.

In December 1999, I, as Chair of the Governing Board, received a voluminous correspondence, mostly from member organizations and registrants within UKCP, an overwhelming number of which wished to protest strongly against the extension of the use of the title "psychoanalyst" to sixty-three psychoanalytic psychothera-pists in the UKCP Register. There were similar letters from non-UKCP organizations such as the BP-AS, the British Association of Psychotherapists, and the Society of Analytical Psychologists.

As a result of this correspondence, the UKCP AGM in January 2000 devoted a great deal of time to discussing this issue and it was finally agreed that the use of the term "psychoanalyst" by indi-viduals on the Register would be deferred for twelve months pend-ing wide-ranging discussions. These discussions were envisaged to take place within UKCP as well as between the organization and other interested outside bodies, and meetings have indeed taken place.

This matter continues to provoke a great deal of interest and discussion within the psychoanalytic and psychotherapy field in the United Kingdom. The BP-AS, for instance, has put out on its website a notice calling attention to this issue alongside its own list of psychoanalysts for reference by members of the public seeking psychoanalysis.

Conclusion

This chapter has concentrated on questions surrounding the usage of the title "psycho-analyst" in the United Kingdom since the 1920s. This is an on-going issue and is likely to be contentious for some-time to come, particularly with psychotherapy statutory regulation in the air. This has given a new impetus to the whole question of entitlement to be registered as a "psycho-analyst"—with or without the hyphen.

References

British Medical Association (1929). *Report of the Psycho-Analysis Committee*. London: Printed at the Office of the British Medical Association, BMA House, Tavistock Square.

King, P., & Steiner, R. (Eds.) (1991). *The Freud–Klein Controversies 1941–45*. London: Routledge.

CHAPTER SEVEN

What has happened to psychoanalysis in the British Society?[1]

Pearl King

Introduction

In 1942, in a paper on Object Relations, Marjorie Brierley wrote prior to what are known as the "controversial discussions":

> One way of stating the problem before us is to ask the question: Is a theory of mental development in terms of infantile object relationships compatible with a theory in terms of instinct vicissitudes? [Brierley, 1942, pp. 110–111]

She felt that the answer was in the affirmative, and she quoted Freud's own most recent definition of instinct (Freud, 1933) in support of her opinion that an instinct may be described as having a source, an object and an aim.

In 1992, fifty years later, the British Society organized an English Speaking Conference in London and the topic was to assess the status of some of the topics that had been so hotly discussed then. I read the opening paper and I dared to suggest that

> Fifty years have now passed and when I listen to clinical material from some members of the British Society, I wonder if she [Brierley]

was right, as they tend to work in terms of the analysis of the vicis-situdes of the current Object relationships of the patient and the analyst, and there is little reference to the vicissitudes of instincts, indicating that perhaps the two theories have not proved compati-ble, but that one theory has replaced the other. [King, 1994]

When I read that sentence there was a gasp from some members of the audience.

I am pleased to contribute to this book because I am very worried about what is happening to psychoanalysis in the British Society. Furthermore, what is happening is being covered up with a fudge that implies that there is very little difference between the conceptual and clinical points of view of most of the members of the British Society. This is conveyed by the following statements, which are made at International Conferences and Congresses, to the effect that in the British Society, we all work in the "here and now"! Such people try to give a message to those outside the British Society that those who do not agree with this statement are not worth taking seriously, and the message to those in the British Society is that if you want to get on in this Society, you had better agree with this way of working. I think that this is sick, and I feel that those of us who are unhappy about this state of affairs, should stand up and be counted for I know that I am not alone in my disquiet.

It is not just that there is only one way of interpreting transfer-ence that is acceptable, but that this approach to the interpretation of transference as the current relationship between the patient and the analyst in the "here and now", excludes the use of many of the key technical concepts of Freud. If you dare to discuss with students in clinical seminars other ways of looking at clinical mate-rial, drawing on some of Freud's formulations, you are considered old-fashioned, and told: "We would not be allowed to work like that." This was said to me when I asked the question of a student: "Who do you think that you are in the transference?" The student replied that they had to ask the question: "What is the patient doing to you now?" The whole past of the patient was ignored and the idea of the operation of the repetition compulsion was either alien, "forbidden" or felt to be disapproved of.

What is so sad is that so much of the fun, the excitement of exploring with a patient their whole life span, has been lost. This is not the kind of psychoanalysis that I was taught in this Society and it would have been anathema to most of my teachers and colleagues. I think that support for this approach to analysing comes from two main directions. The first source of support for this approach comes from most of the Kleinians and their followers in the Independent Group. This has developed slowly over many years. The second source of support comes from the Sandlers and their idea of splitting the Unconscious into a Present Unconscious and a Past Unconscious (Sandler & Sandler. 1995).[2] Clifford Yorke has given a critique of these ideas and a discussion of their theory (Yorke, 1996, 2001).

Their contribution to metapsychology might not have had much effect on psychoanalytical thinking had it not been used to support one of the rationales for restricting technique to working on the present relationship between the patient and the analyst, which becomes a restrictive, relationship-based technique for therapy, with its taboo on working with the past in the present when it occurs.

I was wondering when these changes and the development of this restrictive technique started developing. I first became a Training Analyst in 1955. At that time it was made quite clear to us that we should not take part in any other training for any psychotherapy course. Prior to the war, in order that those accepted for training with us would be enabled to keep their experience of psychoanalysis separate from the psychotherapies that were practised at the Tavistock Clinic, applicants who worked at that Clinic were told that they had to give up their work there if they wanted us to train them as psychoanalysts. One result of the Second World War was that members of both organizations, the Institute and the Tavistock Clinic, who had worked together during that war, made friends and sorted out their roles to their mutual advantage.

During the 1950s other trainings in psychotherapy began to be developed. The Institute supported the training in child psychotherapy, under Anna Freud at the Hampstead Clinic, provided that it was not called psychoanalysis. The Tavistock Clinic soon followed with their own training in child psychotherapy, under the direction of John Bowlby. We were permitted to analyse their candidates as their training was initially based on five sessions a week both for the candidates and their patients.

However, as time went on, analysts found that their patients were finding their way into various forms of psychotherapy training for adults. When this happened it was thought that we could not refuse to continue to treat them. It was explained to us that they were training to see patients for only three sessions a week and that they would only work on their relationship between themselves and their patients, so that there would be no transference created or interpretations from the past.[3] It was therefore a different form of therapy and it should not get confused with what we were trained to do as psychoanalysts (Bibring, 1954).

When I realized how I had just described the way these psychotherapists were supposed to work, a bell rang in my mind. Is this not a description of how I had just been complaining that many colleagues were now working as "psychoanalysts" in the British Society? No wonder it is so difficult to describe the difference between what goes on in the Institute and what psychotherapists do.

It reminded me of a story about a man travelling in the desert on a camel. It was a beautiful day, but as evening drew on a sand storm started to blow up, and the man got off his camel and pitched a small tent for himself, and tethered his camel outside the tent. Soon the camel put his head into the tent and asked if he could keep it there, as the sand was getting into his eyes. The man agreed, and went to sleep again. The camel then woke him up and asked if he could come further inside the tent, as the sand was uncomfortable on his coat, while the man had a cloak to protect him. So the camel came even further into the tent and the man pulled his cloak around him to keep out the sand. When he woke up in the morning the man found himself sitting outside the tent, while the camel was comfortably established inside it. As he had pulled his cloak over his head, he had not even noticed that the camel had taken over his tent.

Now, could this be a parable to explain what has happened between the "here and now" way some psychoanalysts in the British Society work and the description of the way psychotherapists would be trained to work in the psychotherapy trainings that had been set up? The only difference between the way they work and the way many of our members work is that they see patients three times a week, though, when they can, they see them more often, and we see them five times a week. I must say that I am not very familiar with the work done now by colleagues in these psychotherapy organizations, but I do not think that they follow strictly the lines laid down initially, nor do they cut themselves or their patients off from the past.

What makes me so unhappy about what is happening to psychoanalysis in the British Society, is that we have lost the high ground that we once held. We are also in danger of losing Freud and, I think, Melanie Klein also!

I would now like to comment on the term "here and now" as it is used today. In my opinion, it is emasculated compared with the way it was used in the late 1940s when I was a student and first encountered it. I think that John Rickman was the first to use it. I remember telling him that the Theravada Buddhists also used this phrase. He replied that he had first heard it from David Eder, one of the early British analysts. He said that David Eder, who was an ardent Zionist, was also interested in Buddhism.

John Rickman was very concerned to put things in their correct chronological order, and to show the link, for example, between Freud's contributions and thoughts and those of his colleagues. I have a long scroll that he has produced to help him to explain to students the development of Freud's thoughts and their influence on his colleagues. The years were marked out along the top of the scroll and, underneath, at the appropriate date, he entered the works of Freud on one line, and on a line below the works of his colleagues are entered.

The sequence of events was as important to him as the sequence of the patient's free associations. He was very aware of the timelessness of unconscious processes and the extent to which that which has not been digested from the past will continue to influence the present. Thus, to him, the past was very present in his version of the "here and now", but it was the task of the analyst to discover the age or developmental stage that the patient felt he was re-experiencing at any particular moment during any session, alongside who or what the patient was experiencing his analyst to be, either from the past or in the current moment that was contained by the psychoanalytical setting or situation.

As I understand the way the phrase "here and now" is presently used by many people in the Society, from all three groups, i.e. many Kleinians, some Contemporary Freudians and some Independents, they use it to refer to the actual relationship in the session and what the analyst thinks that the patient is doing to him, what the analyst thinks that his patient is feeling about what he is doing to him, which he gathers not only from what his patient says, but from his own affective reaction to what he thinks is going on in the present of the analytic relationship and what he feels about it. I was told that to refer to any past affect or behaviour that was possibly being repeated might divert a patient to his past and away from the affects related to the current person of the analyst, even though it might help the patient to understand himself and his past better. Thus, the concept of the transference, by which affects, memories, and experience from the past are transferred to and still exist in the mind of the patient, is ignored, and is replaced by equating the transference with a relationship. So, if an analyst interprets his relationship, he is thought to be interpreting "the transference" or "working in the transference".

I understand this concept of transference differently. To me, following Freud, transference is the process by which a patient, as a result of the repetition compulsion, repeats and relives in the present of the psychoanalytic relationship unconscious conflicts, traumas, and pathological phantasies from his past, and re-experiences them, together with affects, expectations, and wishes appropriate to those past situations and relationships, in relation to his analyst, who is then felt to be the person responsible for whatever distress he is re-experiencing.

> In this way, the symptoms of the patient's illness are given a new transference meaning and his neurosis is replaced by a transference-neurosis of which he can be cured by the therapeutic work. The transference thus creates an intermediate region between illness and real life through which the transition from the one to the other is made. [Freud, 1914g, p. 154]

The analytic relationship, and what happens within it, is both within time and beyond time. It is also out of time. I suppose that we are dealing with a paradox. The psychoanalytic relationship takes place in time, and keeping time, with its intimate link with space, and therefore with place (which links with togetherness and with separation), has to be acknowledged in the present of the session. Yet, according to Freud, we have to be able to work and to see our patients within the context of their whole life span.

Before discussing the concepts that analysts are unable to use, or feel that they have no need to use, if they adopt the version of the "here and now" that is current in the British Society, I want to present a quote to you. It is from Melanie Klein's description of her way of working, which you will find in Part 3 of the *Freud–Klein Controversies*. I was looking for a quote from her that I could use to blame her for the state of affairs that we now find ourselves in, but to my chagrin, I realized that she had described well how I myself have used, and still think about, transference. She describes beautifully how one has to pass backwards and forwards through time in one's understanding of a patient. I then remembered that I started my training as a Kleinian, and when Rickman quarrelled with her, I became a member of the "Middle Group"!

In my experience, the transference situation permeates the whole actual life of the patient during the analysis. When the analytic situation has been established, the analyst takes the place of the original objects, and the patient, as we know, deals again with the feelings and conflicts that are being revived with the very defences he used in the original situation. Therefore, while repeating in relation to the analyst some of his early feelings, phantasies, and sexual desires, he displaces others from the analyst to different people and situations. The result is that the transference phenomena are in part being diverted from the analysis. In other words, the patient is "acting out" part of his transference feelings in a different setting outside the analysis.

These facts have an important bearing on technique. In my view, what the patient shows or expresses consciously about his relation to the analyst is only one small part of the feelings, thoughts, and phantasies that he experiences towards him. These have, therefore, to be uncovered in the unconscious material of the patient through the analyst following up, by means of interpretation, the many ways of escape from the conflicts revived in the transference situation. By this widened application of the transference situation the analyst finds that he is playing a variety of parts in the patient's mind, and that he is not only standing for actual people in the patient's present and past, but also for the objects that the patient has internalized from his early days onwards, thus building up his super-ego. In this way we are able to understand and analyse the development of his ego and his super-ego, of his sexuality and his Oedipus complex from their inception.

If during the course of the analysis we are constantly guided by the transference situation, we are sure not to overlook the present and past actual experiences of the patient, because they are seen again and again through the medium of the transference situation.

Provided the interplay between reality and phantasy, and thus between the conscious and the unconscious, is consistently interpreted, the transference situation and feelings do not become blurred or obscured.

This constant interaction between conscious and unconscious processes, between phantasy products and the perception of reality, finds full expression in the transference situation. Here we see at certain stages of the analysis how the ground shifts from real experiences to phantasy situations and to internal situations—by which I mean the object world felt by the patient to be established inside—and again back to external situations, which later may appear in either a realistic or phantastic aspect. This movement to and fro is connected with an interchange of figures, real and phantastic, external and internal, which the analyst represents.

There is one more aspect of the transference situation that I should emphasize. The figures whom the analyst comes to represent in the patient's mind always belong to specific situations, and it is only by considering those situations that we can understand the nature and content of the feelings transferred on to the analyst. This means that we must understand what in the patient's mind analysis unconsciously stands for at any particular moment, in order to discover the phantasies and desires associated with those earlier situations—containing always elements of both actuality and phantasy—which have provided the pattern for the later ones.

Moreover, it is in the nature of these particular "situations" that in the patient's mind other people besides the analyst are included in the transference situation. This is to say, it is not just a one to one relation between patient and analyst, but something more complex. For instance, the patient may experience sexual desires towards the analyst, which at the same time bring up jealousy and hatred towards another person who is connected with the analyst (another patient, somebody in the analyst's house, somebody met on the way to the analyst, etc.) who, in the patient's phantasy, represents a favoured rival. Thus we discover the ways in which the patient's earliest object relations, emotions, and conflicts have shaped and coloured the development of his Oedipus conflict, and we elucidate the various situations and relationships in the patient's history against the background of which his sexuality, symptoms, character, and emotional attitudes have developed.

What I want to stress here is that it is by keeping the two things together in the transference—feelings and phantasies on the one hand and specific situations on the other—that we are able to bring home to the patient how he came to develop the particular patterns of his experiences (King & Steiner, 1990, pp. 635–637).

I shall now present some of Freud's concepts, particularly those referring to the technique of working with patients, although some of his metapsychological concepts to do with the way the mind functions and is organized can also be affected by our assumptions about the role of the past in our work as psychoanalysts. In putting forward these ideas, I realize that I have my own assumptions and hypotheses on how psychoanalysis functions to help my patients, and others may not always agree with them.

If I give some examples of what I think has happened to some of Freud's concepts, I hope that this will inspire others to develop ideas of their own, for I have only touched the fringe of the problem under consideration. It seems important to me that thought should be given to how we could salvage some of these concepts, that once seemed so central to our understanding of how psychoanalysis functioned. It may also emerge, as I suspect, that more analysts secretly make use of the past, are aware of the extent to which the past is still active in the present of their patients, and are alive to the importance of their patient's history, than they would be prepared to let the senior colleagues in their group know, or would include in a paper that they read or published.

I have selected the following concepts to comment on, which in my opinion can only make sense together with an appreciation of the patient's past history.

1. *Free association* by the patient, who should be free to bring up and communicate whatever comes to his mind, relevant to his past, his present, or his future. However, when an analyst relates everything

that his patient says to himself in the present, ignoring what may come from his past, patients soon pick this up. Thus, the concept of free association will have already become devalued.

At an unconscious level, our patients quickly discover our rules, regulations, and assumptions and have little difficulty in making use of them for their own neurotic purposes. Therefore, any analyst who feels he has to adhere too rigidly to certain lines of conduct or modes of interpretation can soon find himself (except that he seldom becomes aware of it himself) in the situation where his very technique is used as a defence and resistance to protect the patient's illness. I sometimes have to say to students, "Listen to the order of the patient's communications to you, see what is the meaning of the links between one statement or memory and the next one. So often, that is where there is an important key to what is going on at an unconscious level in your patient's mind."

2. *The free floating attention of the analyst* is the parallel concept to the request to our patients to associate freely, and not to censor their thoughts, which, of course, they cannot always do. Any rigid rules as to what may or may not be taken up or interpreted by the analyst, must cloud the openness of the analyst to their own UCS perceptions and awareness. Their perception of themselves as being treated by their patient as the patient's mother could have treated the patient, would be missed if only current events could be accepted or recognized by the analyst.

3. *The repetition compulsion*, which leads to unsatisfactory experiences, intra-psychic or interpersonal, being repeated in various internal or external contexts. This is one of the mechanisms behind the operation of transference, whereby the past is kept alive and brought into the present. Drawing the patient's attention to what is being repeated, empowers the patient very often to be aware of such repetitions occurring in his everyday life and to begin to be less at the mercy of past impulses. By cutting out the use and understanding of the repetition compulsion, analysts reduce to an affect or emotion the meaning of the term *transference*.

4. *Regression* to infantile experiences occurs when the patient brings their past into the session, feeling themselves to be re-experiencing

their infantile feelings and frustrations, and perhaps treating their analysts as their infantile mother. If an analyst cannot put these experiences into the historical context of the patient's life, the patient's analysis is seriously impoverished.

5. *Developmental approach*, which helps us to be aware of the patient's need to re-experience his bodily functions and frustrations at different phases of growth, e.g., the patient as a baby, hungry or being breast-fed by the words/interpretations of his analyst. This concept also helps analysts to tune into what is being repeated from past periods of the patient's life, so that the analyst can more easily discover what significant person from his past, the patient is experiencing the analyst as: e.g., mother, father, nurse, or sibling

6. *Infantile sexuality leading to adult sexuality*, and the operation of instinctual impulses in the patient's inner world and in his relationships, cannot be explored outside the context of the whole of the patient's past and present. Acceptance of the concept of infantile sexuality was the key difference between the early Jungians and early psychoanalysts. It is crucial to bodily, affective, and cognitive development, and crucial also to the working through of the Oedipus complex, with its important role in facilitating the growth of the capacity for object relationships.

7. *The super-ego* is a concept which changes over time, and refers to a function of the patient's mind whereby he internalizes authority figures from his childhood, which can become both supportive and also punishing, sometimes sadistically so, to the young child. As growth and/or psychoanalysis proceeds, the severity of the super-ego should be diminished. Some time ago, I was invited as a guest at a seminar of students to introduce a discussion on criteria for the termination of analysis, which was being run by a senior Kleinian. I put forward the idea that one criteria would be the reduction of the severity of the super-ego. I was immediately told by him that we do not use concepts like that nowadays. I was staggered, and pointed out that it was a very important and useful concept, particularly in the context in which I had used it. I realized sadly that "modern" Kleinians had gone a long way from Freud, as well as from Melanie Klein.

Other basic concepts suggested:

8. *Reconstruction* and the importance of discovering what was still influencing and damaging a patient's present as well as what made them ill.

9. *Psychosomatic concepts* that link body and psyche/mind together, but which are mostly excluded in "current" psychoanalytic writing and thinking.

In the paper that was read at the First Extraordinary Business Meeting of the British Society, which is reported in the *Freud–Klein Controversies*, Sylvia Payne wrote:

> The basic conceptions of psychoanalysis were laid down by Professor Freud, and this Society and Institute were founded on them.

> It might be said why should we limit our basic principles to those laid down by Freud. My answer to this is that we have in the past done so publicly and voluntarily, both by adherence to the International Psycho-Analytical Association and by acclaiming our intention to the Committee set up by the British Medical Association, who passed the resolution that only those analysts adhering to the conceptions of Freud had the right to call themselves Psycho-Analysts.

Sylvia Payne continues:

> The basic conceptions of Psycho-Analysis are:
> (l) The concept of a dynamic psychology (2) The existence of the Unconscious (3) The theory of instincts and of repression (4) Infantile sexuality (5) The dynamic of the transference. In my view all work which really recognizes and is built upon these conceptions has a right to be called psychoanalysis. [King & Steiner, 1990, pp. 53–54]

This is our heritage. If we want to continue to call ourselves psychoanalysts, those of us who value this heritage and what we have learnt from Freud have an obligation to understand and to explain his contributions to our colleagues, and especially to those who come after us.

Notes

1. This paper was first presented for a private discussion in the "Forum" on 31 January 1996 and later revised in 2003.
2. I selected this reference as it is the most recent statement of the Sandler's point of view.
3. Margret Tonnesman reminded me that a number of discussions had taken place in the United States between 1952 and 1955 on the difference between psychoanalysis and psychotherapy, and they had come to the same conclusion. She quoted the paper by Edward Bibring (1954) as an example.

References

Bibring, E. (1954). Psychoanalysis and the psychotherapies. *Journal of the American Psychoanalytic Association, 2*: 745–770.

Brierley, M. (1942). Internal objects and theory. *International Journal of Psycho-Analysis, 23*: 107–112.

Freud, S. (1914g). Remembering, repeating and working through. *S.E., 12*: 154. London: Hogarth.

Freud, S. (1933a). New introductory lectures on psycho-analysis. *S.E., 22*: 3. London: Hogarth.

King, P. H. M. (1994). The evolution of controversial issues. *International Journal of Psycho-Analysis, 75*(2): 335–342.

King, P. H. M., & Steiner, R. (1990). *The Freud–Klein Controversies in the British Psycho-Analytical Society 1941–1945.* (Sections 1, 2, 3, 4 and 5) The New Library of Psychoanalysis. No.11. London: The Institute of Psychoanalysis/Routledge.

Sandler, J. J., & Sandler, A.-M. (1995). The past unconscious and the present unconscious: a contribution to a technical frame of reference. *Psychoanalytic Study of the Child, 29*: 278–292.

Yorke, C. (1996). Childhood and the unconscious. *American Imago, 53*: 227–256.

Yorke, C. (2001). The unconscious, past present and future. In: R. Steiner & J. Johns (Eds.), *Within Time and Beyond Time. A Festschrift for Pearl King.* London: Karnac.

CHAPTER EIGHT

An historical view

Paul Roazen

Freud proved to be an altogether remarkable political leader. Once he had achieved the theory that made up the insights going into his "The interpretation of dreams" (1900a), he quickly saw the implications that he put into his *The Psychopathology of Everyday Life* (1901a), one of his most popular texts. And, although he did not publish his case history of Dora (1901) until 1905, it provided him with a concrete illustration for how richly psycho-analysis could illuminate an individual patient's life (1905c). Once he pulled the informal strings, which were the necessary steps required to getting, in 1902, his titular professorship at the University of Vienna, he proceeded to invite potential local followers to start assembling in his waiting room for regular meetings and discussions.

Yet, even before he had formally founded the "movement" for what he had called psycho-analysis, as early as 1901 in his "On dreams" he had remarked on how he

> had been led to fresh conclusions on the subject of dreams by applying to them a new method of psychological investigation which had done excellent service in the solution of phobias, obsessions and delusions, etc. [Freud, 1901a, p. 635]

It would be another generation before he would distinguish between neuroses and psychoses; and his orientation towards "solving" clinical problems amounted to a kind of reductionism that would require subsequent correction. As of 1901 he was so sure already of his future success, as well as the manner by which he would accomplish it, that he could be proclaiming about the progress of his work that "since then, under the name of 'psycho-analysis', it has found acceptance by a whole school of research workers" (Freud, 1901a, p. 635).

Even if Freud had yet to create what he had envisaged as that "whole school of research workers", presumably by 1901 he already knew something of the power his therapeutic approach would be capable of exerting. He was generous enough about the teachings he felt he could offer that he began gathering together the students who could forward the "cause" he had initiated. We should not be surprised to find that by 1908, even before psycho-analysis could be considered widely recognized within medicine, he could write rather grandly about what "every doctor who has practised psycho-analysis knows . . ." (Freud, 1908b, p. 173). However much of Old World sceptical misanthropy Freud may have shared, he was still far less closed off and distant from human contact than he would be once he first got cancer of the jaw in 1923.

Freud's assumption that he was developing a science capable of being neutral, is somewhat negated by the fervour associated with his approach. Here I think that Freud found it all too easy to mislead himself into thinking that he had come up with "findings" that had been verified by others; the suggestive impact of the psycho-analytic setting was immense and easily missed, enabling Freud to deceive himself about the degree of his detached accomplishments. Psycho-analysis was capable of becoming a way of life, reorientating both morality and the understanding of social life. The full-scale nature of the appeal of psycho-analysis helps to account for how passionately people came to feel about it. Outsiders were able to spot the cult-like aspects to Freud's cause. It would not be going too far to say that participants in his movement reorientated their souls around what they thought of as the "discovery" of the unconscious. Freud was not alone in thinking that he had come up with "findings"; Jung, too, would insist that he had been an empiricist. No matter how heated the differences between

Freud and Jung became, neither readily acknowledged the artistic, philosophic, and non-scientific nature of their dispute. The opposition Freud succeeded in stirring up can be traced not just to the weaknesses in his approach that he neglected to pursue, but to the ethical stakes that were thought to be at issue.

In Vienna Freud never attained in his lifetime the influence that a follower of his, Alfred Adler, managed to secure, so it would be the students he attracted from abroad that largely spread his message. Once a Vienna Psychoanalytic Institute was set up in late 1924, a centre for educating future analysts was able to attract students from abroad. But right from the beginning internationalizing psycho-analysis had special organizational costs of its own. Once Freud undertook in 1910 to transfer the centre of the new movement to Zurich, under the leadership of the Swiss Jung, the complicated political effects of having created the International Psychoanalytical Association (IPA) at the Nuremberg Congress would already be evident. Victor Tausk's observations at the time look, in hindsight, prescient; as he maintained in a discussion at the Vienna Psychoanalytic Society, he felt in 1910, according to the notes that the then secretary Otto Rank compiled, that

> something very saddening is taking place. He [Tausk] cannot make any positive statements because he did not take part in the Congress, and therefore would like only to express his view with regard to some of what he heard here today. No soil is so well suited as that of Vienna for the dissemination of Freud's teachings, and that is, probably, precisely because it is a sick soil. It won't do to consider psycho-analysis merely from the medical standpoint; this does not offer a true picture of what our conception of psycho-analysis should be. Tausk then makes a comparison with Darwinism, which was a scientific religion just as psycho-analysis is; no society for the dissemination of Darwinism was founded, and yet today it is part of the consciousness of every civilized man. It is out of these considerations that the speaker expresses his opinion against the formation of an association. [Nunberg & Federn, 1967, p. 467]

At the same time that Jung became IPA president, Freud elevated Adler (with the support of Tausk) to head the Vienna Psychoanalytic Society. Still the Viennese remained resentful of the full results of what Freud had initiated with the creation of the IPA.

Adler's own intellectual ambitions were simultaneously encouraged by his new position of local leadership, until Freud decided to draw the line and boot Adler, along with his followers, out. Freud had all along felt more comfortable with the meetings of the Vienna psychoanalytic group, made up of his committed adherents, than at the more heterogeneous audience for his university talks. But he found he could not tolerate the presumptuousness of the differences Adler, who was a socialist, had with him. After a full-scale examination of Adler's views at the Vienna Psychoanalytic Society, in proceedings that even those who took Freud's side thought of as a trial, Adler withdrew to found his own group. Freud insisted on making a thorough housecleaning of the views of those he deemed heretical, and insisted that members of his society could not also belong to that of Adler. In the end Freud had driven away just about half of his tiny Vienna following, but he remained confident that the future would redeem the wisdom of his militancy. Not unlike Lenin's thinking in pre-First World War Zurich, Freud felt that the purity of his message would survive better without any dilution by views, seemingly broad-minded, that might adulterate his convictions.

No sooner had Freud in 1911 settled Adler's hash when the long-standing ideological differences between Freud and Jung also boiled over. Even after almost a century has now passed these legendary disputes have been hard for many to reconsider, and on the whole intellectual historians have been surprisingly apt to echo Freud's own viewpoint at the time. For him these were not personal or even theoretical conflicts, but rather scientific ones; and Freud allowed himself to believe that psycho-analysis itself, and not his own individual position, was at stake. Freud proceeded to put into print in his pamphlet "On the history of the psychoanalytic movement" (1914d) his own side of things, while the Adlerians, altogether less committed to the power of the written word, largely failed to counter-attack in writing. Although by the mid-1920s Jung had occasion to use a seminar for answering Freud, and he challenged many parts of Freud's thinking in the course of his own various publications, essentially the die had been cast by Freud's pre-emptive literary 1914 strike. Sorting out the merits of who was right or wrong, clinically as well as theoretically, remains, I think, an enduring challenge for future intellectual historians to untangle.

In the course of presenting the official biography of Freud around the 100th anniversary of his birth, publicists like Ernest Jones were able to promote Freud's own partisan view of things. Intellectuals in general were initially immensely credulous about what an important bit of statecraft Jones's books amounted to. And the excellent scholarly edition of Freud's writings prepared by James Strachey, with the help of Freud's daughter Anna and others when it came to English translations, meant that the scales were heavily weighed in Freud's favour. Freud's life, right up until his death in 1939, would have many other controversies associated with it, besides those connected with his pre-First World War difficulties. But the same pattern endured, as he personally felt entitled to define what was or what was not to be deemed legitimately psycho-analysis. In 1909 Freud had cautiously said that his name was "linked with the topic of psycho-analysis", and "if it is a merit to have brought psycho-analysis into being, that merit is not mine" (Freud, 1910a, p. 9). In those days Freud was rather using his mentor Josef Breuer as a stalking horse for himself. But by the time of "On the history of the psychoanalytic movement" Freud had assumed the role of having created psycho-analysis, and he henceforth insisted on being able to decide what was or what was not a legitimate extension of his work. As Freud, starting in the 1920s, also defended his daughter Anna against the innovations of someone like Melanie Klein, it came to appear that it was a family business Freud had founded.

Right from the beginning of the difficulties with Adler and Jung, Freud had found it difficult to tolerate "deviations," not only for personal reasons, but also because the organization he headed was not yet successful enough to permit much range of opinion. Once psycho-analysis became established, numbering thousands of practitioners and influencing countless others, the limits of the permissible area of disagreement should have expanded. But the model persisted of how Freud had fought more bitterly against backsliders than against the outside world, lest psycho-analysis become hopelessly confused with other techniques and theories. Freud had identified with Hannibal and other warriors, and internecine quarrels have afflicted the world he initiated.

Freud thought he had special property rights to his field (Szasz, 1973), even though at the same time he wanted to think of psychoanalysis as independent of human will and a part of Western science. Freud insisted upon one main point against the two "secessions", led by Adler and Jung, that made up what he called the "two opposition" groups:

> I am not concerned with the truth that may be contained in the theories which I am rejecting, nor shall I attempt to refute them . . . I wish merely to show that these theories controvert the fundamental principles of analysis . . . and for that reason they should not be known by the name of analysis. [Freud, 1914d, pp. 49–50]

Oddly enough, intellectual historians have still been inadequately attentive, following Freud's leadership, precisely to the issue of the "truth contained in the theories" that he had rejected. Freud's opening paragraph in "On the history of the psychoanalytic movement" had made the point that

> psycho-analysis is my creation; for ten years I was the only person who concerned himself with it . . . Although it is a long time now since I was the only psycho-analyst, I consider myself justified in maintaining that even today no one can know better than I do what psycho-analysis is, how it differs from other ways of investigating the life of the mind, and precisely what should be called psycho-analysis and what would better be described by some other name. [Freud, 1914d, p. 7]

Freud felt he was repudiating with Adler and Jung what seemed to him "a cool act of usurpation . . ." (Freud, 1914d, p. 7). Although Freud prided himself on being a rebel in the history of ideas, he did not seem to realize that that the quality of his work had attracted people who were similarly disposed to assault received wisdom. Like other would-be revolutionaries before him, Freud struggled to bring a halt to any further upheavals.

Freud had singled out what he called the "facts" of transference and resistance, which he feared were going to get lost in the ideas and approaches that Adler and Jung were proposing.

> Any line of investigation which recognizes these two facts and takes them as the starting point of his work has a right to call itself psycho-analysis, even though it arrives at results other than my

own. But anyone who takes up other sides of the problem while avoiding these two hypotheses will hardly escape a charge of misappropriation of property by attempted impersonation, if he persists in calling himself a psycho-analyst. [Freud, 1914d, p. 16]

It has to be worth noticing how Freud was waffling about calling transference and resistance "facts" as well as "hypotheses". Jung, too, shared Freud's naïve attitude toward scientific method, and therefore, as I have already mentioned, Jung also could claim to be a mere empiricist. Instead of Freud's acknowledging how the creation of the IPA had helped set off these problems he had then encountered, Freud dug in his heels: "There should be some head-quarters whose business it would be to declare: 'All this nonsense is nothing to do with analysis; this is not psycho-analysis'" (Freud, 1914d, p. 43). Instead of Freud seeing the personal bases for the quarrels that had ensued after the founding of the IPA, he felt enti-tled to insist on what sounds like a claim to his personal copyright:

Jung has given us a counterpart to the famous Lichtenberg knife. He has changed the hilt, and he has put a new blade into it; yet because the same name is engraved on it we are expected to regard the instrument as the original one. [Freud, 1914d, p. 55]

Freud was insistent on his claim to priorities, a subject that has still not been adequately incorporated in the literature (Roazen, 1969, pp. 59–93).

Ever since Freud's day there have been organizational fanatics, within the IPA as well as its affiliate groups, determined to exclude innovations on the grounds that they contravene that which quali-fies as proper psycho-analysis. Ostracism, with the consequences of being marginalized, has been the penalty to be dreaded. The danger nowadays is not so much that some prominent psycho-analytic leader will try to expel anyone for being "deviant", but that the long-term consequences of those pre-First World War battles will mean that unspoken conformist pressures will intimidate people from entertaining ideas lest they become possibly "heretical". Even after Freud had been gone from the scene since 1939, Anna Freud, right up to her own death in 1982, was able to stigmatize certain ideas (like those of Heinz Kohut) as "anti-psychoanalytic". At the same time nobody is likely to suffer organizationally from being accused of intolerance or sectarianism, since that was never cited by Freud as any kind of special crime. Although Freud's tentative image that ideas like transference and resistance might be "hypotheses" rather than "facts" should have seemed to encourage tolerance, the ideal of toleration as a valuable ideal in itself has never succeeded in being established within psychoanalysis (Roazen, 2002, pp. 277–288).

Even within those groups stigmatized as "deviant" similar difficulties have been apt to recur. So there have been heretical movements within the followers of Adler as well as among the students of Erich Fromm. The relevant general principle within political science would be that wherever power resides then there is apt to be competition for the possession of the grail. Among the Lacanians, whose combined numbers of practitioners today must be in the thousands, titanic-seeming disputes have been endemic. Cartesian French conflicts may be easier for logicians to follow than the rather more muffled controversies among the Jungians. And the followers of Otto Rank have been too unworldly ever to achieve much of any institutionalization.

Nevertheless, despite all this interesting history, as a field psychoanalysis has been notably anti-historical or ahistorical. (Roazen, 2003, pp. 27–40). For example, the whole series of steps by which the institution of training analyses became a requirement for future practitioners of psycho-analysis have rarely been explored. (Roazen, 2003, pp. 51–57). In reality it was Jung who had first suggested the idea of mandating training analyses, while Freud was initially on the reluctant side. The needs of a bureaucratizing movement, for example the creation of the Berlin Psychoanalytic Institute following the First World War, made the practice seem desirable, although Freud himself only looked on training analysis as an inevitable accepted institution after his falling ill with cancer in 1923. It would no longer be possible for him to hope to control his movement personally, and he bowed to what a great sociological theorist like Max Weber once called the routinization of charisma. (Within Jung's own movement of "analytical psychology" he only reluctantly accepted the creation of a training organization in Zurich after his own heart difficulties during the Second World War.) Although privately many analysts have thought the root source of authoritarianism in the field was the submission of candidates to training analyses, it is only relatively rarely that leaders have spoken out on the subject; and few institutional corrections have succeeded in being implemented. It would, for example, be not only desirable to ensure that there were no reports about candidates from analysts to training centres, but to split off personal analyses entirely from training institutes. Private therapeutic experiences could remain eminently desirable for future psycho-analysts, but without there being so much formalized oversight.

The striking anti-historical bias in the field remains possible to miss since so many psycho-analytic treatises begin by giving lip-service to the past professional literature. It has been largely left to historians of ideas, not analysts, to rummage through the fascinating details of past controversies, for example the truths to be found in Adler or Jung. Contemporary analysts, for example, if asked to defend Freud's criticism of someone like Adler, would find themselves in an embarrassing position. Freud's cherished notion of "libido" rarely appears in papers today. By 1954 a leading orthodox analyst, Rudolf Loewenstein, could maintain that

> as compared to the past, we now pay increased attention not only to early childhood but also to events and conflicts occurring in our patients in later life and in the present. [Loewenstein, 1954, p. 189]

Erik H. Erikson emphasized what he called the "prospective aspects of the life cycle." (Evans, 1967, p. 100). In the early period of psycho-analysis,

> regressive pulls in human life were . . . much more emphasized than what pulls a child out of the past, out of the family and out to wider experiences. [Evans, 1967, p. 27]

It is no longer heresy for psycho-analysts to practice short-term, supportive psychotherapy. And few could share Freud's old disdain for Adler's concern with character problems as well as normal psychology. Adler also pioneered on racial relations, gender discrimination, as well as family therapy. I am concentrating on his ideas now, not because Freud rated Adler a more significant opponent than Jung, who went on to succeed in creating a much larger and more influential following than Adler, but because the literature on Adler remains so notably thin (Roazen, 1975, pp. 174–211; Singer, 2003).

It has to appear odd that the metaphor Freud initiated of psycho-analysts being an embattled minority should still extend to today's IPA with its membership of over ten thousand. The heritage Freud left has been unfortunate in that psycho-analysis became so identified with an organizational bureaucracy rather than with the life of the mind. One of Freud's most loyal apostles, Hanns Sachs, was willing as early as 1939 to protest about the point being reached "where the scientific movement and the organization were bound to drift apart . . ." (Sachs, 1939, p. 462). Sachs thought then that "the scientific trends in psycho-analysis have been separated and are bound to become still more divorced from the organization which, by its inherent law, becomes progressively more conservative, directed towards practical aims and a self-preservative purpose." (Sachs, 1939, p. 463). Sixty years later a Paris analyst, Rene Major, wrote in a similar spirit:

> Psychoanalytic institutions themselves, created to preserve the Freudian inheritance and to promote psychoanalytic research, have inevitably at times developed rigidities which stand in the way of the aims they pursue. An analytic establishment is necessarily called upon to be conservative since its tasks are to protect basic principles and to establish standards of excellence for teaching and practice, while analytic procedure is called upon to be innovative, and even subversive, always working in inquiry for new and original understandings and insights. [Roazen, 2003, p. 56]

The issue remains: what ought we to consider "the Freudian inheritance"? Instead of the more standard view that either ignores the existence of past psychoanalytic controversies or minimizes their significance, I believe that that is precisely where the potential richness of the field is to be found. The ideal of toleration would have allowed for even more varieties of thought to get expressed; without the possible upshot of threatened excommunications there would be more room for disagreement, without the consequent fanaticism. Still, it has to be in the long run a great tribute to Freud that he was capable of attracting to this field such a wide divergence of different sorts of beliefs and opinions. And disputes about the course psycho-analysis should pursue reflect a variety of different moral beliefs and contrasting ethical values, a discussion of which can only enhance the vitality of the field. Disagreements

about the nature of the good life, and how therapy should be conducted, ought to be considered a wholly desirable part of intellectual life, as opposed to the habit of cutting off debate. Sectarianism
should be the identifiable enemy, as opposed to questions of trademark.

Thousands of psycho-analytic practitioners are excluded from
today's IPA. It is not just the many followers of figures like Jung as
well as Jacques Lacan who automatically enhance the arena of
possible thinking. But there would be a whole list of other analysts
from the past whose names, most of which I have not yet mentioned, automatically serve to broaden the spectrum of possible
discussion: Otto Rank, Wilhelm Reich, Erich Fromm, Sandor
Ferenczi, Franz Alexander, Sandor Rado, Harry Stack Sullivan, to
name only some of the most prominent. Some of these people had
personal difficulties with Freud, but not all of them. In any event,
the real question should be no longer the matter of loyalty, or the
clash of personalities, but whether we need the input that the work
of these thinkers might add.

As a matter of fact I think we ought not by any means to confine
psycho-analysis simply to therapeutic practitioners. Freud thought
he had created a system of thought that would not just change the
future of scientific understanding, but moral and social thinking as
well. Herbert Marcuse, for example, made his own use of Freud's
thinking, and even though Marcuse relied on "orthodox" theorizing for the sake of revising Marxism, the Frankfurt school of sociology has to be considered one variety of social philosophy that has
paid significant attention to psycho-analysis. Jean-Paul Sartre, and
the whole tradition of thinking associated with existentialism, can
provide a breath of fresh air within psycho-analysis. (Roazen, 2002,
pp. 212–213). No matter how Freud might have sought to exclude
philosophic speculation from his realm of thought, in hindsight it
should be readily apparent that he himself was not only indebted
to special sorts of philosophizing, but his work reflected certain
unverifiable moral, ethical, and epistemological points of view. In
truth I think that the people in the best position to broaden the hori-
zons of psycho-analysis are intellectual historians, as well as literary people, who should be able in principle to take the most
detached sorts of positions vis-à-vis the most hotly contested issues.
In practice, however, these outsiders have been at times capable

of being more naïve than practising clinicians, curiously enough less apt to be aware of clinical flexibilities; and so we should be on our toes about how propagandizing can arise from surprising directions.

We are living in a time when the consequences of trade unionism within psycho-analysis can be especially dangerous. In Germany today, for example, the oldest psycho-analytic group in existence there, whose origins go straight back to Freud's first Berlin disciple Karl Abraham, has been kept out of the IPA because the number of times a week it commits itself to seeing patients falls below the threshold required for IPA entrance. Yet the members of few existing IPA societies today fulfil the mandatory figures that once were considered "ideal" and still now necessary for admission to the IPA.

In his own time Freud was a great heretic, which is precisely why he could not win conventional academic recognition and felt he had to create an organizational structure of his own. Its designated leadership would long outlive his own death. Even in Freud's own lifetime he came to experience what a Frankenstein-like monster he had been responsible for making, since prominent leaders of the IPA, jealous for example of all the favours Freud had for years showered on Otto Rank, eagerly and successfully sought to drive a wedge between Freud and Rank. The difficulties with Rank were to be one of the main tragedies of Freud's final years (Roazen, 1975, pp. 392–418). Freud knew that because of his age and poor health never again would he be capable of being as generous towards an adopted son like Rank. Yet it proved easier to assimilate Rank's name to the usual so-called suspects who had led prior insurrections in the history of psycho-analysis than to appreciate either the unique aspects to Rank's falling-out with Freud, not to mention the evaluation of the merits of Rank's innovative ideas.

Although it was contrary to Freud's declared intentions, in those countries where psycho-analysis has been most closely allied to philosophy and literature, as in France for example, Freud's work has remained at the centre of intellectual life. But in North America, for instance, where practical therapeutics have always been more central, the medical pendulum has swung radically toward the psychopharmacological direction. Drug companies have in general attained a tremendous amount of power within medical schools, and young practitioners are being trained in an atmosphere notable for a degree of formalism and brain mythologizing that is reminiscent of what once was fashionable at the beginning of the twentieth century. Diagnoses and classification have swept the board, so that categories which were once designed largely for purposes of insurance reimbursement have acquired a falsely scientific-seeming stature.

By now the ethics of psychopharmacology seems as esoteric a subject as once the subject of the ethics of psychoanalysis appeared to be. It is rarely the case that the degree to which every clinical encounter is simultaneously an ethical and moral one gets appreciated. (Lomas, 1999). What might be considered a legitimate disappointment in love, or how we should evaluate what a good marriage consists in, remain open questions. I believe Karen Horney deserves the credit for insisting on the unsettled nature of what could we mean by normality in the first place. Family life does not come defined by nature, but rather is imbedded in cultural forces. All great philosophers and writers in the past have been interested in the issue of what might be "natural". Symptoms only appear in human beings as they are mediated by means of social definitions. And most modern medication is unlike the magic of Aldous Huxley's "soma", and therefore the existence of possible side-effects raises the question of what are the human costs involved in any choice of pills. Even Huxley in his *Brave New World* was unhappy with what the implications for human dignity of soma might be (Roazen, 2003, pp. 210–212).

Instead of relegating the study of so-called deviant schools, and this might include Klein and Lacan as well as Adler and Jung, to the outskirts of psychoanalytic educational life, I think that the past of this field can be unusually helpful in making us aware of what we might be otherwise apt to overlook. History provides us with necessary challenges to the present, and only by being aware of the past as we can best reconstruct it are we able to deal with the present and future with an awareness of the varieties of options that we could have.

The use of the couch, as opposed to a chair, for instance, is a question of technique that has consequences that should be open for exploration and discussion. As far as I have been able to tell, even before Jung's falling out with Freud, Jung was not relying on the couch, and there is no sign that I know of that Freud objected in principle to how he was proceeding. Later on, to be sure, Freud in writing to both A. A. Brill and Edoardo Weiss could chastise these loyal followers for their freedom in allowing patients to sit up. But this bit of the institutionalizing of how Freud personally chose to proceed should not be allowed to wipe out the examination of the pros and cons of any aspect of the use of therapeutic furniture. Jung was in fact one of the earliest in print to point out some of the unfortunate authoritarian consequences of relying on putting patients in a horizontal position. Erik Erikson once suggested that "the classical psychoanalytic treatment situation is an exquisite deprivation experiment" (Roazen, 1976, p. 70). If the treatment setting can be an artefact, a form of sensory deprivation, how do we conceive the phenomenon of transference? Jung for example believed that a lack of rapport between analyst and patient helped account for what once might have appeared as rock-bottom evidence of transferential material from the patient's past.

As our thinking is enabled to go beyond the box that Freud might have in his last dying years defined as properly psycho-analytic, it becomes possible then to entertain questions about psychotherapeutic procedure in general. Psychotherapy is not, as once might have been thought, to be considered supposedly as a second-rate activity in contrast to psycho-analysis itself. When Ernest Jones was travelling to America in order to speak in connection with Freud's 100th birthday in 1956, Anna Freud wrote to him:

> I am now thinking of a subject for you which might be equally [as lay analysis] dangerous for Chicago. What about the relations between psychoanalysis and psychotherapy with a strong warning about the latter? [Anna Freud to Ernest Jones, 1955).

Although she might have in those days been leading the movement of "orthodox" analysis, within the past generation her position has been so eroded that she no longer appears as part of the family romance of British psycho-analysis. Kleinianism has become as distinctive in Britain as Lacanianism in France. And although once Klein was viewed as a heretical threat, clinically her inheritance has meant some interesting therapeutic possibilities. Someone like Donald W. Winnicott, a member of the so-called Middle Group in London, owed much to Klein's inspiration, even though he baulked at what he took to be the intransigence of the ways her ideas were implemented. Some of her apostles came to regard Winnicott as "worse" than Ferenczi (Roazen, 2004). It is necessary to keep one's eyes open for where might be the sources of intolerance, and which figures are in need of being resuscitated. While the Hungarians have substantially succeeded in re-establishing Ferenczi's position as a leading figure in psychoanalytic psychotherapy, Anna Freud and her own contributions have been in danger of being forgotten.

Child analysis, which was Anna Freud's special field, had special moral problems of its own. Even if the Anna Freud Centre, the successor to the Hampstead Clinic she ran for so many years, is no longer going to be concerned with training but devoted instead to research, she raised principles associated with approaching children clinically that deserve to be remembered, especially in our own psychopharmacological era. She properly questioned the ease with which children are capable of being diagnosed, since symptoms can be so different, and more transient, than with adults. The best paediatricians I know have been quietly warning us that it is going to be years before anyone really knows the long-term effects of the latest chemicals that are being given to children. Childhood itself should not be allowed to be medicalized, and I think every possible ethical restraint on the influence of drug companies should be sought. In terms of the power of money, billions are at stake here.

One difficulty we have stems from Freud's reluctance to have psycho-analysis associated with university life. He advocated the setting up of training institutes that would be self-sustaining, and by and large that model has prevailed even today. But the question does still remain what should be taught, and at which time of day; the educational objectives should be to emancipate people as much as possible from local prejudices. But in fact it has been hard to ensure that national provincialism does not become prevalent, ensuring a kind of local brainwashing that ought to be at odds with the emancipation that ideally would be the goal of a good grounding in psycho-analysis. Teaching that takes place at a time of day when everyone is more or less exhausted cannot be satisfactory. At the same time perfectionism can be a special problem all its own.

It may be more necessary than ever to try to establish some general principles by which we can guide the relation between medical as opposed to non-medical ("lay") practitioners. In the USA there are certain limited jurisdictions in which psychologists are being allowed, after special training, to prescribe medication. Although some physicians have been the loudest in protesting against such an intrusion on their traditional monopoly when it comes to drugs, the danger is that such squabbling over professional boundaries may leave the field in the hands of the people who are wholly devoted to a strictly biological orientation.

Conclusions

American medical schools are currently having trouble attracting residents to the field of psychiatry. And psychiatric departments themselves risk losing their accreditation without such training facilities. But few prospective candidates want to go into a field where the model is spending a few minutes with a client before a prescription for medication gets written out. It may be one of the central tasks of psycho-analysis today to keep reminding health-care professionals that there is a person behind the troubles of every patient, and that getting in contact with the unique struggles for personhood can be central to establishing any therapeutic alliance (Havens, 1986). And even though that counsel may seem a come-down from the most ambitions aims that psycho-analysis once had in mind, it may still be an essential part of the humanitarian heritage to be extracted from the psycho-analysis Freud first created.

Hospitals' departments of psychiatry in the USA that psycho-analysts helped found in the 1930s are today being threatened with extinction. The expense and financing of maintaining psycho-therapy seem to exclude the necessary care, time, and attention. In my view young residents, many of whom come from abroad, need to be reminded that the history of psychiatry is to today's practices nothing like the history of dentistry would be to modern dentists. There is little progress in the humane sciences, and no matter how impressive the latest chemical technologies may be there will always remain the elusive human interaction between therapist and patient. The better educated practitioners can become, the more likely they will be able to meet the challenges of today's distressed clients.

Humanism is as embattled now as in the era when Freud first started out, a time when heredity and diagnosis were considered overwhelmingly central considerations. When he introduced the concept of neurosis, he was challenging pre-existing outlooks, and he erred on the side of being so imperialistic as to propose the notion of what he called "narcissistic neuroses". By the 1920s he was ready to concede, without acknowledging that Jung had been right, that psychoses were a domain separate from neurosis.

Nowadays the imperialistic threat comes from insurance handbooks like *DSM-III* and *DSM-IV*, so that diagnoses arising from insurance needs seem to be swamping the still worthwhile idea, first put forward by Freud, of the existence of neurotic suffering. It has to be true that we are as likely to embody our own preconceptions in how we approach psychology today as ever were the early pioneers in the field. An historical over-view can, I hope, help promote an appropriate kind of humility and modesty, so hard to sustain in a field as filled with uncertainties as psycho-analysis has to remain.

References

Evans, R. I. (1967). *Dialogue With Erik Erikson*. New York: Harper & Row.

Freud, A. (1955). Letter of October 20 to Ernest Jones. Jones's Archives.

Freud, S. (1900a). The interpretation of dreams. *S.E.*, 4–5. London: Hogarth.

Freud, S. (1901b). The psychopathology of everyday life. *S.E.*, 6. London: Hogarth.

Freud, S. (1901a). On dreams. *S.E.*, 5; 635. London: Hogarth.

Freud, S. (1905e). Fragment of an analysis of a case of hypnotism. *S.E.*, 7. London: Hogarth.

Freud, S. (1908b). Character and anal eroticism. *S.E.*, 9: 173. London: Hogarth.

Freud, S. (1910) [1909]. Five lectures on psychoanalysis. *S.E. Edition, 11*: 9. London: Hogarth.

Freud, S. (1914). On the history of the psycho-analytic movement. *Standard, 14*. London: Hogarth.

Havens, L. (1986). *Making Contact: Uses of Language in Psychotherapy*. Cambridge, MA: Harvard University Press.

Loewenstein, R. (1954). Some remarks on defenses, autonomous ego and psychoanalytic technique. *International Journal of Psychoanalysis*, 35: 189.

Lomas, P. (1999). *Doing Good? Psychotherapy Out of Its Depth*. Oxford, Oxford University Press.

Nunberg, H., & Federn, E. (Eds.) (1967). M. Nunberg (Trans.). *Minutes of the Vienna Psychoanalytic Society, Vol. II: 1908-1910*, New York: International Universities Press.

Roazen, P. (1969). *Brother Animal: The Story of Freud and Tausk* New York: Knopf. Second edn with new Introduction, New Brunswick, NJ: Transaction, 1990.

Roazen, P. (1975). *Freud and His Followers*. New York: Knopf [reprinted New York: Da Capo, 1992].

Roazen, P. (1976). *Erik H. Erikson: The Power and Limits of a Vision*. New York: The Free Press [reprinted, Northvale, NJ: Jason Aronson, 1997].

Roazen, P. (2002). *The Trauma of Freud: Controversies in Psychoanalysis*. New Brunswick, NJ: Transaction.

Roazen, P. (2003). *On the Freud Watch: Public Memoirs*. London: Free Association.

Roazen, P. (2004). Review of Rodman's *Winnicott: Life and Work*. *Psychoanalysis and History*, 6(1): 117–220.

Sachs, H. (1939). The prospects of psychoanalysis. *International Journal of Psychoanalysis*, 20: 462–463.

Singer, P. (2003). *Pushing Time Away: My Grandfather and the Tragedy of Jewish Vienna*. New York: Harper Collins.

Szasz, T. (1973). Freud as a leader. In: F. Cioffi (Ed.), *Freud: Modern Judgements* (pp. 146–156). London: Macmillan.

PART III
POLITICAL

CHAPTER NINE

The New York State psychoanalytic licence:

An historical perspective

Pearl Appel

Background

This chapter begins with historical background and leads up to current realities in New York State, concerning the conflict about who has claim to, and who has the right to practise and to train others in, psychoanalysis.

The details presented are from the point of view that psychoanalysis is a distinct and independent mental health profession to be practised by anyone who receives the proper training. In New York State, during the last fifty years, work by many teams of dedicated and persistent advocates for this position has culminated in the legal acceptance of "original discipline" status for psychoanalysis.

Already certified by the State of Vermont in 1994 and the State of New Jersey in 2000, New York in 2002 became the first state in the USA to recognize psychoanalysts with a "scope of practice" licence that applies to all appropriately trained psychoanalysts from all psychoanalytic theoretical perspectives. Simultaneously, the psychologists received a scope of practice licence in psychology that included psychoanalysis in its scope of practice, with exemptions for MDs, social workers, and registered nurses.

A certification licence protects only the title of a profession. No one uncertificated can use that title, but one can practise the profession. A scope of practice licence protects both the title and the practice of a profession.

Introduction

Since Freud's memorable visit to lecture at Clark University in September of 1909, there have been many theoretical differences concerning the understanding and the clinical practice of psychoanalysis in the USA. The reaction to these differences and the political forces at work in New York State constitutes a century of factional disputes within the field. New York City has been a major arena where these controversies have been played out. The New York Psychoanalytic Institute (NY Psychoanalytic) and its parent organizations, the American Psychoanalytic Association (the American) and the International Psychoanalytical Association (the International) have dominated psychoanalysis for many years. In 1927, the NY Psychoanalytic declared that New York State had passed a law allowing only psychiatrists to practise psychoanalysis (Jones, 1957, 293). Although no record was ever found of such a law, the NY Psychoanalytic trained only MDs for the practice of psychoanalysis. The American insisted, furthermore, that the International must refuse membership to all USA psychoanalysts and Institutes that are not affiliated with the American. Freud was very unhappy about the medicalization of psychoanalysis by the American and, especially, the New York Psychoanalytic.

Medical Control: NY Psychoanalytic and American

The NY Psychoanalytic had almost complete control of the profession. The strict methods by which they censured anyone who differed with their interpretation of psychoanalysis and how it should be practised are legendary. The NY Psychoanalytic, however, could not prevent the psychoanalytic practice of psychologists who trained at Institutes not affiliated with the American, such as the William Alanson White Institute, founded in 1941, and the Karen

Horney Institute founded in 1944, or the New York University Post-doctoral programme in Psychotherapy and Psychoanalysis founded in 1945. They also could not stop the psychoanalytic practice of non-medical students by Institutes such as the National Psychological Association for Psychoanalysis, founded in 1948.

The MDs in New York were concerned that the psychoanalysts who were psychologists were going to invade their territory. They fought them every step of the way: against allowing psychoanalytically trained psychologists to practise, then against PhD level psychologists obtaining a New York State certification licence, and finally against amending the psychologists' certification to a scope of practice licence. They used their political influence to prevent licensing for any mental health profession, especially psychoanalysis, which they considered a medical speciality. The MD licence with Board certification in psychiatry was the only mental health practice licence in the state. This gave the psychiatrists a powerful, prestigious, and financial monopoly until 1956 when the psychologists obtained a certification licence.

Four psychologists, totally backed by the American Psychological Association (APA), filed a lawsuit in 1985 against the American, the New York Psychoanalytic, and the International. The suit charged the organizations with discrimination and violation of Federal antitrust laws by denying them admittance for training because they were not physicians. The goal of the suit was to provide the public with the best possible range of trained psychoanalysts, a goal that cannot be achieved (they claimed) when training is restricted to psychiatrists. They also sued for access to membership of the International. Freud was quoted in the suit as saying "psychoanalysis is part of psychology and not of medicine" (Freud, 1927, 252). Another relevant quote of Freud's that is conveniently not mentioned in the suit, says, in effect, that psychoanalysis is a branch of the psychology of the mind but not of academic psychology. The lawsuit was settled out of court in 1989. After the settlement, the NY Psychoanalytic did allow carefully screened PhDs in psychology and social work to train at their Institutes. Previously, Institutes from the American had trained non-medical professionals provided they signed a waiver not to practise clinically. The International no longer denied membership to United States psychoanalytic training Institutes or to individual psychoanalysts solely because they were not members of the American.

The medical psychoanalysts disagreed with Freud's many comments during his lifetime about medicine not being a particularly appropriate background for a psychoanalyst. The psychologists referred to several arguments from Freud to substantiate their claim that psychoanalysis is a post-doctoral specialty of psychology. The independent psychoanalysts also used quotes from Freud to demonstrate that psychoanalysis is a distinct profession, such as the following from Freud's postscript, published in 1929 to "The question of lay analysis", the book written in defence of Theodor Reik in 1927.

> the important question is not whether an analyst possesses a medical diploma but whether he has had the special training necessary for the practice of analysis. [Freud, 1927, p. 252]

The important question did not get an official answer in New York State until seventy-three years after Freud posed it. On 9 December 2002, New York Governor George Patake signed a bill establishing psychoanalysis as an independent profession. The history of the events that led to the scope of practice licence in New York State for psychoanalysis is the essence of this chapter.

National Psychological Association for Psychoanalysis

A major event occurred after the Second World War that was pivotal in establishing psychoanalysis as an independent profession in New York. The National Psychological Association for Psychoanalysis (NPAP), the first non-medical psychoanalytic Institute in the Western Hemisphere, was founded in New York City in 1948, as already mentioned. Theodor Reik, a psychologist and member of Freud's original circle, with a nucleus of followers, founded NPAP. Reik came to the USA in 1939, having escaped the Nazis in 1934 by going to live in Holland. He had expected to be greeted with open arms by the New York Psychoanalytic Society, as he had been by the Dutch Psychoanalytic Society. Instead, the NY Psychoanalytic offered him a limited membership and a stipend to teach and do research if he would sign a waiver not to practise since he was a psychologist and not an MD. Reik was told that were he to see some patients, his New York colleagues would look the other way. Some European and American psychoanalysts, who had come to New York after training in Vienna, reluctantly accepted these terms. Reik's refusal and his founding of NPAP, instead, saved psychoanalysis from being a "handmaiden" (Freud's phrase) of psychiatry, psychology, and social work, at least in New York State. In fifteen states, however, primarily in the west and south, after the lawsuit, the psychologists changed their licensing laws to state that psychoanalysis is within their scope of practice. No non-psychologist psychoanalysts can practise in these states unless they are licensed in another mental health field.

NPAP was the first psychoanalytic institute in the USA that opened its doors to suitable candidates from a wide variety of fields. Candidates were accepted for their "depth of character, innate intelligence, emotional stability, and commitment". Students were required to have at least an accredited Masters of Arts or Science degree to establish academic competence and to fulfil state charter requirements. All candidates entered NPAP from diverse backgrounds in fields such as teaching, anthropology, and philosophy, as well as law, psychology, social work, nursing, and occasionally medicine. Eventually more institutes with similar admission policies formed, such as the Center for Modern Psychoanalytic Studies founded in 1971 and Westchester Institute for Training in Psychoanalysis and Psychotherapy founded in 1974. Although these Institutes declared that psychoanalysis is an independent profession, it took until 2002 before there was to be any legal recognition. The medical establishment maintained power over the New York State legislature regarding the practice of mental health. They used their influence to prevent New York from licensing psychologists. The psychologists also encountered strong opposition from psychoanalytic groups and especially NPAP. The independent psychoanalysts feared that non-university institute training of psychoanalysts would be subsumed by the licensing of degree granting university programmes in psychology. The psychologists formed the Joint Council of New York State Psychologists on Legislation and included the opposing psychoanalytic groups, offering them an incentive to support rather than fight their psychology certification bill. A letter of intent was crafted stating that the proposed psychology licence would include psychoanalytic training in an independent institute as equivalent to PhD training in psychology. Finally, the psychologists did become state certified in 1956, with strong support from NPAP and the other psychoanalytic groups. A psychoanalytic equivalency, however, was never included in the final wording of the psychology licensing law. NPAP, on behalf of its members and others, appealed to the New York State Supreme Court, claiming that the statute denied equal protection to trained psychoanalysts in violation of the Fourteenth Amendment of the Constitution. The appeal was denied (NPAP, 1996, pp. 146–149). (The social workers obtained a certification in social work in 1963.)

In 1961 the American Psychological Association (APA) claimed that psychoanalysis was a post-doctoral specialty of psychology. The APA formed Division 39, a psychoanalytic division, in 1979, and lobbied to change their existing psychology certification licence to a scope of practice licence. The proposed licence was to include psychoanalysis in their scope of practice, allowing psychologists to practise psychoanalysis, even if they had little or no specific training in it. However, the MDs, NPAP, NAAP, and groups such as pastoral counsellors, and marriage and family therapists, mental health counsellors, and others, lobbied successfully against a scope of practice licence for psychologists in New York State for almost fifty years

National Association for the Advancement of Psychoanalysis

The formation of the National Association for the Advancement of Psychoanalysis (NAAP), in 1972, created another powerful force within an already contentious field. NAAP was a democratically run organization that included all legitimately established institutes, representing a variety of theoretical orientations (e.g. Jungian, Adlerian, Kohutian, modern Freudian, contemporary Freudian, classical Freudian) in contrast to the American's policy of tight control and exclusion of all "non-Freudian" psychoanalytic institutes.

NAAP's primary goal was to work toward the acceptance of psychoanalysis as an independent profession. An autonomous accreditation committee was formed, the American Board for the Accreditation of Psychoanalysis (ABAP) (later, separately incorporated and called ABAP Inc.). A survey was taken to determine the standards of all psychoanalytic training programmes in the country. ABAP's member institutes accredited their programmes by standards that were established from the survey. The standards were designed to accommodate educational programmes with diverse theoretical perspectives. An individual who was a graduate from an ABAP accredited institute or from an equivalent institute was accepted for membership and listed in a registry as a NAAP-registered certified psychoanalyst (NCPsyA).

Accreditation is voluntary participation by professional training bodies who consensually establish standards for training that ensures diversity, quality education, and protection of academic freedom.

NAAP has yearly conferences. At the third conference, on 19 November 1974, the title "psychoanalyst" was adopted for all theoretical models represented within the organization, setting the tone for future government and state interactions. NAAP's member institutes had also voted, by consensus, to respect academic freedom and to judge the quality of each programme autonomously, providing mechanisms for innovation and growth in the individual analytic schools (NAAP, 1998, pp. 12–16).

The MDs had more than turf to worry about when NAAP organized the non-medical psychoanalytic institutes, and ABAP was advancing standards that were a departure from those set years earlier and rigidly controlled by the American and the International. The American applied to the US government for recognition as the only legitimate accreditor of psychoanalytic institutes in the USA in 1975. NAAP countered with testimony revealing the narrow population of analysts the American represented. The APA's and NAAP's testimony, in opposition, were probably major factors in the government's denial of the American's application.

The 1990s—COPA, the Consortium, APA Diplomate in Psychoanalysis

In the 1990s, three important events occurred in this ongoing struggle to establish psychoanalysis as an independent profession. One event was that ABAP, after beginning to work on an application to the Council on Post-secondary Accreditation (COPA) in 1989, formally applied for recognition in 1991. Another was the formation of the Psychoanalytic Consortium, also in 1991, consisting of several previously opposing factions: the American Academy of Psychoanalysis, the American Psychoanalytic Association, the American Psychological Association (Division 39), and the National Committee on Psychoanalysis in Clinical Social Work. The third event was that a diplomate in psychoanalysis was created by the American Psychological Association in 1996.

The MDs allied with the psychologist psychoanalysts within the APA Division 39 and social worker psychoanalysts to protest against COPA recognition of ABAP in 1991. The irony in this union is that Division 39 had no set standards for psychoanalytic training. A psychologist with an interest in psychoanalysis even without any training can become a member of Division 39. APA bylaws did not allow Division 39 to credential psychoanalysts or accredit affiliated institutes. A separate board, the American Board of Psychoanalysis in Psychology (ABPP) was established in 1996, and for the first time, Division 39 applicants could be examined at their request for "diplomate" status in psychoanalysis. To quote from the APA regulations

> APA also sponsors a diplomating board, the ABPP in Psychology. This board diplomates psychologists in the specialty of psychoanalysis from many diverse fields of psychoanalysis. Such issues as frequency of session, and content of interpretations shall be left to the candidate's self-identified theoretical orientation.

Another irony is that the standards for diplomate status invoke the same acceptance of diversity in schools of thought embraced by NAAP. The psychoanalytic consortium set up the Accreditation Council for Psychoanalytic Education (ACPE) whose standards included a minimum of three times per week analysis, and Candidates in Training are required to have mental health backgrounds before beginning their analytic training. It took the Consortium a decade to develop the standards. The last member to ratify them was the American, on 3 May 2001. The American and Division 39 have such widely disparate psychoanalytic orientations and methods of training that one can only speculate as to how many compromises were agreed to. The psychologists can use the diplomate designation when an exception is needed for the ratified standards. New York Psychoanalytic also has its exception for admitting trainees that do not have a mental health background. In other words, in order to discredit ABAP, standards were established that compromised the positions of all the members.

ABAP's application for COPA recognition should have been a routine matter. But, while ABAP was involved with COPA business, psychologists' licensing laws were being amended to include psychoanalysis in their scope of practice in several of the fifteen states already mentioned. The states chosen had no or few NAAP members and very few if any training institutes. NAAP did not get an opportunity to protest. Distinguished and well-trained independent psychoanalysts were disenfranchised from practising in those states because they did not have a licence in the mental health field that those states licensed. The COPA board was informed by members of the Psychoanalytic Consortium and by members of the Confederation of Independent Psychoanalytic Societies (known as IPS) that ABAP accredited institutes were not warning incoming students that these laws existed. The IPS institute members were the Institute for Psychoanalytic Training and Research (IPTAR), the New York Freudian Society, the Psychoanalytic Center of California (PCC), and the Los Angeles Institute and Society for Psychoanalytic Studies (LAISPS). In addition, the medical members of the Consortium solicited letters from the presidents of all the medical schools around the country to tell COPA that ABAP should not be granted national recognition because their standards were low. The major objections were that incoming students did not need to have mental health backgrounds and that the number of times per week a patient needed to be seen for psychoanalytic treatment was not specified. The letters were all the same and from people who assumed an expert role in psychoanalytic standards. COPA had a regular board, called the committee on recognition, and an appeals board. After COPA's appeals board overturned two deferrals by COPA's committee on recognition, COPA itself disbanded. A transition board, the Committee on Recognition of Post-secondary Accreditation (CORPA) then deferred ABAP as their final action before closing its doors in 1996. It was a five-year dog fight, and there was a strong indication that COPA's regular board and appeals board were in disagreement. One of the main reasons given for the rejection was that there were too many third party objections.

State licensing other than New York

Meanwhile, NAAP has maintained an active involvement in the licensing of psychoanalysts on the state level. Along with the pursuit of New York State licensing since NAAP's inception, there have been opportunities for NAAP to support a psychoanalytic licence in Pennsylvania, Vermont, Connecticut, and New Jersey.

In July 1994, Vermont became the first state to offer a licence to psychoanalysts, and it legally recognized that psychoanalysis is an independent profession. The legislatures had passed a scope of practice licence for psychologists on 1 July 1993 that would prevent independent psychoanalysts from practising psychoanalysis. The governor of Vermont had signed the bill into law but then he placed a moratorium on the law when complaints were registered by Jungian and Modern psychoanalysts whose livelihood would be curtailed. The Vermont psychoanalysts found sponsors who helped them successfully to obtain a certification licence. The consortium lobbied the Vermont Licensing Board to rescind the certification licence in psychoanalysis that it had passed. The State of Vermont did not comply with the Consortium's request. In Connecticut, the four member organizations of the Psychoanalytic Consortium and the Connecticut Psychiatric Society, the State Medical Society, Psychological Association, Society for Clinical Social Work, Society for Psychoanalytic Psychology, and the National Association of Social Workers—Connecticut Chapter, and the Western New England Psychoanalytic Society were successful in preventing a licence for psychoanalysts. Three pages of complaint about the inadequacy of NAAP registered–certified psychoanalysts were sent to every legislature in Connecticut on 3 April 1998, just before a vote in favour of a certification licence for psychoanalysts was to take place. The false negative statements made about NAAP, signed by eleven organizations, were so strong that the sponsors of the bill didn't even want to read a rebuttal because the issue was too controversial.

In several states, there were efforts to licence two, three, or four mental health professions (such as counsellors and marriage and family therapists) in one bill. The psychologists agreed not to block the licensing of these professions as long as the psychoanalysts were excluded from the bill. This tactic was successful in Pennsylvania and Massachusetts. In New Jersey, the Board of Psychological Examiners (NJBPE), in July of 1993, announced a plan to change the rules of the Psychology Licensing Act and claim psychoanalysis as a subspeciality, allowing only licensed psychologists to practise psychoanalysis in the state. This followed the success of the APA's efforts to subsume psychoanalysis by enacting scope of practice laws in several southern and western states, as previously mentioned. However, as in Vermont, with many NAAP members living and practising in New Jersey, the psychologists were unsuccessful in another eastern state. An effective letter-writing campaign brought about a hearing before the NJBPE on 18 October 1993. Many prominent psychoanalysts sent written documents and several others testified at the meeting about psychoanalysis being a separate profession. The outcome was a postponement of any rule change by the NJBPE. With the help of a lawyer, lobbyist, and Senate sponsor, and a very dedicated group of psychoanalysts campaigning, a bill was passed in 1994 to exempt the psychoanalysts from the scope of practice law. The Governor encouraged an actual licence instead and ultimately vetoed the bill in January of 1996. Governor Whitman did sign into law a certification licence bill on 6 July 2000, and New Jersey became the second state to pass legislation for the certification of psychoanalysis as an independent profession.

State licensing—New York 1970–2003

To fully understand how New York State arrived at recognition for psychoanalysis it is necessary to go back to the 1970s, throughout which there was a severe threat to the existence of independent institutes by the New York Psychoanalytic and the American psychiatrists and the New York State Psychological Association (NYSPA) psychologists. The psychologists continued to submit licensing bills to Albany legislators that would include psychotherapy and psychoanalysis in their scope of practice. They were consistently defeated by the MDs and the unlicensed mental health practitioners, including psychoanalysts.

NPAP and NAAP together, with other mental health professional groups including marriage and family therapists, mental health counsellors, and pastoral counsellors, formed the New York Joint Council for Psychotherapy and Related Mental Health Services on 3 May 1968, which later became the Joint Council for Mental Health Services/Coalition. The Joint Council actively pursued licensing legislation for the unlicensed professions. Lobbyists were hired and grass-roots efforts were organized. Many clinical psychologists, who were trained psychoanalysts, were also against the psychologists' bills. They formed the "Psychologists for the Independence of Psychoanalysis" group. Most of them were state-certified psychologists who worked in the independent psychoanalytic institutes and supported the philosophical belief in psychoanalysis as a separate profession.

Mental health bills are introduced to the legislature by the Chairs of the Higher Education Committees in the Assembly and in the Senate. The Chairs have the power to influence the bills' fate by moving them out of the higher education committee, through the finance committee, and into the rules committee, where the heads of the Assembly and the Senate control when and if bills are placed on the calendar for a vote.

The Chair of the Higher Education Committee (HEC) of the Assembly, who was appointed in 1979, met with all interested parties, from consumers to professional groups. NAAP testified before this committee in March of 1981. The Chair then studied the mental health situation thoroughly and became convinced that New Yorkers needed assurance that they were being treated by competent practitioners. He dismissed arguments by the psychologists and social workers that mental health treatment should be limited to them and pointed out that similar arguments had been made against the psychologists and social workers years earlier by the psychiatrists. He finally introduced a bill for mental health practitioners, including independent psychoanalysts, and was determined to see it pass. However, it never reached the floor for a vote and the following year a new Chair was appointed, a move that contributed to the delay in regulating the unlicensed professions for more than a decade. The new Chair was not in favour of more mental health licences in the belief that licensing could disenfranchise good therapists who may not have the necessary credentials.

The 1990s

In the beginning of the 1990s, the Regents (the New York State governing board) and the New York State Department of Education (DOE) directly acknowledged the psychoanalysts and other unlicensed mental health professionals. The Office of Professions in the DOE regulates professional licences with the advice of regulatory boards and with the approval of the Regents. The lobbyist for the mental health practitioners approached the Regents with the serious problem that existed for New York citizens. He discussed how people who sought help could not distinguish between qualified and unqualified practitioners. The Regents requested that the DOE review the issues and come up with a legislative solution. At a meeting with the lobbyist, the DOE expressed interest in creating a fifth profession to join medicine, nursing, psychology, and social work, while the practitioners stressed a need to recognize their individual titles. The Joint Council lobbyist for the unlicensed professions submitted an omnibus bill proposal to the DOE that would protect the titles of the mental health groups. The DOE came up with its own plan to have a fifth profession, called mental health counsellor, because "the professional titles must refer to an already recognized educational field". Their bias against recognizing psychoanalysis as an independent field was influenced by the psychology and social work professions. The DOE advisory mental health regulatory boards (including the psychology board, in existence since the late 1950s, and the social work board, in existence since the early 1960s) are headed by members of the DOE staff, who are also psychologists and social workers.

A letter from NAAP was sent to the meeting coordinator stating all the reasons why "therapist" rather than "counsellor" would be a more accurate term for the fifth profession. Finally a bill was introduced that included the endorsement "at the request of the State Education Department" calling the "fifth" profession mental health therapist. The bill defined the practice of mental health therapy and the use of the various titles. Some features needed work, but it was a beginning. The psychologists registered strong opposition to the

DOE's endorsement and blamed the coordinator (a psychologist employed by the DOE) and the Regents. Not so coincidentally, that year, the chair of the Regents and the coordinator from the Office of Professions changed, and the sponsorship by the Regents was withdrawn. An exchange of letters by the practitioners with the DOE confirmed that the DOE's major concern was the interests of the certified psychologists and social workers.

By the mid-1990s, the psychologists were again preparing a major thrust for a scope of practice law, and the New York State Chapter of the National Association of Social Workers was lobbying the legislatures to pass licensing laws for various levels of social workers. A massive campaign by the psychoanalysts and their mental health allies was launched to educate all legislators that a mental health practice bill for all the professions was the only workable solution to the needs of the New York citizens. In 1996, the bill being proposed for the unlicensed professions changed from certification to "Licensed Mental Health Practitioners" and defined the scope of practice of the individual professions.

The new Chair of the Higher Education Committee was reluctantly dragged into the fray by pressure from all sides of the issue. He conducted a public hearing before his committee in November 1996.

The psychoanalysts' testimony concentrated on the specific training requirements of independent institutes. The NPAP bulletin was used to show that the coursework, the personal analysis, the control analysis under supervision, and the supervised clinical experience is the necessary preparation for the practice of psychoanalysis for suitable candidates from one of a variety of Masters and PhD level backgrounds, as well as for candidates from medicine, psychology, and social work. The important point was made that both were psychoanalysts because of their graduation from a psychoanalytic training programme. Testimony opposing the mental health practitioners was given by representatives for the psychologists and social workers.

Shortly after the public meeting, a forum was convened by the Committees of the State Legislature and the DOE's Office of the Professions. The participants included consumer and professional organizations as well as legislators and regulators. The topic was regulation of psychotherapy and the other mental health services that affect New Yorkers. The consensus by the people in the room was that a scope of practice licence would best protect the consumer against unqualified therapists and that another meeting should convene very soon with only representatives of the professions directly involved in licensure.

When the next meeting was announced by the sponsors, all the mental health players were invited including the MDs and nurses. The lobbyist for the Joint Council Coalition (the mental heath counsellors, creative arts therapists, and psychoanalysts) was informed that the Coalition should send only one representative. (The marriage and family therapists had left the Coalition, had hired their own lobbyist, and had submitted their own bill. However, they had also remained as one of the four professions in the practitioners' bill.) The response from the Coalition's various organizations was a request that the Coalition representative for each of their professions (mental health counselling, creative arts therapy, and psychoanalysis) speak as they have at all legislative meetings for the past thirty years. It was a tense and anxious period but all representatives did attend and all were heard. At the last minute, the Coalition lobbyist had advised the two psychoanalysts to present evidence that psychoanalysis is an independent profession. One produced a document that had been requested in 1991 from the DOE executive director that stated the requirements of the DOE for the establishment of a separate profession. The other presented psychoanalytic journals, conference and workshop brochures, institute catalogues, and other proof that validated psychoanalysis as a profession according to the DOE criteria.

In the autumn of 1997, the psychologists were assured by the NYS Office of Professions and by the State Assembly Higher Education Committee (HEC) that they would be helped to obtain their long sought-after scope of practice licence. The reason the psychologists gave for requiring a protected scope of practice licence is that a title licence is not sufficient in a court of law and leaves the consumer without protection from unqualified practitioners of psychology. However, the psychologists made their scope too broad by including psychoanalysis, psychotherapy, and counselling in it without a means of differentiating between those psychologists who were trained and those who were untrained in these mental health professions.

The practitioners confronted the Chair of the Assembly HEC at a private meeting in June 1997 outlining why their professions needed to be recognized. He was convinced, and reassured the representatives of these groups that before a licence was granted to the psychologists there would be protection for the unlicensed professions. A few weeks later the HEC Chair submitted a bill to his committee with the title "certified professional counsellor" for everyone practising mental health who is not a psychiatrist, psychologist, or social worker. The minimum educational requirement for this certification was a Bachelor's degree, creating a two-tiered system. The licensed professions would command a higher fee than the certified professions, increasing profits for the psychologists and social workers. When confronted with a deluge of complaints by members of the mental health practitioners, the Chair of the HEC acknowledged that his certified counsellor bill "sank like the *Titanic*" and was withdrawn.

The year 1998 was critical. Another effort was made to leave the independent psychoanalysts out of the Mental Health Practitioners' Bill. Amendments are often circulated after important negotiations occur. One such draft excluded listing psychoanalysis with the mental health professions. The lobbyist for the coalition told the psychoanalysts that the opposition insisted that psychoanalysis was a speciality of the existing professions of medicine, psychology, social work, and nursing. A plea was sent out to distinguished psychoanalysts in Europe and the USA for letters affirming the importance of an independent profession for psychoanalysis. It brought an overwhelming positive response. When asked how many psychoanalysts were not licensed, lists of NAAP members and other institute graduates were tabulated and sent to Albany. Letters, faxes, and telephone calls from NAAP members and others flooded the offices of the HEC Chairs, the Leaders of the Assembly and the Senate, and all the legislators. The lobbyist and the psychoanalytic representatives had meetings in Albany with the HEC Chairs. Years of testimony by NAAP psychoanalysts had been reviewed by the Senate's HEC staff. The Council of the Senate HEC was convinced. Everyone agreed. Psychoanalysis does qualify and yes, the psychoanalysts will remain in the next official bill printing with their own title and definition of practice. The bipartisan Omnibus bill, introduced in the final days of the 1998 legislative session, provided licensure and a scope of practice for the psychologists and social workers and the four unlicensed professions. On its way to a vote on the floor of both chambers, the bill was withdrawn. Last minute details needed to be worked out with the unions of the social workers.

In the following year, 1999, the lobbyists were told that the Mental Health Practitioners Act in the Omnibus Mental Health Bill was the most talked about bill in Albany. Still, no vote was in sight at the end of the session. With six professions to work with, the MDs and anyone else who wanted to keep licensed mental health professionals to a minimum could keep the negotiations going forever. The social worker issues were unresolved and the Medical Society for the State of New York came up with a new condition. The newly licensed professionals to be (psychoanalysts, marriage and family therapists, mental health counsellors, and creative arts therapists) must send all patients for consultation to a physician before treating them, and, in addition, the psychoanalysts must have a mental health background before entering a psychoanalytic training programme. The session ended with no bill but with encouragement from the lobbyists to have faith: the Medical Society would not prevail with their impossible demands.

The lobbyists for the six professions met with representatives from the Medical Society of the State of New York and the New York State Psychiatric Association before the start of the 2000 legislative session. The MDs and the psychologists still had concerns with all the professions to be licensed. The session ended with no bill and the MDs and psychologists having concerns about each other, too.

Months of groundwork by the lobbyist in 2001 culminated in meetings in the first week of June by the unlicensed professions and the counsels of the Senate and Assembly sponsors, the Senate leader, and the Assembly speaker. The unacceptable restrictions the medical society had demanded on our ability to treat mental illness were withdrawn. They had finally accepted that, in lieu of a mental health background, courses included in the beginning years of psychoanalytic training in a state chartered institute are equivalent to coursework required for a Master's degree in a health or mental health field.

The social workers, the psychologists, and the mental health practitioners now each had their own bills. The feedback on the practitioners' chances for success was very positive.

With the use of sophisticated software, a system was set up to send faxes to targeted legislators. Nearly 7,000 faxes were sent from the four unlicensed professions. Rumour had it that it was the largest grass-roots response ever. The assembly had already passed the psychologists' bill and the unlicensed practitioners' bill. On the last day of the Senate session, both the practitioners' and the psychologists' bills were on the floor. While watching the Senate proceedings live on the Internet, one could see and hear that the psychologists' bill number was placed on the calendar and was ready to be voted on. The practitioners' bill was not. The vote was imminent. Someone in the Speaker of the Senate's chamber had pulled a fast one in cooperation with the psychologists and man-oeuvred to bring the psychologists' bill up for a vote and not the practitioners' bill. Within seconds, the Chair of the HEC was alerted by an advocate for the practitioners, who was also in the Speaker of the Senate's chamber. The Chair instantly conveyed to the proper authority that they (the psychologists' and the mental health professions' bills) will move together for a vote or not at all. The psychologists' bill ended up in the "return to rules" pile. The psy-chologists' bill and the practitioners' bill were combined and one bill was printed, instead, with a section for each of the original bills. The session ended with a positive note if not a vote.

In the year 2002 similar manoeuvres occurred: letters, e-mails, and faxes continued to pressure the legislatures. The Speaker of the House and the Leader of the Senate were determined to go ahead with a vote. In the final hours of the 2002 session, the legislators in both houses voted unanimously to regulate psychoanalysis and all the mental health professions. With the governor signing the bill into law in New York State, the legal acceptance of psychoanalysis as an independent profession now exists side by side with its legal acceptance as a post-doctoral specialization of psychology. The psychologists received a scope of practice licence in psychology that included psychoanalysis in its scope of practice, with exemp-tions for MDs, social workers, and registered nurses. The New York solution does not give priority to either the psychologists or the independent psychoanalysts.

Conclusion

One can assume that, in New York State, a truce will not be forth-coming from psychologists just because of the stroke of a gover-nor's pen. Also, one must not lose sight of the fact that there is a core group of psychoanalysts in New York City belonging to the American, and/or the International who have considered them-selves "anointed" (Kirsner, 2000, pp. 13–71) as guardians of "legiti-mate" psychoanalytic standards for nearly a century. They appear to be most unhappy that New York State has sanctioned psycho-analysis as an independent profession, and they will undoubtedly attempt to establish control of what they consider their rightful property.

In most parts of the USA and in many other countries, the controversy as to who can train in and who can practise psycho-analysis rages on. One can only hope that during the next 100 years, mutual respect for differences in psychoanalytic orientation will develop and allow energy to be spent on psychoanalytic inquiry rather than on fighting restrictive standards that inhibit the freedom necessary for further growth and development of the field.

Acknowledgement

Many thanks to Dr Natalie Becker for reading several drafts of this chapter: her invaluable criticisms and challenging suggestions stimulated my telling the whole story.

References

Freud, S. (1927). Postscript to "Discussion on lay analysis". *S.E.*, *20*: 293. London: Hogarth.

Jones, E., (1957). *The Life and Work of Sigmund Freud, Volume 2* (p. 393). New York: Basic Books.

Kirsner, D. (2000). *Unfree Associations: Inside Psychoanalytic Institutes* (pp. 13–21). London: Process Press.

National Association for the Advancement of Psychoanalysis (1998). *Twenty Five Years 1972–1997* (pp. 12–16). Lviv, Ukraine: Limited Edition.

National Psychological Association for the Advancement of Psychoanalysis, (1996). *Fifty Years 1948–1998* (pp. 146–149). New York City,
USA: Limited Edition.

CHAPTER TEN

The geography of psychoanalysis: sovereignty, ownership, and dispossession

Elisabeth Roudinesco

Introduction

The chapter takes as its starting point the fact that psycho-analysis belongs to no one, but as a discipline in the field of the human sciences, it is part of humankind's legacy. It then goes on to unravel the historical and institutional reasons behind the appropriation drive to which psychoanalysis has been sub-ject, and shows how, as a movement, psychoanalysis has gone from being a sovereignist institution with a living Freud or his direct heirs at its helm, to becoming a splintered mass move-ment. In a parallel line of argumentation, the chapter shows that the conceptual foundations of psychoanalysis, which propose the decentring of the subject, also deconstruct the very principle of a sacred sovereignty and render psychoanalysis incompatible with any form of dictatorship or fascism and enable it only to thrive in the regions of the world where a rule of law exists. However, psychoanalysis as a discipline has often been misrepresented and betrayed by those who practise in its name. Finally, the ques-tion of the ownership of psychoanalysis is further developed by examining debates around its transmission, specifically the uneasy relationship between universities and dedicated psychoanalytic training institutions.

Who owns psychoanalysis?

Truth be told, this is a strange formulation. Never would such a question be posed in France, nor, in all likelihood, in any Latin-American country. Similarly, one would never ask who it is that owns anthropology or philosophy. Thus, I have had to make quite an effort to understand just why this particular line of questioning, apparently so par for the course in contemporary Anglophone culture, seems so strange to me. Nevertheless, I have attempted to address it with as much sincerity as possible.

As a discipline, psychoanalysis belongs to no one: to no state, to no country, to no institution. And while professional societies appear to wish to represent it exclusively, for the most part it over-flows from the framework that attempts to constrain it. In a way, psychoanalysis belongs to humankind's legacy, as in fact do other disciplines born at the same time, such as sociology or anthropology. In this respect, its place is firmly in the field of the human sciences, since its object of study is the *psyche*, which was formerly in philosophy's domain. From this vantage point, and since it presupposes the existence of an unconscious unanchored in roots, ethnicity, or a beyond consciousness, psychoanalysis stands in opposition to its predecessor, psychology.

As a form of psychotherapy, psychoanalysis is heir to those ancient therapies of the soul to which it has brought a body of concepts and a doctrine. Finally, it would appear to belong to those who, since 1910, the date when Freud founded the International Psychoanalytical Association (IPA), have formed psychoanalytic associations either by laying claim to the name of the founding father or by giving institutional form to post-Freudian variants. However, this gives rise to an obvious contradiction. If psycho-analysis is, as I believe it to be, a discipline in its own right, distinct from psychology on the one hand, and from psychiatry on the other, it cannot under any circumstance be the property of the vari-ous organizations that claim to represent it in an orthodox fashion, even if they are Freud's historic heirs.[1]

To understand better this question of ownership—and to show that psychoanalysis belongs to no one, even as it is the object of a permanent appropriation drive—I will begin by describing what is nowadays the geography of the psychoanalytic world.

Invented by a Jew of the Haskala, at the heart of a central Europe still in thrall to the feudal order that the 1789 Revolution had ended a century before, psychoanalysis wished from the outset to symbolically reassert the value of the paternal function and simultaneously contribute to its deconstruction. Through its vision of a humanity steeped in the tragedy of Oedipus, it brought to the world a fascinating utopia, a new science of the unconscious. In a word, Freud and his first disciples, the famous pioneers of the Wednesday Psychoanalytic Society (Nunberg & Federn, 1962–1976),[2] were seeking to change man, not through a social revolution, but through an awakening of consciousness: the awakening of a consciousness capable of admitting that its freedom might be linked to the destiny of the dream, of sexuality, and of desire, to the destiny of an unsteady rationality.

It is possible to identify forty-one countries where psychoanalysis has had an impact since the beginning of the twentieth century. However, it is only in thirty-two of these that it was able to constitute itself either as a powerful institutional movement, or as something limited to a group or even to a few individuals. It is not by chance that it has blossomed, save for a few exceptions (such as Japan or India) in the arena of so-called Western civilization (Europe, North and South America, Australia, Israel, Lebanon), albeit with considerable differences from one country to the next.

Everywhere in the world, psychoanalysis is an urban phenomenon carried by industrialization, by the weakening of religious belief and traditional patriarchy, in other words, by the waning of autocratic, theocratic, or monarchic power, and therefore by the instauration of democratic rule and the emancipation of women. It dispenses its teaching, founds its associations and creates its training institutes in the big cities whose inhabitants are, for the most part, cut off from their roots, withdrawn into a restricted familial nucleus, and immersed in anonymity and cosmopolitanism. Apt for the exploration of the depths of private life, psychoanalysis is nourished by a conception of subjectivity, which presupposes the solitude of man faced with himself: a renunciation of any form of tribal allegiance.

In this respect, the apparatus of the couch is but the clinical translation of such a detachment: a *tête-à-tête* with one's self in confrontation with an alterity reduced to its simplest manifestation. As for transference, a major concept introduced by Freud, it is none other than the transposition, on an intersubjective mode, of a hold that has in reality weakened, but whose power the subject imaginarily reconstructs for therapeutic ends.

As we know, Freud preferred the model of British Constitutional Monarchy to the Republican Constitution, voted by the Convention in Year II, the 24th of June 1793. In his eyes, the former embodied a culture of the ego (Schorske, 1998), a puritan ego capable of mastering its passions, a moral righteousness, an ethics of constraint, whereas the latter inhabited the terrain of the id, the aesthetic of disorder, of the libido, of the group under the sway of the drives; in sum, it represented an irruption of uncontrollable forces, which were not, however, lacking in seductiveness. On the one hand there was the masculine, taken together with an admiration for Cromwell, on the other hand, the feminine, with a fascination for Charcot and the performances of the Salpêtrière.

Beyond this effective polarization and this inscription of sexual difference within his cultural preferences, Freud constantly emphasized from "Totem and taboo" (1912–1913) to "Moses and monotheism" (1939), that the murder of the father was always necessary for the building of human societies. But once the act was accomplished, the said societies could only emerge from murderous anarchy if the act was followed up with a penalty and with a reconciliation with the image of the father. In other words, Freud believed at the same time in the necessity of the murder and the interdiction of the murder, in the necessity of the act and the recognition of guilt punished by law. He believed that every human society is traversed by the death drive, a drive which cannot be eradicated. However, he also maintained that every society where the rule of law exists, supposes the existence of forgiveness, of mourning, of redemption (Derrida, 1999).

From this standpoint, one can no doubt extrapolate the idea that psychoanalysis is simultaneously a form of regicide—since it is based on this Freudian thesis of the necessity of the murderous act—and hostility to any form of juridical killing, of torture, or death penalty. This is because the murderous act, even if it occurs repeatedly in the history of revolutions, must be followed by a sanction whose effect tends to abolish the possibility of the crime, and thus of capital punishment.[3]

Similarly, coming back to that which defines the conditions under which psychoanalysis is practised in the world, one can say, as I have already suggested, that psychoanalysis has no homeland, no borders, even as the form that its implantation takes on the specific traits of the cultures that have made it their own. Psychoanalysis is not sovereignist in its essence, as it does not recognize any form of sacred sovereignty—of the nation, of the leader. This holds true even if historically, its forms of transmission have always been supported by the principle of filiation, or that which Michael Balint called "apostolic succession" (Balint, 1952), meaning a form of initiation into its knowledge and its practice taking place between a master and a disciple through the experience of the training analysis. But it is precisely because it does not admit a sacred sovereignty that psychoanalysis is a discipline which supposes the uprooting of man from himself, the decentring of the subject. Or, as Freud puts it, an interior exile proceeding through three narcissistic humiliations: to no longer be at the centre of the universe, to no longer be outside the animal kingdom, to no longer be master of his own house (Freud, 1917a). This necessary exile is an indication that the geography of psychoanalysis derives from a kind of melancholy sovereignty that passes through the deconstruction of the great figures of narcissism.

Therefore, one understands why it is that in all the countries of the world the implantation of psychoanalysis has followed upon a particular psychiatric gesture, that gesture said to be "Pinelian"[4], born in the eighteenth century and ratified by the Convention that substantiated the wresting of madness from the universe of religion and demonic possession. One also understands why psychoanalysis was always forbidden or persecuted in countries where a rule of law has never existed, and even more so by those political regimes where all the fundamental freedoms which characterize a rule of law have been suppressed. The Nazi regime is the prime example of this, designating psychoanalysis as a "Jewish science", and subjecting it to an eradication by striking off its concepts and its vocabulary. It was also the case with the Stalinst regime where, stigmatized as a "bourgeois science" since 1949, psychoanalysis found itself tormented, despite the fact that it had in effect disappeared from Soviet territory for twenty years.

In 1976, Michel Foucault rightly pointed out that Freud, finding himself in opposition to the theories of heredity–degeneration, and reacting to the great upsurge of racism which was contemporaneous to it, was to "ground sexuality in the law—the law of alliance, tabooed consanguinity, and the Sovereign-Father, in short, to surround desire with all the trappings of the old order of power". And he added, "it was owing to this that psychoanalysis was—in the main, with a few exceptions, in theoretical and practical opposition to fascism" (Foucault, 1990, p. 198).

This Foucaldian judgment, to which I readily subscribe, concerns the discipline itself. It is effectively *as a discipline* that psychoanalysis is in its essence incompatible with the dictatorial forms of fascism and with all manner of discrimination associated with it (racism, anti-Semitism, xenophobia, etc.). This holds true independently from the actions of its representatives who, in given historical circumstances, have failed to honour what the discipline demanded of them, to the point of unhesitatingly collaborating with the very regimes that persecuted psychoanalysis (Major, 1986; Roudinesco & Plon, 1997).

It is precisely because psychoanalysis demonstrates that the death drive, murder, violence, hatred of the self and of the other are the affective invariants of the human condition, that it owes it to itself to combat them even as it emphasizes the principle of their repetition *ad infinitum.*

The double process of a wresting away from the principle of sovereignty and a freeing of a symbolic function of the father characterizes the psychoanalytic movement itself. If need be, the evolution of its institutions can attest to this. For the first Freudians, psychoanalysis was the property of a founding father who described his followers as a "savage horde". Those who left him defined themselves as dissidents who no longer belonged to the circle of the chosen.

From 1910 onwards, the sovereign function of power was delegated by Freud to the IPA. For almost twenty years, this association was the only legitimate representative of psychoanalysis, led not by the founder who continued to embody its creativity, but by the disciples of the first generation. This type of oligarchic power structure was very well suited to a psychoanalytic movement which was still modelled on a theatre production straight out of the Ancient Greek or Shakespearian heritage: between the city of Thebes and the Kingdom of Denmark.

With the splits starting in 1927, the IPA progressively ceased to embody the sovereignty of psychoanalysis, but still remained, for some time to come, its only legitimate representative. In effect, those who split no longer left the community whose principal operative remained a living Freud. Instead, they sought to create other internal currents within it. The splits of the inter-war years were in this respect symptomatic of the impossibility for psychoanalysis to be represented in its entirety by a single government or to be defined by a single measure of belonging. This form of splitting reflected that which was the essence of Freudianism: the decentring of the subject, the abolition of mastery, the defeat of monarchical authority, dispossession, or even "disbelonging".

That is why the IPA was no longer regarded after the Second World War as the only institution capable of uniting the sum total of psychoanalytic tendencies into an indivisible community. At this point there appeared not only associations that sought to stay in the midst of one single empire, but also groups that refused the very principle of a unique kind of belonging. At times, they laid claim to their allegiance to the lost father and his doctrine, at times they rallied around a going beyond or even an abandonment of his system of thought. This form of splitting signalled the transformation of psychoanalysis into a mass movement.

The present situation reflects this history. One knows now that no international organization can claim to embody the unique legitimacy of psychoanalysis. Consequently, all of its institutions are either marked by the mourning for a sovereignty lost for ever, or else are born out of an interminable mourning for this figure of a master to whom everybody wishes to be faithful, thereby risking his being remade into a simulacrum.

Today there is not one international association but international associations, each of which regroup many societies, themselves either non-homogeneous or in a permanent state of flux. There are at least four international associations in addition to the IPA

(Roudinesco & Plon, 1997). As for the various societies, schools, groups, their number extends into the hundreds throughout the world, assembling around thirty thousand registered practitioners. To this number can be added the independents, who are steadily on the increase, and who either belong to no institution, or on the contrary, to many.

Psychoanalysis' success in the world has been accompanied by constant attacks. During the first half of the twentieth century, it was considered to be a kind of pan-sexualism and accused of lowering civilized morality. It was charged with corrupting behaviour and sowing discord in families. After 1960, when more open sexual practices had gained ascendance in the West, psychoanalysis was taken to task for its so-called clinical inefficiency, its absence of scientificity. After its rebel spirit had got it banished from the city of the *bien-pensants*, psychoanalysis was excluded from the academy of scientific greats for its attachment, deemed conservative, to the tradition of Greek and Judaeo-Christian humanism.

But it was also attacked by the churches and religions, with the help of an "essentialist" conception of sexual difference that privileges the masculine to the detriment of the feminine. In religion, as one knows, woman is always sanctified as wife or mother and demonized as temptress or as the object of sexual desire. However, the female emancipation movement, originating in the eighteenth century with the Enlightenment, progressively challenged these founding myths. And psychoanalysis was a significant heir to this.

Within this context, the three monotheistic religions, Judaism, Christianity, and Islam, judged psychoanalysis to be responsible for the sexualization of women's bodies. However, the full frontal assault was conducted during the inter-war years by the Catholic church. which regarded Freudianism and Marxism as two manifestations of the Anti-Christ, as two new religions of reason without faith.

Only since 1945, when the Holy See adopted the principles of psychological and psychiatric expertise to examine the notion of vocation, has the relationship between the faithful and the followers of positive science begun to normalize. This process implied subjecting priests to the scrutiny of an expert knowledge in order to distinguish that which in their religious commitment was due to the effect of a true faith and that which was neurotic (Roudinesco, 1990)

Fascinated by this quest for truth, a number of priests volun-tarily chose the path of psychoanalysis in order to test the nature of their faith. Some became psychoanalysts, particularly in France where the development of Lacanian thought was attractive to Christians. Culturally a Catholic, Lacan was much more interested than Freud in the question of mysticism, which he saw as a category in its own right, and did not reduce it to neurosis

After sixty years of battles and conflicts, French Catholicism became increasingly secularized. Hence, it is less prone today to fundamentalism than are Protestantism and Judaism. Nowadays, it is with political Islam that psychoanalysis is in conflict (Benslama, 2002),[5] that is to say with an Islam which exerts a real coercion on the "sexed" body of women, through the intermediary of the state and its institutional representative, the family. Stoning, female circumcision, polygamy, the forbidding of any kind of coeducation, the obligation to wear the veil, arranged marriages, or worse, the enslavement of subjectivity through the cultivation of a voluntary enslavement, these are but the most visible practices of a new obscurantism, all the more dangerous since it serves as an organiz-ing link to the rejects of the liberal economy.[6]

To invoke an anecdote, I once said quite casually to a Lebanese psychoanalyst that it seemed to me difficult to analyse a veiled woman. This provoked a bit of a row as he misunderstood what I meant. So he answered that he did indeed see in his consulting room Muslim women wearing the veil, something to which, of course, I had no objection. But this man thought that it was enough to produce magnificent Lacanian interpretations in order to be heard by his patients. To this utopia, I was opposing the idea that it is impossible to accede to the unconscious of a subject when she inscribes on her body the signs of an enslavement aiming to isolate any relation with an alterity judged "impure". How to speak openly, how to enter into a transferential relationship freely when one exhibits on one's self the paradigms of a vestimentary servitude whose goal is to forbid an engagement in an intersubjective rela-tionship?

The fact that psychoanalysis has been attacked, condemned, or eradicated through its history has not prevented it from being used as an instrument of domination or discrimination by its own prac-titioners. The way in which homosexuality has been treated by all factions of the Freudian movement can attest to this, among other possible examples.

Freud had taken a big step by refusing to classify homosexuality among the defects or anomalies of sexuality, in the manner of the sexologists of his time. He did not think that homosexuals were committing "acts against nature" and he was refusing to partake in any form of stigmatization founded on the idea of degeneration. In other words, he was not separating homosexuals from other human beings, and considered that every subject could potentially make this object choice, as a psychic bisexuality exists in all of us.

In other words, if Freudian man is marked by the tragedy of desire, the homosexual is none other, in terms of this general human tragedy, than a subject even more tragic than the ordinary neurotic, since his sexual choice alienates him from bourgeois society. His only recourse would be creativity, in order to assume ownership of his own drama.[7] By refusing to classify homosexuality as a sexual perversion, Freud universalized perversion. His universalization was much more progressive than the affirmation of difference promulgated by the sexologists and psychiatrists of the nineteenth century who were treating homosexuals as abnormal or mentally ill, thus returning to the Christian conception of the sodomite (Ferenczi, 1980, 1994).

In the history of the psychoanalytic movement, it was Ernest Jones and Anna Freud who held, contrary to Freud, a repressive attitude towards homosexuality.

From December 1921, for an entire month, the question of homosexuality divided the members of the famous comity that was secretly leading the IPA. The Viennese amongst them showed much more tolerance than the Berliners in this respect. Supported by Karl Abraham, this latter camp suggested that homosexuals were incapable of becoming psychoanalysts, since analysis did not cure them of their perversion. With Freud's approval, Otto Rank opposed the Berliners and declared that homosexuals should accede normally to the profession of psychoanalyst, judged on the basis of their competence. Jones refused to agree to this. He argued with the Berliners and declared openly that "to the world homosexuality is an abhorrent crime the committal of which by one of our members would discredit us seriously" (Lieberman, 1985, p.175). From then on, homosexuality was banished from the Freudian empire through an unwritten rule.

Gradually, over more than fifty years, with the increasing influence of North-American psychoanalytic societies, the IPA reinforced its repressive arsenal. After turning away from the stand that Freud took, it did not hesitate to qualify homosexuals as sexual perverts and to consider them as either unresponsive to psychoanalytic treatment, or else treatable only if the goal of the treatment was to orient them towards heterosexuality.

This position was not counterbalanced by the Kleinian psychoanalytic current, which envisaged homosexuality (whether latent or actual) as being in its female version, an identification with a sadistic penis, and, in its male version, a schizoid troubling of the personality or a means of facing up to excessive paranoia.

It is only now that the famous unwritten rule instituted by the secret comity in 1921 has been effaced, although not abolished. This is thanks to the activities of the American gay movement and specifically to the self-outing of certain psychoanalysts, members of the IPA, who began openly to declare their homosexuality, notably in 1997, at the International Congress in Barcelona.

As for Lacan, he did not have the same conception of homosexuality as Freud. In his eyes, it was not a sexual orientation as such. A transgressive character, Lacan was influenced by his reading of de Sade and his contact with Georges Bataille. His fascination with Greek homosexuality made him on the one hand turn the figure of the pervert into the incarnation of a higher intellect, even though it was one which was damned, and on the other hand, to see all forms of love, or even desire, as something perverse. It is within this context that he understood homosexuality to be a perversion and not a sexual orientation. He did not re-establish the old conceptual system of sexology, but this did not prevent some of his heirs from being as homophobic as the psychoanalysts from the IPA (Roudinesco, 2002, 2003).

Even though its death has been foretold a thousand times, and even as it was being used in a repressive manner by its own practitioners, psychoanalysis has survived. It has been carried by many different currents of thought claiming a connection to Freudianism, to be sure, but also to its numerous interpretative variants. Some of its schools took on the name of the masters who founded then

(Anna Freud, Melanie Klein, Jacques Lacan), while others, to the contrary, chose a name signalling a conceptual marker of belonging. One can identify five main schools (in addition to classical Freudianism), divided amongst the various geographic areas I mentioned at the beginning of this article: Ego Psychology, Self Psychology, Kleinianism, Existential Analysis, Annafreudianism, Lacaniansim; each of these schools, in turn, divides into various branches. The force of the expansion is so strong that some ask themselves if one true psychoanalytic community can still exist and whether, in the various corners of the world, the practitioners of the unconscious are still willing to speak to each other across these movements and outside their respective schools.

In this respect, there is a veritable "crisis of psychoanalysis" in the present context of the globalization of cultural exchange. If the nineteenth century was the century of psychiatry and the twentieth century was that of psychoanalysis, this crisis is none other, in my understanding, than psychoanalysis's attempt to mark its specificity in a twenty-first century world where there is a great expansion of diverse psychotherapies: over a thousand different ones to date. The success of these psychotherapies is due in part to psychiatric knowledge becoming stuck in a mire of cognitive and behaviourist classifications which reduce the human being to a sum of symptoms. The interminable "diagnostic" quarrels around the *DSM* attest to this state of things (Kirk & Kutchins, 1992; Roudinesco, 2001). But this success is also the consequence of a transformation having taken place in Western society. In the West, especially among the middle classes, the cult of happiness, the quest for health, the interest in the body, and the privilege accorded to the success of a narcissistic individuality, in sum, the entire area of "personal development" has substituted itself to a social or political engagement relying on a subjectivity simultaneously subversive and universalist. Instead of thinking the world, the Narcissus-individual thinks himself as the centre of the world in order to better sell himself or herself to the highest bidder.

Adaptable to every case, every group, every individual, and therefore taken up by the middle classes jealous of their well-being, these therapies have developed slowly, first in the USA from the 1960s onwards, then during the past ten years, in all Western countries as the world evolved towards a globalized economy. After the fall of communism in 1989, it had no other enemy than the ghosts of a self that has become master once more in his own house and projects its fantasies on to the other: on to another who embodies the stranger to itself, the stranger to the homeland, to private life, to the nation (Lasch, 1991).

To the opposite of psychoanalysis, but on the very terrain on which it is practised, these therapies allow for the belief that individual will is more powerful than the weight of the past, that it is this will that determines the destiny of the subject much more than repression or the anchoring in an unconscious genealogy. Thus, we have moved from a historical situation where psychoanalysis offered the subject the means to reconstruct his undone subjectivity, to a state of social globalization where the subject, gripped by depression, wants nothing more to do with his unconscious. To the detriment of the possible elucidation of desire, this "post-modern" subject lays claim to pornographic sexual practices while valuing the instauration of a puritan Moral Order, founded on an ever greater legislation of the conflict between the sexes.

Therefore, psychoanalysis, which has nothing to do with a fascination with pornography, nor with the restitution of a Moral Order, no longer seems equal to the task of elucidating a given psychic conflict. Assimilated by its patients to a simple psychotherapy among others, it seems to be put to the test by a challenge that it has never accepted, only to be rejected like a drug past its sell-by date. As for its practitioners, careful to respond to the new demands of the civil society, they have become, almost despite themselves, and due to their sectarian withdrawal, psychotherapies shorn of their ancient prerogatives.

Nevertheless, in this beginning of the twenty-first century, it is possible to see that the attraction of these therapies, as indeed that of the *DSM*, is in decline. It is possible to discern a return to the psyche through the ruins of an organicism and a behaviourism incapable of fulfilling what they had promised. One could therefore suppose that psychoanalysis would still be able to provide original answers to new social rebellions. But it is likely that in the future its appearance will be very different to the one that we have known. Would it be in accordance with the vagaries of a democratic populism seeking to seduce the masses through the market, profit, or profitability, or would it be, on the contrary, in such disaccord

with the evolution of society, that it radically contested its principles? Democracy, or the rule of law, are insufficient in themselves to
ensure the survival of psychoanalysis. There should be, within the
spaces where it exists, the enabling of a certain subjective freedom
without which no individual could accede to his or her unconscious.

Even though psychoanalysis has always relied on specific institutions to train its practitioners, it does not, for that matter, belong
to the clinicians who are the agents of its expansion. For this reason,
it needed to be taught at the university in order to flourish.

In a famous article written in the autumn of 1918, and published
in Hungarian in March 1919[8] Freud clearly differentiated undergoing a treatment that permitted one to become a psychoanalyst
from the teaching of the discipline, which does not rely on the treatment in order to exist.

Moreover, he emphasized that if it was taught in an academic
fashion, theoretical knowledge derived from psychoanalysis could
help doctors to better understand the psychical problems of their
patients, so that they need not rely on healers or charlatans whose
methods might seem more efficient. Thus he is full of praise—once
is hardly sign of habit—for the fact that psychoanalysis is studied
in the USA as an introduction to psychiatry. In conclusion, he imagines a radiant future where the human sciences would be cross-
fertilized by the ideas of psychoanalysis.

However, Freud does not consider for an instant the specific
problem posed by the relationship between the university and
psychoanalytic societies. He does not imagine that one can create a
faculty of psychoanalysis independent from the IPA, where teaching could be done by professors who are not analysts or not even
analysed. He seems to think of himself in 1918 as the owner of the
discipline that he invented:

> The fact that an organisation of this kind exists is actually due to the
> exclusion of psycho-analysis from universities. And it is therefore
> evident that these arrangements will continue to perform an effec-
> tive function as long as this exclusion persists. [Freud, 1919j, p. 171]

Consequently, he makes the principle of lay psychoanalysis rely
exclusively on the existence of psychoanalytic institutions. And

within this perspective, he regards the university as a locus of power, susceptible of staking its claim on psychoanalysis and of which one has to beware. It is the university, he writes, which must prove that it does not seek to deform the content of the doctrine it tries to transmit.[9]

Evidently, Freud did not think that the university could play a role in the laicization of psychoanalysis. That is why he does not predict that one day psychoanalysts would come to wish to pursue an academic career in order to insist on their autonomy from schools of psychoanalysis, felt to be rigid, constraining or dogmatic.

Freud does not understand what it is in fact that the modern university, derived from the great medieval European model and developed by democratic states, represents. Here I speak of the University, with a capital U, and thus of the Idea of the University, which demands that nations unconditionally recognize its freedom, in other words, the right to state in public that which research demands, a knowledge, an idea of the truth (Derrida, 2001). And if Freud does not take into account this principle of unconditionality, it is because it does not fit in with the claims to ownership, characteristic of the psychoanalytic community. Following the example of the founding father, psychoanalysts have considered themselves for several generations to be the owners of Freudian knowledge. Thus, they resisted psychoanalysis becoming a lay discipline that might escape from the control of their schools. An intractable misunderstanding derives from this. Everywhere in the world, what we can call the impossible teaching of psychoanalysis at the university rests on this misunderstanding.

To move from abstract definitions to concrete situations, one can take as examples three countries where the relationship between psychoanalysis and the university has taken shape in three different ways: the USA, Brazil, and France.

In the first instance, the guarantee of truth that the university proposes relies on the principle of liberal competition inscribed at the heart of a country which is profoundly religious and puritanical. In the second case, it leans on a model derived from Auguste Comte's positivism, and later on the inspiration of Fernand Braudel, under whose influence the Catholicism of the Jesuits became more missionary than colonial. Finally, in the third case, that of France, it refers back to a Republican spirit, for which only the existence of a state secularism, separate from religion, can authorize the very idea of a freedom of knowledge.

During the first half of the twentieth century, psychoanalysis became implanted in the USA almost exclusively via a medical path and according to a model of therapeutic efficiency unique in the world. Consequently, the discipline was taught first of all in the schools of psychoanalysis affiliated to the IPA, and which were extended into various university medical faculties. From 1910 to 1960, psychoanalysis had a considerable popular success throughout America. But this enthusiasm rested on a misundersanding, since analytic therapy was thought to be a therapy of happiness (Hale, 1971, 1995).

Since the end of the 1960s, despite its formidable institutional power and its expansion into all the sectors of psychiatry, psychoanalysis was attacked with as much strength as it had previously been lionized. Using in reverse the empirical arguments of the pioneers of Freudianism, the enemies of psychoanalysis started to refute psychoanalytic practice by criticizing its so-called therapeutic inefficiency. The various therapies discussed previously were brought into opposition to it.

In other words, if psychoanalysis had flourished on American soil by adopting an ideal that Freud had always rejected, by promising to liberate man from the weight of guilt, it was then rejected because it never fulfilled any of the claims which were used to transform it into a therapy of happiness.

With the onset of this decline in popularity, a cleavage took place between the doctors, centred upon the clinic, and the teachers who worked on the Freudian corpus without being practitioners. This investment in Freudian knowledge in Humanities departments gave rise to a generation of Freud scholars, specialists in Freud in the academic sense, who transposed into the academic field the quarrels which had hitherto opposed psychoanalysts. In this context, chairs of psychoanalytic studies were created occupied by specialists who were not clinicians but strictly academics. Since then, the conflicts that opposed analytic schools became less important than quarrels in historiography or interpretation. It is primarily in this academic context, dominated by gender studies, that the study of the work of Lacan, which only had a small following within North American psychoanalytic associations, gained ascendance.

If, from the USA, one descends geographically towards the South American continent, one realizes that in this world where the seasons are inversed, psychoanalysis "belongs" above all to Argentina, and in Argentina it belongs to the city of Buenos Aires, in other words, to a new Vienna, a new Athens, a new Jerusalem, that the Freudian West could only dream of. But this affirmation can only hold true because in Buenos Aires psychoanalysis represents, first and foremost, Europe; a Europe without limits, multiplied, without borders; a Europe of cities: Vienna, Berlin, Paris, London (Vezzetti, 1996; Valladares, 2001).

This Latin American continent has shown Europe, even more than the USA had done, that psychoanalysis continues to be in all places expressive of a great migratory flux. And even when urban Europeans arrive in Buenos Aires, they get a sense of déjà vu, of the uncanny, having the impression of arriving in a city already visited, whether Barcelona or Madrid, and similarly, upon meeting an Argentinian psychoanalyst, they have the impression of meeting not only their double but a curiously inversed image of themselves.

In this twisted world, everything takes place as in a Borges story, like a test of cosmopolitanism à la Borges. The words are the same, the references are identical, the men and women are like us. Yet, everything there is enunciated like the Japanese translation of a Western book whose pages are turned from right to left, rather than left to right. As for the city, it resembles a tower of Babel, a virtual city *par excellence*, which contains all possible worlds; to such an extent that the ego no longer knows if it exists, if it dreams or if it is dreamt.

If, coming from Argentina and Europe, one then journeys to a Brazilian city, the impression is similar yet different. Certainly, the seasons are the reverse of ours, but it also seems as if every city contained a microcosm of all possible seasons: winter in the morning, spring at noon, summer in the afternoon, autumn in the evening. Consequently, the Brazilian city participates, not in the same Borgesian cosmopolitan cosmos, but in an extremely violent hierarchical hybridization. The relationship between the intellect and the body is of a cannibalistic, colonialist, bisexual nature. To eat the other, to repress the other, to spit out the other, in other words, the enemy, the stranger, the Amazonian Indian, the neighbour, the hybrid, the relative, the pauper, the man or the woman within oneself, that is how Brazil incorporates the image it has of its relationship to the European world, a world it always engages with as a vacillating projection between love and rejection.

While psychoanalysis was for urban Argentines, and especially for the *portenōs*, a means of elucidating a genealogical history carried by successive waves of migration, and while it became implanted there with the help of a heroic dynasty, in the guise of a reconfigured Oedipal family from Europe, it remained in Brazil the accomplished expression of a rational knowledge, simultaneously capable of responding to cultural interrogations and of tempering the excesses of a feudal urban society, still prone to magical thinking: a society of healers, of choreographers of the trance, or else, charismatic leaders of sects.

Thus, psychoanalysis is in Brazil both ailment and remedy, reason and transgression against reason, the norm and the rebellion against the norm, the law of the father and the irruption of a maternal heterogeneity. At times it sees itself as submitting to the universal that links it to Europe or to the other America, at times it thinks itself at odds with this ideal to the point of giving in to a frantic quest for an impossible "Brazilianism". Dare I say that it changes seasons at any time of day and night, and for this reason it dazzles us, Europeans, by offering us the spectacle of a remarkable vitality that has been lost for over two decades to European and American psychoanalysis, because of its rivalry with the neurosciences.

It is not by chance that the University plays a great role in this country where all psychoanalytic schools, of all tendencies, have allied themselves not to departments of medicine, human sciences, or literature, but to those of psychology, thus managing to put in place a complete osmosis between clinical practice and the transmission of the doctrine and the corpus. Taught like a rational knowledge, instead of and in the place of psychology, psychoanalysis has acquired a crucial position in Brazilian urban society at a time when, in Europe and in the USA, it is being subject to the full force of the after-effects of a crisis which has forced it to develop more and more outside of a university system dominated by scientism.

Taking now the situation in France as an example, we see that to this day, it is the only country in the world where psychoanalysis has fertilized the totality of the intellectual and clinical field, and has been carried as much by psychiatry as by literature or philosophy,[10]

There exists in this field a real "French exception". Its origin dates back to the Revolution of 1789, which has given scientific and juridical legitimacy to the dominance of reason over madness, thus signing the institutional birth certificate of psychiatry. Later, the Dreyfus affair instituted a self-consciousness within the intellectual class. By declaring themselves of the "avant-garde", intellectuals were able to take hold of the most innovative ideas and make them bear fruit in their own way. To these factors I might also add the existence of a literary modernism, which gave expression in a new style of writing, that of Charles Baudelaire, Arthur Rimbaud, and Lautréamont, to the idea of changing man through an "I is an other (*je est un autre*)".

The French exception owes something to the status that grammar, words, vocabulary, the lexicon, have always had in France. Far from regarding language as an empirical instrument of communication, the French elite have always granted it a unique place: first of all as a written language with a function of homogenizing the nation, and then the Republic. Thus, the French language must represent the ideal of language, something like the symbolic function of language, a law, a categorical imperative. From this derives the importance accorded not only to the Academy, whose role it is to legitimate good usage in speech and in writing, but also to writers in general. This conception of language is strange to other European countries. It explains why a grammarian, Edouard Pichon, could have played such a great role in the genesis of French Freudianism, whose traces we find in the work of Jacques Lacan. Lacan, in fact, was the only Freudian in the world to make his mark as the instigator of a system of thought capable of entirely renewing psychoanalysis through structural linguistics and the German philosophical tradition (Roudinesco, 1997).

Despite its position as exception, France, the most Freudian country in the world, together with Argentina and Brazil, has never had a department of psychoanalysis in its great institutions of Higher Education, the College de France or the Ecole des Hautes Etudes en Sciences Sociales.[11] This astonished American specialists in Freud's work, who have succeeded in having such Chairs created in American universities.

It is to Daniel Lagache[12] that we owe the fact that a French model of teaching psychoanalysis, via clinical psychology and

psychopathology, was put in place at the University. It was instituted in order to practise a politics of unification in psychology, a
perfectly imaginary unification, actually, whose effect was to trap
the teaching of psychoanalysis between experimental psychology,
social psychology, and later, between all the different branches of
psychology, themselves more interested in tipping over into the
neurosciences than in preserving a clinical presence.

Between 1945 and 1968, clinical psychology served as a means
for the implantation of the teaching of psychoanalysis. Clinical
psychologists were led, in their training, towards the analytical
schools, and hence the conflicts between the various schools were
transposed into the academy, with each camp occupying its own
university bastion.

The changes in law that transformed the universities following
the student revolution of 1968, were instrumental in ushering in a
new generation and another politics: that of Jean Laplanche, and
subsequently of Pierre Fédida and Roland Gori.[13]

If, in the inter-war years, Lagache's objective was to consolidate
the status of the psychoanalytic movement by transposing its stakes
to the university sector, his successors were looking for a means to
escape from their respective psychoanalytic societies. New quarrels
regarding ownership and the carving up of the territory derived
from this situation. Could one be at the same time a psychoanalyst
and a teacher? Could one belong at the same time to a psychoanalytic school and respect the lay character of the Republican
University?

If Lagache and his heirs implanted psychoanalysis in the departments of psychology, Serge Leclaire[14] took another path by creating,
for the first time in France, a department of psychoanalysis entirely
cut off from any link to psychology, and even hostile to the idea of
forming any link with it.

Supported by Michel Foucault, Jacques Derrida, and Georges
Canguilhem, the experiment took place at the University of Paris
VIII in the context of the renewal of philosophy education.
However, Lacan himself attacked it, denouncing for four years the
transformation of psychoanalysis into a "university discourse"
(Lacan, 1991). He subsequently changed his mind, and his theory,
in order to give his support to his son-in-law, Jacques-Alain Miller.
Miller founded another department of psychoanalysis at the same

university, The Freudian Field, which became an annex of the Ecole de la Cause Freudienne.[15]

Conclusion

Whether through its own institutions, or alternatively outside these, in other words, at the University, psychoanalysis has been subject to rather strange relations of belonging and "disbelonging, of inclusion and exclusion, which have no equivalent in any discipline of the human or social sciences. Taught as such in institutions created by practitioners, psychoanalysis has never been recognized as a discipline in its own right within the university in the manner of, say, anthropology or sociology. Thus, it has always been through the intermediary of another discipline, psychology, psychiatry, medicine, history, literature, etc., that it has been admitted into the space reserved for academic knowledge, sometimes as a doctrine, sometimes as a psychotherapy, sometimes as an interpretative method, and then only in those parts of the world where a rule of law exists.

It is from this that all of its strengths and its weaknesses derive. Forced to put itself to the test of society in order to continue to exist, psychoanalysis must constantly redefine its boundaries, which nevertheless disappear at the least sign of a storm. And it is no doubt due to this dialectic that it oscillates between presence and absence, disappearance and affirmation, dispossession and reconquest, that it has managed to construct an empire that continues to bother its critics through the very fact of its splintering.

However, in the absence of any academic or juridical status capable of cutting through the question of what is and is not psychoanalysis, it is attacked in three different ways. At times, it is attacked from the outside by the various "sciences" of cognition and behaviour which try to eradicate it. At times it is attacked from the inside, by the bureaucratic rigidity of its institutions. Finally, it is also under attack at its very borders by the schools of psychotherapy on the one hand, and on the other hand, by the various sects which have no qualms in claiming its name.[16] This is why it seems important at this point in time when historical studies in the field have taken the lead over theoretical renewal, to carefully mark the ways in which psychoanalysis belongs to its history, its concepts, its movement; in other words, to the indelible event that was Freud's discovery. But only by being permanently unfaithful to it (Derrida & Roudinesco, 2001). For to reinvent the force of a founding act, one must detach it from its old markers of belonging, but without for that matter, rejecting these.

Acknowledgement

My thanks go to Julia Borossa for translating this chapter, and for her excellent work in putting together the Introduction for me.

Notes

1. It is interesting to note that the British Psycho-Analytical Society (BP-AS), founded by Ernest Jones, is the only psychoanalytic association in the world to have received the exclusive right to appropriate the name of the discipline, to the disadvantage of other groups, thus forced to class themselves amongst psychotherapists. This is due to the fact that Freud moved to London during the last year of his life, and his daughter obtained this unique privilege from the British government.
2. I take up again here certain themes that I discussed in the opening address to the Estates General of psychoanalysis which took place in Paris in July 2000 and which assembled practitioners from thirty four countries. See Major, 2003.
3. It is in a conversation with Theodor Reik that Freud pronounced himself in favour of the abolition of the death penalty, not only as a private citizen, but also in the name of psychoanalysis. See Reik, 1957.
4. From the French alienist Philippe Pinel (1745–1826), founder of modern psychiatry.
5. Let us note that psychoanalysis cannot thrive in regions dominated by political Islam.
6. Bensalma writes of a barbarism linked to a indentitary despair.
7. One finds this position in Freud's writings on Leonardo Da Vinci. And it is this work of 1910 that he renounces the term "invert" in favour of "homosexual" (Freud, 1905d, 1910c)
8. Only the Hungarian version of this article is known, and it served as the basis of the translation into other languages. During the three

months when the Bolchevik Commune of Bela Kuhn was in power Ferenczi was given a professorship in psychoanalysis in the faculty of medicine at the university of Budapest. This was a pioneering experiment, albeit shortlived.

9. In another project, that would never see the light of day, Freud imagines that one could one day found a Higher School of psychoanalysis which would unite all the scholars of all disciplines who wish to fertilize the new discipline. It is René Major who has taken it upon himself to see this project through in the year 2000. See Major, 2003.

10 Except for the field of history and historiography, where I am the only one to teach in a department of history with an academic background in history.

11. When specialists in psychoanalysis have succeeded in acceding to these places it was always within the context of another discipline: history, philosophy, anthropology

12. Daniel Lagache (1903–1972) was a French psychiatrist and psychoanalyst. A philosopher by training, he introduced psychoanalysis to the university through the teaching of clinical psychology. He was a great rival of Lacan and founded the Societié française de psychanalyse at the time of the 1953 split with the Paris psychoanalytical society, and in 1964, the Association psychanalytique de France.

13. Pierre Fédida (1934–2002). A psychoanalyst and philosopher, he was a student of Ludwig Binswanger and member of the Association psychanalytique de France. Roland Gori (1943–) is a professor at the University of Aix en Provence and co-founder with Pierre Fédida of an inter-university seminar in psychoanalysis and psychopathology.

14. Serge Leclaire (1924–1992). A psychiatrist and psychoanalyst, he was Jacques Lacan's first disciple and a member of the Ecole Freudienne de Paris.

15. The Ecole de la cause freudienne was a school founded by Jacques-Alain Miller in January 1981, after the dissolution of the Lacan's Ecole Freudienne, a few months before Jacques Lacan's death.

16. This is the case with the school of analytic psychology founded by Carl Gustav Jung, some of whose heirs, to the contrary of their master, are seeking to come under the banner of psychoanalysis. They do not see that there is an insurmountable theoretical contradiction in this, since analytical psychology rests on a different conceptual basis than the different Freudian lines of thought. As for the sects, they use and abuse without any form of control of the term psychoanalysis in order to associate it to all kind of magical or esoteric forms of practice: tantric psychoanalysis, astropsychoanalysis, etc.

References

Balint, M. (1952). *Primary Love and Psychoanalytic Technique*. London: Tavistock.

Benslama, F. (2002). *La psychanalyse à l'épreuve de l'Islam*. Paris: Aubier.

Derrida, J. (December 1999). Le siècle du pardon, entretien avec Michel Wieviorka, *Le monde des débats*.

Derrida, J. (2001). *L'université sans conditions*. Paris: Galilée.

Derrida, J., & Roudinesco, E. (2001). *De quoi demain. . . . Dialogue*. Paris: Fayard.

Ferenczi, S. (1980) *On the Nosology of Male Homosexuality. First Contributions to Psychoanalysis*. London: Karnac.

Ferenczi, S. (1994). Etats sexuels intermédiaires. Les écrits de Budapest, G. Kurtz & C. Lorin, (Eds.). Paris: EPEL.

Foucault, M. (1990). *The History of Sexuality, Volume 1*. Harmondsworth: Penguin.

Freud, S. (1905d). Three essays on the theory of sexuality. *S.E., VII*: 125–293.

Freud, S. (1910c). Leonardo Da Vinci and a memory of his childhood. *S.E., XI*: 59–137.

Freud, S. (1912–1913). Totem and taboo. *S.E., XIII*.

Freud, S. (1917a). A difficulty in the path of psychoanlysis. *S.E., XVII*: 136–144.

Freud, S. (1919j). On the teaching of psychoanalysis in universities. *S.E., XVII*: 170–173.

Freud, S. (1939). Moses and monotheism. *S.E., XXIII*: 3–137.

Hale, N. (1971). *Freud and the Americans. The Beginnings of Psychoanalysis in the United States 1876–1917*. New York & Oxford: Oxford University Press.

Hale, N. (1995). *The Rise and Crisis of Psychoanalysis in the United States*. New York & Oxford: Oxford University Press.

Kirk S., & Kutchins, H. (1992). *The Selling of DSM. The Rhetoric of Science in Psychiatry*. New York: Walter de Gruyter.

Lasch, C. (1991). *The Culture of Narcissism*. New York: Norton.

Lieberman, J. (1985). *Acts of Will. The Life and Work of Otto Rank*. New York: Macmillan Free Press.

Major, R. (1986). *De l'élection. Freud face aux ideologies américaine, allemande et soviétique*. Paris: Aubier.

Major, R. (Ed.) (2003). *Etats généraux de la psychanalyse*. Paris: Aubier.

Nunberg, H., & Federn, E. (Eds.) (1962–1976). *Minutes of the Vienna Psychoanalytical Society 1912–1918*, 4 vols. New York: International Universities Press.

Reik, T. (1957). *Myth and Guilt: the Crime and Punishment of Mankind*. New York: George Braziller.

Roudinesco, E. (1990). *Jacques Lacan and Co. A History of Psychoanalysis in France 1925–1985*. J. Mehlman (Trans.) London: Free Associations.

Roudinesco, E. (1997). *Jacques Lacan: Outline of a Life, History of a System of Thought*. B.Bray (Trans.). New York: Columbia University Press.

Roudinesco, E. (2001). *Why Psychoanalysis?* R. Bowlby (Trans.). New York: Columbia University Press.

Roudinesco, E. (2002a). *La famille en désordre*. Paris: Fayard.

Roudinesco, E. (2002b). Psychoanalysis and homosexuality. *Journal of European Psychoanalysis*, 15.

Roudinesco, E., & Plon, M. (1997). *Dictionnaire de la psychanalyse*. Paris: Fayard.

Schorske, C.(1998). *Thinking with History: Explorations in the Passage to Modernism*. Princeton University Press.

Valladares Montechi, L. (2001). La psychanalyse au Brésil et à Sao Paulo. Unpublished Doctoral Thesis in the department of history of University Paris VII.

Vezzetti, U. (1996). *Aventuras de Freud en el pais de los Argentinos*. Buenos Aires: Paidos.

CHAPTER ELEVEN

Knowledge in failure:

On the crises of legitimacy within Lacanian psychoanalysis

Dany Nobus

Introduction

From its inception during the early 1950s until the present day, Lacanian psychoanalysis has triggered numerous debates pertaining to its theoretical and clinical legitimacy. These debates have been entertained by non-Lacanian psychoanalysts, non-psychoanalytic adversaries and Lacanians alike. This chapter first of all concentrates on Lacan's own re-appropriation of Freud, in the aftermath of the first schism within the French psychoanalytic community. It then focuses on Lacan's inventions of the variable-length session and the pass, and investigates how these procedures have divided generations of psychoanalysts, both within and outside the Lacanian movement. Finally, some suggestions are made for opening a properly Lacanian perspective on the vexed issue of "ownership" in psychoanalysis. It is suggested here that in the discourse of the analyst knowledge is always in failure and that if psychoanalysis is to be owned, the only agency capable of owning it in a perfectly legitimate fashion would be (the unconscious of) the analysand.

Disputed legacies

Of all the different strands of psychoanalysis that developed after Freud, the Lacanian tradition has been most animated, permeated, and devastated by debates concerning theoretical credibility, clinical legitimacy, and intellectual property. These issues presided over the birth of Lacanian psychoanalysis, they continued to affect its institutions until the very end of Lacan's life, and they may very well be responsible one day for the downfall of its entire edifice. Also, much more than within any other psychoanalytic community, the debates pervading Lacanian psychoanalysis have been sustained by three different adversaries, none of whom is very willing to compromise: anti-Lacanian psychoanalysts wanting to protect disciplinary orthodoxy against the infiltration of purportedly metaphysical forces; external (non-psychoanalytic) agencies perceiving the Lacanian "ideology" as the pinnacle of an inherently abusive scheme; and Lacanian psychoanalysts themselves, pitting one interpretation of the master's narrative against the other, in an attempt to preserve the purity of his doctrine, be it as a non-doctrinal type of inquiry. Amongst these detractors, the last have not so much acted as latter-day Jung- or Adler-style intellectual dissidents, since they have generally disputed the legitimacy of the Lacanian party-line for its unfaithfulness to Lacan's own discourse, not disagreeing with one or the other of Lacan's radical principles but exposing the low Lacan-content of a certain type of Lacanianism.

Within this quagmire of stakes, interests, parties, and stakeholders, the Anglo-American reader is probably most familiar with the acrimonious argument that prompted Lacan to present himself, during the early 1950s, as the figurehead of a maverick group of French psychoanalysts. This conflict, which has been documented in many a primer of Lacanian psychoanalysis, ignited the first schism within the French psychoanalytic world, signalled Lacan's historical departure from the psychoanalytic mainstream, and features most conspicuously in Lacan's own writings. Subsequently, Lacan proposed his famous "return to Freud" as an alternative to the reigning doctrinal tendencies of ego-psychology and, to a lesser extent, object-relations within the International Psychoanalytical Association (IPA). Yet whereas this antagonism generated a new set of loyalties, it did not suffice to maintain the unity of the Lacanian group. As Lacan gained more recognition and admiration as a *maître à penser*, his authority as the self-proclaimed recipient of Freud's legacy came more and more under attack from people who had initially supported him. As ego-psychology disappeared from the Lacanian scene as the psychoanalytic bugbear *par excellence* and Lacan progressively moved from fairly intimate seminars on Freud's texts to large-scale public events promoting his own theory, he himself started to occupy a place of contention for his followers. This eventually led to a series of institutional implosions, crowned by Lacan's unilateral "dissolution" in January 1980 (Lacan, 1987b) of the "Ecole freudienne de Paris", the School he had single-handedly created some fifteen years earlier (Lacan, 1987a).

Since Lacan's demise, in September 1981, the newly established "Freudian Field" (*Le Champ freudien*) has been in constant turmoil, on the one hand losing valuable strategic parts of its territory, while on the other continuously expanding its realm of influence beyond the geographical and linguistic boundaries of its homeland. At an institutional level this has coincided with the eruption, in increasingly rapid succession, of new formal and informal groups devoted to Lacanian psychoanalysis, some of which are strictly controlled in their function as satellite units of the central governing body, whereas others are more devolved and therefore allowed to run a more independent and self-governing course. At an intellectual level, the tumultuous existence of the "Freudian Field" has coincided with the emergence of new rivalries over the moral ownership of Lacan's intellectual heritage and ardent discussions over the preservation of Lacanian theory as an anti-dogmatic corpus. These conflicts have no doubt been exacerbated by the fact that both the institutional and the intellectual centres of the "Freudian Field" are, if not directed, at least closely monitored by Jacques-Alain Miller, Lacan's son-in-law, who has come to represent for many adversaries the conflation of doctrinal concerns and genealogical authority at the highest level of Lacanian officialdom.

Teasing out the intricacies of this complex dynamics constitutes a huge task, which I have refused to set myself for this chapter. Interested parties will be able to bite off more than they can chew from two exceedingly detailed, if sometimes slightly overwritten books by Roudinesco (1990, 1997) and an absorbing study by Turkle

(1992), not to mention the numerous critical accounts of the situational variables that are available in French. Instead, I have decided to restrict myself to a brief sketch of how the issue of "ownership" has affected Lacan's trajectory, in its theoretical, technico-clinical, and institutional ramifications, and how it divides the Lacanian community even in the present day. In the first section of my chapter, I outline how Lacan himself endeavoured to re-own Freud's discourse, and how his intellectual parentage influenced the conception and development of the "French Freud" (Dufresne, 1997). Following on from this, I concentrate on Lacan's most controversial contributions to psychoanalytic theory and practice, and how some of these ideas have managed to antagonize generations of psychoanalysts, including those trained by Lacan himself. In the final section, I attempt to present the gist of ongoing discussions over the ownership of Lacan's assets, including the vexed question of the transcription of his seminars, the publication and translation of his writings, the correct implementation of his training principles, and the general dissemination of his ideas. Simultaneously, I try to open a critical perspective on what a Lacanian interpretation of "ownership" in psychoanalysis might entail.

Re-appropriating Freud

In a famous quote from his 1953 "Rome discourse", a text which may be regarded simultaneously as the intellectual bedrock, the organizational mission statement, and the political manifesto of Lacanianism, Lacan justified his polemical intervention in the field of psychoanalysis as follows:

> In any case, I consider it to be an urgent task to isolate, in concepts that are being deadened by routine use, the meaning they recover when we re-examine their history and reflect on their subjective foundations. That, no doubt, is the teacher's function—the function on which all the others depend—and the one in which the value of experience figures best. If this function is neglected, the meaning of an action whose effects derive solely from meaning is obliterated, and the rules of analytic technique, being reduced to mere recipes, rob analytic experience of any status as knowledge [*connaissance*] and even of any criterion of reality. [Lacan, 2002a, p. 34]

Like so many of Lacan's statements, this proposition probably requires some clarification, if only because of the characteristically elliptic and allusive style in which it is couched.[1] The "concepts" Lacan is referring to here are, of course, those employed by Freud when he explained the mechanisms of the human mind and the clinical process of psychoanalysis. According to Lacan, these concepts and, by extension, Freud's entire theory, had completely lost their cutting edge—the French refers to "notions qui s'amortis-sent", which literally means a "softening" or "blunting" of notions —through the uprooted fashion in which they were being applied and transmitted within the psychoanalytic training institutions. Lacan even went so far as to accuse his colleagues of no longer being interested in Freud's works and preferring, for instance, Marie Bonaparte's watered-down manual on the theory of the drives (1934) over the founder's original contributions to sexual-ity—similar to how undergraduate students would these days acquire knowledge of their discipline via a series of textbooks rather than via the study of primary source materials (Lacan, 2002a, p. 40). The inevitable upshot, Lacan argued, was a symptomatic de-Freudianization of psychoanalysis, somehow in need of analysis itself (Lacan, 1988a, p. 24; 2002a, p. 36). Lacan's proposed solution to the conceptual deadlock thus entailed the implementation of the very principles Freud had adduced as the defining characteristics of the psychoanalytic treatment: an in-depth investigation of the historical origins of the materials at hand and a profound reflection upon their subjective significance.

The main difference between this "analysis of analysis" and the traditional, clinical application of analytic principles lay in the posi-tion Lacan reserved for its initiator, in this case himself. Only by adopting the position of a teacher, and therefore not as an analyst, would the analyst be capable of overcoming the stalemate of the analytic discourse. Yet when Lacan subsequently commenced his public seminars at Sainte-Anne Hospital in Paris, he remained quite careful not to identify with the omniscient professors and intellec-tual guides, whose unassailable knowledge had contributed to the disappearance of the spirit of discovery within contemporary psychoanalysis. As a teacher, Lacan preferred the auspices of the Zen-master, who "conducts his search for meaning" without teach-ing "ex cathedra a ready made science", and who "supplies an answer when the students are on the verge of finding it", thus exemplifying the "refusal of any system" and favouring the revelation of "a thought in motion" (Lacan 1988a, p. 1). And indeed, Lacan's so-called "early seminars" were perfect illustrations of interactive, learner-orientated instruction, geared towards uncovering the elusive meaning of Freud's texts. In the presence of a small group of enthusiastic seekers, Lacan would often formulate more questions than answers, continuously prompting his audience to read, work, and present their way through the conceptual maze of Freud's papers, and testing the results of this procedure against the hallowed interpretations of the same ideas. True to his own motto, Lacan also regularly referred to the original, German version of Freud's texts, sometimes inviting selected participants of the seminar to flesh out the nitty-gritty details of one entire document, as in the case of the renowned Hegel-scholar and translator Jean Hyppolite, who was charged with the task of commenting on Freud's notoriously difficult paper "Negation" (Freud, 1925h; Lacan, 1966a, 1966b, 1988a, pp. 289–297).

With hindsight, Lacan's strategy was unique, exciting, and clever. It was unique because the format of weekly, small-scale interactive lectures on a sharply delineated set of texts was virtually unheard of within the existing psychoanalytic training institutions. When reading the transcriptions of these seminars one is involuntarily reminded of the atmosphere surrounding a group of conscientious students discussing a "great book" in a far-away corner of an academic library. There is no doubt that Lacan stood out as the focal point of intellectual convergence, yet it is equally indubitable that the participants felt capable and confident enough to push forward, to extrapolate and sometimes to challenge his ideas. One could compare Lacan's early seminars to a jazz-workshop in which the leader brings together a group of trusted sidemen, known for their technical skills, their ability to empathize and their improvisational talents, in order to extract a new creative piece of music from a long established melody. Lacan may have based this format on what he himself had experienced during the 1930s at Kojève's seminar on Hegel (Kojève, 1969), which would also explain why he decided to give absolute priority to the *reading* of Freud. In any case, the seminars at Sainte-Anne Hospital bore more resemblance to a scientific laboratory in which young researchers are on a quest for a new formula than to an academic lecture theatre in which students quietly assimilate grand narratives of solid knowledge. In trying to rescue Freud's spirit of discovery from the clutches of his contemporaries, Lacan definitely managed to create surroundings in which people could also breathe this same spirit.

For precisely these reasons, perhaps, Lacan's early seminars were also incredibly exciting, although one should not discount the importance of the transference towards Lacan, especially amongst the younger generation. In a barely concealed moment of nostalgia, Wladimir Granoff, one of the most active figures during the first ten years of Lacan's teaching, captured the events by saying:

> One day the historian will be faced with the task of explaining why Lacan's teaching, notably during this introductory phase, was received with so much enthusiasm. No doubt it is partly to do with fortunate circumstances concerning the quality of the first epigones. . . . I nonetheless believe that the essence was elsewhere. On the side of the joy of revenge. It is a common observation that school results and the taste for study improve amongst students who were previously described as bad when a person who is heavily invested with transference condemns the masters, the manuals and the taught materials. From the start of the game, Lacan told us that we were being taught stupid things and that those who taught us were fools. I still believe he had a point. [Granoff, 1986, p. 38]

For the record, and drawing on my own experience as a teacher, I should add that Granoff's enthusiastic commitment may also have been sustained by the way in which Lacan was able to handle the transference within the classroom, refusing to employ it as a lever for driving home distinct units of knowledge, but letting it run as the silent engine of a mutual influencing process. In other words, apart from their being taught less stupid things, the students' interest may also have been stimulated by the fact that Lacan modified the process of teaching itself, so that participants felt less objectified and infantilized.

Above all, Lacan's early seminars were exceedingly clever. Here was a dyed-in-the-wool, charismatic analyst who did not so much define his position *per via di porre*, by adding lots of new things to the established canon of ideas, but *per via di levare*, by taking away the dirt that had settled over the Freudian constructions in the unfriendly climate of the psychoanalytic institutions, in order to let it shine again in all its naked glory. Thus, paradoxically, Lacan became an innovator less by presenting something entirely new, but more by recovering the old and forgotten, that is to say, by resuscitating discarded fragments of the past, more specifically the precise significance of Freud's original insights. This was the overarching objective of what came to be designated as "the return to Freud" or, as Lacan himself put it in a famous line from the mid-1950s: "The meaning of a return to Freud is a return to Freud's meaning" (Lacan, 2002b, p. 110).

To justify the necessity of such a project, Lacan had to show that the psychoanalytic establishment had completely mis-appropriated Freud's corpus. He had to prove that the existing versions of Freud were erroneous, misguided, and potentially destructive for the future of psychoanalysis. During the early 1950s, Lacan carried out this critique of psychoanalysis—in the name and for the sake of Freud—on at least four different levels. Textually, he pointed out that Freud's works had filtered through the French psychoanalytic community in appalling translations, which sometimes failed to convey important nuances in Freud's writing, and quite often also rendered his words in phrases carrying completely different meanings (Lacan, 1988a, pp. 38–51). At a theoretical level, Lacan argued that the reigning psychoanalytic doctrine tended to look at Freud's entire oeuvre from the perspective of the so-called "second topography", i.e., the threefold distinction between the Ego, the Id, and the Superego, thus promoting one particular model to the highest ranks of conceptual achievement, at the expense of numerous other structural distinctions (Lacan, 1988b, pp. 11–12). In terms of clinical practice, Lacan scorned contemporary psychoanalysts for transforming Freud's flexible recommendations on how to conduct the treatment into a formalistic set of simplistic and rigid algorithms that discourages the analyst from taking initiative (Lacan, 2002a, p. 33) and that potentially turns the entire experience into a professionally conducted obsessional neurosis (*ibid.*, pp. 37–38). Beyond these technical issues, Lacan also exposed the accepted goals of analysis within the various post-Freudian schools as non-psychoanalytic deviations: the ego-psychological aim to re-adapt the patient to external reality reduces psychoanalysis to behavioural engineering; modelling to the patient an image of a strong, mature personality in view of her becoming an active, competent citizen drives psychoanalysis into the realm of social re-education; restoring the patient's genital object-relations in order to induce the degree of sexual normalization necessary for the appearance of a solid character structure infects psychoanalysis with spurious moralistic ideals (*ibid.*, pp. 35–40). Finally, at an institutional level, Lacan reacted against the authoritarian principles presiding over the existing psychoanalytic training institutes, on the one hand through the maintenance of strict hierarchical distinctions between training analysts, "simple" analysts, and analytic trainees, and on the other through the way in which they organized and dispensed clinical experience. In a bitterly sarcastic comment he posited that the predominant conception of analytic training was "like that of a driving school which, not content to claim the unique privilege of issuing drivers' licenses, also imagines that it is in a position to supervise car construction" (*ibid.*, p. 34).

During the 1950s, all of this contributed to the conception and development of the so-called "French Freud", as distinct from the Anglo-American Freud, although the "French" incarnation remained less confined to its geographical boundaries than the "Anglo-American" avatar. Indeed, Lacan was not so much struggling with enemies on the other side of the Atlantic, but with "Americanized" psychoanalysts at home and around Europe. The "French Freud", who is much more conflict-ridden, restless, and dialectical than its counterpart, is therefore not even typically French, since the majority of the French psychoanalysts, at least during the 1950s, "owned" the Anglo-American Freud. It was only after Lacan's progressive "disowning" of the psychoanalytic establishment, and his concurrent re-appropriation of the "original Freud" that the "French Freud" started to spread across Europe. For many of Lacan's followers this "French Freud" would have been "Lacan's Freud", since they would have been eager to emphasize the idiographic factor over national identity. For Lacan himself, however, the Freud he succeeded in disseminating would have been neither French nor Lacanian, but simply "Freudian".

Lacan's assets

This complex dynamics of re-appropriation, which eventually gave rise to a genuine cult of Lacanianism, did not trigger the institutional schism within the French psychoanalytic community that I mentioned in my introduction. It is not Lacan's vituperative dismissal of his contemporaries' ideas, their shared conception of psychoanalytic theory and practice, and their proposed organization of psychoanalytic training, which elicited the earthquakes that divided the French psychoanalytic landscape, neither the first time (in 1953) nor the second time (in 1963). Indeed, it was exactly the other way round, Lacan's "return to Freud" emanating from and consolidating itself through the institutional split. Lacan's re-invention of Freud thus occurred on the ruins of an institutional collapse, instead of the institution collapsing in the aftermath of Lacan's project.

At the same time, Lacan did play a major part in the institutional conflict, not in the least because the crisis revolved mainly around the clinical legitimacy of one of his technical assets: the infamous principle of the "variable-length session" (Eissler, 1954). This contentious principle, which allows the psychoanalyst to interrupt the session at will and therefore also, for instance, after five or ten minutes, contravened the rule of the fifty-minute hour within the IPA and was regarded by its representatives as a dangerous deviation from the norm—abusive when applied in the treatment of regular patients and unethical when utilized within the context of a training analysis. Whatever else they may have (dis)liked about Lacan's uncompromising character, the leading figures within the French psychoanalytic society were consequently concerned about the clinical authority that he granted himself by manipulating the temporal structure of the treatment and, even more seriously, about the possible ineffectiveness of the training analyses which he was conducting. The latter issue was considered more pressing because training analyses had always been more strictly regulated than "regular" analyses, and any failure to comply with these regulations on the side of the training analyst could have resulted in trainees being badly trained and subsequently practising as insufficiently trained ("wild") psychoanalysts. The possibility of patients being mistreated by these psychoanalysts could not only have posed a problem, then, for the legitimacy (and the survival) of the psychoanalytic training institution, but also for the assurance of public health. Also, if the IPA refused to ratify Lacan's practice of variable-length sessions, those trainees who had been allocated to him for their training analysis would never have been able to become members of the Association, unless they started all over again with a different training analyst.

Aggravated by personal rivalries and exacerbated by Lacan's ostensible intransigence, discussions over the principle (and associated institutional matters) reached a breaking point in June 1953, when Lacan was forced to resign as president of the French psychoanalytic society and a dissident psychoanalytic group was created, uniting Lacan, a handful of loyal colleagues, and a substantial number of trainees (Miller, 1976, p. 11). Throughout the 1950s and, indeed, throughout his entire career, Lacan refused to budge on the vexed question of the variable-length sessions, which, especially during the later years of Lacan's life, when his clinical practice expanded as exponentially as the audience attending his seminars, often developed into "short sessions". Reflecting upon his analysis with Lacan, the American scholar Stuart Schneiderman recalled:

> Short sessions usually lasted only a few minutes. Their time was the time of a dream, the few minutes of sleep eked out before the inevitable awakening of the real; Lacan called it an exemplary instance of the real. [Schneiderman, 1983, p. 132]

Schneiderman's testimony of the short session tallies with that given by other analysands of Lacan (Godin, 1990; Haddad, 2002; Rey, 1989), so that one must not jump to the conclusion that Lacan may simply have been challenging analytically the popular American belief that "time is money".

Quite remarkably, perhaps, in none of these patient accounts does it transpire that the short session was a form of "cheap" clinical charlatanism, practised by Lacan with the sole purpose of self-enrichment. And although some of these testimonies were produced by people who later committed themselves to the Lacanian cause, and are therefore everything but neutral, others included in Roudinesco's volume on the history of psychoanalysis in France (Roudinesco, 1990) strike the same tone of respect. Hence, if the psychoanalytic officials brandished Lacan's technique as a totally unacceptable instance of malpractice, his analysands seemed to accept it quite easily as an appropriate analytic intervention, sometimes retroactively saturating the act with Lacanian meaning. In Schneiderman's recollection, for instance, the short session had a clear relationship to the experience of death:

> The gesture of breaking the session, of cutting it off, was a way of telling people to put things on the side, to move forward, not to get stuck or fascinated by the aesthetics of the dream . . . There was something of the horror of death in the short sessions, in these psychoanalytic sessions whose time could not be known in advance, whose time was not counted by the ticks of the clock . . . The combined pressure of the shortness of the sessions and the unpredictability of their stops creates a condition that greatly enhances one's tendencies to free-associate . . . Almost by definition the ego cannot be the master of the short session. [Schneiderman, 1983, pp. 133–134]

Lacan's own theoretical justification for the "variable-length session" was much more prosaic: the analyst who manipulates the time of the session operates with a supplementary, non-verbal tool of interpretation, since patients will experience the interruption as a punctuation of their discourse (Lacan, 2002a, p. 44). These temporal scansions, Lacan continued, may also facilitate productive "moments of concluding" in the analysand, and reduce the negative effects of protracted attempts at enhanced self-understanding (*ibid.*, p. 48).

As I mentioned previously, Lacan never compromised on the legitimacy of this technique, yet it proved to be an insurmountable problem for the IPA.[2] After separating from the French psychoanalytic society, the renegade group of psychoanalysts attempted to re-affiliate with the official professional body, which also proves somehow that Lacan did not completely repudiate the latter's hegemonic status (Etchegoyen & Miller, 1996, pp. 48–49). The investigative committees took ten years to make up their mind, yet they eventually concluded that the "French situation" was really a "Lacan-problem" and so they proposed that the group could be re-adopted on the condition that Lacan be excluded from his position as a teacher and training analyst (Miller, 1977, pp. 41–45). On the evening of 19 November 1963, a majority voted in favour of re-affiliating and accepted the condition, which left Lacan being betrayed by his former allies, stripped of his teaching responsibilities, and "excommunicated", as he later called it, from psychoanalytic officialdom (Lacan, 1994, pp. 1–13). Not for long though, for within the space of a couple of months, Lacan found a new niche for his seminar—thanks to the support of Louis Althusser and Claude Lévi-Strauss—and a new, larger, younger, and more devoted audience, who were less interested in the "return to Freud" and more hungry for innovative critical knowledge. Opening up to this new generation of followers, and professing his allegiance to the fashionable doctrine of structuralism, Lacan's seminar at once changed dramatically from an intimate reading group to a massive intellectual performance with little or no audience participation.

In June 1964, Lacan proceeded to the creation of his own professional organization, the "Ecole freudienne de Paris", which set out with the overtly political aim of reconquering Freud's invention by denouncing "the deviations and compromises that blunt its progress" (Lacan, 1987a, p. 97). Yet rather than re-claiming, once again, the spirit of discovery in psychoanalysis through the reading and interpretation of Freud's texts, Lacan did not suggest a "second return to Freud". Instead he launched an alternative constitution for the management of a psychoanalytic organization, a new set of institutional categories that avoid the classic distinctions between "training analysis", "therapeutic analysis", "training-analyst", "trainee", and a radical set of formal procedures for assessing the effects of training (Lacan, 1995). The most controversial amongst these procedures, for non-Lacanians and Lacanians alike, proved to be the procedure of the pass (Lacan, 2001), which demands that all members of the school who want to apply for recognition as Analyst of the School talk about their analysis to three other analysands (the so-called "passers"), who then convey each individually to a jury (the so-called "cartel of the pass") what they have heard, after which the jury decides whether the candidate has "passed" or not. Less than five years after Lacan's creation of his own school, the pass constituted a thorn in the eye of many a member, some of whom at one point decided to leave the school and form their own organization, thus becoming "Lacanians without Lacan" (Castoriadis-Aulagnier, Perrier, & Valabrega, 1970).

In theory, the structures and procedures Lacan invented for the "Ecole freudienne de Paris" were designed as democratic alternatives to the rigid hierarchical stratification of the "old" institutions. The school was meant to be open to anyone interested in the pursuit of its objectives. Nobody was forced to be in analysis, much less to practise psychoanalysis in order to contribute to its activities. Wanting to train as a psychoanalyst required doing a psychoanalysis oneself, which did not differ from the psychoanalysis someone would start for purely clinical reasons. Applying for recognition by the school entailed an indirect judgment based on an evaluation of what someone was able to transmit about his analysis to people who were fellow-travellers along the psychoanalytic route, and therefore not in a position of authority. Rather than judging someone's capacity on the basis of academic qualifications, professional diplomas or general character, the school only listened to the nature of personal psychoanalytic experience. Lacan expressed the latter principle with the famous formula "The psychoanalyst derives his authorisation only from himself" (Lacan, 1995, p. 1), which has been misunderstood by many as a rejection of any type of professional regulation and a recipe for the proliferation of fraudulent practices. However, what Lacan tried to achieve here was an institutional framework in which psychoanalysis would flourish on the basis of social and professional equality, no member being by definition superior in terms of knowledge and power than any other member, and in which only one's personal psychoanalytic experience would condition access to the psychoanalytic profession.

In practice, the system proved to be a hotbed for narcissistic aspirations, pseudo-paranoid suspicions and acerbic rivalries. And despite thirty-five years of intense debate among Lacanians, a cornucopia of dissensions, and a plethora of new institutional initiatives, these issues continue to devastate the Lacanian community until this very day—more than two decades after Lacan dissolved his school and a new one was created under the leadership of Jacques-Alain Miller. For members of the "Ecole freudienne de Paris" and its successor, the "Ecole de la Cause freudienne", the pass somehow failed to live up to its promises because it gradually acquired new status as the ultimate litmus-test of (Lacanian) "analicity", whose outcome could literally constitute a matter of life and death—in March 1977, Juliette Labin, a younger member of the

"Ecole freudienne de Paris" committed suicide after failing to "pass" the procedure of the pass.

Ever since Jacques-Alain Miller "inherited" Lacan's legacy, the pass has elicited animosity and resentment, predominantly within the ranks of the Lacanian community itself, yet from time to time also externally, from representatives of non-Lacanian institutions. Among Lacanians it has given birth to suspicions that the vagueness of the criteria on the basis of which a candidate is accepted (or rejected)—a filtered narrative of psychoanalytic experience—is an excellent strategy for surreptitiously reinforcing analytic authority. Quite often, both the passers and the "cartel of the pass" would know who the candidate's analyst is, so that the outcome of the pass would inevitably contain a judgment on the quality of the analyst. Given the fact that Analysts of the School are subsequently required to talk about their experience to a large forum, their analyst would then also be able to benefit, narcissistically if not financially, from the public exposure of his clinical achievements. In other words, the analyst of a successful candidate would invariably be regarded as an accomplished practitioner, and the other way round. If the analyst behind the candidate occupies, whether voluntarily or not, a position of authority within the school, the procedure of the pass can also be manipulated purely out of respect for the analyst, or the latter can throw the procedure into doubt whenever its outcome is unfavourable for "his" candidate. Precisely such a suspicion of institutional foul play, amongst numerous other allegations of misuse of authority, triggered a massive crisis in the Lacanian community during the late 1990s, eventually leading to the dissension of literally hundreds of analysts across the globe from Miller's "World Association of Psychoanalysis" (Soler et al., 2000).

More recently, Lacanian training procedures have also come under renewed attack from representatives of the IPA. In June 2001, Gilbert Diatkine, a member of the "Sociéte Psychanalytique de Paris" (SPP)—the oldest French psychoanalytic society and one of the two groups currently affiliated to the IPA—published a paper in which he claimed that the Lacanian principle according to which the psychoanalyst only derives authorization from himself does not offer sufficient guarantees for protecting the public against "wild" practitioners (Diatkine, 2001). As such, the accusation is everything but new—indeed, Diatkine himself had already voiced similar concerns in a small book on Lacan (Diatkine, 1997, pp. 97–101)—yet when the editor of the SPP's journal decided not to publish Jacques-Alain Miller's reply to the allegations, the latter embarked on a large-scale public campaign explaining the stakes of the debate and attempting to re-unite the numerous Lacanian factions against the new enemy (Miller, 2002). Paraphrasing the French satirical magazine *Le canard enchaîné*, which at one point dubbed Miller "Divan the Terrible", one may ask why a relatively minor incident should cause such a huge storm. Miller himself has not ceased underscoring the non-negotiable value of the "right to response", yet from time to time he has also indicated that Diatkine's dismissive account of Lacanian training practices appeared at a rather unfortunate moment in French politics, when the government was moving towards a new regulatory system for the psychotherapeutic professions. What proves to be at stake, therefore, is much more than the "right to response" but the demonstration of clinical legitimacy *vis-à-vis* governmental regulatory bodies.

The delicate issue of the state regulation of psychotherapeutic practice, including psychoanalysis, has been on the European political agenda for many years and has intermittently stirred the psychoanalytic community since the mid 1980s. It was mainly in response to imminent legal initiatives across Europe that, in December 1989, Serge Leclaire, one of Lacan's earliest associates and a key player on the French psychoanalytic scene, suggested the creation of an "ordinal agency of psychoanalysts", to which the government could delegate the juridical, financial, and social control of the psychoanalytic profession, similar to medical practice (Leclaire, 1996). Leclaire's proposal met with strong resistance from various psychoanalytic groupings and was therefore never implemented. In response to the question as to why the "Ecole de la Cause freudienne" refused to endorse Leclaire's idea, Jacques-Alain Miller said:

> The IPA does not want to hear about it because it thinks that it is an Order in itself. The small groups of the Lacanian nebula [the numerous Lacanian groups existing outside Miller's school] don't want it because they know that they are not very presentable . . . The members of the Ecole de la Cause freudienne don't want it

because for essential reasons they are committed to the "pass" even when its practice has effectively not always been perfect. [Miller 1990, p. 28]

It should not come as a surprise, then, that Diatkine's critical reading of the most cherished instrument for the verification of analytic training within Miller's school, as a "not very presentable" procedure which potentially puts the public's health at risk, is perceived by Miller as an extremely damaging attack, requiring swift retaliation. Nor should it come as a surprise that Miller has taken the lead in the most recent debate over the state regulation of the psycho-business which, as am I writing, looks as if it might put an end to psychoanalytic organizations implementing their own training procedures. On 14 October 2003, the French National Assembly voted unanimously in favour of an amendment (the so-called Accoyer amendment, after the person who promoted it) that gives the Health Secretary the right, by state decree, to define which types of psychotherapy are legally sanctioned and under what conditions its practitioners are entitled to exercise their practice. Which concrete measures this amendment will entail remains to be seen, yet Miller has not hesitated to point out that it was passed without any form of public debate and without any consideration of the possibility of dealing with the existing risks to public health in a different way (Miller, 2003), whatever that may be. The story continues . . .

Conclusion: seeking or believing?

Historically, Lacanian psychoanalysis started as a separate movement with a vehement dispute over the clinical legitimacy of Lacan's technical principle of the variable-length sessions, which defied the golden rule of the fifty-minute hour. Apart from justifying this principle theoretically with reference to psychoanalytically appropriate tactics of interpretation, Lacan subsequently disowned his adversaries from the moral right to situate themselves within the theoretical and clinical tradition of Freudian orthodoxy. Arguing in favour of a "return to Freud", he constructed an architectural wonder of ideas, erected on solid Freudian foundations, and built with the same spirit of discovery that had animated the founder throughout his career. With the introduction of the variable-length sessions, Lacan, of course, favoured a technical principle that had not featured as such within Freud's original discourse, and this lack of Freudian justification no doubt contributed to his being perceived as deviating dangerously from a central aspect of psychoanalytic practice. Yet, as is the case with so many of his "innovations", including his famous marriage of psychoanalysis and Saussurean linguistics (Nobus, 2003), Lacan would retroactively situate it back firmly within the intellectual scope of Freud's invention, adding that Freud had never really emphasized either that a psychoanalytic session should always last fifty minutes.

Lacan's theoretical and clinical re-appropriation of Freud's discourse has always constituted a source of rivalry between Lacanians and non-Lacanians, especially representatives of the IPA. The same is true for Lacan's institutional initiatives—the creation of his own school, the implantation of a department for psychoanalysis at the university, the opening of a "clinical section" (Lacan, 1977)—and for the associated procedures regularising psychoanalytic training (the pass), yet these initiatives have also induced sharp divisions within the Lacanian community itself. Indeed, it is for institutional reasons (rather than for theoretical and/or clinical motives) that the first split occurred within the Lacanian community, and for institutional reasons that many dissensions followed.

After Lacan's death, the Lacanian community has also been troubled by ongoing discussions over the legitimate ownership of Lacan's discourse—the transcription of the twenty-eight volumes of his seminars and the copyright over his written texts—prompting Jacques-Alain Miller to undertake legal proceedings during the mid 1980s, which resulted in his being assigned the sole right to transcribe, edit, and publish the seminars (Miller, 1985). This ruling, however, has not stopped people from producing "pirate versions" of the seminars and "privately printed, not for resale" volumes of Lacaniana, nor has it encouraged Miller himself to take legal action against "non-official" documents made available in French bookshops and over the Internet. Most recently, Miller has also indicated that he would be happy to tolerate different versions of Lacan's seminars, alongside the "official" Miller transcription (Miller, 2002, pp. 167–169). Although many critics of the Miller version of the seminars have focused on his distortion of the original (Ecole lacanienne de psychanalyse, 1991), despite the fact that Lacan himself fully endorsed his pupil's work (Lacan, 1973), the complicating factor, of course, is Miller's family ties to Lacan, which have put him in a position of intellectual, legal, and genealogical authority.

This position of unassailable authority, attributed to, if not adopted by, the leader and somehow initiated by Lacan himself during the 1960s, is for some psychoanalysts the reason why the Lacanian community has changed so radically since the early 1950s. Originally, during the good old days, Lacan's seminars were attended by seekers rather than believers. Much like the early Christian movement, the Lacanian setting was originally characterized by diversity, multiformity, and an intense desire to innovate. Gradually, diversity was replaced by a demand for conformity, formulated by a group of apostles-cum-church fathers, which has led, in a Bakhtinian sense, to the disappearance of open debate and discussion and the emergence of dogmatism. Discursive activity and dialogic exchange gave way to the reciting of dogma, dictated by the masters. In Lacanian psychoanalysis, so it is often heard, there are also intellectual guides that do not possess guiding lights, but simply a strong desire to be recognized by the master; there are spiritual teachers who lack the ability to teach; there are prophets who do not even believe in themselves. And there are also heretics who refuse to recite the creed, and who are therefore persecuted, expelled, and annihilated. Whatever the truth of these assertions may be, the religious metaphors, here, are quite inappropriate. Whereas a church, or a sect for that matter, generally welcomes new members but makes it extremely difficult and sometimes impossible for them to leave, anyone who has ever tried to become part of the Lacanian community will have had exactly the opposite experience: it is fairly easy to get out of it, but excruciatingly difficult to get into.

Echoing Derrida in a memorable reflection upon his encounters with Lacan, one is tempted to exclaim: "What wouldn't Lacan have said!" (Derrida, 1998, p. 39) What wouldn't a properly Lacanian, psychoanalytic outlook have been! Isn't psychoanalysis, the discourse of the analyst, a discourse in perpetual crisis precisely because it contravenes "ownership" as such? Doesn't every attempt at "owning" it (its concepts, practice, history) fail to do justice to one of its essential principles, i.e., that its knowledge (from which its practice emanates) is in a state of continuous dispossession? If psychoanalytic knowledge is by definition a knowledge in failure, isn't the crisis of legitimacy a necessary precondition, then, for the discourse of the analyst to sustain itself? Perhaps the only agency that could ever be in the position of owning psychoanalysis is the (unconscious of the) analysand, the Other of psychoanalytic discourse, who tests, directs, evaluates and (without any conscious knowledge whatsoever), advances psychoanalytic knowledge. The analyst may direct the treatment, but it is the patient who paradoxically guides the applicability of psychoanalytic principles.

As one becomes more attuned to the meanderings of the legitimacy crises within Lacanian psychoanalysis, one discovers that these crises invariably revolve around issues concerning the relationship between knowledge and truth, the installation and exercise of a particular social bond, the attribution and adoption of roles, functions and positions, and the delivery of a product whose surplus value is optimal, that is to say, neither exceedingly low nor excessively high, for the maintenance of the production process. As Lacan himself suggested, these issues do not merely constitute a central concern for the discourse of the analyst, but feature high on the agenda of other discourses as well (Lacan, 1991). Regardless of the specific distribution of the relationships, the terms and conditions are exactly the same for the discourse of the analyst (analytical practice), the discourse of the master (ruling practice), the discourse of the university (educational practice), and the discourse of the hysteric (help-seeking practice). It is therefore to be expected that many of the instabilities underpinning the legitimacy crises within Lacanian psychoanalysis, other than occupying psychoanalysis as such, are equally at work in the other so-called "impossible professions" (Freud, 1925f, 1937c). Moreover, history has shown that the discourse of the analyst is by no means better equipped to recognize, solve, and prevent the instabilities than the other, non-analytical discourses. The awareness of conflict, as a potentially productive experience, within psychoanalysis, and *a fortiori* within Lacanian psychoanalysis, does not guarantee better strategic plans for dealing with it.

Notes

1. As a matter of fact, the translation, here, already silently reduces some of the semantic ambiguities in the original French version by adding the adjective "analytic" to the terms "technique" and "experience". For some, this in itself might constitute a sufficient reason for saying that after the de-humanisation of Freud's soul at the hands of Strachey (Bettelheim, 1983) the Anglo-Americans now also "own" a more streamlined, less interpretable Lacanian discourse, and rumour has it that this is precisely what Lacan's literary executor perceives as a potential threat in English translations of Lacan's works.

2. Although it did not prevent Lacan's analysands from subsequently climbing the hierarchical ladder within non-Lacanian institutions. Daniel Widlöcher, the current president of the International Psychoanalytical Association, is a former analysand of Lacan's . . .

References

Bettelheim, B. (1983). *Freud and Man's Soul*, New York: Alfred A. Knopf.

Bonaparte, M. (1934). *Introduction à la théorie des instincts*. Paris: Denoël et Steele.

Castoriadis-Aulagnier, P., Perrier, F., & Valabrega, J.-P. (1970). Lettre à l'adresse du Directeur. *Scilicet*, 2(3), 51–52.

Derrida, J. (1998). *Resistances of Psychoanalysis* (P. Kamuf, P.-A. Brault, & M. Naas (Trans.)). Stanford, CA: Stanford University Press.

Diatkine, G. (1997). *Jacques Lacan*, Paris: Presses Universitaires de France.

Diatkine, G. (2001). Les lacanismes, les analystes français et l'Association psychanalytique internationale. In: A. Green (Ed.), *Courants de la psychanalyse contemporaine* (pp. 389–400).Revue française de psychanalyse-numéro hors-série. Paris: Presses Universitaires de France.

Dufresne, T. (1997). (Ed.) *Returns of the "French Freud": Freud, Lacan, and Beyond*, New York &London: Routledge.

Ecole lacanienne de psychanalyse (1991). *Le Transfert dans tous ses errata*. Paris: EPEL.

Eissler, R. S. (Ed.) (1954). 106th bulletin of the International Psycho-Analytical Association, *The International Journal of Psycho-Analysis*, 35(1): 267–290.

Etchegoyen, R. H., & Miller, J.-A. (1996). *Silence brisé. Entretien sur le mouvement psychanalytique*. Paris: Agalma.

Freud, S. (1925f). Preface to Aichhorn's *Wayward Youth*. *S.E.*, *19*: 271–275.

Freud, S. (1925h). Negation. *S.E.*, *19*, 235–239.

Freud, S. (1937c). Analysis terminable and interminable. *S.E.*, 23: 216–253.

Godin, J.-G. (1990). *Jacques Lacan, 5, rue de Lille*. Paris: du Seuil.

Granoff, W. (1986). D'un fétiche en forme d'article. In: M. Augé, M. David-Menard, W. Granoff, Jean-Louis Lang & O. Mannoni (Eds.), *L'object en psychanalyse. Le fétiche, le corps, L'enfant, la science* (pp. 33–49). Paris: Denoël.

Haddad, G. (2002). *Le jour où Lacan m'a adopté*. Paris: Bernard Grasset.

Kojève, A. (1969). *Introduction to the Reading of Hegel*. A. Bloom (Ed.), J. H. Nichols Jr. (Trans.). New York & London: Basic Books.

Lacan, J. (1966a). Introduction au commentaire de Jean Hyppolite sur la "Verneinung" de Freud. In: *Ecrits* (pp. 369–380). Paris: du Seuil.

Lacan, J. (1966b). Réponse au commentaire de Jean Hyppolite sur la "Verneinung" de Freud. In *Ecrits* (pp. 381–399). Paris: du Seuil.

Lacan, J. (1973). Postface. In: *Le Séminaire, Livre XI: Les quatre concepts fondamentaux de la psychanalyse*, texte établi par J.-A. Miller. Paris: du Seuil.

Lacan, J. (1977). Ouverture de la Section clinique. *Ornicar?*, *9*: 7–14.

Lacan, J. (1987a). Founding act (J. Mehlman (Trans.)). *October*, *40*: 96–105.

Lacan, J. (1987b). Letter of dissolution (J. Mehlman, (Trans.)). *October*, *40*: 128–130.

Lacan, J. (1988a). *The Seminar. Book 1: Freud's Papers on Technique*. J.-A. Miller, (Ed.), J. Forrester (Trans. and Notes). Cambridge: Cambridge University Press.

Lacan, J. (1988b). *The Seminar. Book 2: The Ego in Freud's Theory and in the Technique of Psychoanalysis*. J.-A. Miller (Ed.), S. Tomaselli (Trans.), J. Forrester (Notes). Cambridge: Cambridge University Press.

Lacan, J. (1991). *Le Séminaire, Livre XVII: L'envers de la psychanalyse*, texte établi par J.-A. Miller, Paris: du Seuil.

Lacan, J. (1994). *The Four Fundamental Concepts of Psycho-Analysis*. J.-A. Miller (Ed.), A. Sheridan (Trans.). Harmondsworth: Penguin.

Lacan, J. (1995). Proposition of 9 October 1967 on the Psychoanalyst of the School (R. Grigg (Trans.)). *analysis*, *6*: 1–13.

Lacan, J. (2001). Adresse à l'Ecole. In: *Autres Ecrits* (pp. 293–295). Paris: du Seuil.

Lacan, J. (2002a). The function and field of speech and language in psychoanalysis. In: *Ecrits: A Selection* (B. Fink (Trans.)), (pp. 31–106). New York: W.W. Norton.

Lacan, J. (2002b). The Freudian thing, or the meaning of the return to Freud in psychoanalysis. In: *Ecrits: A Selection* (B. Fink (Trans.)), (pp. 107–137). New York: W.W. Norton.

Leclaire, S. (1996). Proposition pour une instance ordinale des psychanalystes. In: *Ecrits pour la psychanalyse, Vol. 1: Demeures de l'ailleurs (1954–1993)* (pp. 327–348). Paris: Arcanes.

Miller, J.-A. (Ed.) (1976). *La scission de 1953. La communauté psychanalytique en France-1*. Paris: Navarin.

Miller, J.-A. (Ed.) (1977). *L'excommunication. La communauté psychanalytique en France-2*. Paris: Navarin.

Miller, J.-A. (1985). *Entretien sur Le Séminaire avec François Ansermet*, Paris: Navarin.

Miller, J.-A. (1990). Entretien sur la cause analytique avec Jacques-Alain Miller. *l'Âne*, 42: 26–30.

Miller, J.-A. (2002). *Lettres à l'opinion éclairée*. Paris: du Seuil.

Miller, J.-A. (2003). Entretien avec Bernard Accoyer et Jacques-Alain Miller, par Jean-Pierre Elkabbach. Radio broadcast, Europe 1, 31 October 2003, 8:30 a.m.

Nobus, D. (2003). Lacan's science of the subject: between linguistics and topology. In: J.-M. Rabaté (Ed.), *The Cambridge Companion to Lacan* (pp. 50–68). Cambridge: Cambridge University Press.

Rey, P. (1989). *Une saison chez Lacan*. Paris: Robert Laffont.

Roudinesco, E. (1990). *Jacques Lacan & Co.: A History of Psychoanalysis in France, 1925–1985* (J. Mehlman (Trans.)). Chicago, IL: University of Chicago Press.

Roudinesco, E. (1997). *Jacques Lacan* (B. Bray (Trans.)). New York: Columbia University Press.

Schneiderman, S. (1983). *Jacques Lacan: The Death of an Intellectual Hero*. Cambridge, MA & London: Harvard University Press.

Soler, C., Soler, L., Adam, J., & Silvestre, D. (2000). *La psychanalyse, pas la pensée unique. Histoire d'une crise singulière*. Paris: Editions du Champ Lacanien.

Turkle, S. (1992). *Psychoanalytic Politics: Jacques Lacan and Freud's French Revolution* (2nd edn). London: Free Association Books.

CHAPTER TWELVE

Who decides who decides?

Michael R. Pokorny

Introduction

I n this chapter I put forward my thinking about the underlying cause of the acrimonious battles that beset psychoanalysis in the UK. My view is that the psychoanalytic enterprise has become confused since the British Psycho-Analytic Society simultaneously adopted two mutually exclusive functions. This has led to splitting and impoverishment, which in turn undermines both functions. The two functions are the academic/educational, and the external political, which includes clinical practice. These two functions are not reconcilable in one locus, whether in a university, a religious movement, or any scientific or professional body. In that sense psychoanalysis is no different from any public enterprise where academic/educational and external political issues can only be managed independently of each other. Examples are given of the destructive effect of trying to combine the two. Only after reintegration has happened can a rational choice be made between the two functions. The choice suggested is to give up the least successful activity, which is the external political, and focus on what can be done well, the academic and educational.

It was not until the final year of medical school, when I sat down to read endless texts in my anxiety to know enough for the examinations, that I also thought about what I wanted to do subsequently. Having decided on psychiatry, I shelved further such thinking and set about starting my career. Once I was on the first rung of the ladder, in the academic department in Sheffield, I stumbled over psychoanalysis, and at once realized that this was for me. This was what I had been unknowingly seeking. Turning my back on offers of senior appointments and a research job, I came to London and enrolled at the Institute of Psychoanalysis.

Having trained, I plunged into full time private practice, and I spent thirty-one years engaged in running a practice and working within the psychotherapy profession. In spite of my career-long commitment and my love of psychoanalysis, I became increasingly disturbed by the internecine warfare that I encountered. After years of puzzlement, anguish, and much hilarity, I finally came to a particular view of what I think is wrong with the psychoanalytic enterprise as practised and fought over in the UK. Very soon after my idea crystallized, I was asked to write a chapter for this book, *Who owns psychoanalysis?*. Before we can even attempt to answer that question, we must ask "Who decides who decides?" Here is where we run into a debilitating struggle which creates the very splitting that it is intended to prevent. Intended consciously, that is. There seems to be a conflict about who should be in charge of psychoanalysis. If we could all agree on who is in charge, we would in effect agree on who decides. Those who are in charge would have the power to make the decisions about psychoanalysis. But here is the key to the problem.

General outline

There are two separate functions that have to be fulfilled in any profession, the academic function including education and the function of practice in the real world of external political choices. If these two functions are put together under one authority, unavoidable conflicts appear, and in time destroy both functions. I think that this is true of all professions, and that it is a basic structural problem. I also think that it is ultimately destructive of that which it is intended to preserve. It is my belief that this is the key to the problems that beset psychoanalysis in the UK, and that the inability to acknowledge the unmanageable conflict of having these two functions located together in the same place is destroying British psychoanalysis.

Universities that train doctors have no jurisdiction over the employment of doctors, and the NHS, which is the greatest employer of doctors, has no jurisdiction over medical schools. This applies equally to nursing, clinical psychology, and so on. Just as law schools have no say in the practice of lawyers. We all know what happens when universities are politicized. When political considerations start to interfere with academic and educational choices, the end result is the disintegration of the entire university. Neither academic nor political functions survive.

The reason for this is that when the two functions are located in one place they inevitably start to interact. Not only are political considerations allowed to creep into academic decision-making, but academic considerations also creep into political decision-making. The best professor is rarely the best leader of an economic entity such as a university. The most successful businessman is seldom the best person to judge academic merit and the advancement that should go with the merit. A recent example of the politicization of a decision that should have been made purely on merit occurred when the European Association of Psychotherapy wanted to start a journal. They advertised for an editor and had several applicants. The choice came down to two well qualified people, one of whom had a job in which the word "Counselling" formed an integral part of the description. It was agreed by those concerned that one could not have a "counsellor" as editor of a psychotherapy journal, even though he was arguably the most highly qualified person in Europe. What shocks me now about that decision is that when I was told the reason why the excellent, but second-best candidate was chosen, I did not question the idea that the reason given was quite acceptable. I failed to notice that what had been done was to make a decision based on external political criteria, even though I was by then well aware that most of what is called counselling in the UK is called psychotherapy in the rest of Europe. The chosen editor has done a good job, but the other was better qualified by a long way. Whether he would have done a better job we will never know, but if this kind of rejection of merit goes on for long, it is not difficult to see how it can undermine the entire enterprise.

Once the two functions start to overlap, they start to corrode each other. The most dangerous part of the process is the inability to see what is happening and separate out the two basic functions. Instead a hidden collusion is formed which disguises the problem by creating a split image in which the two functions become treated as though they are entirely separate, an unacknowledged "Chinese wall". Once the split has formed, it causes strain which leads to exporting the split from the organization. This leads to an agreement that "they" do not understand the problem. This process is most easily seen in organized religions. The spiritual leaders must eschew politics. Political power destroys the spiritual authority of any religious group that wields it. A simple example is the late Archbishop Makarios, who had to decide whether he wished to be the first president of Cyprus, or be the head of the Greek Orthodox Church. He could not be both. Mixing political power with spiritual leadership would not have worked. What is perhaps surprising about that case is that the conflict was recognized by all concerned at the time. Surprising, because a similar conflict is destroying the Anglican Church, and has been recognized only very recently by the new Archbishop of Canterbury, who is reported in the press as wanting to relinquish the political power of seats in the House of Lords. He seems to have recognized the insoluble conundrum posed by being a "Lord Spiritual". Not only does it not work, it undermines the religious function. Why is this?

A specific example

The Church of England is "established", so its leader is chosen for political reasons, as well as spiritual ones. We can assume that the senior bishops are all spiritually competent, even though they have all been chosen by the prime minister. When a vacancy occurs, a committee assesses the needs of the diocese and then an appointments committee puts forward two names to the prime minister of the day to choose one. When it comes to the Archbishopric of Canterbury, the choice is made by a night of prayer when a small group of senior clergy seek guidance to find a new Archbishop.

What happens is that the prime minister of the day tells them who he wants before their night vigil. If they fail to come up with the right name, their possessions are forfeit to the Crown and they may be thrown in prison. This is an old law, but there was a story that a bishop once wrote to the prime minister to say that he could not in all conscience put forward the desired name. Harold Macmillan, it is said, wrote back thanking him for prior notice of his intention to commit the offence, which has a Latin name, with the very clear implication that the penalty would be exacted if he did not toe the line. So of course he did as he was told. As an exercise in spiritual authority it is laughable, but also serious.

Of course the origins of these practices was the wish of a king to have a divorce, which the Pope would not allow. The king formed his own church, of which he was the head. The authority of the iing was firmly established, and remains to this day, although it is exercised by the prime minister.

The problem here is very clear. How can a spiritual leader have any authority when he has been chosen by a secular prime minister, who may not be an Anglican, or even a Christian? The Anglican Church is disintegrating from within, with decreasing congregations and increasing sexual scandals. In my view, the Anglican Church has been prevented from dealing with sexual misdemeanours by the clergy because of the links with temporal political influence. This contamination has the effect of corrupting the processes by which the clergy minister to the congregation. I am sure that the clergy are not corrupt, although some of them may be, but I think that their functioning has been corrupted over many years by the political elements in their lives, in exactly the same way that the choice of European journal editor was corrupted, without any of us noticing at the time. My recommendation is that the Anglicans must get out of the House of Lords as fast as they can.

I was intrigued that within a few days of my writing my first draft for this chapter, it was reported that the Archbishop of Canterbury had come to the same conclusion. I do not know whether his reasoning is the same as mine, although subsequent press reports indicate to me that he is thinking along similar lines. One of his themes is that of renewal with each generation. The Archbishop is saying that each generation of Anglicans must reinterpret the scriptures in their own way, a recipe that is unthinkable in an established church where the head of state is the head of the church. The result is to get stuck with a particular interpretation that has to be made to apply for evermore. Clearly this is not working within the Established Church, and the solution is to become disestablished as quickly as possible. Whether there is still time to rescue the Anglicans from schism and self-destruction remains to be seen. But the matter is one of great urgency for them. I think that exactly the same matter is of great urgency for the psychoanalytical community.

British Psycho-analysis

When we turn to the psycho-analytic scene we find an essentially similar conflict, unrecognized by the participants. Indeed, I have only come to my ideas long after giving up my psycho-political activities, and after much hard thinking. I was very much concerned with the evolution of the problem when I first came to my incompatibility theory, and I think that I was as intrigued by the chronology as by the diagnosis and the prescription.

I have come to the view that what prevents the British Psycho-Analytic Society from developing the psychoanalytic enterprise is its self-imposed inhibition on exploring the boundary between psychoanalysis and psychoanalytic psychotherapy. The inhibition is the consequence of the fact a hidden split exists, which cannot be acknowledged. Just like the established church, they are not able to allow themselves the reality of a continual re-interpretation of what psychoanalysis is. Like the established church, they have become stuck in a particular view of psychoanalysis, that is held in place by what are really external political considerations. Like the estab-lished church they have become paralysed both politically and theoretically. They are still trying to hold on to the idea that the number of sessions a week is in some way a critical factor, long after all the evidence clearly shows that it is not. They are stuck with maintaining a position, no matter how absurd that position may have become.

Writing in the *Journal of the American Psychoanalytic Association*, Otto Kernberg states that the only distinction that he can discern between psychoanalysis and psychoanalytic psychotherapy is the intention of the practitioner. If the intention is to be helpful, that is psychotherapy, if the intention is to find out more, that is psycho-analysis. On that basis Kernberg says that we all do psychotherapy some of the time and psychoanalysis some of the time, thus driving a coach and horses through the political distinction that is said by some to exist between psychoanalysts and psychotherapists.

This article was published whilst Otto Kernberg was president of the International Psychoanalytical Association. It is clear that with this as the yardstick, a sharp distinction between the two activities melts away. Yet the British Psycho-Analytic Society is stuck with keeping the distinction for political reasons. Reasons that I think they do not understand.

Background

Psychoanalysis was brought to the UK by a few pioneers who had read Freud in German and who went to Vienna to be analysed. They were the first in this country to appreciate that what Freud had done was, for the first time, to give meaning to the symptoms of mental disorder. They set up the British Psycho-Analytic Society as a scientific body, and founded the Institute of Psychoanalysis to undertake the training of psychoanalysts. In doing this they captured the psychoanalytic market, and became the arbiters of psychoanalysis in the UK. Later, they came to an arrangement with the International Psychoanalytical Association that only the British Psycho-Analytic Society could decide who could be a psychoanalyst in the UK. So this gives us the first chronological answer to the question "Who decides?". The original founders set themselves up and secured their position; a position that their successors are defending vigorously.

As psychotherapy in the UK developed slowly, the British Psycho-Analytical Society managed to keep its grip on the psychoanalytic title and largely ignored the emergence of humanistic, integrative, behavioural, cognitive, and person-centred psychotherapies. Jacques Lacan having been dismissed from the International Psychoanalytical Association meant that the British Lacanian psychoanalysts could be safely ignored. One could have an interesting debate about why Fairbairn's contribution was so much more highly valued in the UK than Lacan's. That debate would be as much a political as an academic one.

"Rugby" and the UKCP

When the psychotherapy organisations got together in the "Rugby Psychotherapy Conference" and began to create a profession with a boundary, the British Psycho-Analytical Society found themselves in a peculiar difficulty. They were regarded quite openly as the spiritual leaders of psychotherapy in the UK. Unfortunately the British Psycho-Analytical Society could not be content with this status. They did not recognize the paradoxical position that they occupied of also demanding to be the political arbiters of the boundaries of psychotherapy. They were unable to see that they had taken a position that is inherently impossible, and that they were, and are, suffering the consequences. They did not do this just in response to the new organization of the psychotherapy profession, they had edged their way into this position over a good many years. Indeed, it could be said to have started with the agreement that they made with the International Psychoanalytical Association long ago. Their main hidden problem is that inhabiting a paradox made them vulnerable to exploitation, and they have been ruthlessly exploited in a most skilful manner by being seduced into the creation of the British Confederation of Psychotherapists, the BCP.

The British Society imagine that they thought of the BCP and that they have led the creation of it. Nothing could be further from the truth. The split in their own thinking has left them unable to address political issues in a rational way, so that when a senior psychoanalyst told them that they were consorting with their enemies and shunning their friends they were unable to take the message on board. This was around the time that they were edging toward leaving the national psychotherapy organization.

The problem was the wish of the British Society to keep the title Psycho-Analyst to themselves. Only their own members should be recognised as psycho-analysts. At the same time they had to play down the importance of the developments in psychoanalytic psychotherapy that had flowed naturally from the developments in psychoanalysis. In spite of this rather artificial attitude, they also demanded that only they could be the arbiters of the psychoanalytic enterprise, and only they could decide what was kosher and what was not. It is easy to see the difficulty that they got into when it is spelled out like this. Psychoanalytic psychotherapists who had their training analysis with British Society training analysts and their control case supervision with other British Society training analysts, were still not really psychoanalysts, because they were not members of the British Psycho-Analytical Society, but "only" of the British Association of Psychotherapists, or some other equally prestigious training organizations.

This split attitude towards the psychotherapy profession is actually hidden in the British Society, who are not aware that they behave as though they despise the very organizations that are their staunchest supporters. Some years ago a survey showed that about half the work of the members of British Psycho-Analytical Society consists of conducting training analysis and clinical supervision for trainees of the psychotherapy training organizations. So there is a captive market for psychoanalysis, which the British Society continues to exploit while continuing to deny that there is no longer a visible boundary between what their members do and what their psychoanalytic psychotherapy colleagues do. They are largely dependent for their livelihoods on the very psychotherapists whom they are trying to keep in what they regard as their place in the scheme of things. Any organization that tries to manage by controlling its market comes to grief in due course. Controlled markets always fail.

In spite of the overt strategic aim of keeping the title psychoanalyst to themselves, they now find that they are forced to take seriously the claim of the British Association of Psychotherapists, the BAP, to be doing the same work as the psycho-analysts. Having been strongly supported by the BAP in the formation of the British Confederation of Psychotherapists, the British Society now find themselves in serious talks with the BAP leading to recognition of the BAP by the International Psychoanalytical Association, so that then there will be, for the first time, two psychoanalytic institutes in the UK. No doubt the other BCP organizations will follow suit, and the BCP will become an organization of psychoanalytic societies, plus of course the Jungian "Society of Analytical Psychology". This is the exact opposite of the intention of British Psycho-Analytical

Society when they abandoned the UK national psychotherapy organization.

So the way that this has come about is of great interest and importance. It is also an example of the political ineptitude of British Society. In trying to preserve their status they find that they have donated their status piecemeal to adjacent organizations. What is the BCP and how was it formed, and by whom and why? I propose to explain the process partly by chronology, otherwise it gets too jumbled up, and partly by inserting my own suppositions into the story. I hope to be clear about what is factual and what are my inferences.

The (dis)organisation of UK psychotherapy

Long ago the Foster Report advised that psychotherapy should be regulated, and a working party was set up. No agreement was reached, and it all fell into abeyance. Then an MP called Graham Bright got lucky in the ballot for Private Member's Bills and, having had a serious complaint from a constituent, he put forward a Bill to regulate psychotherapy. His Bill fell at second reading, as many such Bills do, just because Parliamentary time ran out. It was not "called" and therefore fell, never to be revived. As all went quiet on the legislative front, the British Association of Counselling invited as many psychotherapy organizations as they could find to a Conference at their headquarters in Rugby. Thus, the Rugby Conferences began, and flourished, and led to the formation of the UK Standing Conference of Psychotherapy and in turn that became the UK Council for Psychotherapy, the UKCP, which publishes a National Register of Psychotherapists. I was sent to the second Rugby Conference as a delegate by the Lincoln Clinic. Being pushed on to the working party for the third conference, I was asked to chair the working party when it met to start planning the third Rugby Psychotherapy Conference. I continued to chair the working party and the Rugby Conferences, and was the chair of the Standing Conference. When the UK Council for Psychotherapy was formed, I became chair of the Registration Board, with the task of making the first national register. After four years I retired and began to recoup my private life. I have to say that it had been a very exciting period in my life. It took over every minute. We spoke of almost nothing else at home. I used to say that we, my wife and I, were working thirty-six hours a day eight days a week. That was what it felt like. And it was by no means plain sailing, there were decisions to make all the time, which would have echoes and reverberations over future possibilities and decisions. So it felt risky, and that was part of the excitement. We were doing what had never been done before, and what many thought was impossible. In my speech to the delegates when we formed the Standing Conference, I said that I wished that I had a shilling for every time someone had said to me " You will never get that lot to agree to anything". One of the surprises all along was how sensible the delegates turned out to be.

Jubilant though we were, we also managed to upset the existing order, and in particular, we created serious discomfort for the Tavistock Clinic. After many years of struggle, they had become recognized by the Department of Health as the post-graduate training institute for psychotherapy and had obtained ring-fenced funding to enable them to continue training National Health Service (NHS) psychotherapy practitioners. Just as they were poised to be the arbiters of psychotherapy nationally, they found themselves dealing with the new national psychotherapy organization, the boundaries of which were not exactly to their liking. Before they could blink twice over their new-found status, they were being usurped by this hybrid newcomer, of dubious parentage. The idea that the profession itself would regulate psychotherapy did not go down at all well, so resort was had to other means.

The British Confederation of Psychotherapists

The Tavistock Clinic was central to the plans to create the British Confederation of Psychotherapists, and the first few drafts of the BCP constitution were written in the Tavistock Clinic building in Swiss Cottage. It was the Tavistock group who conceived the idea of the single membership policy, and it was they who drove it through. The point of it was that as long as psychotherapy organizations belonged to both BCP and UK Council for Psychotherapy, the credibility of BCP would be questionable as it was so much smaller and contained only a fragment of the psychotherapy profession. To boost its apparent importance, it was decided that BCP organizations had to choose either to belong to BCP, or to belong to UKCP. This single membership policy was referred to the Office of Fair Trading, which decided that BCP is a Trade Association and that the single membership policy is a restrictive practice. How a group of organizations that are registered charities is allowed to promote and fund a trade association for its members is an interesting question, which does not seem to have been taken seriously by anyone. This may be in part because the problem has been skilfully hidden. The BCP now has a small group of trustees, whose names are at the front of their register of practitioners. This could easily give the impression that the BCP is a charitable trust, although such a claim is not made explicitly. Indeed, I think that most of the members of British Psycho-Analytical Society are not aware that BCP is legally a trade association. What matters to them is that the creation of the BCP produced a split in the psychoanalytic community, and thus exported the hidden split in the British Society, thus benefiting them by keeping their own split hidden provided that the split in the psychoanalytical community is regarded as "external". This requires the British Society to see the "others" as different from "us", while remaining oblivious to the fact that the division between "them" and "us" has been created quite artificially. Inevitably the split has now reappeared inside the BCP in terms of those who may and those who may not call themselves psychoanalysts. As we all know, each time that a hidden split is shifted, so as to temporarily decrease discomfort, it inevitably diminishes the original holder of the split. This split is now shifting within the BCP; when it finally appears as the split between the psychoanalytic organizations and the Jungian organizations, the British Association of Psychotherapists will move from its comfort zone to partially holding the split because the BAP has both Freudian and Jungian analysts in its membership. Thus, in the end, a form of splitting that originated in the British Psycho-Analytical Society will come to reside in the BAP. After all the hard work and political manoeuvring that BAP has undertaken, this seems very unfair to its members. The split between the Freudian and the Jungian organizations is, of course, nothing new, but it will be very interesting to see just what form it will take in its new incarnation within the BCP.

The British Psycho-Analytical Society will derive no lasting benefit from forming the BCP, and by the impoverishment contingent on exporting the splitting, will actually suffer. The only real beneficiaries of the BCP and its single membership policy, on this view, is the Tavistock and Portman Clinic NHS Trust. They have little, if any, concern about who may or may not call themselves a psychoanalyst, as long as they have power within the NHS to appoint only those psychotherapists whom they deem to be good enough. So they are perfectly happy that the BCP register came to be advertised as though it were a professional qualification, and they have no interest in the British Psycho-Analytical Society having to share its exclusive title with the British Association of Psychotherapists, and with whoever else among the BCP organizations is resolute enough to press their claim. It could even be argued that this dilution of the title suits the Tavistock very well, as it dilutes the effectiveness of the British Society even further and thereby promotes their own power. Thus, in the external political arena, which the British Society should never have entered, they have lost at every turn.

The "Alderdice" working group

Worse was to come. A working party was set up which has led to much recrimination and confusion. In an astute move the composition of the parties who might represent psychotherapy if regulations were to be introduced has been altered, with the particular aim of reducing the representation of non-analytic modalities, and especially to reduce the voice of the UK Council for Psychotherapy. Slowly but surely that working party has changed the perception of how psychotherapy is to be viewed and even whether it is a coherent profession.

This subtle shift has been masterminded by Lord Alderdice, who has skilfully steered things in exactly the way that I regard as the preference of the Tavistock Clinic. Getting Lord Alderdice to chair the working group was a masterstroke. He is a psychiatrist who did a psychotherapy training at the Tavistock Clinic. The conjecture of some of us is that it would have been the Tavistock who approached John Alderdice and who persuaded the British

Psycho-Analytical Society into thinking that it would be to their advantage to go along with his working group. If Lord Alderdice understands psychotherapy, he appears to show no concern for some of its modalities, and his lack of apparent concern coincides with the line of thinking that I attribute to the Tavistock Clinic.

The sad part is that the deal that the British Psycho-Analytical Society rejected when they left the UK Standing Conference for Psychotherapy would have been much better for them than anything that is now offered by the working group. They were to have their own seat on the Conference's Governing Board and they would have continued to inhabit the Psychoanalytic Section, which was distinct from the Psychoanalytic and Psychodynamic Psychotherapy Section. Most British Society members are unaware that this is the deal that they rejected, as it was never debated properly in the British Society meetings. Instead scorn was poured on the UK Standing Conference and all its works, which I found incomprehensible at the time, but with hindsight and thought, I now see that what was at stake was the threat that the hidden split within the British Society would emerge if any serious negotiating had taken place. This was such an intolerable prospect that it was carefully avoided. At the time it seemed to me very strange that the part of the profession that laid claim to be the supreme authority on the talking cure was unable to talk to us about their views, needs, wishes at any stage of the process of joining and then leaving the Rugby Conference, Standing Conference, UK Council for Psychotherapy process. Instead of talking to us, they attempted to split the conference from within, and when that failed they were a sitting target for the political skills of their Tavistock Clinic masters.

Inhibitions, symptoms and anxiety

The symptoms of the condition that British Psycho-Analytical Society have got into are actually typical of any individual or organisation that has this particular affliction. They are having increasing difficulty in recruiting trainees, and their membership is ageing steadily. They are living beyond their means, so that although they have sold their expensive palace in the West End of London and moved to more modest premises, they are still struggling financially.

Having put up their fees too much, they are now seeing an exodus of older members who are retired, or partly retired, because they cannot afford to pay the new rates. In spite of years of discussing their growing financial crisis they continue to have many committees, all of which require servicing by a secretariat. It seems to make no difference that they cannot afford the level of secretarial resource that their internal structure demands. At the same time their influence in the external world is waning rapidly, and that will accelerate when the British Association of Psychotherapists becomes a psychoanalytic institute. Already it is clear that training at the Institute of Psychoanalysis no longer leads to a good and steady livelihood. Many psychoanalysts are having increasing difficulty in filling their timetable, even though many also offer psychotherapy, for which they may or may not be trained. There is here an issue of whether psychotherapy should be restricted to those practitioners who have had a training that is distinct from the psychoanalytic training. Here, too, there is a necessary muddle, because it engages the very problem that is evaded by the split that I am describing.

While the British Society claim that the public identify analysts with themselves, any cursory perusal of the broadsheet press will show that terms like analyst, counsellor, psychologist, shrink, are used interchangeably and at random with no distinction being made between them. Penguin is about to publish a new translation of the works of Sigmund Freud, and the editor in charge is not a member of British Psycho-Analytical Society.

Reparation

Now that I have spelled out my diagnosis, what can be done about it? What would be the treatment and what the prognosis? I am quite clear in my own mind that without appropriate treatment the condition is terminal, after a lengthy period of increasing debility. The treatment suggests itself, the split must be taken back inside where it belongs and resolved internally, as any psychotherapist will tell you. Whatever model of psychotherapy is practised, all agree that a split projected out and invested elsewhere is untreatable until it is internalized again in something like its original form, and resolved in a quite different way. The prescription that I have come to is for British Psycho-Analytical Society to relinquish their pretensions to be the political masters of the psychoanalytic enterprise in the UK. I expect that this is likely to be painful but effective. It will require turmoil within the Society and a fair amount of anguish, but it is better in the medium and the long term than the alternative, which is disintegration, and probable annihilation. In my opinion, the solution is parallel to the solution that Canterbury is wanting to adopt, give up political pretensions, and take your place in the world just as you are. Bishops should stick to spiritual leadership, and psychoanalysts should stick to the elucidation and teaching of unconscious processes. I am aware that my prescription may not be the only solution, and that the British Society will have to engage in an internal process in the hope of finding the best solution for them. But having said that, I should like to offer something concrete as a starting point. I think that the optimum solution is to give up entirely all pretence at exclusivity, and to recognize that the psychoanalytic enterprise is much broader than one group. The reality of embracing trade in place of eminence may be painful to some, but in the medium and the long term, it is the least painful route.

All those who strive to understand the unconscious and who want to work on the basis of the unravelling of unconscious processes, should be made welcome into the federation of the psychoanalytic movement. Some will want to argue theory, some will want to practise full psychoanalysis, others will want to offer a variety of therapy modes and modules to the public, maybe in the NHS and maybe in private practice, or maybe in a variety of clinics. But there should be no class distinction made between these different aspirations, they are all as psychoanalytically based as each other. My prediction is that if they did this, the British Psycho-Analytical Society would quickly regain their ascendancy, but in a very different form. They would be judged on the thoroughness of their practice, and not on any other criteria. They would not be the regulators of psychoanalysis, which they are unable to achieve anyway, but would be the main source of clinical and perhaps theoretical excellence. They would again be appreciated for what they can realistically achieve, and they would be spared the torment of their failed political aspirations. They would also reoccupy their unique position as the pre-eminent training group in the UK. It is a paradox that while all this is going on, the British training in psychoanalysis is greatly admired within the International Psychoanalytical Association. Of course, it may be that regional psychoanalytical institutes may appear in the UK, but that would be better than the present situation where psychoanalysis has hardly moved out of London at all. In my view such moves can only strengthen the psychoanalytic enterprise and make it less of an arcane curiosity and less the butt of poor jokes about shrinks. In one sense, of course, to be the butt of jokes is a sort of accolade, at least it forms one kind of celebrity status, but not the sort that the psychoanalytical profession should seek.

Conclusion

So there it is; my diagnosis of splitting and projection, with the inevitable impoverishment of the collective "ego" of the British Psycho-Analytical Society, and the subsequent stumbling from one disappointment to the next, punctuated by varying degrees of wishful thinking, or, one might say, varying degrees of grandiosity. None of the aspirations that inform their present predicament is capable of realistic solutions, having already been submerged in the BCP. Returning to the issue of who should decide about who should decide, we have to acknowledge that just as astronomy does not belong to the Astronomer Royal, psychoanalysis does not belong to the British Psycho-Analytical Society. Psychoanalysis must belong to everybody who takes the trouble to study the subject in depth. It is open to all who want to take part, just like any other enterprise that is in the public domain.

Certainly there is a place for a professional authority to influence training and practice, and there is a place for an authority to have oversight of the safety of the public who seek professional help. The question of whether those two authorities are better put in one place, or separated into two distinct functions starts us on another set of issues about whether two functions like regulating training and regulating practice can be put together without leading to the difficulties that I have described, or whether the public would be better served by separating them entirely. That is another argument for another day.

CHAPTER THIRTEEN

Can there be a monopoly on psychoanalysis?

Darian Leader

Introduction

This chapter explores the history of the question of the owner-ship of psychoanalysis and the attempts to define the nature and parameters of psychoanalytic treatment. It shows how psychoanalysis has evolved into a plurality of practices with their own traditions and that hence it is not possible to provide a single model of psychoanalytic theory or practice today. Recent attempts to claim a monopoly on psychoanalytic training are discussed and the conclusion reached that there are no serious arguments to support this, only appeals to an imagined authority. All forms of therapy, in contrast, ought to have as one of their goals a question-ing of appeals to irrational forms of authority.

There are many questions that only make sense at a particular time and place. When the historian and philosopher of science Thomas Kuhn was describing the genesis of his celebrated theory of paradigm shifts, he singled out the importance of what he saw as the conditions of possibility of posing questions. What mattered, he thought, was less to see how a particular scientific theory answered a question than to explain how that question could have been asked in the first place (Kuhn, 1977).

Rather than assuming that the history of science consisted of attempts to solve the same riddles, it could be shown—by taking what seemed to be odd or absurd questions seriously—to be tackling fundamentally disparate problems. Thus, Kuhn could argue that Aristotle had not been writing bad Newtonian physics, as he had first assumed, but good Greek philosophy. This technique of studying the history of science was inspired, he said, by his experience of psychoanalysis (Hoyningen-Huene, 1993, 1997).

We might be tempted to apply the same logic to the question, "Who owns psychoanalysis?" To pose this question in, say, 1926, may be quite different from posing it in 2003. Although the form of the question is the same, our framework for making sense of it has changed. Where in 1926 it may have been necessary to warn the public of the activities of what seem to have been a number of rather unscrupulous practitioners, today the landscape of the psychoanalytic world has altered. Indeed, for many of today's psychoanalysts, the question "Who owns psychoanalysis?" provokes puzzlement. How, they ask, could the claim ever be made for ownership of a discipline and a diverse set of therapeutic practices?

As we cast an eye over psychoanalytic history, however, our separation of epochs seems slightly less secure. If the first and second generation of analysts were worried about fairground-booth clinicians boasting of the Freudian therapy they could dispense, their energies were still much more bound up with their own internal territorial disputes. The debate about lay analysis in the mid-1920s would be one example of this, and, on a more general level, the whole question of who could and could not practise psychoanalysis in the USA. The sheer scale of this latter dispute is becoming clearer with the ongoing publication of historical studies and correspondences (Hale, 1995; Kirsner, 2000a). These demonstrate that the problem was less the occasional maverick setting up shop than the threat posed, precisely, by other psychoanalysts.

The tangled histories of psychoanalytic groups are hardly edifying. They are histories of splits, struggles, and sometimes open warfare, of broken allegiances, broken promises, and broken friendships. Theoretical differences have led to political differences, and, just as frequently, political differences have disguised themselves as theoretical ones. All of those who have studied the institutional politics of the psychoanalytic world agree on one thing: that the key issues revolve around psychoanalytic training. Who should the so-called training analysts be, and what should a proper psychoanalytic training consist of?

Freud's most sustained contribution to this debate came at a time when the question of a monopoly on the use of the term "psychoanalyst" was first raised. The term, it was claimed, should be reserved for medical doctors who had undergone some form of analytic training (Freud, 1926e). Freud was unreservedly opposed to this notion. Medical training, he thought, had nothing to do with psychoanalytic training. Psychoanalytical training, on the contrary, had to do with the establishment of an analytic attitude; a focus on handling transference, battling resistance, and the skills of inter-preting. As he put it in his study of the history of the psychoanalytic movement, any line of investigation that recognizes the facts of transference and resistance as a starting point in its work has a right to call itself psychoanalysis (Freud, 1914d, p.16; Tardits, 2000).

Freud went on to elaborate a blueprint for psychoanalytic train-ing, and curiously, despite the fact that what holds psychoanalysis together is supposed to be a common foundation in the work of Freud, a majority of Freud's students at that time chose to disagree with him. Medical training, they thought, was in fact a requirement, and his blueprint for a college of psychoanalysts a chimera. The various interventions at the Innsbruck Congress in 1927 by Freud's students for the most part contest his own position (Jones et al., 1927).

This set of disagreements is significant since it shows that there was no consensus on training at the time that psychoanalysis began to be organized into its institutes (Costecalde et al., 1995, Safouan, 2000). It was the 1920s, after all, that saw the establishment of the first sets of training criteria for psychoanalysis. Differences between the psychoanalytic styles of Vienna and Berlin were made much of at the time, and it was the Berlin Institute that became the model for much of the subsequent psychoanalytic training that would be developed around the world. Despite this, the actual practice of psychoanalysis within institutes was varied. The supposedly uniform, classical technique that Freud practised, and that genera-tions of later analysts so often referred to like a lost Eden, turned out to have existed only in their imagination. Enough data exists on Freud's technique to demonstrate this quite clearly (Roazen, 1995).

Subsequent debates on the question of defining psychoanalytic technique failed to find any model of practice that everyone agreed on. This is relevant to us today in the context of the problem of mapping out the relations of psychoanalysis to psychoanalytic psychotherapy. As analysts tried to say what classical treatment was, they ended up by charting how technique had to be altered to deal with problematic cases. No one could agree on what the "standard treatment" or "cure type" consisted of, but everyone recognized that "adaptations" were being made to meet the clinical demands of working with specific patients. The fruit of this debate, which ran from about 1949 to 1956, was not a consensus on what psychoanalysis was but rather the creation of a new clinical category: the borderline (Leader, 1993).

The fact that by the 1940s so many different styles of psychoanalytic practice were in evidence generated, for some analysts, the search for a treatment that everyone could agree upon. As the mythical, pure Freudian style was now lost in a myriad of technical diversity, a gold standard had to be found. And as analysts realized that they were all using very disparate modes of interpretation with their patients, the debate began to focus on defining what classical interpretation would consist of. This would solve, they hoped, the problem of defining what exactly psychoanalysis was, as distinct from other therapeutic practices.

At the London Congress in 1953, Edward Glover asked his colleagues what modifications in technique could take place "without forfeiting the right to use the term psycho-analysis". He contrasted the more "flexible" styles of treatment advocated by Alexander with what could be called the "standard treatment". His conclusion consisted of an appeal to regiment the actions of the analyst:

> Without some reliable form of standardization of technique there can be no science of psychoanalysis, for if we cannot standardize the behaviour of the patient, we must at least be able to standardize the behaviour of the analyst. [Glover, 1954, p. 383]

Although Glover singles out the handling of free association here as a criterion of proper analytic functioning, he shies away from an investigation of the properties of language in psychoanalysis. This might surprise us given the fact that most of the contributions to the debate at that time were concerned with applying theories of language to the analytic encounter, as part of the attempt to clarify the nature of standard treatment.

Summing up the American Psychoanalytic Association's Panel on variations in analytic technique, Elizabeth Zetzel claimed that

> the differences in technical procedure appear to be clearly related to a basic difference in respect to one point, namely, the extent to which analysis may be carried to a successful conclusion by verbal methods directed towards the acquisition of insight. [Zetzel, 1953, p. 537].

This was a problem that the so-called ego psychologists had been working on for some time, and their main research instrument was the language theory of Karl Buehler. Buehler had divided language into a number of different functions, ranging from the cognitive to the expressive, and the idea was that proper psychoanalysis could be defined as the systematic movement through this series of functions to reach the expressive level (Hartmann, 1951, Loewenstein, 1956).

The only hitch was that, as both Hartmann and Loewenstein admitted, the patient's ego wasn't always ready for this linguistic trajectory, and hence had to be prepared for it. But preparing an ego would mean introducing a number of technical procedures that seemed to deviate from classical technique! In an effort to distinguish such procedures from the purity of psychoanalysis as such, several new terms were minted: Bibring proposed "clarification", Devereux "confrontation", Nacht "the presence of the analyst", and Eissler "parameter". This latter term was defined as a deviation from pure interpretation necessitated by a problem in the ego structure of the patient (Eissler, 1953). Parameters, however, were only to be employed if they eventually led to their own "self elimination": by the end of analysis, they had to be abolished and only then could the ego attain its "integrity".

Eissler's formulations bring out the central thread to this debate. An unmodified ego will be the perfect partner for "standard treatment" and an ego with structural defects will call for the introduction of technical variations. Now, whereas analysts such as

Loewenstein were trying to use a theory of language to situate technical diversity, the more it became apparent that everyone was "deviating", the more the cause of deviation was shifted to the problematic ego structure of the patient. This was so much the case that by the Paris Congress in 1957, the question of the relation of modes of analytic intervention to language had been replaced by that of cataloguing defective ego structures. The debate on variations in technique became a debate on what was known at the time as "ego distortion", and it was in this fertile soil that the notion of borderline would take root.

If the debates of the 1950s on variations in psychoanalytic technique died down and metamorphosed into rather separate considerations, they would be revived again in the 1980s and 1990s when many psychoanalytic groupings tried to distinguish themselves from the growing number of psychotherapies. Without going into the details of the various positions put forward, it should be noted that in contrast to the 1950s, internal diversity and the absence of a standard treatment was no longer a trade secret. As Robert Wallerstein, a former president of the International Psychoanalytical Association (IPA) and the APA, pointed out in 1988, we live in a time of "worldwide theoretical diversity", with an "established pluralism of psychoanalysis in Europe and in Latin America. . . . We have several, or many psychoanalyses today, and not one" (Wallerstein, 1988, pp. 11–12).

This recognition of difference was still not the same thing as saying that psychoanalysis and psychotherapy were one. But nor was it saying that if difference there was, it was only difference internal to the IPA. Evoking Freud's emphasis on transference and resistance, Wallerstein argued that "the decision about whose work and whose theoretical views then belong within psychoanalysis is not a political-administrative issue of who remained within the organized institutional framework of the IPA.". And as the later president of the IPA, Horacio Etchegoyen, added, "there are institutions outside the IPA that train analysts and we ought to stimulate contact with them" (Etchegoyen & Miller, 1996).

Although the IPA certainly had the privilege in the early years of psychoanalysis of being the sole international organization aiming to propagate the work of Freud, the many splits and divergences in the movement led to the creation of new schools and new analytic traditions. Today, for example, there are several hundred different analytic training organizations in Europe, the USA, and Latin America.

Times have changed. No one owns psychoanalysis, just as no one owns physics or chemistry. As Jacob Arlow pointed out almost twenty years ago, this new era of psychoanalysis is one in which "no one will be able to substantiate a claim to being the confirmed representative of the fountainhead of psychoanalytic authority" (Arlow, 1985).

Naturally—and unfortunately—enough, this pluralism has generated territorial disputes. Analysts have disparaged the work of colleagues who do not share their own institutional affiliation—and probably always will. The accusation of not being a proper psychoanalyst has been levelled at just about everyone, from the Kleinians in London and in California to the members of the Columbia Institute in New York, to Anna Freud, and the Lacanians. Such attempts at impeachment do not just occur between schools, but within them: the Chairman of the Education Committee at the New York Psychoanalytic Institute said in the 1960s that 95% of its members were not qualified to work as analysts (Kirsner, 2000a).

Yet historically, the last two decades have seen a general acceptance of diversity in the States and on the Continent. In the States, the Federal Office of Education has ruled that a broad range of heterogeneously trained professionals have the right to call themselves analysts (Spezzano, 1990). Within the IPA, and running against the cultural current, Britain is the exception here, and the British Psycho-Analytical Society (BP-AS) makes the remarkable claim that it is the only body authorized to train psychoanalysts in the United Kingdom.

Anyone accessing the website of the BP-AS in the summer of 2002 would have found an icon titled "Note concerning imposters in the world of psychoanalysis" and a series of statements aiming to discredit those who had followed other training routes. A list of BP-AS members was—and still is—preceded by the claim

> There follows a list of the names of all qualified UK psychoanalysts. All those listed here, and only those listed here, are properly entitled to hold themselves out the public as psychoanalysts

because of their internationally recognized training and membership of the British Psycho-Analytical Society and Institute of
Psychoanalysis.

These amazing claims are, to my knowledge, not made by any other
IPA society in the world.

The website also asserts that "psychoanalytic psychotherapist"
and "psychoanalyst" are "distinct professional titles which imply
different training requirements". The training of analysts in the UK,
we are told, requires five-times-weekly analysis, whereas in some
other IPA societies "four times a week suffices, but not less". This is
another surprising statement, given the well-known fact that IPA
societies in France, Spain, Germany, and other countries are perfectly happy to allow less than four-times-weekly, with one French
IPA society noting that "Analysis is most usually three times a
week" (Parker, 2003).

The BP-AS, in contrast to other IPA societies around the world,
claims a UK monopoly on the term "psychoanalyst" (unless the
practitioner has trained with another IPA society abroad). Given the
confidence of its claims, one might expect robust arguments to back
them up. Despite much searching, only two arguments seem to
emerge, and neither has much scientific credibility. The first is that,
as Peter Fonagy claims, the BP-AS offers the "best models of practice" (Fonagy, 2000, paper presented at UKCP debate). The second
is that the IPA training, as administered through the Institute, is the
only one to be recognized by the British Medical Association
(BMA). Now, as for the first claim, we find no evidence for this
"best models of practice", despite the fact that the claim is made by
an author who is well known for the deluge of academic references
to be found in his writings. Even if we think the claim true, it in no
way sanctions a monopoly. Arguing that one psychotherapy training is better than another is not to say that the other is not a
psychotherapy training.

While this is not the place to go into any details of the Institute's
customs, we might note that it was one of the very last of the
IPA societies to continue the practice of contact between training
analyst and training committee, a practice that the last president of
the IPA deemed "unethical" (Kernberg, 2000, p. 114). It is also the
only society to have failed to respond to the recent IPA task-force

investigation into the relations between analytic and psychotherapeutic practice in the work of its members, and this without giving
any explanation (Israel, 1999).

Now, the second argument for a monopoly appeals to the old
BMA ruling. The BMA had reported in 1929 that the term psychoanalyst is reserved for any person

> who uses Freud's technique and anyone who does not use this tech-
> nique should not, whatever other methods he may apply, be called
> a psychoanalyst. In accordance with this definition and for the
> purpose of avoiding confusion, the term psychoanalyst is properly
> reserved for members of the IPA (Supplement to the *British Medical
> Journal*, 1929, p. 266).

In this pre-Training Standards era, the criterion for membership of
the IPA is defined as "an adequate knowledge of the subject". Now,
note first that the IPA was certainly the only international psychoanalytic organization at the time, whereas today this is no longer
the case. And note second that, on this definition, there can be
no more than half a dozen members of the BP-AS who currently
qualify as psychoanalysts. Practically no one today "uses Freud's
technique", and, as we have seen, defining this technique has never
been easy.

Seventy years of analytic theory and technical reformulations
testify to this. Since the 1930s, and probably even before, there have
been a variety of ways of practising psychoanalysis. Indeed, some
would argue that there have always been as many ways of practising psychoanalysis as there have been individual patients. In terms
of technical styles associated with different groupings, the range is
rather wide. As Arlow says, psychoanalysts have "altered radically
the technical procedures they inherited from their teachers" (Arlow,
1985). Kleinian work is proof of this, differing in quite extreme
ways from the general parameters of Freudian practice. Despite
these facts of psychoanalytic history, Jennifer Johns could say at the
United Kingdom Council for Psychotherapy (UKCP) debate on the
subject that the "BMA report . . . has stood us in good stead over
many years" (Johns, 2000, paper presented at UKCP debate).

Clearly, apart from the fact that hardly anyone even knows
about the British Medical Association (BMA) report, this is not a

rational argument but an appeal to authority, and a strange one at that, as if the medical profession had the last word in the legit-imization of psychoanalysis. BMA rulings tend to be quite ephemeral, with frequent changes and updates, an attention that psychoanalysis never received from the BMA subsequently. We might note that the BP-AS had, at that time, the highest percentage of non-medical analysts in the IPA, and that the background contro-versy to the BMA report had a highly specific context (Richards, 2000). As the historian of psychoanalysis Douglas Kirsner points out, the Institute has no legal right to the exclusive use of the term psychoanalyst "but they can threaten strike action against those that employ this term, a power ploy. In a sense, I can't blame them for pursuing their power aims; most institutions do" (Kirsner, 2000b).

Now, what happens in the absence of rational arguments based on theories of training? In this country, there has been an appeal to formal criteria, in particular, the number of sessions per week. There are no serious theories about why five is the best number, only vague references to this frequency being "deeper" or more "intense". The Institute is relatively isolated here: in fact, it is the only IPA Society in the world, apart from the Australian, to insist on it. Elsewhere, as we have seen, three or four times a week is seen as adequate. And clearly, the frequency of sessions is not a defining feature of psychoanalysis, as Freud and later Otto Kernberg, the last IPA president, have stressed (Kernberg, 2000). What matters is what the analysand achieves, not the number of times per week it took him or her to achieve it.

We cannot deny the diversity of psychoanalytic practices in the world today, and at a time when all forms of psychodynamic work are under threat, it is saddening to see political struggles and terri-torial disputes absorb the energies of some parts of the analytic community, who would no doubt be better served by talking to each other and learning from each other's approaches. As BP-AS member Christopher Bollas asked recently, "Who has the right to call him or herself a psychoanalyst?" And he answered:

> While it is undeniable that some institutes offer superior training, not unlike colleges or universities, it is time for all psychoanalysts . . . to agree that anyone who has qualified in a psychoanalytic or

psychoanalytic psychotherapy training program may practice psychoanalysis. (Bollas & Sundelson, 1995 pp. 196–197]

And, as Bollas then points out, whatever differences there may be between psychoanalysis and psychoanalytic psychotherapy, they are minimal compared to their shared differences from other forms of treatment.

The idea of establishing a monopoly on a discipline is inherently absurd, and is clearly ruled out by UKCP philosophy. As their Training Standards documentation tells us, psychotherapy training should be "intentionally designed to challenge and critique [its received] traditions and practices". If one group has exclusive use of a title such as "psychoanalyst", what would happen if some, perhaps most, of its members were to become disenchanted with its institutional practices and decide to form a new group? Would they therefore cease to be psychoanalysts?

None of these questions has been addressed by the Governing Board of the UKCP, who in July 2003 accepted a report by a working party appointed by their Registration Board on the use of the term "UKCP-Registered Psychoanalyst" in the UKCP Register. This report was not impressive. Apart from its misspellings of names like "Lacan" and "Anna Freud", it suffered from a complete failure to research its subject matter. Claiming an "inclusive consulting process" and a "rigorous and fair" approach, it neglected to consult a single specialist on the question of psychoanalytic training, just as its meagre bibliography failed to include a single one of the standard books on the subject. IPA facts and figures were paraded, while no comparable data from non-IPA trainings were included. The document is, to my mind, a catalogue of misinformation and one's sympathy for the philistinism of the authors is only countered by the presence of a series of patently biased comments that will irritate anyone who has chosen a training route outside the IPA.

Crowning all of this is the report's conclusion that the application form for the label "UKCP-Registered Psychoanalyst" was not filled in properly. It should have come from individual member organizations and not from the Psychoanalytic and Psychodynamic Section as such. Given the fact that initial enquiries to the UKCP about the application were met with the instruction that it should be the Section that applied, not member organizations, this is odd.

Yet it is even odder that, if the "mistake" was made that the Section applied, it wasn't simply sent the application back and told that it should have come from member organizations! The circularity of the procedure has all the credentials of a short story by Kafka, yet the comedy of this situation is sadly offset by the seriousness of its stakes.

What emerges as the central bias of the report is the claim that it is the status quo that a psychoanalyst is simply someone who has graduated from the Institute of Psychoanalysis. Although there is no problem in finding people who will subscribe to this opinion, it is in fact a minority view in the culture we live in today, to which the hundreds of books, articles, and journals published each year by analysts who do not work within the IPA testify. It would be very difficult, likewise, to find anyone in the many university depart-ments of psychoanalysis that have sprung up over the last two decades who would give credence to such a view. Indeed, despite the publication over the last fifty years of innumerable studies that purport to demonstrate the scientific instability and clinical dubi-ousness of several mainstream IPA positions, the majority of these texts are not held by the Institute of Psychoanalysis's library and hence are potentially unavailable to its trainees.

The Institute's sustained efforts to exert a monopoly have even gone so far as to evoke the need to protect the public from unscrupulous practitioners. One might be tempted to argue here that its neglect of making many critiques of its own practices avail-able to its trainees is in itself constitutive here of potentially putting the public at risk. Rather than following this path, we should recog-nize appeals for the protection of the public as possibly constitut-ing instead a rather shabby alibi for a trade war. Members of the public who have the opportunity to find out what psychoanalysis is will learn about the different traditions that the term embraces. The UKCP encourages promotion of public knowledge of these differences and it should endeavour, together with the Institute, to inform the public about the different styles of psychoanalytic treat-ment available.

Psychoanalysis is a field of enquiry and a set of therapeutic practices. It is not a unified body of knowledge with a unified prac-tice, but a movement with multiple traditions. These traditions deserve respect, study, and critique, although they so often tend to deny each other's worth—and even existence. When Anne-Marie Sandler set about exploring different training traditions in Europe, this was her initial reaction:

> I was profoundly shocked to discover my own very strong preju-
> dices and my difficulty in digesting the information sent to me . . .
> I found myself wanting to deride those methods which were differ-
> ent from those I was accustomed to, and it took me some time to
> overcome my culture shock and to accept, at an emotional level, the
> reality that they were outstanding analysts who have followed a
> different training route. [Sandler, 1990, p. 49]

This respect for differences is something we should take seriously, rather than pandering to appeals to some mythic status quo
or authority, and we should question the nature of our own transferences in this debate. We often hear it said that all forms of
psychotherapy are about freeing ourselves from the tyranny of irrational forms of authority, forms which are established and consoli-
dated by transference. If most analysts agree that an analyst is
someone who has graduated from an institute, isn't it time for some
of them to recognize that this doesn't necessarily mean their institute? And that if there is a genuine question about monopolies, it is
not about whether there is or even could be a monopoly on psychoanalysis, but rather, as Lord Sutch once asked, why there is only one
Monopolies Commission?

Summary

The history of psychoanalysis has seen many attempts to define and
clarify the nature of psychoanalytic theory and practice. These
attempts have often been fruitful, but they have not led to any standardization or, indeed, to any monopoly on psychoanalytic training. This situation seems to be accepted today although one
psychoanalytic institution in the UK thinks otherwise. This chapter
has shown how there are no grounds for a monopoly on psychoanalysis: there is no appeal to a rational argument here and it is
generally agreed that formal criteria cannot be used to define
psychoanalytic practice. What we have instead is something that

bears a certain resemblance to a territorial battle or trade war. This is a regrettable state of affairs given the fact that the place of psychoanalysis in contemporary culture is increasingly under threat. Different psychoanalytic orientations should realize that they have more in common with each other than they do with other orientations in mental health that are working against the effects of psychoanalytically based practice.

References

Arlow, J. (1985). Issues in the evaluation of psychoanalysis. In: C. Settlage & R. Brockbank (Eds.), *New Ideas in Psychoanalysis* (pp. 5–18). Hillsdale: Lawrence Erlbaum.

Bollas, C., & Sundleson, D. (1995). *The New Informants*. London: Karnac.

British Medical Association (BMA) (1929). Supplement to the *British Medical Journal*, 29 June.

Costecalde, A. et al. (1995). *Devenir Psychanalyste*. Paris, Denoel.

Eissler, K. (1953). The effect of the structure of the ego on psychoanalytic technique. *Journal of the American Psychoanalytic Association*, 1: 104–143.

Etchegoyen, H., & Miller, J.-A. (1996). *Silence Brise, Entretien sur le Mouvement Psychanalytique*. Paris: Seuil.

Fonagy, P. (2000). Paper given at UKCP conference "The Future of Psychoanalysis", London, 6 May

Freud, S. (1914e). On the history of the psycho-analytic movement. *S.E.*, 14: 7–66. London: Hogarth.

Freud, S. (1926d). The question of lay analysis. *S.E.*, 20: 183–258. London: Hogarth.

Hale, N. (1995). *The Rise and Crisis of Psychoanalysis in the United States*. New York: Oxford University Press.

Hartmann, H. (1951). Technical implications of ego psychology. *Psychoanalytic Quaterly*, 20: 31–43.

Hoyningen-Huene, P. (1993). *Reconstructing Scientific Revolutions: Thomas S. Kuhn's Philosophy of Science*. Chicago: Chicago University Press.

Hoyningen-Huene, P. (1997). Thomas S. Kuhn. *Journal for General Philosophy of Science, 28*: 235–256.

Israel, P. (1999). Report of the Committee on Psychoanalysis and Allied Therapies. *IPA Newsletter, 8*(1): 15–17.

Johns, J. (2000). The Tower of Babel and the ivory tower. Paper given at UKCP conference "The Future of Psychoanalysis", London, 6 May.

Jones, J. et al (1927). Diskussionen der "Laienanalyse". *Internationale Zeitschrift fur Psychoanalyse, 13*: 171–326.

Kernberg, O. (2000). A concerned critique of psychoanalytic education. *International Journal of Psycho-Analysis, 81*: 97–120.

Kirsner, D. (2000a). *Unfree Associations, Inside Psychoanalytic Institutes.* London: Process Press.

Kirsner, D. (2000b). Personal communication.

Kuhn, T. (1977). *The Essential Tension: Selected Studies in Scientific Tradition and Change.* Chicago: Chicago University Press.

Leader, D. (1993). Note sur la strategie et la tactique. *La Lettre Mensuelle de l'Ecole de la Cause Freudienne, 117*: 21–24.

Loewenstein, R. (1956). Some remarks on the role of speech in psychoanalytic technique. *International Journal of Psychoanalysis, 37*: pp. 460–468.

Parker, I. (2003). The label "UKCP Registered Psychoanalyst": diversity of practice inside and outside the IPA. *The Psychotherapist, 20*(Spring/Summer): 10–11.

Richards, G. (2000). Britain on the couch: the popularization of psychoanalysis in Britain 1918–1940. *Science in Context, 13*: 183–230.

Roazen, P. (1995). *How Freud Worked.* New York: Aronson.

Safouan, M. (2000). *Jacques Lacan and the Question of Psychoanalytic Training* J. Rose (Trans.). London: Macmillan.

Sandler, A.-M. (1990). Comments on varieties of psychoanlytic training in Europe. In: M. Meisels & E. Shapiro (Eds.), *Tradition and Innovation in Psychoanalytic Education* (pp. 45–58). Hillsdale: Lawrence Erlbaum.

Spezzano, C. (1990). A history of psychoanalytic training for psychologists in the United States. In: M. Meisels & E. Shapiro (Eds.), *Tradition and Innovation in Psychoanalytic Education* (pp. 63–76). Hillsdale: Lawrence Erlbaum.

Tardits, A. (2000). *Les Formations du Psychanalyste,*.Paris: Eres.

Wallerstein, R. (1988). One psychoanalysis or many? *International Journal of Psycho-Analysis, 69*, 5–21.

Zetzel, E. (1953). The traditional technique and its variations. *Journal of the American Psychoanalytic Association, 1*: 526–537.

PART IV
SCIENCE

CHAPTER FOURTEEN

Critique of psychoanalysis

Adolf Grünbaum

Background

As we know, classical long-term psychoanalytic treatment has fallen on hard times in the USA. But the membership of Division 39 of the American Psychological Association, which is concerned with psychoanalytic psychology, is quite active, and so-called *"psychoanalytically-oriented"* psychotherapy of shorter duration still needs to be reckoned with in this country. Indeed, I venture to claim that some key Freudian notions remain quite influential in psychotherapeutic practice, though sometimes unbeknownst to both the practitioners and their patients.

In my essay "Critique of psychoanalysis", which first appeared in the 2002 *Freud Encyclopedia* (ed. Edward Erwin), I have distilled from my writings a systematic critique of the fundamental hypotheses of the psychoanalytic enterprise, both theoretical and therapeutic, employing a philosophy of science perspective. And I have done so in the hope that psychologists from the spectrum of various schools of thought will find my article useful.

I. Introduction

The most basic ideas of psychoanalytic theory were initially enunciated in Josef Breuer's and Sigmund Freud's "Preliminary communication" of 1893, which introduced their "Studies on hysteria". But the first published use of the *word* "psychoanalysis" occurred in Freud's 1896 French paper on "Heredity and the aetiology of the neuroses" (1896a, p. 151). Therein Freud designated Breuer's method of clinical investigation as "a new method of psycho-analysis". Breuer used hypnosis to revive and articulate a patient's unhappy memory of a supposedly *repressed* traumatic experience. The *repression* of that painful experience had occasioned the first appearance of a particular hysterical symptom, such as a phobic aversion to drinking water. Thus, Freud's mentor also induced the release of the suppressed emotional distress originally felt from the trauma. Thereby Breuer's method provided a catharsis for the patient.

The cathartic *lifting* of the repression yielded relief from the particular hysterical symptom. Breuer and Freud believed that they could therefore hypothesize that the *repression*, coupled with affective suppression, was the crucial cause for the development of the patient's psychoneurosis (Breuer & Freud, 1893a, pp. 6–7; 1893h, pp. 34–35).

Having reasoned in this way, they concluded in Freud's words:

> Thus one and the same procedure served simultaneously the purposes of [causally] investigating and of getting rid of the ailment; and this unusual conjunction was later retained in psychoanalysis. [Freud, 1924f, p. 194]

In historical retrospect, Freud acknowledged the pioneering role of Breuer's cathartic method:

> The cathartic method was the immediate precursor of psychoanalysis; and, in spite of every extension of experience and of every modification of theory, is still contained within it as its nucleus. [Freud, 1924f, p. 194]

Yet Freud was careful to highlight the contribution he made himself after the termination of his collaboration with Breuer. Referring to himself in the third person, he tells us:

Freud devoted himself to the further perfection of the instrument left over to him by his elder collaborator. The technical novelties which he introduced and the discoveries he made changed the cathartic method into psycho-analysis. [Freud, 1924f, p. 195]

These extensive elaborations have earned Freud the mantle of being the *father* of psychoanalysis.

By now, the psychoanalytic enterprise has completed its first century. Thus, the time has come to take thorough *critical* stock of its past performance qua theory of human nature and therapy, as well as to have a look at its prospects. Here I can do so only in broad strokes.

It is important to distinguish between the validity of Freud's work qua *psychoanalytic* theoretician, and the merits of his earlier work, which would have done someone else proud as the achievement of a lifetime. Currently, Mark Solms, working at the Unit of Neuro-surgery of the Royal London Hospital (Whitechapel) in the UK, is the editor and translator of the forthcoming four-volume series *The Complete Neuroscientific Works of Sigmund Freud* (Karnac Books) for publication in all of the major European languages. One focus of these writings is the neurological representation of mental functioning; another is Freud's discovery of the essential morphological and physiological unity of the nerve cell and fibre. They also contain contributions to basic neuroscience such as the histology of the nerve cell, neuronal function, and neurophysiology. As a clinical neurologist, Freud wrote a major monograph on aphasia (Solms & Saling, 1990). As Solms points out in his preview "An introduction to the neuro-scientific works of Sigmund Freud" (2002, pp. 25–26), Freud wrote major papers on cerebral palsy that earned him the status of a world authority. More generally, he was a distinguished paediatric neurologist in the field of the movement disorders of childhood. Furthermore, Freud was one of the founders of neuropsychopharmacology. For instance, he did scientific work on the properties of cocaine that benefited perhaps from his own use of that drug. Alas, that intake may well also account for some of the abandon featured by the more bizarre and grandiose of his psychoanalytic forays.

As Solms has remarked (private conversation), it is an irony of history that Freud, the psychoanalyst who postulated the ubiquity of bisexuality in humans, started out by deeming himself a *failure* for having had to conclude that eels are indeed bisexual. In a quest to learn how they reproduce, one of Freud's teachers of histology and anatomy assigned him the task of finding the hitherto elusive testicles of the eel as early as 1877, when he was twenty-one years old. After having dissected a lobular organ in about 400 specimens in Trieste, Freud found that this organ apparently had the properties of an ovary no less than those of a testicle. Being unable to decide whether he had found the ever-elusive testicles, Freud inferred that he had failed, as he reported in a rueful 1877 paper.

In 1880, he published a (free) translation of some of J. S. Mill's philosophical writings (Stephan, 1989, pp. 85–86). Yet he was often disdainful of philosophy (Assoun, 1995), despite clearly being indebted to the Viennese philosopher Franz Brentano, from whom he had taken several courses: the marks of Brentano's (1995) quondam representationalist and intentionalist account of the mental are clearly discernible in Freud's conception of ideation (see "Brentano, Franz" this volume). And the arguments for the existence of God championed by the quondam Roman Catholic priest Brentano further solidified the thoroughgoing atheism of Freud, the "godless Jew" (Gay, 1987, pp. 3–4).

II. History and logical relations of the "dynamic" and "cognitive" species of the unconscious

Freud was the creator of the full-blown theory of psychoanalysis, but even well-educated people often don't know that he was certainly *not at all* the first to postulate the existence of *some kinds or other of unconscious mental processes* (Freud, 1915e, p. 166). A number of thinkers did so earlier in order to explain conscious thought and overt behaviour for which they could find no other explanation. As we recall from Plato's dialogue *The Meno*, that philosopher was concerned to understand how an ignorant slave boy could have arrived at geometric truths under mere questioning by an interlocutor with reference to a diagram. And Plato argued that the slave boy had not acquired such geometric knowledge during his life. Instead, he explained, the boy was tapping prenatal but *unconsciously stored* knowledge, and restoring it to his conscious memory.

At the turn of the eighteenth century, Leibniz gave psychological arguments for the occurrence of *sub-threshold* sensory perceptions, and for the existence of unconscious mental contents or motives that manifest themselves in our behaviour (Ellenberger, 1970, p. 312). Moreover, Leibniz pointed out (1981, p. 107) that when the contents of some forgotten experiences subsequently emerge in our consciousness, we may *misidentify* them as *new* experiences, rather than recognize them as having been unconsciously stored in our memory. As he put it:

> It once happened that a man thought that he had written original verses, and was then found to have read them word for word, long before, in some ancient poet. . . . I think that dreams often revive former thoughts for us in this way. [Leibniz, 1981, p. 107]

As Rosemarie Sand has pointed out (private communication), Leibniz's notion anticipates, to some extent, Freud's dictum that *"The interpretation of dreams is the royal road to a knowledge of the unconscious activities of the mind"* (Freud, 1900a, p. 608).

Before Freud was born, Hermann von Helmholtz discovered the phenomenon of "unconscious inference" as being present in sensory perception (Ellenberger, 1970, p. 313). For example, we often unconsciously infer the *constancy* of the *physical* size of nearby objects that move away from us, when we have *other* distance cues, although their *visual* images decrease in size. Similarly, there can be unconsciously inferred constancy of brightness and colour under changing conditions of illumination, when the light source remains visible. Such unconscious *inferential compensation* for visual discrepancies also occurs when we transform our *non*-Euclidean (hyperbolic) binocular *visual* space into the "seen" Euclidean physical space (Grünbaum, 1973, pp. 154–157).

Historically, it is more significant that Freud also had other precursors who anticipated some of his key ideas with impressive *specificity*. As he himself acknowledged (1914d, pp. 15–16), Arthur Schopenhauer and Friedrich Nietzsche had speculatively propounded major psychoanalytic doctrines that Freud himself reportedly developed independently from his clinical observations only thereafter. Indeed, a recent German book by the Swiss psychologist Marcel Zentner (1995) traces the foundations of psychoanalysis to the philosophy of Schopenhauer.

Preparatory to my critical assessment of the psychoanalytic enterprise, let me emphasize the existence of major differences between the unconscious processes hypothesized by current cognitive psychology, on the one hand, and the unconscious contents of the mind claimed by psychoanalytic psychology, on the other (Eagle, 1987). These differences will show that the existence of the *cognitive* unconscious clearly fails to support, or even may cast doubt on, the existence of Freud's *psychoanalytic* unconscious. His so-called *"dynamic"* unconscious is the supposed repository of repressed forbidden wishes of a sexual or aggressive nature, whose re-entry or initial entry into consciousness is prevented by the defensive operations of the ego. Though socially unacceptable, these instinctual desires are so imperious and peremptory that they recklessly seek immediate gratification, independently of the constraints of external reality.

Indeed, according to Freud (1900a, pp. 566–567), we would not even have developed the skills needed to engage in cognitive activities, if it had been possible to gratify our instinctual needs without reliance on these cognitive skills. Thus, as Eagle (1987, p. 162) has pointed out:

> Freud did not seem to take seriously the possibility that cognition and thought could be inherently programmed to reflect reality and could have their own structure and development—an assumption basic to cognitive psychology.

After the Second World War, the psychoanalyst Heinz Hartmann was driven, by facts of biological maturation discovered *non*-psychoanalytically, to acknowledge in his so-called "ego psychology" that such functions as cognition, memory, and thinking can develop autonomously by innate genetic programming, and independently of instinctual drive gratification (Eagle, 1993, pp. 374–376). In the cognitive unconscious, there is great rationality in the ubiquitous computational and associative problem-solving processes required by memory, perception, judgement, and attention. By contrast, as Freud emphasized, the wish-content of the dynamic unconscious makes it operate in a highly illogical way.

There is a further major difference between the two species of unconscious (Eagle, 1987, pp. 161–165): the dynamic unconscious acquires its content largely from the unwitting repression of ideas in the form they originally had in consciousness. By contrast, in the generation of the processes in the cognitive unconscious, neither the expulsion of ideas and memories from consciousness nor the censorious denial of entry to them plays any role at all. Having populated the dynamic unconscious by means of repressions, Freud reasoned that the use of his new technique of free association could *lift* these repressions of instinctual wishes, and could thereby bring the repressed ideas back to consciousness *unchanged*. But in the case of the cognitive unconscious, we typically cannot bring to phenomenal consciousness the intellectual processes that are presumed to occur in it, although we can describe them theoretically.

For example, even if my life depended on it, I simply could not bring into my phenomenal conscious experience the elaborate scanning or search-process by which I rapidly come up with the name of the Czarina's lover Rasputin when I am asked for it. Helmholtz's various processes of "unconscious inference" illustrate the same point. By glossing over the stated major differences between the two species of unconscious, some psychoanalysts have claimed their compatibility within the same genus without ado (Shevrin *et al.*, 1992, pp. 340–341). But Eagle (1987, pp. 166–186) has articulated the extensive modifications required in the Freudian notion of the dynamic unconscious, if it is to be made compatible with the cognitive one.

More importantly, some Freudian apologists have overlooked that even after the two different species of the genus "unconscious" are thus made logically *compatible*, the dynamic unconscious as such cannot derive any *credibility* from the presumed existence of the cognitive unconscious. None the less, faced with mounting attacks on their theory and therapy, some psychoanalysts have made just that fallacious claim. Thus, the Chicago analyst Michael Franz Basch (1994, p. 1) reasoned in vain that since neurophysiological evidence supports the hypothesis of a *generic* unconscious, "psychoanalytic theory has passed the [epistemological] test with flying colors". On the contrary, we must bear in mind that evidence for the cognitive unconscious does not, as such, also furnish support for the dynamic unconscious as such.

III. Has psychoanalytic theory become
a staple of Western culture?

In appraising psychoanalysis, we must also beware of yet another logical blunder that has recently become fashionable: the bizarre argument recently given by a number of American philosophers (e.g., Nagel, 1994), that the supposed pervasive influence of Freudian ideas in Western culture vouches for the validity of the psychoanalytic enterprise. But this argument is demonstrably untenable (Grünbaum, 1994).

Even its premise that Freudian theory has become part of the intellectual ethos and folklore of Western culture cannot be taken at face value. As the great Swiss scholar Henri Ellenberger (1970, pp. 547–549) has stressed in his monumental historical work *The Discovery of the Unconscious*, the prevalence of vulgarized *pseudo*-Freudian concepts makes it very difficult to determine reliably the extent to which *genuine* psychoanalytic hypotheses have actually become influential in our culture at large. For example, *any* slip of the tongue or other bungled action (parapraxis) is typically yet incorrectly called a "Freudian slip".

But, Freud himself has called attention to the existence of a very large class of lapses or slips whose psychological motivation is simply *transparent* to the person who commits them or to others (Freud, 1916–1917, p. 40). And he added commendably that neither he nor his followers deserve any credit for the motivational explanations of such perspicuous slips (1916–1917, p. 47). In this vein, a psychoanalyst friend of mine provided me with the following example of a *pseudo*-Freudian slip that would, however, be wrongly yet widely called "Freudian": a man who is at a crowded party in a stiflingly hot room starts to go outdoors to cool off, but is confronted by the exciting view of a woman's *décolleté* bosom and says to her: "Excuse me, I have to get a *breast* of *flesh* air". Many otherwise educated people would erroneously classify this slip as Freudian for two *wrong* reasons: first, *merely* because it is motivated, rather than a purely mechanical *lapsus linguae*, and, furthermore, because its theme is sexual.

Yet what is required for a slip or so-called "parapraxis" to qualify as *Freudian* is that it be motivationally *opaque* rather than transparent, precisely because its psychological motive is *repressed*

(Freud, 1916–1917, p. 41). As the father of psychoanalysis declared unambiguously (Freud, 1901b, p. 239): if psychoanalysis is to provide an explanation of a parapraxis, "we must not be aware in ourselves of any motive for it. We must rather be tempted to explain it by 'inattentiveness', or to put it down to 'chance'". And Freud characterized the pertinent explanatory unconscious causes of slips as "motives of unpleasure". Thus, when a young man forgot the Latin word *aliquis* in a quotation from Virgil, Freud diagnosed its interfering cause as the man's distressing unconscious fear that his girlfriend had become pregnant by him (Freud, 1901b, p. 9). *If* that latent fear was actually the motive of the slip, it was surely *not apparent* to anyone.

Once it is clear what is *meant* by a *bona fide* Freudian slip, we need to ask whether there *actually exist* any such slips at all, that is, slips that *appear* to be psychologically *unmotivated* but are actually caused by repressed unpleasant ideas. It is very important to appreciate how difficult it is to provide cogent evidence for such causation. Schüttauf *et al.* (1997) claim to have produced just such evidence. They note that, according to psychoanalytic aetiologic theory, obsessive–compulsive neurosis is attributable to an unconscious conflict whose repressed component features anal-erotic and sadistic wishes, which are presumably activated by regression. Then they reason that when such conflict-laden material is to be verbalized by obsessive–compulsive neurotics, Freudian theory expects a higher incidence of misspeakings (slips of the tongue) among them than among normal subjects. And these researchers report that all of their findings bore out that expectation.

This investigation by Schüttauf *et al.* differs from Bröder's (1995) strategy, which was designed to inquire into "the possible influence of unconscious information-processing on the frequency of specific speech-errors in an experimental setting". Thus, Bröder and Bredenkamp (1996, Abstract) claim to have produced experimental support for the "weaker Freudian thesis" of verbal slip generation by unconscious, rather than repressed, thoughts: "Priming words that remain unconscious induce misspeaking errors with higher probability than consciously registered ones".

As for the soundness of the design of Schüttauf *et al.*, Hans Eysenck (private communication to Rosemarie Sand, 1 March 1996; cited by permission) has raised several objections:

(i) "as the author [Schüttauf] himself acknowledges, this is not an experiment, as ordinarily understood; it is a simple correlational study . . . correlation cannot be interpreted as causation, which he unfortunately attempts to do".

(ii) The members of the experimental group were severely neurotic, while the control group were normals. But "the proper control group would have been severely [disturbed] neurotics suffering from a different form of neurosis than that of obsessive compulsive behaviour".

(iii) "Freudian theory posits a causal relationship between the anal stage of development and obsessive compulsive neurosis; the author does not even try to document this hypothetical relationship".

(iv) "[O]bsessive–compulsive neurotics suffer from fear of dirt and contamination, so that on those grounds alone they would be likely to react differentially to stimuli suggesting such contamination. . . . It is truly commonsensical to say that people whose neurosis consists of feelings of dirt will react differentially to verbal presentations of words related to dirt".

Naturally, I sympathize with Schüttauf and his co-workers in their avowed effort (Section 4) to escape my criticism (Grünbaum, 1984, pp. 202–205) of an earlier purported experimental confirmation of Freud's theory of slips by M. T. Motley (1980). I had complained that the independent variable Motley manipulated in his speech-error experiments did *not* involve *unconscious* antecedents—but only conscious ones. As Schüttauf *et al.* tell us, precisely in order to escape my criticism of Motley, they relied on Freud's aetiology of obsessive–compulsive neurosis to infer that subjects who exhibit the symptoms of that neurosis fulfil the requirement of harbouring repressions of anal-sadistic wishes. Thus, *only* on that aetiologic assumption does their use of compulsive subjects *and* their manipulation of words pertaining to anal-sadistic themata warrant their expectation of a higher incidence of verbal slips in this group than among normals.

Surely one could not reasonably expect the authors themselves to have carried out empirical tests of the aetiology on which their entire investigation is *crucially predicated*. But, none the less, Eysenck's demand for such evidence is entirely appropriate:

without independent *supporting* evidence for that aetiology, their test is definitely *not* a test of Freud's theory of slips of the tongue, let alone—as they conclude—a confirmation of it.

Thus, as long as good empirical support for the Freudian scenario is unavailable, we actually don't know whether any *bona fide* Freudian slips exist at all. Just this lack of evidence serves to undermine Nagel's thesis that cultural influence is a criterion of validity. After all, if we have no cogent evidence for the existence of genuinely Freudian slips, then Freud's theory of bungled actions ("parapraxes") might well be false. And if so, it would not contribute one iota to its validity, even if our entire culture unanimously believed in it, and made extensive explanatory use of it: when an ill-supported theory is used to provide explanations, they run the grave risk of being bogus, and its purported insights may well be *pseudo*-insights.

A second example supporting my rejection of Nagel's cultural criterion is furnished by the work of the celebrated art historian Meyer Schapiro of Columbia University. Schapiro saw himself as greatly influenced by Freud in his accounts of the work of such painters as Paul Cézanne, who died in 1906 (Solomon, 1994). Of course, Schapiro never actually put Cézanne on the psychoanalytic couch. But he subjected artists indirectly "to his own [brand of speculative] couch treatment" (Solomon, 1994). In his best-known essay, Schapiro "turns the Frenchman into a case history". Indeed, a recent tribute to Schapiro's transformation of scholarship in art history (Solomon, 1994) says that his "accomplishment was to shake off the dust and open the field to a style of speculation and intellectual bravura that drew . . . most notably [on] psychoanalysis" (Solomon, 1994, p. 24). Reportedly, "his insights into . . . the apples of Cézanne" (*ibid.*) make the point that Cézanne's "depictions of apples contain [in Schapiro's words] 'a latent erotic sense'".

But if apples are held to symbolize sex unconsciously for Cézanne or anyone else, why doesn't *anything else* that resembles apples in *some* respect (e.g., being quasi-spherical) do likewise? Yet we learn that Schapiro's 1968 publication "The apples of Cézanne" is "His best known essay" (Solomon, 1994, p. 25). Alas, if Schapiro's claim that Cézanne was "unwillingly chaste" is to be a psychoanalytic insight gleaned from his art, rather than a documented biographical fact, I must say that Schapiro's psycho-diagnosis is an instance of what Freud himself deplored as "'Wild' Psycho-Analysis" (1910k, pp. 221–227). In any case, *pace* Nagel, such art-historical invocation of Freud, however influential, does nothing, I claim, to enhance the *credibility* of psychoanalysis.

For centuries, even as far back as in New Testament narratives, both physical disease and insanity have been attributed to demonic possession in Christendom, no less than among primitive peoples. That demon theory has been used, for example, to explain deafness, blindness, and fever as well as such psychopathological conditions as epilepsy, somnambulism, and hysteria. Our contemporary medical term "epilepsy" comes from the Greek word *epilepsis* (for seizure), and reflects etymologically the notion of being seized by a demon. Since exorcism is designed to drive out the devil, it is the supposed *therapy* for demonic possession. In the Roman Catholic exorcist ritual, which has been endorsed by the present Pope and by Cardinal O'Connor of New York, the existence of death is blamed on Satan. And that ritual also survives in baptism as well as in blessing persons or consecrating houses.

How does the strength of the cultural influence of such religious beliefs and practices compare to that of Freud's teachings? Though Freud characterized his type of psychotherapy as *"primus inter pares"* (1933a, p. 157), he conceded sorrowfully:

> I do not think our [psychoanalytic] cures can compete with those of Lourdes. There are so many more people who believe in the miracles of the Blessed Virgin than in the existence of the unconscious. [Freud, 1933a, p. 152]

Clearly, the psychoanalytic and theological notions of aetiology and of therapy clash, and their comparative cultural influence cannot cogently decide between them. But, if it *could*, psychoanalysis would be the loser! This alone, I claim, is a *reductio ad absurdum* of the thesis that the validity of the psychoanalytic enterprise is assured by its wide cultural influence.

Nor can Nagel buttress that thesis by the dubious, vague declaration that psychoanalysis is an "extension" of common sense. As I have shown elsewhere (Grünbaum, forthcoming), the term "extension" is hopelessly unable to bear the weight required by his thesis, if *actual* psychoanalytic theory is to square with it. What, for example, is *common sensical* about the standard psychoanalytic aetiologic explanation of male diffidence and social anxiety by repressed adult *"castration* anxiety" (Fenichel, 1945, p. 520), or of a like explanation of a male driver's stopping at a *green* traffic light as if it were red (Brenner, 1982, pp. 182–183)? Common sense rightly treats such explanations incredulously as bizarre, and rightly so: as I have shown (Grünbaum, 1997), these aetiologic explanations rest on quicksand, even if we were to grant Freud's Oedipal scenario that all adult males unconsciously dread castration by their fathers for having lusted after their mothers.

IV. Critique of Freudian and post-Freudian psychoanalysis

Let me now turn to my critique of the core of Freud's original psychoanalytic theory and to a verdict on its fundamental modifications by two major post-Freudian sets of hypotheses called "self-psychology" and "object relations theory".

The pillars of the avowed "cornerstone" of Freud's theoretical edifice comprise several major theses:

1. Distressing mental states induce the operation of a psychic mechanism of repression, which consists in the banishment from consciousness of *unpleasurable* psychic states (Freud, 1915d, p. 147).

2. Once repression is operative (more or less fully), it not only banishes such negatively charged ideas from consciousness, but plays a *further* crucial multiple causal role: it is *causally necessary* for the pathogens of neuroses, the production of our dreams, and the generation of our various sorts of slips (bungled actions).

3. The "method of free association" can identify and lift (undo) the patient's repressions; by doing so, it can identify the pathogens of the neuroses, and the generators of our dreams, as well as the causes of our motivationally opaque slips; moreover, by lifting the pathogenic repressions, free association functions therapeutically, rather than only investigatively.

Freud provided two sorts of arguments for his cardinal aetiologic doctrine that repressions are the pathogens of the neuroses:

his earlier one, which goes back to his original collaboration with Josef Breuer, relies on purported *therapeutic successes* from lifting repressions; the later one, which is designed to show that the pathogenic repressions are *sexual*, is drawn from presumed re-enactments ("transferences") of infantile episodes in the adult patient's interactions with the analyst during psychoanalytic treatment.

It will be expositorily expeditious to deal with Freud's earlier aetiologic argument within Section B below, and to appraise the subsequent one, which goes back to his "Dora" case history of 1905, in Section C. But, also for expository reasons, it behooves us to devote a prior Section A to his account of the actuation of the hypothesized mechanism of repression by "motives of unpleasure".

A. Negative affect and forgetting

As Freud told us, "The theory of repression is the cornerstone on which the whole structure of psycho-analysis rests. It is the most essential part of it" (Freud, 1914d, p. 16). The *process* of repression, which consists in the banishment of ideas from consciousness or in denying them entry into it, is itself presumed to be unconscious (Freud, 1915d, p. 147). In Freud's view, our neurotic symptoms, the manifest contents of our dreams, and the slips we commit are each constructed as "compromises between the demands of a repressed impulse and the resistances of a censoring force in the ego" (Freud, 1916–1917, p. 301; 1925d, p. 45). By being only such compromises, rather than fulfilments of the instinctual impulses, these products of the unconscious afford only *substitutive* gratifications or outlets. For brevity, one can say, therefore, that Freud has offered a unifying "compromise-model" of neuroses, dreams, and parapraxes.

But what, in the first place, is the *motive* or cause that initiates and sustains the operation of the unconscious mechanism of repression *before* it produces its own later effects? Apparently, Freud assumes *axiomatically* that distressing mental states, such as forbidden wishes, trauma, disgust, anxiety, anger, shame, hate, guilt, and sadness—all of which are *unpleasurable*—almost always actuate, and then fuel, *forgetting* to the point of repression. Thus, repression regulates pleasure and unpleasure by defending our consciousness against various sorts of *negative affect*. Indeed, Freud claimed perennially that repression is the paragon among our *defence* mechanisms

(Thomä & Kächele, 1987, volume 1, pp. 107–111). As Freud put it dogmatically: "The tendency to forget what is disagreeable seems to me to be a quite universal one" (Freud, 1901b, p. 144), and "the recollection of distressing impressions and the occurrence of distressing thoughts are opposed by a resistance" (Freud, 1901b, p. 146).

Freud tries to disarm an important objection to his thesis that "distressing memories succumb especially easily to motivated forgetting" (Freud, 1901b, p. 147). He says:

> The assumption that a defensive trend of this kind exists cannot be objected to on the ground that one often enough finds it impossible, on the contrary, to get rid of distressing memories that pursue one, and to banish distressing affective impulses like remorse and the pangs of conscience. For we are not asserting that this defensive trend is able to put itself into effect *in every case* . . . [Freud, 1901b, p. 147, my italics]

Indeed, he acknowledges as "also a true fact" that "distressing things are particularly hard to forget" (Freud, 1916–1917, pp. 76–77).

For instance, we know from Charles Darwin's autobiography that his father had developed a remarkably retentive memory for painful experiences (cited in Grünbaum, 1994), and that a half century after Giuseppe Verdi was humiliatingly denied admission to the Milan Music Conservatory, he recalled it indignantly (Walker, 1962, pp. 8–9). Freud himself told us as an adult (Freud, 1900a, p. 216) that he "can remember very clearly," from age seven or eight, how his father rebuked him for having relieved himself in the presence of his parents in their bedroom. In a frightful blow to Freud's ego, his father said: "The boy will come to nothing".

But Freud's attempt here to uphold his thesis of motivated forgetting is *evasive* and *unavailing*: since some painful mental states are vividly remembered while others are forgotten or even repressed, I claim that *factors different from their painfulness determine whether they are remembered or forgotten.* For example, personality dispositions or situational variables may in fact be causally relevant. To the great detriment of his theory, Freud never came to grips with the *unfavourable* bearing of this key fact about the mnemic effects of painfulness on the tenability of the following pillar of his theory of repression: when painful or forbidden experiences are forgotten, the forgetting is tantamount to their repression *due to their negative affect*, and thereby produces neurotic symptoms or other compromise formations. Thomas Gilovich, a professor of psychology at Cornell University (USA), is now doing valuable work on the conditions under which painful experiences are *remembered*, and on those *other* conditions under which they are forgotten.

The numerous and familiar occurrences of vivid and even obsessive recall of negative experiences pose a fundamental *statistical* and explanatory challenge to Freud that neither he nor his followers have ever met. We must ask (Grünbaum, 1994): just what is the *ratio* of the forgetting of distressing experiences to their recall, and what *other* factors determine that ratio? Freud gave no statistical evidence for assuming that forgetting them is the *rule*, while remembering them is the exception. Yet, as we can see, his theory of repression is devastatingly undermined from the outset if forgettings of negative experiences do not greatly outnumber rememberings statistically. After all, if forgetting is *not* the rule, then what *other* reason does Freud offer for supposing that when distressing experiences are actually forgotten, these forgettings are instances of genuine repression due to affective displeasure? And if he has no such other reason, then, *a fortiori*, he has no basis at all for his pivotal aetiologic scenario that forbidden or aversive states of mind are usually repressed and thereby cause compromise formations.

Astonishingly, Freud thinks he can parry this basic statistical and explanatory challenge by an evasive dictum as follows:

> ... mental life is the arena and battle-ground for mutually opposing purposes [of forgetting and remembering];

> ... there is room for both. It is only a question ... of what effects are produced by the one and the other. [Freud, 1916–1917, pp. 76–77]

Indeed, just that question cries out for an answer from Freud, if he is to make his case. Instead, he cavalierly left it dangle epistemologically in limbo.

B. The epistemological liabilities of the psychoanalytic method of free association

Another basic difficulty, which besets all three major branches of the theory of repression alike, lies in the epistemological defects of

Freud's so-called "fundamental rule" of free association, the supposed microscope and X-ray tomograph of the human mind. This rule enjoins the patient to tell the analyst without reservation whatever comes to mind. Thus, it serves as the fundamental method of clinical investigation. We are told that by using this technique to unlock the floodgates of the unconscious, Freud was able to show that neuroses, dreams, and slips are caused by repressed motives. Just as in Breuer's cathartic use of hypnosis, it is a cardinal thesis of Freud's entire psychoanalytic enterprise that his method of free association has a twofold major capability, which is both investigative and therapeutic: (i) it can *identify* the unconscious causes of human thoughts and behaviour, both abnormal and normal, and (ii) by overcoming resistances and lifting repressions, it can remove the unconscious pathogens of neuroses, and thus provide therapy for an important class of mental disorders.

But on what grounds did Freud assert that free association has the stunning investigative capability to be *causally probative* for aetiologic research in psychopathology? Is it not too good to be true that one can put a psychologically disturbed person on the couch and fathom the aetiology of her or his affliction by free association? As compared to fathoming the causation of major somatic diseases, that seems almost miraculous, *if at all true*. Freud tells us very clearly (1900a, p. 528) that his argument for his investigative tribute to free association as a means of uncovering the causation of neuroses is, at bottom, a *therapeutic* one going back to the cathartic method of treating hysteria. Let me state and articulate his argument.

One of Freud's justifications for the use of free association as a *causally probative* method of dream investigation leading to the identification of the repressed dream thoughts, he tells us, is that it

> is identical with the procedure [of free association] by which we resolve hysterical symptoms; and there the correctness of our method [of free association] is warranted by the coincident emergence and disappearance of the symptoms. [Freud, 1900a, p. 528]

But as I have pointed out elsewhere (Grünbaum, 1993, pp. 25–26), his original German text here contains a confusing slip of the pen. As we know, the patient's symptoms hardly first emerge simultaneously with their therapeutic dissipation. Yet Strachey translated

Freud correctly as having spoken of "the coincident emergence and disappearance of the symptoms". It would seem that Freud means to speak of the *resolution* (German: *Auflösung*), rather than of the emergence (*Auftauchen*), of the symptoms as coinciding with their therapeutic dissipation. Now, for Freud, the "resolution of a symptom", in turn, consists of using free association to uncover the repressed pathogen that enters into the compromise formation that is held to constitute the symptom. This much, then, is the statement of Freud's appeal to therapeutic success to vouch for the "correctness of our method" of free association as causally probative for aetiologic research in psychopathology.

To articulate the argument adequately, however, we must still clarify Freud's original basis for claiming that (unsuccessful) repression is indeed the pathogen of neurosis. Only then will he have made his case for claiming that free association is aetiologically probative, because it is uniquely capable of uncovering repressions. The pertinent argument is offered in Breuer and Freud's "Preliminary communication" (1893a, pp. 6–7). There they wrote

> For we found, to our great surprise at first, that *each individual hysterical symptom immediately and permanently disappeared when we had succeeded in bringing clearly to light the memory of the event by which it was provoked and in arousing its accompanying affect, and when the patient had described that event in the greatest possible detail and had put the affect into words.* Recollection without affect almost invariably produces no result. The psychical process which originally took place must be repeated as vividly as possible; it must be brought back to its *status nascendi* and then given verbal utterance. [*ibid.*, p. 6, original italics]

Breuer and Freud make an important comment on their construal of this therapeutic finding:

> It is plausible to suppose that it is a question here of unconscious suggestion: the patient expects to be relieved of his sufferings by this procedure, and it is this expectation, and not the verbal utterance, which is the operative factor. This, however, is not so. [Breuer & Freud, 1893a, p. 7]

And their avowed reason is that, in 1881, i.e., in the "'pre-suggestion' era", the cathartic method was used to remove *separately* distinct symptoms, "which sprang from separate causes" such that any one symptom disappeared only after the cathartic ("abreactive") lifting of a *particular* repression. But Breuer and Freud do not tell us why the likelihood of placebo effect should be deemed to be lower when several symptoms are wiped out *seriatim* than in the case of getting rid of only one symptom. Thus, as I have pointed out elsewhere (Grünbaum, 1993, p. 238) to discredit the hypothesis of placebo effect, it would have been essential to have comparisons with treatment outcome from a suitable control group whose repressions are *not* lifted. If that control group were to fare equally well, treatment gains from psychoanalysis would then be placebo effects after all.

In sum, Breuer and Freud inferred that the therapeutic removal of neurotic symptoms was produced by the cathartic lifting of the patient's previously ongoing repression of the pertinent traumatic memory, not by the therapist's suggestion or some other placebo factor (see Grünbaum, 1993, Chapter Three for a very detailed analysis of the placebo concept). We can codify this claim as follows:

T. Therapeutic hypothesis. Lifting repressions of traumatic memories cathartically is *causally relevant* to the disappearance of neuroses.

As we saw, Breuer and Freud (1893a, p. 6) reported the immediate and permanent disappearance of each hysterical symptom after they cathartically lifted the repression of the memory of the trauma that occasioned the given symptom. They adduce this "evidence" to draw an epoch-making inductive *aetiologic* inference (*ibid.*), which postulates "a causal relation between the determining [repression of the memory of the] psychical trauma and the hysterical phenomenon". Citing the old scholastic dictum "*Cessante causa cessat effectus*" ("when the cause ceases, its effect ceases"), they invoke its contrapositive (*ibid.*, p. 7), which states that as long as the effect (symptom) persists, so does its cause (the repressed memory of the psychical trauma). And they declare just that to be the pattern of the pathogenic action of the repressed psychical trauma. This trauma, we learn, is *not* a mere *precipitating* cause. Such a mere *agent provocateur* just releases the symptom, "which thereafter leads an independent existence". Instead, "the [repressed] memory of the trauma . . . acts like a foreign body which long after its entry must continue to be regarded as an agent that is still at work" (ibid., p. 6).

The upshot of their account is that their observations of positive therapeutic outcome upon the abreactive lifting of repressions, which they interpret in the sense of their therapeutic hypothesis, spelled a paramount aetiologic moral as follows:

E. Aetiologic hypothesis. An ongoing repression accompanied by affective suppression is causally necessary for the initial pathogenesis and persistence of a neurosis.

This formulation of the foundational aetiology of psychoanalysis supersedes the one I gave as a result of a suggestion by Carl Hempel and Morris Eagle (Grünbaum, 1984, p. 181). The revised formulation here is faithful to Breuer and Freud's reference to "accompanying affect" (Breuer & Freud, 1893a, p. 6) à propos of the traumatic events whose repression occasioned the symptoms.

Clearly, this aetiologic hypothesis E permits the valid deduction of the therapeutic finding reported by Breuer and Freud as codified in their therapeutic hypothesis T: the cathartic lifting of the repressions of traumatic memories of events that occasion symptoms engendered the disappearance of the symptoms. And, as they told us explicitly (Breuer & Freud, 1893a, p. 6), this therapeutic finding is their "evidence" for their cardinal aetiologic hypothesis E. But I maintain that this inductive argument is vitiated by what I like to call the "fallacy of crude hypothetico–deductive (H–D) pseudo-confirmation". Thus note that the remedial action of aspirin consumption for tension headaches does not lend H–D support to the outlandish aetiologic hypothesis that a hematolytic aspirin deficiency is a causal sine qua non for having tension headaches, although such remedial action is validly deducible from that bizarre hypothesis. Twenty-five years ago, Wesley Salmon called attention to the fallacy of inductive causal inference from mere valid H–D deducibility by giving an example in which a deductively valid pseudo-explanation of a man's avoiding pregnancy can readily give rise to an H–D pseudo-confirmation of the addle-brained attribution of his non-pregnancy to his consumption of birth-control pills. Salmon (1971, p. 34) states the fatuous pseudo-explanation: "John Jones avoided becoming pregnant during the past year, for he had taken his wife's birth control pills regularly, and every man who regularly takes birth control pills avoids pregnancy".

Plainly, this deducibility of John Jones's recent failure to become pregnant from the stated premisses does not lend any credence at all to the zany hypothesis that this absence of pregnancy is *causally attributable* to his consumption of birth-control pills. Yet it is even true that any men who consume such pills *in fact* never do become pregnant. Patently, as Salmon notes, the fly in the ointment is that men just do not become pregnant, whether they take birth-control pills or not.

His example shows that neither the empirical truth of the deductively inferred conclusion and of the pertinent initial condition concerning Jones nor the deductive validity of the inference can provide bona fide confirmation of the causal hypothesis that male consumption of birth-control pills prevents male pregnancy: that hypothesis would first have to meet other epistemic requirements, which it manifestly cannot do.

Crude H–D confirmationism is a paradise of spurious causal inferences, as illustrated by Breuer and Freud's unsound aetiologic inference. Thus, psychoanalytic narratives are replete with the belief that a hypothesized aetiologic scenario embedded in a psychoanalytic narrative of an analysand's affliction is *made credible* merely because the postulated aetiology then permits the logical deduction or probabilistic inference of the neurotic symptoms to be explained.

Yet some apologists offer a facile excuse for the fallacious H–D confirmation of a causal hypothesis. We are told that the hypothesis is warranted by an "inference to the best explanation" (Harman, 1965). But in a careful new study, Wesley Salmon (2001) has argued that "the characterization of nondemonstrative inference as inference to the best explanation serves to muddy the waters . . . by fostering confusion" between two sorts of why-questions that Hempel had distinguished: *explanation*-seeking questions as to why something is the case, and *confirmation*-seeking why-questions as to why a hypothesis is *credible*. Thus, a hypothesis that is pseudo-confirmed by some data cannot be warranted qua being "the only [explanatory] game in town". Alas, "best explanation" sanction was claimed for psychoanalytic aetiologies to explain and treat the destructive behaviour of sociopaths *to no avail* for years (cf. Cleckley, 1988, Section 4, esp. pp. 238–239 and 438–439).

I can now demonstrate the multiple failure of Freud's therapeutic argument for the aetiologic probativeness of free association in psychopathology, no matter how revealing the associative contents may otherwise be in regard to the patient's psychological preoccupations and personality dispositions. Let us take our bearings and first encapsulate the structure of his therapeutic argument.

First, Freud inferred that the therapeutic disappearance of the neurotic symptoms is *causally attributable* to the cathartic lifting of repressions *by means of the method of free associations*. Relying on this key therapeutic hypothesis, he then drew two further major theoretical inferences: (i) the seeming removal of the neurosis by means of cathartically *lifting* repressions is good inductive evidence for postulating that repressions accompanied by affective suppression are themselves *causally necessary* for the very existence of a neurosis (Freud, 1893h, pp. 6–7), and (ii) granted that such repressions are thus the essential causes of neurosis, *and* that the method of free association is uniquely capable of uncovering these repressions, this method is uniquely competent *to identify the causes* or pathogens of the neuroses. (Having convinced himself of the causal probativeness of the method of free associations on therapeutic grounds in the case of those neuroses he believed to be successfully treatable, Freud also felt justified in deeming the method reliable as a means of unearthing the aetiologies of those *other* neuroses—the so-called "narcissistic ones," such as paranoia—which he considered psychoanalytically *untreatable*.)

But the argument fails for the following several reasons: in the first place, the durable therapeutic success on which it was predicated did not materialize (Borch-Jacobsen, 1996), as Freud was driven to admit both early and very late in his career (Freud, 1925d, p. 27; 1937c, pp. 23, 216–253). But even in so far as there was transitory therapeutic gain, we saw that Freud *failed* to rule out a rival hypothesis that undermines his attribution of such gain to the lifting of repressions by free association: the ominous hypothesis of placebo effect, which asserts that treatment ingredients *other than* insight into the patient's repressions—such as the mobilization of the patient's hope by the therapist—are responsible for any resulting improvement (Grünbaum, 1993, Chapter Three). Nor have other analysts ruled out the placebo hypothesis during the past century. A case in point is a forty-five-page study "On the efficacy of psychoanalysis" (Bachrach, Galatzer-Levy, Skolnikoff, & Waldron, 1991), published in the official *Journal of the American Psychoanalytic Association*. Another is the account of analytic treatment process by Vaughan and Roose (1995).

Last, but not least, the repression aetiology is evidentially ill-founded, as we saw earlier and will see further in Section C. It is unavailing to the purported *aetiologic* probativeness of free associations that they may lift repressions, since Freud failed to show that the latter are pathogenic. In sum, Freud's argument has forfeited its premisses.

C. Freud's aetiologic transference argument

Now let us consider Freud's argument for his cardinal thesis that *sexual* repressions in particular are the pathogens of all neuroses, an argument he deemed "decisive". Drawing on my earlier writings (Grünbaum, 1990, pp. 565–567; 1993, pp. 152–158), we shall now find that this argument is without merit.

According to Freud's theory of transference, the patient *transfers* on to his psychoanalyst feelings and thoughts that originally pertained to important figures in his or her earlier life. In this important sense, the fantasies woven around the psychoanalyst by the analysand, and quite generally the latter's conduct toward his or her doctor, are hypothesized to be *thematically recapitulatory* of childhood episodes. And by thus being recapitulatory, the patient's behaviour during treatment can be said to exhibit a thematic kinship to such very early episodes. Therefore, when the analyst interprets these supposed re-enactments, the ensuing interpretations are called "transference interpretations".

Freud and his followers have traditionally drawn the following highly questionable causal inference: precisely in virtue of being thematically recapitulated in the patient–doctor interaction, the hypothesized earlier scenario in the patient's life can cogently be held to have originally been a *pathogenic* factor in the patient's affliction. For example, in his case history of the Rat-Man, Freud (1909d) infers that a certain emotional conflict had originally been the precipitating cause of the patient's inability to work, merely because this conflict had been thematically re-enacted in a fantasy the Rat-Man had woven around Freud during treatment.

Thus, in the context of Freud's transference interpretations, the thematic re-enactment is claimed to show that the early scenario had originally been *pathogenic*. According to this aetiologic conclusion, the patient's thematic re-enactment in the treatment setting is also asserted to be *pathogenically* recapitulatory by being pathogenic in the adult patient's here-and-now, rather than only thematically recapitulatory. Freud extols this dubious aetiologic transference argument in his "On the history of the psycho-analytic movement," claiming that it furnishes the most unshakable proof for his sexual aetiology of all the neuroses:

> The fact of the emergence of the transference in its crudely sexual form, whether affectionate or hostile, in every treatment of a neurosis, although this is neither desired nor induced by either doctor or patient, has always seemed to me the most irrefragable proof [original German: "unerschütterlichste Beweis"] that the source of the driving forces of neurosis lies in sexual life [sexual repressions]. This argument has never received anything approaching the degree of attention that it merits, for if it had, investigations in this field would leave no other conclusion open. As far as I am concerned, this argument has remained the decisive one, over and above the more specific findings of analytic work. [Freud, 1914d, p. 12]

On the contrary, the patient's thematically recapitulatory behavior toward his doctor *does not show* that it is also *pathogenically* recapitulatory. How, for example, does the re-enactment, during treatment, of a patient's early conflict show at all that the original conflict had been pathogenic in the first place? Quite generally, how do transference phenomena focusing on the analyst show that a presumed current replica of a past event is *pathogenic* in the here-and-now?

Therefore, I submit, the purportedly "irrefragable proof" of which Freud spoke deserves more attention *not* because its appreciation "would leave no other conclusion open," as he would have it; instead, I contend that the Rat-Man case and other such case histories show how baffling it is that Freud deemed the aetiologic transference argument cogent *at all*, let alone unshakably so.

Marshall Edelson has offered a rebuttal to my denial of the cogency of the aetiologic transference argument:

. . . in fact, in psychoanalysis the pathogen is not merely a remote event, or a series of such events, the effect of which lives on. The pathogen reappears in all its virulence, with increasing frankness and explicitness, in the transference—in a new edition, a new version, a reemergence, a repetition of the past pathogenic events or factors. [Edelson, 1984, p. 150]

And Edelson elaborates:

The pathogen together with its pathological effects are, therefore, under the investigator's eye, so to speak, in the psychoanalytic situation, and demonstrating the causal relation between them in that situation, by experimental or quasi-experimental methods, surely provides support, even if indirect, for the hypothesis that in the past the same kind of pathogenic factors were necessary to bring about the same kind of effects. [*ibid.*, p. 151]

But how does the psychoanalyst demonstrate, within the confines of his clinical setting, that the supposed *current* replica of the remote, early event is *presently* the virulent *cause* of the patient's neurosis, let alone that the original pathogen is replicated at all in the transference? Having fallaciously identified a conflict as a pathogen because it reappears in the transference, many Freudians conclude that pathogens must reappear in the transference. And, in this way, they beg the key question I have just asked. How, for example, did Freud show that the Rat-Man's marriage conflict depicted in that patient's transference fantasy was the *current* cause of his *ongoing death obsessions*? Neither Edelson's book nor his later paper offers a better answer. Thus, in the paper he declares:

The psychoanalyst claims that current mental representations of particular past events or fantasies are constitutive (i.e., *current* operative) causes of current behavior, and then goes on to claim that therefore past actual events or fantasies are aetiological causes of the analysand's symptoms. [Edelson, 1986]

And Edelson concludes: "Transference phenomena are . . . nonquestion-begging evidence for . . . inferences about causally efficacious psychological entities existing or occurring in the here-and-now" (*ibid.*, p. 110).

In sum, despite Edelson's best efforts, the aetiologic transference argument on which both Freud and he rely is ill-founded: (i) they employ epistemically circular reasoning, when inferring the occurrence of infantile episodes from the adult patient's reports, and then claiming that these early episodes are thematically recapitulated in the adult analysand's conduct towards the analyst; (ii) they beg the *aetiologic* question by inferring that, qua being thematically recapitulated, the infantile episodes had been pathogenic at the outset; (iii) they reason that the adult patient's thematic re-enactment is *pathogenically* recapitulatory such that the current replica of the infantile episodes is pathogenic in the here-and-now.

Indeed, Freud went on to build on the quicksand of his aetiologic transference argument. It inspired two of his further fundamental tenets: first, the *investigative* thesis that the psychoanalytic dissection of the patient's behaviour toward the analyst can reliably identify the *original pathogens* of his or her long-term neurosis; second, the cardinal therapeutic doctrine that the working through of the analysand's so-called "transference neurosis" is the key to overcoming his or her perennial problems.

D. Free association as a method of dream interpretation

Yet, as we learn from Freud's opening pages on his method of dream interpretation, he *extrapolated* the presumed causally probative role of free associations from being only a method of aetiologic inquiry aimed at therapy, to serving likewise as an avenue for finding the purported *unconscious* causes of dreams (Freud, 1900a, pp. 100–101; see also p. 528). And, in the same breath, he reports that when patients told him about their dreams while associating freely to their symptoms, he extrapolated his compromise-model from neurotic symptoms to manifest dream contents. A year later, he carried out the same twofold extrapolation to include slips or bungled actions.

But what do free associations tell us about our dreams? Whatever the manifest content of dreams, they are *purportedly wish-fulfilling* in at least two logically distinct specific ways as follows: for every dream *D*, there exists at least one normally unconscious infantile wish *W* such that (i) *W* is the motivational cause of *D*, and (ii) the manifest content of *D* graphically displays, more or less disguisedly, the state of affairs desired by W. As Freud opined (1925d, p. 44):

> When the latent dream-thoughts that are revealed by the analysis [via free association] of a dream are examined, one of them is found to stand out from among the rest . . . the isolated thought is found to be a wishful impulse. [Freud, 1925d, p. 44]

But Freud manipulated the free associations to yield a distinguished wish-motive (Glymour, 1983).

Quite independently of Freud's abortive therapeutic argument for the causal probativeness of free association, he offered his analysis of his 1895 "Specimen Irma Dream" (Freud, 1990a, p. 97) as a *non-therapeutic* argument for the method of free association as a cogent means of identifying hypothesized hidden, forbidden wishes as the motives of our dreams. But in my detailed critique of that unjustly celebrated analysis (Grünbaum, 1984, Chapter Five), I have argued that Freud's account is, alas, no more than a piece of false advertising: (i) it does not deliver at all the promised vindication of the probativeness of free association, (ii) it does nothing toward warranting his foolhardy dogma that *all* dreams are wish-fulfilling in his stated sense, (iii) it does not even pretend that his alleged "Specimen Dream" is evidence for his compromise-model of manifest-dream content, and (iv) the inveterate and continuing celebration of Freud's analysis of his Irma Dream in the psychoanalytic literature as the paragon of dream interpretation is completely unwarranted, because it is mere salesmanship.

Alas, Freud's 1895 neurobiological wish-fulfilment theory of dreaming was irremediably flawed from the outset (Grünbaum, forthcoming). Furthermore, he astonishingly did not heed a patent epistemological consequence of having abandoned his 1895 *Project's* neurological energy-model of *wish-driven* dreaming: by precisely that abandonment, he himself had *forfeited* his initial biological *rationale* for claiming that at least all "normal" dreams are wish-fulfilling. *A fortiori*, this forfeiture left him without any kind of energy-based warrant for then *universalizing* the doctrine of wish-fulfilment on the psychological level to extend to *any* sort of dream. Yet, unencumbered by the total absence of any such warrant, the *universalized* doctrine, now formulated in psychological terms, rose like a Phoenix from the ashes of Freud's defunct energy-model.

Once he had clearly *chained* himself gratuitously to the universal wish-monopoly of dream-generation, his interpretations of dreams were constrained to reconcile *wish-contravening* dreams with the decreed universality of wish-fulfilment. Such reconciliation demanded imperiously that all other parts and details of his dream-theory be obligingly *tailored* to the governing wish-dogma so as to sustain it. Yet, Freud artfully obscured this *dynamic* of theorizing, while begging the methodological question (Freud, 1900a, p. 135). Wish-contravening dreams include anxiety dreams, nightmares, and the so-called "counter-wish dreams" (1900a, p. 157). As an example of the latter, Freud reports a trial attorney's dream that he had lost all of his court cases (1900a, p. 152).

Freud's initial 1900 statement of his dual wish-fulfillment in dreams had been: "*Thus its content was the fulfilment of a wish and its motive was a wish*" (1900a, p. 119). But the sense in which dreams are wish-fulfilling *overall* is purportedly *threefold* rather than only twofold: one motivating cause is the universal *preconscious* wish-to-sleep, which purportedly provides a generic causal explanation of dreaming *as such* and, in turn, makes dreaming the guardian of sleep (Freud, 1900a, pp. 234, 680); another is the individualized *repressed* infantile wish, which is activated by the day's residue and explains the *particular* manifest *content* of a given dream; furthermore, as already noted, that manifest content of the dream graphically displays, more or less disguisedly, the state of affairs desired by the unconscious wish. The disguise is supposedly effected by the defensive operation of the "dream-*distortion*" of the content of forbidden unconscious wishes.

But this theorized distortion of the hypothesized latent content must not be identified with the very familiar *phenomenological bizarreness* of the manifest dream content! That bizarreness stands in contrast to the stable configurations of ordinary waking experiences. By achieving a compromise with the *repressed* wishes, the postulated distortion makes "plausible that even dreams with a distressing content are to be construed as wish-fulfilments" (Freud, 1900a, p. 159). Accordingly, Freud concedes:

> The fact that dreams really have a secret meaning which represents the fulfillment of a wish must be proved afresh in each particular case by analysis. [Freud, 1900a, p. 146]

But in a 1993 book (Grünbaum, 1993, Chapter Ten; forthcoming), I have argued that this dream theory of universal wish-fulfilment should be presumed to be false at its core rather than just ill-founded.

More conservatively, the psychoanalysts Jacob Arlow and Charles Brenner (1964) had claimed, for reasons of their own, that "A dream is not simply the visually or auditorily hallucinated fulfill-ment of a childhood wish" (Arlow & Brenner, 1988, p. 7). And they countenanced a range of dream motives *other than* wishes, such as anxiety, though ultimately still rooted in childhood (*ibid.*, p. 8).

But this modification did not remedy the fundamental episte-mological defect in the claim that the method of free association can reliably identify dream motives. Undaunted, Arlow and Brenner declare:

> The theory and technique of dream analysis [by free association] in no way differs from the way one would analyze . . . a neurotic symptom, . . . a parapraxis, . . . or any other object of [psycho]analytic scrutiny. [Arlow & Brenner, 1988, p. 8]

By the same token, these analysts insouciantly announce: "Dreams are, in fact, compromise-formations like any others" (*ibid.*, pp. 7–8). Yet this ontological conclusion is predicated on the ill-founded epis-temological thesis that free associations reliably identify repressions to be the causes of symptoms, dreams, and slips.

Indeed, careful studies have shown that the so-called "free" associations are not free but are strongly influenced by the psycho-analyst's subtle promptings to the patient (Grünbaum, 1984, pp. 211–212). And recent memory research has shown further how patients and others can be induced to generate *pseudo*-memories, which are false but deemed veridical by the patients themselves (Goleman, 1994).

As a corollary of the latter epistemological defects of the method of free association, it appears that such associations *cannot* reliably vouch for the *contents* of presumed past repressions that are lifted by them. Thus, the products of such associations cannot serve to justify the following repeated claim of the later (post-1923) Freud: the mere painfulness or unpleasurableness of an experience is *not itself* the prime motive for its repression; instead, its negativity must involve the conscious emergence of an instinctual desire that is recognized by the super-ego as illicit or dangerous (Freud, 1933a, pp. 57, 89, 91, 94; 1937c, p. 227; 1940a, pp. 184–187).

But since Freud had also stressed the well-nigh universal tendency to *forget* negative experiences *per se*, his later view of the dynamics of repression disappointingly leaves dangling theoretically (i) the relation of forgetting to repression, and (ii) why some forgettings, no less than repressions, supposedly cannot be undone without the use of the controlled method of free association. In James Strachey's *Standard Edition*, (1901b, p. 301), the General Index lists two subcategories, among others, under "Forgetting": (i) "motivated by avoidance of unpleasure," and (ii) "motivated by repression". But alas, Freud himself leaves us in a total quandary whether these two categories of Strachey's represent a distinction without a difference.

E. The explanatory pseudo-unification generated by Freud's compromise-model of neuroses, dreams, and slips

My indictment of the compromise-model, if correct, spells an important lesson, I claim, for both philosophical ontology and the theory of scientific explanation. Advocates of psychoanalysis have proclaimed it to be an explanatory virtue of their theory that its compromise-model gives a *unifying* account of such *prima facie* disparate domains of phenomena as neuroses, dreams, and slips, and indeed that the theory of repression also illuminates infantile sexuality and the four stages hypothesized in Freud's theory of psychosexual development. In fact, some philosophers of science, such as Michael Friedman, have hailed explanatory unification as one of the great achievements and desiderata of the scientific enterprise. Thus, one need only think of the beautiful way in which Newton's theory of mechanics and gravitation served all at once to explain the motions of a pendulum on earth and of binary stars above by putting both terrestrial and celestial mechanics under a single theoretical umbrella.

Yet, in other contexts, unification can be a vice rather than a virtue. Thales of Miletus, though rightly seeking a rationalistic, rather than mythopoetic, picture of the world, taught that everything is made of water. And other philosophical monists have enunciated their own unifying ontologies. But the chemist Mendeleyev might have said to Thales across the millennia in the words of Hamlet: "There are more things in heaven and earth, Horatio, than are dreamt of in your philosophy" (Shakespeare, *Hamlet*, Act I, Scene V).

As I have argued, the same moral applies to Freud: by invoking the alleged causal cogency of the method of free association as a warrant for his compromise-model, he generated a *pseudo*-unification of neurotic behaviour with dreaming and the bungling of actions. This dubious unification was effected by conceiving of the *normal* activities of dreaming and occasionally bungling actions as *mini*-neurotic symptoms, of-a-piece with *abnormal* mentation in neuroses and even psychoses. To emphasize this monistic psycho-pathologizing of normalcy, Freud pointedly entitled his magnum opus on slips "The psychopathology of everyday life" (1901b). To this I can only say in metaphorical theological language: "Let no man put together what God has kept asunder", a gibe that was used by Wolfgang Pauli, I believe, against Einstein's unified field theory.

F. The "hermeneutic" reconstruction of psychoanalysis

The French philosopher Paul Ricoeur (1970, p. 358), faced with quite different criticisms of psychoanalysis from philosophers of science during the 1950s and 1960s (von Eckardt, 1985, pp. 356–364), hailed the *failure* of Freud's theory to qualify as an empirical science by the received standards as the basis for "a counter-attack" against those who deplore this failure. In concert with the other so-called "hermeneutic" German philosophers Karl Jaspers and Jürgen Habermas, Ricoeur believed that victory can be snatched from the jaws of the *scientific failings* of Freud's theory by abjuring his scientific aspirations as misguided. Claiming that Freud himself had "scientistically" misunderstood his own theoretical achievement, some hermeneuts misconstrue it as a *semantic* accomplishment by trading on the multiply ambiguous word "meaning" (Grünbaum, 1984, Introduction, Sections 3 and 4; 1990; 1993, Chapter Four). In Freud's theory, an overt symptom manifests one or more underlying unconscious causes and gives evidence for its cause(s), so that the "sense" or "meaning" of the symptom is constituted by its latent motivational cause(s). But this notion of "meaning" is different from the one appropriate to the context of *communication*, in which *linguistic* symbols *acquire semantic* meaning by being used deliberately to designate their referents. Clearly, the relation of being a manifestation, which the symptom bears to its cause, differs from the semantic relation of designation, which a linguistic symbol bears to its object.

The well-known academic psychoanalyst Marshall Edelson is in full agreement with this account and elaborates it lucidly:

> For psychoanalysis, the *meaning* of a mental phenomenon is a set of unconscious psychological or intentional states (specific wishes or impulses, specific fears aroused by these wishes, and thoughts or images which might remind the subject of these wishes and fears). The mental phenomenon substitutes for this set of states. That is, these states would have been present in consciousness, instead of the mental phenomenon requiring interpretation, had they not encountered, at the time of origin of the mental phenomenon or repeatedly since then, obstacles to their access to consciousness. If the mental phenomenon has been a relatively enduring structure, and these obstacles to consciousness are removed, the mental phenomenon disappears as these previously unconscious states achieve access to consciousness. [Edelson, 1988, pp. 246–249]

That the mental phenomenon substitutes for these states is a manifestation of a causal sequence (*ibid.*, pp. 247–248).

And drawing on Freud's compromise-model of symptoms in which symptoms are held to provide *substitutive* outlets or gratifications, Edelson continues:

> Suppose the question is: "Why does the analysand fear the snake so?" Suppose the answer to that question is: "A snake stands for or symbolizes, a penis". It is easy to see that by itself this is no answer at all; for one thing, it leads immediately to the question: "Why does the analysand fear a penis so?" The question is about an inexplicable [unexplained] mental phenomenon (i.e., "fearing the snake so") and its answer depends on an entire causal explanation. . . . "A snake stands for, or symbolizes, a penis" makes sense as an answer only if it is understood as shorthand for a causal explanation. . . . Correspondingly, "the child stands for, or symbolizes, the boss" is not a satisfactory answer (it does not even sound right) to the question, "Why does this father beat his child?"

For my part, in this context I would wish to forestall a semantic misconstrual of the perniciously ambiguous term "symbol" by saying: in virtue of the similarity of shape, the snake *causally* evokes the unconscious image of a feared penis; thereby the snake itself becomes a dreaded object.

Speaking of Freud's writings, Edelson says illuminatingly:

Certain passages (occasional rather than preponderant) allude, often metaphorically, to symbolizing activities in human life. I think it could be argued that these indicate an effort on Freud's part to clarify by analogy aspects of the subject matter he is studying, including in some instances aspects of the clinical activity of the psychoanalyst—while at the same time perhaps he paid too little attention to disanalogies—rather than indicate any abandonment on his part of the [*causally*] explanatory objectives he so clearly pursues. There is no more reason to suppose that just because Freud refers to language, symbols, representations, and symbolic activity (part of his subject matter), he has rejected, or should have rejected, canons of scientific method and reasoning, than to suppose that just because Chomsky studies language (his subject matter), his theory of linguistics cannot be a theory belonging to natural science and that he cannot be seeking causal explanations in formulating it. [Edelson, 1988, p. 247]

The "hermeneutic" reconstruction of psychoanalysis slides illicitly from one of two familiar senses of "meaning" encountered in ordinary discourse to another. When a paediatrician says that a child's spots on the skin "*mean* measles", the "meaning" of the symptom is constituted by one of its *causes*, much as in the Freudian case. Yet, the analyst Anthony Storr (1986, p. 260), when speaking of Freud's "making sense" of a patient's symptoms, conflates the fathoming of the *aetiologic* "sense" or "meaning" of a symptom with the activity of making *semantic* sense of a text (Grünbaum, 1986, p. 280), declaring astonishingly: "Freud was a man of genius whose expertise lay in semantics". And Ricoeur erroneously credits Freud's theory of repression with having provided, *malgré lui*, a veritable "semantics of desire".

In a German book by Achim Stephan (1989, Section 6.7, "Adolf Grünbaum", pp. 144–149), which appeared before a relevant article and book of mine (Grünbaum, 1990, 1993, Chapter Four), he takes issue with some of my views by reference to my earlier book *The Foundations of Psychoanalysis: A Philosophical Critique* (Grünbaum, 1984) and to its German translation (Grünbaum, 1988). Quotations from Stephan below are my translations of his German text. He does *not* endorse Ricoeur's "hermeneutic" construal of psychoanalysis as a "semantics of desire". But Stephan does object to my claim that in Freud's theory, an overt symptom manifests one or more of its underlying unconscious causes and gives evidence for its cause(s), so that the psychoanalytic "sense" or "meaning" of the overt symptom is constituted by its latent motivational cause(s). (For my most recent detailed elaboration of that claim, see Grünbaum, 1999.)

As Stephan recognizes (1989, p. 27), Freud (1913j, pp. 176–178) avowedly "overstepped" common usage, when he generalized the term "language" to designate not only the verbal expression of thought but also gestures "and every other method . . . by which mental activity can be expressed" (*ibid.*, p. 176). And Freud declared that "the interpretation of dreams [as a cognitive activity] is completely analogous to the decipherment of an ancient pictographic script such as Egyptian hieroglyphs" (*ibid.*, p. 177). But surely this common challenge of *problem-solving* does not license the assimilation of the *psychoanalytic* meaning of manifest dream-content to the *semantic* meaning of spoken or written language (Grünbaum, 1993, p. 115).

Stephan does countenance (1989, p. 148) my emphasis on the distinction between the relation of manifestation, which the symptom bears to its cause, and the semantic relation of designation, which a linguistic symbol bears to its object. Yet, his principal objection to my view of the psychoanalytic "sense" of symptoms as being causal manifestations of unconscious ideation is that I assign "exclusively non-semantic significance" to them by *denying* that they also have "semiotic" significance like linguistic symbols (*ibid.*, pp. 148–149). He grants that Freud did not construe the sense or meaning of symptoms as one of semantic reference to their causes. Yet according to Stephan's own reconstruction of Freud's conception,

> he did assume that the manifest phenomena [symptoms] semantically stand for the same thing as the (repressed) ideas for which they substitute, [i.e.,] they stand semantically for what the

repressed (verbal) ideas stand (or rather would stand, if they were expressed verbally). [Stephan, 1989, p. 149]

Searle (1990) has noted illuminatingly (p. 175) that, unlike many mental states, language is *not intrinsically* "intentional" in Brentano's directed sense; instead, the intentionality (aboutness) of language is *extrinsically imposed* on it by deliberately "decreeing" it to function referentially. Searle (1990, pp. 5, 160, and 177) points out that the mental states of some animals and of "pre-linguistic" very young children do have intrinsic intentionality but *no* linguistic referentiality.

I maintain that Stephan's fundamental hermeneuticist error was to slide illicitly from the *intrinsic, non*-semantic intentionality of (many, but *not* all) mental states to the *imposed*, semantic sort possessed by language. Moreover, *some* of the neurotic symptoms of concern to psychoanalysts, such as diffuse depression and manic, undirected elation even *lack* Brentano-intentionality.

Finally, the aboutness (contents) of Freud's repressed conative states is avowedly different from the intentionality (contents) of their psychic manifestations in symptoms. But Stephan erroneously insists that they are the same.

Yet some version of a hermeneutic reconstruction of the psychoanalytic enterprise has been embraced with alacrity by a considerable number of analysts no less than by professors in humanities departments of universities. Its psychoanalytic adherents see it as buying absolution for their theory and therapy from the criteria of validation mandatory for causal hypotheses in the empirical sciences, although psychoanalysis is replete with just such hypotheses. This form of escape from accountability also augurs ill for the future of psychoanalysis, because the methods of the hermeneuts have not spawned a single new important hypothesis. Instead, their reconstruction is a negativistic ideological battle cry whose disavowal of Freud's scientific aspirations presages the death of his legacy from sheer sterility, at least among those who demand the validation of theories by cogent evidence.

G. Post-Freudian psychoanalysis

But what have been the contemporary *post*-Freudian developments in so far as they still qualify as psychoanalytic in content rather than only in name? And have they advanced the debate by being on firmer epistemological ground than Freud's original major hypotheses (Grünbaum, 1984, Chapter Seven)? Most recently, the noted clinical psychologist and philosopher of psychology Morris Eagle (1993) has given a comprehensive and insightful answer to this question on which we can draw.

Eagle begins with a caveat:

> It is not at all clear that there is a uniform body of thought analogous to the main corpus of Freudian theory that can be called contemporary psychoanalytic theory. In the last forty or fifty years there have been three major theoretical developments in psychoanalysis: ego psychology, object relations theory, and self-psychology. If contemporary psychoanalytic theory is anything, it is one of these three or some combination, integrative or otherwise, of the three. [Eagle, 1993, p. 374]

Eagle makes no mention of Lacan's version of psychoanalysis, presumably because he does not take it seriously, since Lacanians have avowedly forsaken the need to validate their doctrines by familiar canons of evidence, not to mention Lacan's wilful, irresponsible obscurity and notorious cruelty to patients (Green, 1995/1996).

Previously (Section II), we had occasion to note that Heinz Hartmann's ego-psychology departed from Freud's instinctual anchorage of the cognitive functions. But, more importantly, both Heinz Kohut's self-psychology and the object relations theory of Otto Kernberg and the British school more fundamentally reject Freud's compromise-model of psychopathology. Indeed, self-psychology has repudiated virtually every one of Freud's major tenets (Eagle, 1993, p. 388). Thus, Kohut supplants Freud's conflict-model of psychopathology, which is based on the repression of internal sexual and aggressive wishes, by a psychology of self-defects and faulty function caused by hypothesized *environmental events* going back to the first two years of infancy. Relatedly, Kohut denies, contra Freud, that insight is curative, designating instead the analyst's empathic understanding as the operative therapeutic agent (Kohut, 1984). Again, the object relations theorists deny that the aetiology of pathology lies in Freudian (oedipal) conflicts and traumas involving sex and aggression, claiming instead that the quality of maternal caring is the crucial factor.

Yet these two post-Freudian schools not only diverge from Freud but also disagree with one another. Thus, the orthodox psycho-analysts Arlow and Brenner speak ruefully of "the differences among all these theories, so apparent to every observer" (1988, p. 9), hoping wistfully that refined honing of the psychoanalytic method of free association will yield a common body of data, which "would in the end resolve the conflict among competing theories" (*ibid.*, p. 11). But their hope is utopian, if only because of the severe proba-tive limitations of the method of free association. How, for example, could a method of putting adults on the couch possibly have the epistemological resources to resolve the three-way clash between the Freudian and two post-Freudian schools in regard to the *infantile* aetiologies of psychopathology? Otto Kernberg's (1993) account of the "Convergences and divergences in contemporary psychoana-lytic technique" does not solve that problem. And, as other psycho-analysts themselves have documented, there are several clear signs that the future of the sundry clinical and theoretical enterprises that label themselves "psychoanalytic" is now increasingly in jeopardy. For example, the pool of patients seeking (full-term) psychoanalytic treatment in the USA has been steadily shrinking, and academic psychoanalysts are becoming an endangered species in American medical schools (Reiser, 1989). No wonder that the subtitle of the 1988 book *Psychoanalysis* by the well-known analyst Marshal Edel-son is "*A Theory in Crisis*" (Edelson, 1988).

But what about the *evidential* merits of the two post-Freudian developments that are usually designated as "*contemporary* psycho-analysis"? Do they constitute an *advance* over Freud? The answer turns largely, though not entirely, on whether there is *better eviden-tial support* for them than for Freud's classical edifice. But Eagle argues that the verdict is clearly negative:

> . . . the different variants of so-called contemporary psychoanalytic theory . . . are on no firmer epistemological ground than the central formulations and claims of Freudian theory. . . . There is no evidence that contemporary psychoanalytic theories have remedied the epistemological and methodological difficulties that are associ-ated with Freudian theory. [Eagle, 1993, p. 404]

H. What are the future prospects of psychoanalysis?

Finally, what are the prospects for the future of psychoanalysis in the twenty-firstst century? In their 1988 paper on that topic, the psychoanalysts Arlow and Brenner reached the following sanguine conclusion about both its past and its future:

> Of some things about the future of psychoanalysis we can be certain. Fortunately, they are the most important issues as well. Psychoanalysis will continue· to furnish the most comprehensive and illuminating insight into the human psyche. It will continue to stimulate research and understanding in many areas of human endeavor. In addition to being the best kind of treatment for many cases, it will remain, as it has been, the fundamental base for almost all methods that try to alleviate human mental suffering by psychological means. [Arlow & Brenner, 1988, p. 13]

By contrast, a dismal verdict is offered by the distinguished American psychologist and psychoanalyst Paul E. Meehl. Since one of my main arguments figures in it, let me mention that à propos of my critiques of Freud's theories of transference and of obsessional neurosis (Rat-Man), I had demonstrated the *fallaciousness* of inferring a *causal* connection between mental states from a mere "meaning" or thematic connection between them. Meehl refers to the latter kind of shared thematic content as "the existence of a theme" and writes:

> His [Grünbaum's] core objection, the epistemological difficulty of inferring a causal influence from the existence of a theme (assuming the latter can be statistically demonstrated), is the biggest single methodological problem that we [psychoanalysts] face. If that problem cannot be solved, we will have another century in which psychoanalysis can be accepted or rejected, mostly as a matter of personal taste. Should that happen, I predict it will be slowly but surely abandoned, both as a mode of helping and as a theory of the mind [reference omitted]. [Meehl, 1995, p. 1021]

Returning to Arlow and Brenner, I hope I have shown that, in regard to the last 100 years, their rosy partisan account is very largely ill-founded, if only because the lauded comprehensiveness of the core theory of repression is only a *pseudo*-unification, as I have argued. Among Arlow and Brenner's glowingly optimistic statements about the future, just one is plausible: the expectation of a continuing heuristic role for psychoanalysis. Such a function does *not* require the correctness of its current theories at all. As an example of the heuristic role, one need only think of the issues I raised *à propos* of Freud's dubious account of the relation of affect to forgetting and remembering. These issues range well beyond the concerns of psychoanalysis. As the Harvard psychoanalyst and schizophrenia researcher Philip Holzman sees it (Holzman, 1994, p. 190): "This view of the heuristic role of psychoanalysis, even in the face of its poor science, is beginning to be appreciated only now". Holzman (private communication) mentions three areas of inquiry as illustrations: (i) the plasticity and reconstructive role of memory as against photographic reproducibility of the past, (ii) the general role of affect in cognition, and (iii) the relevance of temperament (e.g., shyness) in character development, as currently investigated by Jerome Kagan at Harvard.

References

Arlow, J., & Brenner, C. (1964). *Psychoanalytic Concepts and the Structural Theory*. New York: International Universities Press.

Arlow, J., & Brenner, C. (1988). The future of psychoanalysis. *Psychoanalytic Quarterly, 57*: 1–14.

Assoun, P. (1995). *Freud, la Philosophie, et les Philosophes*. Paris: Presses Universitaires de France.

Bachrach, H. M., Galatzer-Levy, R., Skolnikoff, A., & Waldron, S. J. (1991). On the efficacy of psychoanalysis. *Journal of the American Psychoanalytic Association, 39*: 871–916.

Basch, M. (1994). Psychoanalysis, science & epistemology. *The Bulletin of the [Chicago] Institute for Psychoanalysis, 4*(2): 1; 8–9.

Borch-Jacobsen, M. (1996). *Remembering Anna O.: 100 Years of Psychoanalytic Mystification*. New York: Routledge.

Brenner, C. (1982). *The Mind in Conflict*. New York: International Universities Press.

Brentano, B. (1995). *Psychology from an Empirical Standpoint*. New York: Routledge & Kegan Paul.

Breuer, J., & Freud, S. (1893a). On the psychical mechanism of hysterical phenomena: Preliminary communication. *S.E., 2*: 1–17. London: Hogarth.

Bröder, A. (1995). *Unbewusstes Semantisches Priming Laborinduzierter Sprechfehler*. Bonn: University of Bonn. "Diplomarbeit" in psychology.

Bröder, A., & Bredenkamp, J. (1996). SLIP-Technik, prozessdissoziationsmodell und multinomiale modellierrung: neue werkzeuge zum experimentellen nachweis "Freudscher versprecher"? *Zeitschrift für Experimentelle Psychologie, 43*: 175–202.

Cleckley, H. (1988). *The Mask of Sanity* (5th edn). Augusta, GA: Emily S. Cleckley.

Eagle, M. (1987). The psychoanalytic and the cognitive unconscious. In: R. Stern (Ed.), *Theories of the Unconscious and Theories of the Self* (pp. 155–189). Hillsdale, NJ: Analytic Press.

Eagle, M. (1993). The dynamics of theory change in psychoanalysis. In: J. Earman, A. I. Janis, G. J. Massey, & N. Rescher (Eds.), *Philosophical Problems of the Internal and External Worlds: Essays on the Philosophy of Adolf Grünbaum* (Chapter 15). Pittsburgh; Konstanz: University of Pittsburgh Press; University of Konstanz Press.

Edelson, M. (1984). *Hypothesis and Evidence in Psychoanalysis*. Chicago: University of Chicago Press.

Edelson, M. (1986). Causal explanation in science and in psychoanalysis. *Psychoanalytic Study of the Child, 41*: 89–127.

Edelson, M. (1988). *Psychoanalysis: A Theory in Crisis*. Chicago: University of Chicago Press.

Ellenberger, H. (1970). *The Discovery of the Unconscious*. New York: Basic Books.

Fenichel, O. (1945). *The Psychoanalytic Theory of Neurosis*. New York: Norton.

Freud, S. (1893h). On the psychical mechanism of hysterical phenomena. *S.E., 3*: 27–39.

Freud, S. (1896a). Heredity and the aetiology of the neuroses. *S.E., 3*: 143–156.

Freud, S. (1900a). *The Interpretation of Dreams. S.E., 4–5*: 1–621.

Freud, S. (1901b). *The Psychopathology of Everyday Life. S.E., 6*: 1–279.

Freud, S. (1905e). Fragment of an analysis of a case of hysteria. *S.E., 7*: 249–254.

Freud, S. (1909d). Notes upon a case of obsessional neurosis. *S.E., 10*: 155–318.

Freud, S. (1910k). 'Wild" psycho-analysis. *S.E., 11*: 219–230.

Freud, S. (1913j). The claims of psycho-analysis to scientific interest. *S.E., 13*: 165–190.

Freud, S. (1914d). On the history of the psycho-analytic movement. *S.E.*, 14: 7–66.

Freud, S. (1915e). The unconscious. *S.E.*, *14*: 166–215.

Freud, S. (1915d). Repression. *S.E.*, 14: 146–158.

Freud, S. (1916–1917). Introductory lectures on psycho-analysis. *S.E.*, *15–16*: 9–496.

Freud, S. (1924f). A short account of psychoanalysis. *S.E.*, *19*: 191–209.

Freud, S. (1925d). An autobiographical study. *S.E.*, *20*: 7–74.

Freud, S. (1933a). New introductory lectures on psychoanalysis. *S.E.*, *22*: 5–185.

Freud, S. (1937c). Analysis terminable and interminable. *S.E.*, *23*: 209–253.

Freud, S. (1940a). An outline of psycho-analysis. *S.E.*, *23*: 139–207.

Gay, P. (1987). *A Godless Jew: Freud, Atheism, and the Making of Psychoanalysis*. New Haven: Yale University Press.

Glymour, C. (1983). The theory of your dreams. In: R. S. Cohen & L. Laudan (Eds.), *Physics, Philosophy, and Psychoanalysis: Essays in Honor of Adolf Grünbaum* (pp. 57–71). Dordrecht: D. Reidel.

Goleman, D. (1994), Miscoding is seen as the root of false memories. *New York Times* 31 May (Section C): pp. C1 and C8.

Green, A. (1995/1996). Against Lacanism. *Journal of European Psychoanalysis*, (2): 169–185.

Grünbaum, A. (1973). *Philosophical Problems of Space and Time* (2nd edn) Dordrecht: D. Reidel.

Grünbaum, A. (1984). *The Foundations of Psychoanalysis: A Philosophical Critique*. Berkeley: University of California Press.

Grünbaum, A. (1986). Author's response to 40 reviewers: Is Freud's theory well-founded? *Behavioral and Brain Sciences*, *9*(June): 266–284.

Grünbaum, A. (1988). *Die Grundlagen der Psychoanalyse, Eine Philosophische Kritik*. Stuttgart: Philipp Reclam jun. Gmbh & co. This is a German translation of *The Foundations of Psychoanalysis: A Philosophical Critique*.

Grünbaum, A. (1990). "Meaning" connections and causal connections in the human sciences: The poverty of hermeneutic philosophy. *Journal of the American Psychoanalytic Association*, *38*(September): 559–577.

Grünbaum, A. (1993). *Validation in the Clinical Theory of Psychoanalysis: A Study in the Philosophy of Psychoanalysis*. Madison, CT: International Universities Press.

Grünbaum, A. (1994) Letter to the Editor. *New York Review of Books*, 41(14): 54–55. Contra Thomas Nagel's "Freud's Permanent Revolution."

Grünbaum, A. (1997). Is the concept of "psychic reality" a theoretical advance? *Psychoanalysis and Contemporary Thought*, 20(2): 245–267.

Grünbaum, A. (1999). The hermeneutic versus the scientific conception of psychoanalysis: An unsucessful effort to chart a *via media* for the human sciences. In: D. Aerts, J. Boekaert, & E. Mathijs (Eds.), *Einstein Meets Magritte, an Interdisciplinary Reflection: The White Book of Einstein Meets Magritte* (pp. 219–239). Dordrecht: Kluwer.

Grünbaum, A. (2002). Critique of psychoanalysis. In: E. Erwin (Ed.), *The Freud Encyclopedia, Theory, Therap;y, and Culture* (pp. 117–136). New York/London: Routledge.

Grünbaum, A. (forthcoming). Critique of Freud's neurobiological and psychoanalytic dream theories. In: A. Grünbaum, *Philosophy of Science in Action, Volume II, Part 2*. New York: Oxford University Press.

Harman, G. (1965). Inference to the best explanation. *Philosophical Review*, 74: 88–95.

Holzman, P. (1994). Hilgard on psychoanalysis as science. *Psychological Science*, 5(July): 190–191.

Kernberg, O. (1993). Convergences and divergences in contemporary psychoanalytic technique. *International Journal of Psychoanalysis*, 74: 659–673.

Kohut, H. (1984). *How Does Analysis Cure?* Chicago: University of Chicago Press.

Leibniz, G. (1981)[c. 1705]. *New Essays on Human Understanding*. P. Remnant & J. Bennett (Trans.) Cambridge: Cambridge University Press.

Meehl, P. (1995). Commentary: Psychoanalysis as science. *Journal of the American Psychoanalytic Association*, 43: 1015–1021.

Motley, M. (1980). Verification of "Freudian slips" and semantic prearticulatory editing via laboratory-induced spoonerisms. In: V. Fromkin (Ed.), *Errors in Linguistic Performance: Slips of the Tongue, Ear, Pen, and Hand* (pp. 133–147). New York: Academic Press.

Nagel, T. (1994) Freud's permanent revolution. *New York Review of Books*, 41(9): 34–38.

Reiser, M. (1989). The future of psychoanalysis in academic psychiatry: Plain talk. *Psychoanalytic Quarterly*, 58: 158–209.

Ricoeur, P. (1970). *Freud and Philosophy*. New Haven: Yale University Press.

Salmon, W. (1971). *Statistical Explanation and Statistical Relevance*. Pittsburgh: University of Pittsburgh Press.

Salmon, W. (2001). Explanation and confirmation: A Bayesian critique of inference to the best explanation. In: G. Hon & S. S. Rackover (Eds.), *Explanation: Theoretical Approaches and Applications* (pp. 61–91). Dordrecht: Kluwer.

Schapiro, M. (1968). The apples of Cézanne. *Art News Annual, 34*: 34–53.

Schüttauf, K., Bredenkamp, J., & Specht, E. K. (1997). Induzierte "Freudsche Versprecher" und zwangsneurotischer konflikt. *Sprache und Kognition, 16*: 3–13..

Searle, J. (1990). *Intentionality*. New York: Cambridge University Press.

Shevrin, H., Williams, W. J., Marshall, R. E., Hertel, R. K., Bond, J. A., & Brakel, L. A. (1992). Event-related potential indicators of the dynamic unconscious. *Consciousness and Cognition, 1*: 340–366.

Solms, M. (2002). An introduction to the neuroscientific works of Sigmund Freud. In: G. Van De Vijver & F. Geerardyn (Eds.), *The Pre-Psychoanalytic Writings of Sigmund Freud* (pp. 25–26). London: Karnac.

Solms, M., & Saling, M. (Eds. & Trans.) (1990). *A Moment of Transition: Two Neuroscientific Articles by Sigmund Freud*. New York: Karnac.

Solomon, D. (1994). Meyer Schapiro. *The New York Times Magazine*, 14 August: 22–25.

Stephan, A. (1989). *Sinn Als Bedeutung: Bedeutungstheoretische Untersuchungen Zur Psychoanalyse Sigmund Freud's*. Berlin: Walter de Gruyter.

Storr, A. (1986). Human understanding and scientific validation. *Behavioral and Brain Sciences, 9*: 259–260.

Thomä, H., & Kächele, H. (1987). *Psychoanalytic Practice*. Berlin: Springer-Verlag.

Vaughan, S., & Roose, S. (1995). The analytic process: Clinical and research definitions. *International Journal of Psycho-Analysis, 76*: 343–356.

Von Eckardt, B. (1985). Adolf Grünbaum and psychoanalytic epistemology. In: J. Reppen (Ed.), *Beyond Freud: A Study of Modern Psychoanalytic Theorists* (pp. 353–403). Hillsdale, NJ: Analytic Press.

Walker, F. (1962). *The Man Verdi*. New York: Alfred A. Knopf.

Zentner, M. (1995). *Die Flucht Ins Vergessen: Die Anfänge der Psychoanalyse Freud's bei Schopenhauer*. Darmstadt, Germany: Wissenschaftliche Buchgessellschaft.

CHAPTER FIFTEEN

What can developmental psychopathology tell psychoanalysts about the mind?[1]

Peter Fonagy and Mary Target

W hat is the validity of the enterprise of relating psycho-analysis to the developmental sciences? At a Scientific Meeting of the British Psycho-Analytical Society in 2001, Michael Feldman asserted:

> There will always be a pressure to turn to the spurious certainty of premature, over-valued formulations, or to incline in a more radical way to other methods of investigation, which seem to offer a route towards a more comforting sense of certainty and respectability, but which are, in my view, inappropriate for the further study of the mind. [Feldman, 2001, p. 5]

At the same meeting, Egle Laufer took a different perspective suggesting that clinical research and studies of other disciplines might expand the psychoanalytic model and contribute to the enhancement of the scientific status of psychoanalysis. Our livelihoods depend on favouring Dr Laufer's position over Dr Feldman's, so unsurprisingly we cannot agree to an *a priori* decision that other disciplines add nothing pertinent to our psychoanalytic study of the mind.

At this point, we would like to suggest an obvious but crucial distinction. It is agreed that psychoanalysis is, among other things, a method of data gathering and knowledge integration about human subjectivity. Its intensity, the freedom it provides within a relatively strict observational framework, make it unique as a way of discovering the contents and characteristic modes of functioning of another person's mind. Thus, it is truly helpful in explaining why people do things, at the level of the individual, the clinical group or the culture. Furthermore, it has remarkable therapeutic potential through self-understanding, the healing of divisions within the mind, and the freeing of inhibited developmental processes.[2] While clinical psychoanalysis needs little help in getting to know an individual's subjectivity in the most detailed way possible, when we wish to generalize to a comprehensive model of the human mind, the discipline can no longer exist on its own. Historically, perhaps fifty years ago, there were no other fields of inquiry that concerned the mind, with information worth trying to integrate with the psychoanalytic model. This probably lies at the root of our worthy effort "to go it alone"[3] The scientific scene has radically shifted over the past two decades. To put it bluntly, while getting to know an individual mind is perhaps best achieved within an exclusively psychoanalytic framework, a general psychoanalytic model of mind, if it is to be credible, should be aligned with the wider knowledge mind gained from a range of disciplines. Developmental psychology is just one, and by no means the most important, of these.

The millennium editorial of the *New England Journal of Medicine*, in a monumental survey of the most important developments in clinical medicine over the past thousand years, from human anatomy to molecular pharmacotherapy, underlined that progress towards scientific discovery invariably occurs across disciplines.

> None [of these discoveries] was an isolated discovery or event; instead each was a series of notable steps . . . along a broad path that led to a crucial body of knowledge in a particular area. [*New England Journal of Medicine*, 2000, Editorial, p. 42]

Let us introduce a parallel. About eight years ago a group of researchers reported in *Nature* (Rauscher, Shaw, & Ky, 1993) that listening to Mozart's sonata for two pianos (K448) for ten minutes led to a mean improvement in spatial IQ scores of eight or nine points, relative to control conditions that induced a similar amount of relaxation. Not surprisingly, this finding generated considerable additional research (see review by Jenkins, 2001). Most studies have confirmed that the Mozart effect exists (Rauscher, Shaw, & Ky, 1995; Rideout & Laubach, 1996; Wilson & Brown, 1997), cannot be replicated by minimalist music (Rauscher *et al.*, 1997), was associated with enhanced synchrony of the firing patterns of particular regions of the brain (Rideout & Laubach, 1996) and suppressed epileptiform brain activity in severely epileptic patients (Hughes, Daaboul, Fino, & Shaw, 1998; Hughes, Fino, & Melyn, 1999). Perhaps most interesting are related experiments where the long term effects of exposure to classical music was shown to lead to a 30% improvement in the performance of three- to four-year-olds in spatial, temporal reasoning tests compared with a group who had computer lessons for six months (Rauscher *et al.*, 1997) While the working of the Mozart effect is poorly understood, it is a clear illustration of how a particular specific form of subjective experience (in this case familiarity with musical forms) can interact at the level of brain function with an apparently independent, important psychological capacity. The brain is the mind's body and not all the connections that psychological experience makes with subsequent function can be made available through the study of a single domain. While musicology independently identified the double piano sonata (K448) as "one of the most profound and most mature of all Mozart's compositions" (Einstein, cited in Jenkins, 2001, p. 171), its healing and developmentally enhancing effects could never be fully understood in the domain of musicology alone.

Similarly, the impact of psychoanalysis cannot be fully appreciated from clinical material alone. It may be that our difficulty in pinpointing the curative factors in psychoanalytic treatment is directly related to the limitations of our uniquely clinical basis for inquiry. The repetition of patterns of emotional arousal in association with the interpretive process elaborates and strengthens structures of meaning and emotional response. This may have far-reaching effects, we would argue, even on the functioning of the brain and the expression of genetic potential. This is what we will try to briefly outline.

A range of studies have already offered suggestive evidence that the impact of psychotherapy can be seen in alterations in brain activity, using brain imaging techniques (Baxter *et al.*, 1992; Schwartz, Stoessel, Baxter, Martin, & Phelps, 1996; Vinamäki, Kuikka, Tiihonen, & Lehtonen, 1998). These studies as a group provide a rationale for the hope that intensive psychoanalytic treatment might meaningfully affect biological as well as psychological vulnerability. This field is in its infancy but is progressing so fast that it seems highly likely that many future psychoanalytic discoveries about the mind will be made in conjunction and collaboration with biological science

We will concentrate on some links to just one of these fields: behavioral and molecular genetics. A cultural shift characterizes the last decades of this century, with both professionals and the lay public switching from an environmental model of psychopathology to a genetic–biological frame of reference that excludes consideration of psychodynamic aspects. We know that the mind is in important respects inherited, but we also know that genetic influences are in important respects moderated by the mind. We would like to explore how psychoanalytic ideas can contribute to a resolution of this dialectic.

Recently, on the same day one of us saw three new male patients. They were very different: a depressed journalist with potency problems; a young man soon to be married but worried about his history of bipolar illness; and a violent adolescent. During initial assessments we often try to elicit the patient's conscious theory of their problems and ask something like: "Why do you think this has happened to you?" or "Why do you think people like you get depressed?" On this particular day, surprisingly, all three men came up with the same answer: "I think it is well established to be a chemical imbalance caused by my genes," said the groom with the bipolar disorder; "I think from my mother I inherited a tendency to look for the negative," answered the journalist; and "I've been told I have bad genes that make me hit people," replied the adolescent. In each case, as they answered, time seemed to collapse. There was no space between the moment their father's sperm penetrated their mother's ovum and the present moment.[4] There was one simple message: "don't ask what causes my problems, don't probe my memories or thoughts or feelings; there is nothing to know, the answer lies in my genes". [5]

Over the last decade of the twentieth century, perhaps in part triggered by the excitement of the human genome project, but also by research designs of increasing statistical sophistication, ideas from quantitative behaviour genetics have come to dominate developmental research (e.g., Harris, 1998). A number of definitive adoption and twin studies were undertaken in the USA, Scandinavia, UK and elsewhere. Celebrated studies of twins reared apart illustrated remarkable similarities in behaviours, personality, and thinking styles of identical twins (Neubauer, 1996; Plomin, Fulker, Corley, & DeFries, 1997; Reiss et al., 1995; Reiss, Neiderhiser, Hetherington, & Plomin, 2000). These and other studies have shown that genes are more important than environment in almost all psychological illnesses. Some studies seem to indicate that genes are such strong determinants that there is almost no room for environmental influence (e.g., Nigg & Goldsmith, 1998). One of the most surprising results from adoption and twin studies is that adverse, stressful environments appear to be, to a large measure, inherited, and therefore genes probably play a part in the association between stressful environments and symptoms of post-traumatic stress disorder, or symptoms following abuse (e.g., Saudino, Pedersen, Lichtenstein, McClearn, & Plomin, 1997). It is probably true that we have previously exaggerated the importance of parents for development: adoption studies, in particular, show that much of parental influence is illusory.[6] It is likely that personality characteristics in the child that have been thought of as a reaction to the parents' behaviour are, in fact, genetic predispositions. The personality trait and the associated form of parenting (criticism, warmth, or even abuse) are both consequences of the same genes in the parent and the child. Equally, adoption studies suggest that children with genetic tendencies towards—for instance—aggression will elicit more hostile and coercive parenting (Ge, Conger, Cadoret, Neiderhiser, & Yates, 1996). One could say that evocatory projective identification (Spillius, 1992) led to a pattern of interaction that in biologically-related families has been assumed to start with the parents' behaviour. a particular way for the parent to be with the child.

Clinically, this insight from behaviour genetics (the so called "child-to-parent effect") may be quite relevant; we are often baffled by our patients' sense of responsibility for the parents' behaviour, but there may be quite a deep level at which that perception is accurate. These findings help to substantiate projective identification from child to parent as a powerful force in development, both directly and as a representation in the child's mind. This may also help to explain why "parent-blaming" approaches have been so unsuccessful clinically.

While it is important to define the limits of parental influence on child development, the pendulum has swung too far. Behaviour genetics studies of the past two decades have led to a state of affairs where more or less all important psychological capacities, as well as their dysfunctions, are assumed to be innate, and parenting is assumed hardly to matter. Thus, all theories such as psychoanalysis, or even social learning theory, that advocated the key role of early family experience are now seen by many as irrelevant (see Scarr, 1992). For example, the behaviour geneticist Rowe (1994) wrote: ". . . parents in most working to professional class families may have little influence on what traits their children may eventually develop as adults" (p. 7). He went on to say that he doubted whether any undesirable trait displayed by a child could be significantly modified by anything a parent does.

If we are to re-establish a strong position for the psychoanalytic model of the mind within the medical sciences, which is essential if we are to retain our status as a mental health profession, then we have to understand and then address the challenge from behaviour genetics. You may be thinking that it is simply not very relevant to us whether a psychiatric disorder, such as depression, is genetically determined or not; our science is not concerned with the biological level of analysis at all. As psychoanalysts we work with elements of subjective experience and meaning. We will try to show you later that this very subjectivity is a vital missing link in the prevailing genetic developmental models of mind.

Nevertheless, remembering the distinction we started with, while we might be able to relate to behaviour genetics at the level of a general model of the mind, the objection is correct when thinking about the individual patient. It is all very well for adoption and twin studies to demonstrate that psychological disorder has genetic roots, but genetic effects may well be indirect as well as direct. Even a high genetic loading for an environmental risk does not mean that the associated outcome would necessarily be genetically mediated.

For example, even if child abuse and its sequelae were found to have a genetic link, the disturbance of an abused child would still be best understood in terms of the destruction of the child's trust in the world. It is the loss of trust that would have to be addressed in any therapeutic intervention. Behaviour genetic data do not help us much in the individual clinical situation.

In fact, not even the most hard-nosed geneticist claims that genes act independently of a person's environment. In fact, as we increase our understanding of how genes work, we discover that at least part of each gene is a control mechanism for the process of transcription, in other words it determines whether a gene will be expressed. Internal and external experiences, hormones, stress, learning, and social interaction all alter the binding of transcription regulators (Kandel, 1998). There is ample evidence for so-called gene–environment interaction in animals. For instance, rat pups separated from their mother in the first two weeks of life show a permanent increase in the expression of genes controlling the secretion of CRF (cortico-trophin releasing factor), a stress hormone (Plotsky & Meaney, 1993). However, this life-long vulnerability to stress is reversed if the mothers show increased physical care of their pups once they are reunited (Liu et al., 1997). So, the question is, what aspects of the environment influence these control mechanisms in humans?

There are a few dramatic but isolated examples. Adopted-away children of schizophrenic parents only develop the illness if their adoptive families are dysfunctional (Tienari, Wynne, Moring, Lahti, & Naarala, 1994). Similar observations have been made for criminal behaviour (Bohman, 1996). So genetic risk may or may not be fulfilled, depending on the family environment. But behaviour geneticists have run into a problem. Notwithstanding their acceptance of a gene–environment interaction model, there have been few findings so far to demonstrate the moderating effect of the environment on gene expression in humans (Plomin, DeFries, McLearn, & Rutter, 1997). The reason for this disappointing absence of evidence is linked to the way in which psychoanalysis has been relatively sidelined by "naïve innatism", in the past decade.

Human behaviour genetics mostly studies the "wrong" environment. The environment that triggers the expression of a gene is not objective, it is not observable. What counts is the child's *experience of* the environment. The interaction is between gene and *subjective* environment. The way in which environment is experienced acts as a filter in the expression of genotype into phenotype, the translation of genetic potential into personality and behaviour. Here we touch on the crucial importance of psychoanalysis for the understanding of genetic influences on the mind. As psychoanalysts, our primary concern is with the interaction of multiple layers of representations in generating subjective experience in relation to the external world, that is psychic reality (Freud, 1900a, 1912–1913). Data from genetics call for exactly such sophistication. To understand the way that most genes may or may not be expressed in particular individuals we need to understand the internal world of the child or indeed the adult. (It is a common but false assumption that genetic influences are strongest in early childhood. Gene expression continues throughout life and might well be the trigger of its end, in death.)

Whether or not a specific environmental factor triggers the expression of a gene may depend on the way the individual interprets that experience, in its turn determined by conscious or unconscious meanings attributed to it (Kandel, 1998). Thus intrapsychic representational processes are not just the consequences of environmental and genetic effects—they are likely to be the critical moderators of these effects. The Nobel Prize winner, Eric Kandel (1998, 1999) went so far as to suggest that the longer-term and deeper changes associated with psychoanalytic therapy might well come about through the changes in genetic expression brought about by the learning experiences of psychoanalysis. What we are suggesting is that habitual ways of interpreting the world affect brain chemistry, which in turn influences the expression of genes. Clinical psychoanalysis is a powerful technique for *changing* habitual ways of interpreting the world, particularly in the most emotionally stressful contexts, where the impact of subjective meaning might be most intense.

Up until the past five years this could only be abstract conjecture. Links between molecular geneticists and attachment theorists are increasingly making it a realistically testable hypothesis. Let us give an example. In our collaborative follow-up studies of a preschool psychoanalytic treatment programme at the Menninger Clinic, we studied the second dopamine receptor gene (DRD_2), one variant of which has been linked with a number of psychological disorders. We found an interaction between the presence of this variant and sensitivity to attachment trauma: those with this variant were found to be more disturbed as adults if they also represented early experiences as abuse (Fonagy, Stein, & White, 2001). The same individuals showed less accurate understanding of emotional expression, which is known to be characteristic of personality disorder. In contrast, "objective" ratings of the family environment and maltreatment, documented in the childhood records, bore little relationship to adult functioning. We speculate that successful psychotherapy, through increasing emotional awareness, could have reduced the expression of this genetic vulnerability to adult psychiatric problems by elaborating the mental representation of object relationships. Be that as it may, behaviour geneticists will not be able to make sense of the data they collect about the mind unless they become more sophisticated about the environment, extending it to include the subjective meaning—conscious and unconscious—of events, particularly those which could, given certain interpretations, make a substantial emotional impact, for instance triggering sustained anxiety or depression.

The capacity for interpretation, which has been defined recently by the evolutionary biologist Bogdan (1997, p. 7) as "organisms making sense of each other in contexts where this matters biologically", is a characteristic of all complex species and, we suggest, becomes uniquely human when the subject matter of interpretation is in the domain of mental states. This capacity provides the final step in the transcription of genetic influence into a pattern of behaviour. The interpretive mechanism encodes genetic information, in the form of biases, but also moderates genetic influence by modifying the child's perception of his object world. This mechanism is the lifeblood of psychoanalysis; it is the process we observe, and use to observe, in all our work with patients.[7] We also know that this moderator between genotype and phenotype is a capacity that is crucially dependent on the early caregivers' sensitive response to the baby's heightened emotional states. A vital function of early attachment, neglected by Bowlby, was the context the infant–mother relationship provides for the acquisition of the understanding of mental states—the building blocks of both self-organization and intersubjectivity. There is an extensive empirical literature mapping the development of this capacity within early object relationships (e.g. Jaffe, Beebe, Feldstein, Crown, & Jasnow, 2001). We have related particular deficits in parental sensitivity to forms of later psychopathology. For example, evidence we have reviewed in detail elsewhere (Fonagy, Gergely, Jurist, & Target, 2004) strongly suggests that the sensitive responsiveness of the parent in practice involves two parameters: one of correspondence, or "contingency", the other communication of self–other differentiation, or "markedness". Markedness is what the mother does to communicate to the infant in the process of mirroring that what she is showing is not her own feeling but a representation of her perception of the infant's experience.

We have suggested that affect-mirroring, which reflects the baby's feeling but lacks this marking, generates developmental problems within the borderline spectrum. This pattern of mirroring can be expected from mothers who, because of their own difficulties with emotion regulation, are overwhelmed by their infant's distress. Since the mirroring affect-display of distress is not marked, it will not be decoupled from the caregiver and will be felt as the parent's real emotion. The infant will experience his emotional response as more dangerous and frightening, as it seems to be contagious. Since the infant attributes the mirrored affect to the parent, his own distress will be experienced as "out there", belonging to the other, rather than to himself. In the short term, the perception of corresponding distress in the parent will not regulate but escalate the baby's negative state, leading potentially to traumatization rather than containment.

A second major type of deviant mirroring structure would be produced by the dominance of marked, but incongruent, mirroring. Think of an infant whose erotically coloured excitement about physical contact induces anxiety and defensive anger in the mother due to her conflicts in relation to sexuality. The mother might project her defensive hostility on to the infant, and perceive the baby's libidinal excitement as aggression. She may then modulate the (mis)perceived affect in her baby by properly marked mirroring of an *aggressive* display. Due to the markedness of the mirrored aggression, it will be decoupled from the parent. Since the mirroring is contingently responsive to the baby's (miscategorized) affect-state, he will feel the mirrored affect to be linked to his primary emotion-state. However, because the mirrored aggression is incongruent with the infant's actual affect-state of sexual excitement, his secondary representation of his primary emotion will be distorted. He will come to perceive his excitement as hostility. More generally, marked but incongruent mirroring of affects would lead to pathologically *distorted self representations*.

We hope that in this brief chapter we have been able to demonstrate the importance of psychoanalysts engaging with developmental researchers, in order to influence the emerging scientific consensus about the nature of the mind. It is our impression that recent discoveries in the neurosciences mostly confirm psychoanalytic intuitions about the complexity of mental functions. We have chosen to focus on a specific but crucial area, one that may add a further dimension to the understanding of the far-reaching impact of psychoanalytic treatment, and that can at the same time supply a missing link in the chain of explanation from genes to personality and behaviour. This missing link can only be provided by the recognition that it is psychic and not physical reality which holds the key, not the actual environment but the experienced environment. The self-imposed isolation of psychoanalysts, while justified in an individual clinical context and, perhaps, historically, is self-destructive. Depriving ourselves of opportunities to collaborate in scientific progress might all too soon lead to an unjustified loss of scientific credibility and, even more tragically, linked to this, losing our professional respectability in a science-driven clinical market place. Finally we would like to underline that taking these opportunities does not require changing the theory or practice of psychoanalysis, or that many psychoanalysts involve themselves in active collaboration with other developmental sciences. All it requires is that the few who try to build these bridges with neighbouring disciplines can know that they do so with the support and understanding of their colleagues.

Notes

1. This paper was presented as part of the Scientific Meeting of the British Psycho-Analytical Society, 4th July 2001. It is based on Chapter Three of a monograph entitled *Affect Regulation, Mentalization and the*

Development of the Self (Other Press, 2002). The monograph is authored by George Gergely, Elliot Jurist, Peter Fonagy and Mary Target.

2. However, the relationship of psychoanalytic therapy to the psychoanalytic knowledge base is not our subject for this chapter.

3. Not that even in Freud's day was this ideal invariably adhered to. The knowledge base used by Freud to construct a model of the mind included cultural anthropology, embryology, the neurosciences of the day, philosophy, as well as large tracts from the humanities, particularly history, literature, and mythology.

4. Of course, in each case it was possible to call upon the natural human desire to create a meaningful narrative of how their experiences had led them to seek a consultation. Psychoanalysis is based on the biological force to find meaning that is more deeply rooted than an intellectual conviction about the genetic basis of psychological illness.

5. We believe that the devaluing of psychological and environmental explanations lies at the root of both the psychological problems that these individuals brought into the consulting room and of what might be called the naïve innatist perspective of some contemporary culture.

6. Early observations of abnormalities in the parents of autistic children were later discredited, yet most recent evidence indicates that the observations may have been valid: mothers of autistic children are more likely (when interviewed with the Adult Attachment Interview) to be insecure and preoccupied, violent in their imagery and with poor capacity for psychological understanding, than were mothers of children with Downs or Retts syndromes. The genetic evidence, however, suggests that this is not causal, they are simply more likely to carry the genes associated with autism.

7. We have quite a clear idea of where the process takes place in the brain, the evidence is that it is centred in the medial prefrontal cortex.

References

Baxter, L. R., Schwartz, J. M., Bergman, D. S., Szuba, M. P., Guze, B. H., Mazziotta, J. C., Alazraki, A., Selin, C. E., Ferng, H.-K., Munford, P., & Phelps, M. E. (1992). Caudate glucose metabolic rate changes with both drug and behaviour therapy for obsessive-compulsive disorder. *Archives of General Psychiatry, 49*, 618–689.

Bogdan, R. J. (1997). *Interpreting Minds*. Cambridge, MA: MIT Press.

Bohman, M. (1996). Predisposition to criminality. Swedish adoption studies in retrospect. In M. Rutter (Ed.), *Genetics of Criminal and Antisocial Behaviour*. Chichester: Wiley.

Editorial. (2000). Looking back on the millennium in medicine. *New England Journal of Medicine, 342,* 42.

Feldman, M. (2001). What do psychoanalysts know about the mind? The evidential basis for this knowledge. Paper presented at the Scientific Meeting of the British Psycho-Analytical Society, London.

Fonagy, P., Gergely, G., Jurist, E., & Target, M. (2002). *Affect Regulation and Mentalization: Developmental, Clinical and Theoretical Perspectives.* New York: Other Press.

Fonagy, P., Stein, H., & White, R. (2001). Dopamine receptor polymorphism and susceptibility to sexual, physical and psychological abuse: preliminary results of a longitudinal study of maltreatment. Paper presented at the 10th Biannual Meeting of the Society for Research in Child Development, Mineapolis, MI, 21 April.

Freud, S. (1900a). The interpretation of dreams. *S.E., 4, 5:* 1–715). London: Hogarth.

Freud, S. (1912–1913). Totem and taboo. *S.E.,* 13. London: Hogarth Press.

Ge, X., Conger, R. D., Cadoret, R., Neiderhiser, J., & Yates, W. (1996). The developmental interface between nature and nurture: a mutual influence model of child antisocial behavior and parent behavior. *Developmental Psychology, 32:* 574–589.

Harris, J. R. (1998). *The Nurture Assumption: Why Children Turn Out the Way They Do. Parents matter less than you think and peers matter more.* New York: Free Press.

Hughes, J. R., Daaboul, Y., Fino, J. J., & Shaw, G. L. (1998). The Mozart effect on epileptiform activity. *Clinical Electroencephalography, 29*(3): 109–119.

Hughes, J. R., Fino, J. J., & Melyn, M. A. (1999). Is there a chronic change of the "Mozart effect" on epileptiform activity? A case study. *Clinical Electroencephalography, 30*(2): 44–45.

Jaffe, J., Beebe, B., Feldstein, S., Crown, C. L., & Jasnow, M. D. (2001). Rhythms of dialogue in infancy. *Monographs of the Society for Research in Child Development, 66*(2).

Jenkins, J. S. (2001). The Mozart effect. *Journal of the Royal Society of Medicine, 94*(4): 170–172.

Kandel, E. R. (1998). A new intellectual framework for psychiatry. *American Journal of Psychiatry, 155,* 457–469.

Kandel, E. R. (1999). Biology and the future of psychoanalysis: A new intellectual framework for psychiatry revisited. *American Journal of Psychiatry, 156*: 505–524.

Liu, D., Diorio, J., Tannenbaum, B., Caldji, C., Francis, D., Freedman, A., Sharma, S., Pearson, D., Plotsky, P. M., & Meaney, M. J. (1997). Maternal care, hippocampal glucocorticoid receptors, an hypothalamic–pituitary–adrenal responses to stress. *Science, 277*: 1659–1662.

Neubauer, P. B. (1996). *Nature's Thumbprint:The New Genetics of Personality (2nd edn)*. New York: Columbia University Press.

Nigg, J. T., & Goldsmith, H. H. (1998). Developmental psychopathology, personality, and temperament: reflections on recent behavioral genetics research. *Human Biology, 70*: 387–412.

Plomin, R., DeFries, J. C., McClearn, G. E., & Rutter, R. (1997). *Behavioral Genetics* (3rd edn). New York: W. H. Freeman.

Plomin, R., Fulker, D. W., Corley, R., & DeFries, J. C. (1997). Nature, nurture, and cognitive development from 1 to 16 years: A parent–offspring adoption study. *Psychological Science, 8*: 442–447.

Plotsky, P. M., & Meaney, M. J. (1993). Early, postnatal experience alters hypothalamic corticotropin-releasing factor (CRF) mRNA, median eminence CRF content and stress-induced release in adult rats. *Brain Research. Molecular Brain Research, 18*: 195–200.

Rauscher, F. H., Shaw, G. L., & Ky, K. N. (1993). Music and spatial task performance. *Nature, 365*: 611.

Rauscher, F. H., Shaw, G. L., & Ky, K. N. (1995). Listening to Mozart enhances spatial-temporal reasoning: towards a neurophysiological basis. *Neuroscience Letter, 185*(1): 44–47.

Rauscher, F. H., Shaw, G. L., Levine, L. J., Wright, E. L., Dennis, W. R., & Newcomb, R. L. (1997). Music training causes long-term enhancement of preschool children's spatial–temporal reasoning. *Neurological Research, 19*(1): 2–8.

Reiss, D., Hetherington, E. M., Plomin, R., Howe, G. W., Simmens, S. J., Henderson, S. H., O'Connor, T. J., Bussell, D. A., Anderson, E. R., & Law, T. (1995). Genetic questions for environmental studies. Differential parenting and psychopathology in adolescence. *Archives of General Psychiatry, 52*: 925–936.

Reiss, D., Neiderhiser, J., Hetherington, E. M., & Plomin, R. (2000). *The Relationship Code: Deciphering Genetic and Social Patterns in Adolescent Development*. Cambridge, MA: Harvard University Press.

Rideout, B. E., & Laubach, C. M. (1996). EEG correlates of enhanced spatial performance following exposure to music. *Percept Motor Skills, 82*: 427–432.

Rowe, D. (1994). *The Limits of Family Influence: Genes, Experience and Behaviour*. New York: Guilford Press.

Saudino, K. J., Pedersen, N. L., Lichtenstein, P., McClearn, G. E., & Plomin, R. (1997). Can personality explain genetic influences on life events? *Journal of Personality and Social Psychology, 72*: 196–206.

Scarr, S. (1992). Developmental theories for the 1990s: development and individual differences. *Child Development, 63*: 1–19.

Schwartz, J. M., Stoessel, P. W., Baxter, L. R., Martin, K. M., & Phelps, M. E. (1996). Systematic changes in cerebral glucose metabolic rate after successful behavior medication treatment of obsessive–compulsive disorder. *Archives of General Psychiatry, 53*(2): 109–113.

Spillius, E. B. (1992). Clinical experiences of projective identification. In: R. Anderson (Ed.), *Clinical Lectures on Klein and Bion* (pp. 59–73). London: Routledge.

Tienari, P., Wynne, L. C., Moring, J., Lahti, I., & Naarala, M. (1994). The Finnish adoptive family study of schizophrenia: implications for family research. *British Journal of Psychiatry, 23*(Suppl 164): 20–26.

Vinamäki, H., Kuikka, J., Tiihonen, J., & Lehtonen, J. (1998). Change in monoamine transporter density related to clinical recovery: A case-control study. *Nordic Journal of Psychiatry, 52*, 39–44.

Wilson, T. L., & Brown, T. L. (1997). Re-examination fo the effect of Mozart's music on spatial task performance. *Journal of Psychology, 131*: 365–370.

CHAPTER SIXTEEN

Is the brain more real than the mind?[1]

Mark Solms

Introduction

This paper reflects on the place of psychoanalytical thinking in a scientific context in which mental illness is increasingly being reduced to physiological and chemical factors. A small series of neurological patients with severe emotional disturbances is presented, in order to demonstrate that emotional symptoms can be neither described nor explained in physical terms. Even in cases where an organic aetiology is indisputable, physiological factors can only be invoked to explain somatic symptoms and the physiological correlates of mental symptoms. The mental symptoms themselves can only be understood psychologically.

There can be no doubt that mental phenomena are *somehow* related to physical and chemical processes. The mental effects of drinking alcohol (as opposed to water) suffice to prove the point. Yet, psychotherapists get uncomfortable when they are asked to consider the relationship between the mental phenomena they deal with in their patients, and the physical processes occurring in their brains. To think about their patients in this way seems somehow inhuman, and to miss the most essential point of what they are doing. It is as if the very foundations upon which they base their way of thinking about and helping their patients has been brought into question. Behind the question—what is the relationship between the mental phenomena that you deal with in your patients, and the physical processes occurring in their brains?—psychotherapists detect an implicit challenge. This challenge is based on the assumption that the brain is "more real" than the mind.

Of course there are other ways of conceptualizing the relationship between the brain and the mind, but within contemporary psychiatry the assumption that the brain is "more real" is increasingly taking hold. Enormous inroads have been made in pharmacological treatments, not only of the psychoses, but more recently also of the neuroses, and even of ordinary unhappiness. Patients whom we always thought of as having nothing at all wrong with their brains are increasingly being described by our colleagues in biological psychiatry as suffering from neurochemical imbalances. We think of these patients as having personal difficulties, which we situate in their feelings and memories, but our biologically-oriented colleagues think of them as having chemical disorders, which they situate in their brains and their genes. We have a comprehensive, internally coherent way of understanding and treating these patients that has nothing to do with their brains, and we are therefore confronted by a yawning chasm when we try to reconcile this perspective with our own.

There are still some patients whom we all seem to agree have difficulties that are situated either in their minds or in their brains. But the contradictions inherent in dividing the clinical population up in this way is revealed by the very existence of a transitional group, who seem to have difficulties that can be conceptualized and treated in two completely different ways. Thus the relationship between the brain and the mind has ceased to be merely an interesting philosophical problem for us; it has become a matter of urgent and practical concern. In psychiatry today, strange as it may seem, the boundaries of the brain are being extended, and the mind is getting progressively smaller.

In this paper, I am not going to approach these issues from a philosophical point of view. Philosophers themselves admit that the mind–body problem (in the way that they conceive of it) can never be resolved. Instead I will consider the problem in the light of some pertinent clinical material, to see if our psychoanalytical way of thinking about these cases can be reduced to processes occurring in their brains. Although I cannot be comprehensive, I hope that this clinical material will provide a useful basis for at least beginning to address these problems.

Clinical material

I will describe five patients (some treated by my wife and colleague Karen Kaplan-Solms).

Mrs A

This 61-year-old retired nurse was referred from the neurosurgical wards of a large teaching hospital because she was profoundly depressed, following a stroke. She was constantly in tears and she had twice tried to commit suicide, first by throwing herself down a flight of stairs and then by attempting to jump from a third-floor window. The only reason that she did not succeed in the second attempt was because she suffered from such dense hemiplegia, unilateral neglect, and spatial disorientation, that she was unable to negotiate the window.

She had suffered a ruptured aneurysm in the right middle cerebral artery of her brain. The symptoms that she had as a result of her stroke were typical of right-hemisphere cases. The term "left hemiplegia" refers to a spastic paralysis of the left arm and leg, which confined Mrs A to a wheelchair. The term "unilateral neglect" refers to a strange symptom that is quite commonly seen in these cases; they completely ignore everything that they see or hear or feel on the left-hand side of space, even though there is nothing wrong with their senses of vision, hearing, and touch. They seem literally to "forget" that the left-hand side of space, and of their own bodies, ever existed. It sometimes happens with these cases, that, if you show them their own left arm, they will actually deny that it belongs to them, and they will make this assertion with a sense of conviction that you cannot shake no matter how much logical argument or factual evidence you marshall to contradict it. (The symptom of neglect sometimes takes on a different form— one could say, a paradoxical form—whereby the patient, rather than ignore or deny the existence of the left-hand side of the body, becomes completely *obsessed* by it.) The third symptom with which Mrs A presented was spatial disorientation, which is a self-explanatory term, and which is also a common consequence of damage to this part of the brain.

The symptom that caused her to be referred to our service, however, is very unusual in right hemisphere cases. I am referring to her depression. It is a well established clinical fact that, whereas left hemisphere cases are quite frequently depressed, and present with what is called "catastrophic reactions", right hemisphere cases usually display a striking indifference to their symptoms, often actually denying that they are ill at all. They will insist, for example, that they are perfectly capable of walking (or running) despite the obvious fact that they are in a wheelchair and that they cannot even stand. This symptom—which is called "anosognosia"—is closely related to the symptom of neglect. But Mrs A did not suffer from the usual form of anosognosia. She was extremely depressed, and it was for this reasons that we arranged daily sessions for her, in a psychoanalytical setting, to see if we could understand why she felt that she must kill herself, and thereby to see if we could help her.

In the very first minutes of her first session, Mrs A stated that the reason why she was in tears all the time, and feeling suicidal, was because "I keep losing things" and because "everybody hates me". These two thoughts, "I keep losing things" and "everybody hates me" ultimately revealed the basic structure of her depression. This was because, first, her depression was a reaction to loss, and second, it was the product of a self-directed hatred. Mrs A herself explained, reasonably enough, that she was depressed and felt suicidal because, as a result of her stroke, she had lost her independence. Curiously, however, she was not fully aware of the equally obvious fact that she had lost the use of the left-hand side of her body. We are thus faced with a paradoxical situation in which Mrs A was depressed because she had "lost her independence", although she was simultaneously unaware of the essential cause of that lost independence—namely, her dense hemiplegia. This loss, which was the immediate cause of her depression, could only be expressed indirectly, by means of association with other losses, of which she *was* consciously aware, such as the death of her father decades before, an early hysterectomy, and the frequent losses of trivial objects—which resulted from her spatial disorientation and neglect—during her daily life in hospital. (This is what she was *consciously* referring to when she complained that she kept losing things.) This paradoxical situation, of being depressed about a paralysis of which she was unaware, provided a clue as to what had happened to her neglected body-half; a short period of analytic work revealed that she was not consciously aware of having lost her left arm and leg, because *she had denied the loss by means of an introjection*. Thus, the left side of her body was both there and not there at the same time. She neglected her real hemiparetic arm and leg, because in her mind she still had them safely inside her. However, because her attachment to her own body had necessarily been a narcissistic one, her attitude towards these introjected lost objects was decidedly ambivalent. She understandably felt terribly let down by the left side of her body, upon which she—like all of us—had always depended absolutely, without ever realizing it. This part of her own beloved self, which she had naturally assumed was under her omnipotent control, had suddenly revealed itself to be a piece of external reality after all—and moreover, it had revealed itself to be an unreliable piece of reality, an object that she needed and loved, but that had nevertheless abandoned her. Her constant refrain that "everybody hates me" therefore turned out to be a projection of an internal situation in which a previously healthy and independent part of herself was hated by a now-crippled and dependent part of herself.

Her hatred of this introjected image of her lost self could be traced back analytically to its infantile origins in her identification with her mother, that is, it could be traced back to her identification with the woman upon whom she had depended for so long during childhood. The earliest bond to the mother is always a partly narcissistic one, just as the attachment to one's own body is. As Freud (1923, p. 25) has pointed out, the body as an object has a special status; it is simultaneously a part of the ego and a part of external reality. At least one analyst (Laufer, 1982) has demonstrated convincingly in this regard, especially in relation to masturbation, that our own bodies—and particularly our hands—unconsciously represent both our own selves and the physical care that we received from our mothers. Mrs A's internally-directed hatred was thus directed not only towards an introjected image of her lost, fully functioning body; it was ultimately directed also towards her internalized mother, who was narcissistically and ambivalently cathected, and who was an object of absolute dependence, before she let the patient down so terribly.

In this we recognize precisely the configuration which Freud (1916–1917e) described in his classical paper on "Mourning and melancholia". An ambivalently-loved, narcissistically-cathected object is lost, but the loss is denied by means of an introjection of that object; the lost object is thus preserved within the unconscious part of the ego, but it is simultaneoulsy attacked with the ruthless vengefulness of a lover scorned. Thus the self-hatred of the melancholic is revealed to be the internal expression of a repressed hatred towards an external object, whose independent existence was never fully recognized in the first place, before it was lost.

Mrs B & Mr C

Now I would like to describe two somewhat different patients. These two patients, like Mrs A, both suffered strokes in the right hemisphere of their brains—one as a result of a haemorrhage and the other as a result of a thrombosis, also in the distribution of the right middle cerebral artery. They were both middle-aged professionals. Like Mrs A, these two patients were both densely hemiplegic, and they both suffered unilateral neglect and spatial disorientation. However, unlike Mrs A, neither of these patients was depressed. Despite the fact that they suffered exactly the same physical defects as Mrs A, and had damage to precisely the same part of the brain, these patients were indifferent to their symptoms; and in the case of Mr C, he actually denied that there was anything wrong with him at all. In other words these two patients, rather than presenting with depression, presented with varying degrees of anosognosia.

> What was unmistakeable was how narcissistic they were. They were impenetrable, detached, aloof and superior—and although they consciously deplored the idea of being in any way dependent, they were demanding and complaining in a child-like way. Mr C was also rather hypochondriacal in regard to a variety of bodily processes—which created a strange contrast with his near-total denial of his dense hemiplegia. As is so often the case in the non-neurological population, the narcissistic veneer of these two patients turned out to be a rather brittle defence. Their pervasive "indifference" was only apparent. A small amount of psychotherapeutic work revealed an underlying sense of loss, and a profound fear of the humiliation and dependency it involved. These patients, no less than Mrs A, were unconsciously very much aware of the narcissistic blow they had endured, and of how vulnerable they now really were. Consciously they denied any concern about the loss of status and independence which their physical

incapacities implied, but unconsciously these things were very deeply felt. They were constantly on the brink of feeling completely crushed, and *the potential for depression, which this unconscious knowledge brought with it, was constantly threatening to overwhelm them.* This was easy to demonstrate analytically, as appropriate interpretations brought forth floods of tears and an all-consuming sense of loss, with regard to humiliations and failures about which they had apparently been blithely unconcerned just moments before. In these two cases, therefore, no less than in the first case, there was (to use Freud's felicitous phrase) an "open wound" in their narcissism (Freud, 1916–1917, p. 253)—there was a gaping hole in the body image, through which the entire narcissistic supply threatened to drain. Their defence against this intolerable situation—if we think about it in terms of Freud's classical theory—was an introversion of object libido back upon the ego. In this way the anosognosic denial of reality was applied like a patch over the wound in their narcissism. In other words, the ego was—as we say— hypercathected at the expense of reality, and was thereby artificially reinflated. Just as Mrs A had defended herself against conscious awareness of the rent in her ego by means of an introjection of the lost part of herself, so Mrs B and Mr C defended themselves against this same situation by means of an equally narcissistic introversion, which took the form of an all-pervasive denial.

On the basis of these findings, we may conclude that anosognosia can be understood as part of the general tendency in us all to repudiate a breach of our bodily integrity. However, that does not explain why patients with damage to the *right* side of the brain present with this symptom, while patients with damage on the left side of the brain do not, although they suffer an equivalent breach to their bodily integrity (and in fact a greater loss, since in them it is the dominant, right arm which is paralysed). I will return to this question a little later.

Before I do so, I would like to briefly describe a third group of right-hemisphere patients. These were two young men who, like Mrs A, sustained damage to the right hemisphere of the brain as a result of a ruptured middle cerebral artery aneurysm.

Mr D and Mr E

These patients, unlike the previous three cases, were consciously obsessed by their paralysed limbs. This is the paradoxical form of the neglect syndrome, which I mentioned to you earlier. Again, we studied these patients in a psychoanalytic setting.

These two patients, like the other three, were basically narcissistic, but in a different sense of the word. They were in an agitated and aggressive state, constantly blaming the medical and rehabilitation staff for causing their symptoms. Interestingly, both of them demanded that we make good this injustice by amputating the offending limb. They were impatient, imperious, and obsessive; they were hyperactive, and they were intolerant of imperfection, frustration, and doubt of any kind. The notion that they might obtain partial improvement through the slow process and physical effort of a rehabilitation programme, was anathema to them. They wanted their bodies to be restored completely, to the status quo ante, or they did not want them at all. If we could not fix the paralysed arm immediately and perfectly, then we should rather cut it off and replace it with a prosthesis. Even if that meant that they would be left with only the pincer movements of an artificial claw, it would be preferable to the disgusting, malfunctioning append-age that was currently attached to them. Their constant threat to us was that if we did not do as they instructed, they would do it them-selves, or kill themselves, or even kill us. Their unconscious attitude seemed to be, "if you do not give me the breast right now, immedi-ately—exactly when, where, and how I want it—then I will bite my tongue and my mouth, and I will bite the breast, and I will spit out all the pieces, and *that* will teach you a lesson". In fact, Mr E almost said as much when he exploded in one session, saying that he was going to bite his left hand to bits, and spit out all the pieces, and then post them in an envelope to the surgeon who had operated on him. There was no conscious recognition of the fact that the reason why the surgeon had operated on him in the first place, was because the patient had been *born* with a life-threatening arterial abnormality that had now ruptured. The idea that the source of his handicap lay within himself was intolerable; it was the surgeon who had deformed him, and unless he fixed it right now, he would kill himself, or the surgeon, or both. It is important to note, moreover, that in the case I am describing the hemiparesis was actually milder than it was in any of the other four cases—it took the form of an occasional clonus (or involuntary twitching) of the left hand. But this clonus meant that the hand had a life of its own, that it would not do the patient's bidding, that it was no longer under his omnipotent control—and for this reason it *had to be removed*. While he was making these threats, the patient restlessly paced up and down the room, which is something that he frequently did, in order to "let off steam", as he called it.

I hope that this description reveals what the mechanism of the mental disorder was in these two cases. In the first three patients, the hand which had let them down (which straddled the border between the ego and the outside world, and which was therefore unconsciously equated with the ambivalently cathected, earliest mother-figure) was introjected into the ego, where it was violently attacked. However in these two patients the hand was projected outwards, into the hated external reality to which it now so obviously belonged. To these patients, it was intolerable that the hand should remain a part of themselves, because if it did, they would be in the painful situation of the first group of patients—that is, they would have to hate their own beloved selves rather than reality—and that was a positively life-threatening situation. Thus, we can see that in these patients, too, the defence was ultimately directed against the possibility of depression.

I think it can be seen that the patients in the latter group were also distinctly paranoid. For as long as the bad object was perceived as being separate from them, they were constantly under threat from that quarter. In fact, we had a third case of this type at our hospital, who was *extremely* paranoid (and masturbated compulsively). However, it was not possible for us to investigate him analytically, because he was acutely ill, and we had to become involved with the practical management.

Now, considering all of these patients together, we can understand how it happens that the same lesion can give rise to such apparently opposite syndromes. Indifferent neglect of a limb and agitated obsession with it, are in fact two ways of expressing the same psychological conflict; the two syndromes share the same underlying dynamics, but they give rise to different defensive solutions. What all of these cases have in common, is that damage to a part of the normally-functioning body was experienced as a profound narcissistic injury, which was associated with a deep and inseparable sense of loss, accompanied by an awareness of dependency upon the object. But this intolerable situation was avoided, by means of a narcissistic defensive process, which involved a withdrawal of cathexis from the external object back into the ego, which was then split, either by means of introjection, or by projection, together with an all-pervasive denial. In this sense, all cases with right-hemisphere damage that we have so far studied, may be said to present with *a failure of the process of mourning.*

Discussion

In all the above cases there was a demonstrable and unambiguous lesion of the brain. That is why I have chosen to present neurological cases rather than psychiatric ones. If it can be agreed that the emotional symptoms in these cases were correlated with definite abnormalities of the brain, then we can throw into sharper relief the specific issue being considered; and we can separate it off from other controversial issues, such as whether or not we should consider a particular psychiatric disorder to have a neurochemical aetiology or not. In these five cases the matter was beyond dispute, and this allows us to concentrate upon the specific question regarding the nature of the relationship between the neuropathology and the psychopathology. I hope it is evident that despite the presence of a demonstrable lesion is these five cases, and despite the obvious aetiological role of the brain lesions, we still cannot reduce the psychological symptoms to the organic lesions. I believe that this is true for the following reasons.

First, we could have studied these patients' brains for as long as we liked, by every conceivable method, but unless we actually interacted with them as people, we would never have known what had happened to them. We would never have known, for example, that Mrs A was depressed, that Mrs B and Mr C felt indifferent, and that Messrs D and E were obsessed in a very particular way. These emotional symptoms were the fundamental psychiatric facts in these cases. But depression, indifference, and obsessions can never be found in the brain, nor in any other part of the body. Feeling states can, quite simply, only be found in the mind. What I am saying is, of course, quite obvious, and nobody would seriously dispute it. Nevertheless I think that it is worth reminding ourselves that there are things in the world that cannot be seen or heard or touched, but that can still be perceived and known, and that are therefore *real* all the same. Certain things can only be perceived subjectively. If we accept this truism, then we cannot come to any other conclusion than the following one; the mind has a reality of its own. There is both a physical and a psychical reality.

But this does not answer the original question. "Certainly", I hear someone say, "the mind is real—if that's what you wish to call it—but nobody is seriously disputing that; what we are saying is that the reality of the mind *depends* upon the reality of the brain. The mind is *produced* by the brain. Therefore the brain is *more* real than the mind. The states of conscious awareness to which you draw attention may be descriptively or phenomenologically irreducible, but they were *caused* by an event in the brain. If Mrs A had not suffered a stroke, she would not have been depressed; and the same applies to Mrs B's and Mr C's indifference, and to Messrs D's and E's obsessions." The question then seems to be, *why* did these patients experience what they did? Were their subjective symptoms caused by something which happened in their brains, or by something which happened in their minds? This question is more complicated than it seems. In attempting to answer it, I suggest that we be guided by an example from physical neurology.

If we wished to understand what caused Mrs A's *hemiplegia*, for example, we would do so in the following manner. We would begin with the medical history and a thorough clinical examination. This would lead us to formulate an hypothesis—based upon our previous experiences of similar cases, and upon the documented experiences of innumerable colleagues before us—as to what caused this particular hemiplegia. Our hypothesis would be that this hemiplegia was caused by a subarachnoid haemorrhage. We could not have guessed that by *looking* at the hemiplegia, but we could infer it from the clinical history. We could then test this hypothesis by conducting a series of radiological and laboratory investigations. Information derived from these tests, combined with the history and our examination of the patient, would lead us to conclude that the subarachnoid haemorrhage was caused by a constitutional arterial abnormality (known as a cerebral aneurysm) that had now ruptured. We know where in the brain to look for confirmation of this conclusion. The location of the aneurysm—together with the extent and location of the haemorrhage that it produced (and its sequelae)—would fully explain the hemiplegia. As to what caused the aneurysm, we would postulate an inherited disposition. As for the origin of that predisposition, we would infer a genetic variation, which ultimately reflects the laws of natural selection. Proceeding in this way, as you can see, we would be able to reconstruct the entire causal chain, which we describe as the "mechanism" of the symptom. This causal chain unfolds as an unbroken sequence of natural events, over definite physical structures.

But can this type of analysis reveal the mechanism of the *emotional* symptoms? Can these physical investigations and procedures clarify why Mrs A was depressed, for example, or why she felt that she had to kill herself? I believe not. When we investigated the psychological symptomatology in the five cases that I have described, we started from the assumption that the symptoms were real things, even though they were subjective experiences. This reflected the truism that I have discussed already. But if the very nature of a subjective experience renders it inaccessible to physical methods of observation and description, then why should its causal mechanism yield to such methods? A moment's reflection reveals the futility of seeking the cause of a suicidal melancholia (for example) in a CT scan. A scan (or an angiogram, or whatever) can only reveal the cause of the stroke. To say that she was depressed *because* of the stroke (that is, because a part of her brain was not working) begs the question. That is why, in the cases reported above, it seemed natural for us to explore the immediate causal determinants of the patients' subjective experiences by means of a systematic examination of the psychical context out of which those experiences arose. That is, we sought explanations for the psychical symptoms by delving more deeply into the psychical facts. This seemed appropriate, despite our knowledge that something was wrong with their brains. Just as the neurologist set about examining the bodies of these patients, so we set about examining their minds; and just as the neurologist pursued his examination beyond the immediate clinical data with the help of artificial aids such as angiograms and CT scans, so we pursued our investigations beyond the limits of the immediate (conscious) data with the help of artificial psychological aids.

What are these "artificial psychological aids"? They are nothing other than the well-known techniques of psychoanalysis, which enable us to overcome the emotional resistances that conceal a patient's innermost thoughts, and thereby to follow their causal sequence beyond the threshold of consciousness. These techniques are, of course, not easy to master, but they are the only techniques available for investigating the causation of the emotional processes that are of interest to us. The results that these techniques provide do not enjoy the same degree of scientific certainty as the results that are obtained by the neurologist; but we may console ourselves with the knowledge that the difficulty of our techniques, and the controversy surrounding our results, are inevitable consequences of the manner in which the mind is constructed. Unlike physical objects, subjective states of awareness are not sharply delimited things, they are transient and fugitive states, and they cannot be publicly scrutinized. To put it differently, they cannot be perceived via our *external* sensory organs. But this does not mean that they do not exist. For that reason we are able to study them, using appropriate methods.

So, what did the psychoanalytic method of investigation teach us about the causal mechanisms of the emotional symptoms in these cases? We started from the observation that the five patients—all of whom suffered lesions of roughly the same type, in roughly the same part of the brain—presented with radically different emotional symptoms.[2] Analytic investigation revealed that these different symptoms—which I am describing as *depression, indifference,* and *obsession* for short—were produced by three different defensive reactions to a unitary psychical trauma. These defensive reactions were (in varying combinations) *introjection, denial,* and *projection.* These reactions were triggered by a primary breach in the integrity of the bodily ego, which threatened to expose these patients to unbearable states of mental pain, associated with an awareness of loss and dependency. These affective links were traced back to earlier psychological traumata, and ultimately to a primal narcissistic catastrophe which was associated with the process of becoming separate ("weaning"). This established a full causal sequence of psychological events, analogous to the physical sequence which produced the hemiplegia.

We have therefore arrived at the viewpoint that in order to understand the mechanism of emotional symptoms in a case of neurological disease, it is necessary to take account of the whole personality of the patient, including the pre-morbid ego organization. This is not surprising. It simply reflects the fact that by the time that these patients fell ill, they had already been through a life-time of experiences, and that these experiences were different in each case. It also reflects the probable fact that the patients were born with different psychological constitutions. A stroke therefore has different psychological implications for different patients, who have different resources available for dealing with them. However, no matter how we construe these factors, the essential conclusion remains; *the different psychological mechanisms in each case—and therefore the causal chain of psychological events—could only be understood psychologically.* In other words, in marked contrast to the impotence of physical methods of analysis, a psychological approach to the emotional symptoms readily revealed their mechanism.

But this still leaves out of account the specific relationship between the anatomical damage and the emotional symptoms. I have said that the emotional symptoms were attributable to narcissistic injury. But why should bodily-ego disturbances arising from lesions in the *right* cerebral hemisphere in particular, produce severe narcissistic injuries of the sort that we detected at the root of these symptoms? Clearly, the two causal domains described above are linked at this point, and that link calls for an explanation. We must therefore consider how the physiological and psychological mechanisms described above related to one another. This is, in a sense, the crux of the problem we are considering.

If damage to the right hemisphere of the brain necessarily results in a profound narcissistic injury of the type described above, then the implication is that the two causal chains are correlated in a highly specific way. In neurological science this type of correlation is designated by the term "localization". Does this mean that the narcissistically-cathected representation that we call the "bodily ego" (and the introjections based upon it) can be located in the right cerebral hemisphere? As a matter of fact it does not. Just as a narcissistic injury can never be found inside a brain lesion, so a mental function can never be located within an anatomical structure. This is because psychical and physical reality are organized in completely different ways. The nature of the relationship between the two domains is defined by the laws of cerebral localization. In accordance with these laws, we know—for example—that the bodily ego (an elementary mental structure) has a highly complex neural realization. The neurological correlates of the bodily ego begin at the sensory-motor periphery, they include large parts of the spinal cord, all of the cranial nerves, and numerous modality-specific nuclei in the brainstem and diencephalon, in addition to the primary sensory-motor regions of the cerebral cortex, the secondary cortical zones adjacent to them, and much of the association cortex beyond. Each of these structures subserves a physiological function that contributes a different component element to the functional entity known as the bodily ego. They contribute these same elements to numerous other mental functions too. Thus, depending upon the site of the lesion, neurological disease in these different structures correlates with a wide variety of different changes in the mental representation of the body, together with various, simultaneous changes in other aspects of mental life. There is nothing surprising in this finding. Modern neuropsychology has demonstrated that the same principles apply quite generally to human mental functions. Simple mental functions have widely distributed physical correlates, and simple physical structures participate in a wide variety of mental functions. For this reason, mental functions can never be found *inside* neuroanatomical structures; they exist, as it were, *between* them. More importantly, each mental function consists of more than the sum of the component physiological parts that correlate with them. Even if the physiological correlates could somehow be captured and localized, they would still only be correlates of a process of thought, they would not suddenly become the thought itself. This is why mental functions can never be reduced to their physical correlates. Reducing a mental function to the physiological processes that correlate with them is like reducing a poem to the letters of the alphabet. Such reductions are possible in principle, but the object being studied evaporates in the process. Once again, this is a direct expression of the fact that mental and physical states represent two completely different aspects of reality, each irreducible to the other.[3]

Applying these principles to the material at hand, we have found that the right cerebral hemisphere contributes a particular component function to the complex functional system that is the physical correlate of a simple mental presentation known as the "bodily ego". I do not have space to provide a detailed description of this component function here. I can only mention the basic facts. There seems to be a special relationship between the right-hemisphere association cortex and the representation of "things", as opposed to "words". In this respect, the cerebral representation of the body as a "thing" is inextricably linked with the cerebral representation of other "things". Consequently, damage to the right hemisphere of the brain results in a collapse, not only of our conception of bodily space, but also of external objects and of concrete space in general. This reflects the epigenetic (developmental) link between the representation of the body and the representation of the object world. In this sense, the world develops out of the body. Damage to equivalent cortical tissue in the *left* cerebral hemisphere affects symbolic representations of the body, which are bound into a closed system of lexical and semantic connections. Damage to these parts of the brain impair bodily representations only in so far as they are encoded within an abstract system of connections. This has various important consequences, depending upon the aspect of the process involved. But the concrete presentation of the body itself remains largely unaffected. Left hemisphere patients do not "forget" that parts of the body ever existed. This enables them to make realistic adaptations to their physical symptoms, and to institute the necessary process of mourning. These are some of the essential reasons why damage to the left side of the brain does not result in the severe narcissistic reactions which accompany equivalent lesions in the right hemisphere. However, in left hemisphere patients the symbolic functions which words provide are impaired.[4]

The point I am making is this. It would be wrong to infer from the clinical data that I have presented, that the representation of the "thing" to which we are more deeply attached than to any other thing in the world—namely our own beloved selves—can simply be removed like a piece in a jigsaw puzzle from the right hemisphere of the brain. Even the primary trauma involves a complex, dynamic process. Thus, for example, it is impossible to suffer damage to the concrete representation of the bodily ego (the ego as a "thing") without this immediately affecting the representation of external objects and of space. Trauma to this aspect of the bodily ego results in a gross distortion of external objects, to a collapse of external space, and to a withdrawal of object cathexes. This in turn results in a regression from object-love to narcissism, and so on. These interrelationships reflect the fundamental fact that mental life is in its essence a dynamic process, which carries within itself the whole of its developmental history. Processes of this type can never be concretely located in the anatomical structures of the brain.

My general conclusion is this: if it is true that the essential nature and the causal mechanism of a psychological symptom can only be revealed by psychological means in cases where there has been recent physical damage to a specific part of the brain, then how much more that must be so if the physical correlate (or even the aetiological factor) is a neurochemical imbalance, which may or may not have existed for the whole of the patient's life. And if what has happened to a person—and what is happening to them—can only be properly understood by way of their psychical reality, even in cases where the material reality is beyond any reasonable doubt, then how much more that must be so when even the specialists cannot decide what the material reality is. And if we have to take account in neurological cases of the fact that mental processes of the sort that we deal with in psychoanalysis are in a constant state of flux (that they are endlessly organizing, re-organizing and adapting themselves to changing circumstances, and that they not only do so in the present, but that they have also done so in myriad ways throughout the long process of development) then how much more that must be the case if there has not been physical damage to the brain; how much more it must be the case if the physical correlate (or even the aetiology) is a neurochemical imbalance, which is in itself a dynamic thing, and which may or may not have existed for the whole of the patient's life. In short, I think that these cases demonstrate, even in instances in which the aetiological factors are best described in physiological terms, we would be making a serious mistake if we concluded that the associated mental illness itself can be described or understood from a physiological point of view.

These are the essential reasons why I believe that we can never replace a psychological science with a physical one. Of course that does not meant that the two things are unrelated. But what it most certainly does mean is that *the mind is no less real than the brain;* and for that reason, no matter what advances might be made in future in neurological science, it would be foolish to believe that we will ever explain the psychological reality of mental illness by means of anything other than psychology.

In reaching these conclusions, I am not saying anything new; I am simply repeating something that Freud—who was himself a neuroscientist—taught us more than 100 years ago, when he tried to understand the mental symptoms of *his* neurological patients. Given more space I could have described how Freud (1891) arrived at those views on the basis of the mental changes that he observed in cases with damage to the left hemisphere of the brain, and how those observations led him to conclude that psychical reality could never be reduced to material reality, and how that led to the birth of psychoanalysis, and what effect this viewpoint (which Freud first expressed in a famous neurological monograph) had upon subsequent developments in science.

We still do not know how all of the complicated psychological phenomena that we deal with in our consulting rooms are correlated with the material structures of the brain. But if we approach this problem afresh, on the basis of the principles that I have described—in a way that takes as its starting point the primacy and the reality of conscious mental life, and that accepts as given the mental nature of the unconscious processes which determine it— then I see no reason why we should not be able to answer these questions some day. In other words, we will only be able to achieve this goal if we integrate a fully psychological psychiatry into the field of neurobiology. I would like to suggest that if we study psychologically the emotional symptoms that arise from neurological pathology, which necessarily means that we attempt to understand neurological patients using psychoanalytic methods, then I can see no reason why we will not eventually be able to understand the essential changes that have taken place in their lives, and how those changes correlate with the changes that have occurred in their brains. If we do this slowly and carefully, and do not forget the basic principles upon which our discipline was built, then I feel sure that we will gradually be able to differentiate between what is fundamental in those changes, and what is secondary, and between what is generally true for the human mind as a whole, and what is idiosyncratic to the individual concerned. In this way we can build an understanding of how the knowledge that we have gained about the depths of the mind relates to knowledge that has been gained about the brain, without us having to sacrifice any of the valuable insights that the pioneers of our discipline have passed down to us. And if we can do this with structural lesions, I see no reason why we cannot do the same with neurochemical imbalances—if and where they can be demonstrated. I believe that this is an appropriate basis for reconciling our psychoanalytic knowledge with recent advances in the neurological sciences.

In this chapter I have been able only to hint at how this way of approaching the problem actually works in practice, and I have been able to describe only a fragment of the sort of data that it generates, but I hope that I have nevertheless been able to convince readers of the principle that this is a worthwhile way to proceed. Lastly, I hope that if any readers find themselves in a situation in future where a neurological patient is referred to them for psychotherapeutic help, that they will not turn away from the task in horror, but rather that they will grasp the real scientific opportunity that it presents.

Notes

1. Based on a paper presented at the APP conference "Chromosomes on the Couch: addressing biological issues in psychotherapy", on 16 April 1994. Versions of this paper were also presented at St Ann's Hospital, London, (in the Seminars in Psychiatry series, 4 May 1994) and to the BAP South London Network (at a Sunday Morning Discussion Meeting, 8 October 1994) and published in 1995 in *Psychoanalytic Psychotherapy* , 9(2): 107–120.

2. The different symptoms—which in some instances were diametric opposites—cannot be attributed to minor variations in the location and extent of the lesions. All of these patients had damage in the dorsolateral convexity of the right cerebral hemisphere, in the distribution of the middle cerebral artery. Everything that we know about the functional organization of this part of the brain contradicts the view that such major symptomatic differences were due to minor variations in the lesions. In neuropsychology we customarily classify all of the manifestations of right-hemisphere convexity damage under a unitary nosological heading, namely *the* "right hemisphere syndrome".

3. In Freudian metapsychology, we say that consciousness has *two perceptual surfaces*, which represent an underlying reality ("unknowable" in itself) in two completely different ways. These are the terminal points of conscious perception, from which it is simply impossible to free ourselves. The dualistic conception of brain and mind (in the pre-psychoanalytic sense of the word) is abstracted from these two

categories of consciousness; it is therefore determined by the basic structure of the mental apparatus.

4. Words protect us from things. In Freudian metapsychology we speak of "stimulus barriers", and of a process called "binding" which transforms overwhelming concrete realities into manageable "signals" of the same. Accordingly, left-hemisphere patients are frequently unable to use language to distance themselves emotionally from their loss. This produces a characteristic set of emotional symptoms, known as the "catastrophic reaction". (This function of words is also disturbed in certain forms of psychosis.)

References

Freud, S. (1891b)[1953]. *On Aphasia: A Critical Study.* New York: International Universities Press.

Freud, S. (1916–1917e). Mourning and melancholia. *S.E., 14*: 136, 253.

Freud, S. (1923b). The ego and the id. *S.E., 19*: 25.

Laufer, M. E. (1982). Female masturbation in adolescence and the development of the relationship to the body. *International Journal of Psycho-Analysis, 63*: 295–302.

CHAPTER SEVENTEEN

How NOT to escape from the Grünbaum Syndrome: a critique of the "new view" of psychoanalysis

Morris N. Eagle and Jerome Wakefield[1]

Introduction

This chapter discusses the "new view" claims that Grünbaum's critique of Freudian psychoanalysis is irrelevant to contemporary clinicians because the latter have relinquished the traditional idea that analysts uncover hidden mental contents in the patient's mind. Rather, it is claimed, contemporary analysts construct new meanings and narratives. We argue that this response to Grünbaum's criticisms is not only incorrect in its assumptions, but if it were correct, would be more devastating to psychoanalysis than Grünbaum's critique itself. It severs the foundational link between self-knowledge and insight and therapeutic cure and essentially embraces a central role for suggestion. We also argue that the "new-view" theorists confuse vagueness with indeterminacy of mental contents and end up by, in effect, renouncing the idea that psychoanalytic interpretations are the kinds of things that can be confirmed or disconfirmed. This is a case where the attempt to escape criticisms entails a state of affairs that is worse than the criticisms themselves.

In his two books, *The Foundations of Psychoanalysis: A Philosophical Critique* (1984) and *Validation in the Clinical Theory of*

Psychoanalysis: A Study in the Philosophy of Psychoanalysis (1993), Adolf Grünbaum presented cogent and potentially devastating critiques of Freudian psychoanalytic theory. These critiques dealt generally with the empirical and logical foundations of psychoanalytic theory but focused especially on the epistemologically suspect nature of the clinical psychoanalytic data generally cited as the strongest evidence for the theory, including issues regarding the theory of transference in its role as a support for aetiological theory, the problem of suggestion, and Freud's (1916–1917, p. 452) "tally argument", that is, the claim that only interpretations that "tally with what is real [in the patient]") will be therapeutically effective.

Psychoanalysis's response to Grünbaum's critique took several forms. Some analysts thoughtfully attempted to address specific criticisms and thereby to defend Freudian theory. Others responded that Grünbaum's criticisms might apply to classical Freudian theory but not to newer views, but failed to specify what is different about post-Freudian theories that makes them immune to Grünbaum's arguments.

A third response, which we refer to as the "new view", was much more radical and will be our focus here. It held that it is not only that the content of psychoanalytic theory and of clinical interpretations that had changed, but that contemporary analysts no longer conceptualized the very nature of the psychoanalytic situation, interpretation, mind, psychopathology, and cure the way Freud did, and these changes, they argued, are so fundamental that Grünbaum's critique does not apply to this new conceptualization. For example, Stephen Mitchell (1998), a highly influential analyst and the foremost proponent of the new view, acknowledges that "there have been several important features of [traditional] psychoanalysis as a discipline that have contributed to its vulnerability to Grünbaum's kind of critique" and that can lead to what Mitchell refers to as the "Grünbaum Syndrome" (*ibid.*, p. 4).

According to Mitchell (1998, p. 5), analysts become afflicted with the "Grünbaum Syndrome" after exposure to his criticism that "that there is no way of testing their validity [i.e., of psychoanalytic interpretations] in any independent fashion". The syndrome includes

> several days of guilty anguish for not having involved oneself in analytic research . . . And may [also] include actually trying to

remember how analysis of variance works, perhaps even pulling a twenty-year old statistics off the shelf and quickly putting it back. There may also be a sleep disturbance and distractions from work. [Mitchell, 1998, p.5]

However, in virtue of a new conceptualization of the psycho-analytic situation, analysts can avoid the discomfort of the "Grün-baum Syndrome" and can assure themselves of the "almost total irrelevance to contemporary clinicians" (*ibid.*, p. 5) of Grünbaum's critique.

The rendering of Grünbaum's critique as irrelevant, according to Mitchell and other new-view theorists, is accomplished essentially by relinquishing the Freudian idea that analysts uncover or discover hidden pre-existing meanings in the patient's mind and by maintaining instead that analysts construct new meanings and new narratives that benefit the patient. We will argue that this defence of psychoanalysis and approach to curing the Grünbaum Syndrome is not only incorrect in its assumptions but, if it were correct, would be more devastating to psychoanalysis than the Grünbaum Syndrome itself.

But before examining the views of Mitchell and other new-view analysts, we first briefly describe some aspects of the historical and conceptual context in which the current debate arose. Janet (1889) (see Ellenberger, 1970) and other pre-psychoanalytic investigators maintained that hysteria was a product of constitutional weakness interacting with a traumatic event. It was claimed that due to their constitutional weakness, hysterics were unable to integrate traumatic ideas into the overall mental system. Consequently, they suffered a "split in consciousness" and a variety of resulting symptoms. For treatment of hysteria, Janet advocated a technique that followed directly from his assumption that hysterics were deficient in integrative capacity, namely, use of hypnotic suggestion to implant in the region of the patient's mind made accessible by hypnosis the idea of a fictitious benign event to substitute for the unintegratable traumatic event experienced by the patient.

The birth of psychoanalysis was marked by the introduction of what Freud (1914d) referred to as the "cornerstone" concept of repression. Freud's radically new claim was that the splits in consciousness and consequent symptoms characteristic of hysteria were due not to a constitutional weakness that made integration of problematic contents difficult, but rather to an intentional action to, so to speak, dis-integrate consciousness, that is, to prevent integration, in order to keep out of consciousness mental contents that were unacceptable to the individual. The intentional act was referred to as repression. If repression (or the split-off content that resulted) was the pathogen in hysteria, it followed that lifting repression—making the unconscious content conscious—was the means to cure hysteria. The various techniques employed by Freud—hypnosis, the pressure technique, and finally, free association plus interpretation—were all designed to undo repression, that is, to make the unconscious conscious.

If Janet's approach could be described as cure through reassuring falsehood, then Freud's focus on undoing repression could be viewed as a diametrically opposed cure through painful truth, that is, through learning the actual contents of one's repressed unconscious desires, conflicts, and so on. "Know thyself" became not only a Socratic moral imperative, but also a clinical necessity. Thus, through the concept of repression and the central treatment goal of lifting repression, psychoanalysis became part of an Enlightenment vision in which self-knowledge is the path to liberation.

Lifting repression is implemented in analytic work mainly through the analyst's interpretations of the patient's free associations, dreams, and other psychological phenomena. On theoretical grounds, Freud considered the at least approximate truth of interpretations to be crucial to this process. According to Freud's early account, it is partly the degree of correctness of the interpretation that weakens repression and carries the interpretation's therapeutic power. This is because a correct interpretation, through its associative linkages, will be more likely to connect to the repressed idea via intermediate mental states and thus, by forging an associative pathway, overcome the repression and bring the corresponding unconscious content into consciousness. Moreover, because truth and therapeutic progress are linked this way in Freud's theory, the successful therapeutic action of Freudian aetiological interpretations would suggest their likely at least approximate veridicality. Thus, according to Freud, clinical process and outcome can provide verification of psychoanalytic aetiological hypotheses.

With so much in both the theory of therapy and the theory of aetiology riding on the correctness of interpretations, the question immediately arises as to whether psychoanalytic interpretations are, in fact, correct. That is, do the analyst's interpretations correspond to what is contained in the patient's mind, such as the contents of his or her unconscious wishes, fantasies, conflicts, defences, and so on? And, do aetiological interpretations correspond to repressed childhood ideas that are aetiologically related to the patient's symptoms?

One reason this question is of importance is that there is an alternative account of psychoanalytic process and outcome that rejects Freud's theories of cure and aetiology as well as his proposed link between truth and cure, and holds that even seemingly curative interpretations can be false, in the sense that they need not correspond to the contents of representations actually in the patient's mind. This alternative is the "suggestion" account, which in a sense is a Janet-type understanding applied to Freud's approach. The suggestion account maintains that, given the analytic situation, which includes the patient's vulnerable condition and his or her attribution of authority to the analyst, the patient may well comply with the analyst's statements and assent to false interpretations that may be derived from the analyst's pet theory of aetiology rather than from accurate inferences regarding the patient. Because the contents being interpreted are supposed to be unconscious, the patient is not necessarily in a position to directly verify whether they are true and to reject false interpretations. Thus, the patient may become persuaded by the interpretation and come to believe it is true, spuriously "verifying" the analyst's assertion. This alternative account also proposes that the false interpretation might have a placebo effect, or in some other way lead to clinical improvement in the patient. It surely cannot be ruled out, the argument goes, that the acceptance by the patient of a false interpretation might help the patient to overcome a problem or motivate the patient to change his or her life in a useful direction, therefore apparently leading to improvement or even cure. Thus, psychoanalytic interpretations may in the end consist of the implantation of false ideas in the patient's mind which, although not benign in Janet's sense, have curative power for one reason or another. Thus, the therapeutic effect of an interpretation, according to the suggestion account, is no guarantee of the truth.

The idea that suggestion might be a central component of analytic work was anathema to Freud from the first. When Fliess accused him of suggesting ideas to his patients, Freud retorted, "You take sides against me and tell me that the 'thought reader reads his own thoughts into other people', which deprives my work of all its value" (Freud, 1950a, p. 336). If the suggestion account is correct that the analyst's interpretations are nothing more than reading his or her own thoughts into the patient, then, although the content of Freudian interpretations may differ from Janet's, the therapeutic mechanism of Freud's psychoanalysis is not essentially different from that of Janet's "therapeutic" implanting of useful falsehoods. One could no longer think of psychoanalysis as a grand product of the Enlightenment vision marked by the search for self-knowledge and truth.

As Grünbaum (1984) has famously noted, Freud attempted to counter the charge of suggestion by arguing that "only interpretations that tally with what is real in [the patient]" (Freud, 1916–1917, p. 452) will, in the long run, be therapeutically effective. So, interpretations that are mere suggestion, where the analyst reads his or her own meanings into the patient, will be ineffective and will drop out. The problem with Freud's tally argument should be obvious at this point: as a response to the suggestion account, the tally argument blatantly begs the question by presupposing that only a true interpretation can cure. The tally argument thus arbitrarily reasserts the very Freudian claims that the suggestion account aims to dispute. And, as Grünbaum has powerfully argued, the presupposition that only true interpretations cure is without independent warrant. Thus, the tally argument is no counter to the suggestion account.

"The nagging problem of suggestion," as Paul Meehl (1983) has called this seemingly intractable issue for psychoanalysis, leads one to ask: by what independent criteria (that is, independent of therapeutic effectiveness or effects) can one tell whether an interpretation is true, particularly when the interpretation refers to unconscious mental contents? One standard answer is that the patient's ultimate first-person avowal of truth of the interpretation is the critical proof of correctness. For example, Mischel (1963) argues that the acknowledgment of the individual to whom an unconscious wish or motive is attributed is, in the "long run," necessary for establishing the veridicality of the attribution—even if the individual's acknowledgment is delayed. One problem with this thesis is that, as noted, patients may, for a variety of reasons such as suggestibility under the influence of the respected analyst, avow interpretations that are in fact false. Moreover, because of repression or denial, an individual may never acknowledge an unconscious wish or motive that a good deal of convergent evidence (e.g., dreams, free associations, slips of the tongue, symptoms, and other behaviours) might plausibly suggest is operative, and there seems no reason in principle why one could not consider such an interpretation true based on evidence other than first-person avowal. Although first-person insight remains one powerful way that unconscious contents can become known, it does not seem to be the only way.

When faced with such a seemingly intractable epistemological problem of a gap between the evidence one has and the ontological claims about reality that one is making, there is one sure but ultimately unsatisfactory route out of the problem, namely, simply to redefine the ontology in terms of whatever evidence one does have, so the evidence can conclusively demonstrate the truth of one's claims. Thus, for example, behaviourists reduce the mind to behaviours or behavioural dispositions, thus escaping the dilemmas faced by the rest of us as we struggle with the gap between the behavioural evidence and our beliefs about others' internal mental states. Analogously, some contemporary analysts have addressed the epistemological failure of the grounds for psychoanalysis's claims about unconscious mental contents by redefining the claims to make them true in virtue of the available evidence.

One such position, taken by Donald Spence in his influential book *Narrative Truth and Historical Truth* (1980), is to argue that psychoanalytic aetiological interpretations about early experiences do not constitute "historical truths"—which are often difficult, if not impossible, to determine—but rather "narrative truths", that is, narrative accounts that are persuasive to the patient. It is not clear why Spence uses the term "narrative truth" when he means persuasive accounts. After all, outright fiction and lies can be persuasive. Perhaps he intends the idea that the narrative is experienced as the truth by the patient—which, of course, is equivalent to saying that the patient experiences the narrative as persuasive. Perhaps the use of the term "narrative truth" also reflects a nostalgic reluctance to

openly give up any claim to veridicality for psychoanalytic interpretations. Were that to occur, one would have to confront the
disturbing idea that psychoanalytic narratives are not essentially
different from other potentially persuasive accounts promulgated,
say, by cults or religious movements which are also in the business
of altering personality. To give up any claim to truth would be to
openly acknowledge that suggestion is at the core of all these
"narratives". Of course, these narratives are a form of truth only in
virtue of Spence's implicit identification of what we can know, i.e.,
what narratives most effectively persuade the client, with the truth
itself. Thus is ontology reduced to epistemology.

But many analysts would concede to Spence that historical truth
is beyond the grip of the psychoanalytic hour. This concession does
not end the problem of veridicality. In his contrast between "narrative truth" and "historical truth", Spence (1980) focuses his concern
on the question of correspondence of interpretations with past
experiences and events. The difficulty, if not impossibility, of knowing what, in fact, the patient's early experiences were, lead Spence
to settle for "narrative truth" rather than "historical truth". However, although one may not be able to establish the patient's early
experiences, one might still claim that one's interpretations of the
patient's current wishes, conflicts, feelings, defences, transference
reactions, and so on, tally with the patient's current mental states.
So, even if one goes along with Spence and renounces any claim to
accurately capture the patient's early experiences, the issue of
veridicality remains. For example, how does one evaluate the
veridicality of an interpretation in which one attributes current
repressed anger towards the analyst or towards a spouse or a
current defensive manoeuvre, which the patient denies experiencing? Psychoanalysts are disinclined to concede that such current
unconscious contents cannot sometimes be accurately interpreted.

A few psychoanalytic researchers (e.g., Crits-Christoph, Cooper,
& Luborsky, 1988; Silberschatz, Fretter, & Curtis, 1986) have
attempted to address this question empirically by defining accuracy
of interpretations in terms of their agreement with independent
assessments of the patient's dynamics; for example, his or her
stereotypical patterns of wishes. Defined in this way, accuracy of
interpretations has been shown to have a modest but statistically
significant relation to therapeutic outcome.

This brings us back to the new-view theorists and their attempt to render Grünbaum's critique irrelevant by developing conceptions of psychoanalysis and the mind that enable them to bypass the entire question of veridicality. The key move they make is to reject any claim that analysts attempt to uncover or discover anything in the patient's mind. Instead, they argue, analysts construct or, in negotiation with the patient, co-construct new perspectives, new meaning systems, coherent narratives, and even "aesthetic fictions" (Geha, 1984) that are purportedly helpful to the patient. Thus, the analyst need not concern himself or herself with the veridicality of interpretations.

If tallying with something real in the patient is no longer a constraint for analytic interpretations, how are they to be evaluated? The implicit and explicit response to this question by many analysts is that interpretations, or narratives, or new perspectives are to be evaluated by their serviceability and adaptiveness, by the degree to which they contribute to an increase in the patient's well-being and happiness. That is, therapeutic effectiveness—now no longer linked to veridicality or accuracy—is the proper yardstick and remains as the only justification for the psychoanalytic enterprise. However, the new-view theorists provide no evidence that (1) patients do, in fact, adopt new perspectives and narratives; and (2) that, if adopted, they are associated with more positive therapeutic outcome. In this regard, new-view theorists have continued a tradition in which analysts are long on assertions and short on systematic evidence regarding therapeutic outcome.

It should be noted that the foundational link between self-knowledge and insight (into one's unconscious mental life) and therapeutic cure is broken on this account. In this regard, the new view in contemporary psychoanalysis has perhaps more in common with Janet's implantation of ideas into the patient's mind than with Freud's Enlightenment conviction that self-knowledge and learning more of the truth about oneself are the paths to autonomy and liberation. For to proclaim that psychoanalysis is only about "interpretively constructing" the patient's mind and offering new meaning systems and coherent and persuasive narratives is essentially to embrace suggestion rather than attempt to counter it; in effect, psychoanalysis has returned to Janet. Indeed, one influential contemporary new-view analyst, Owen Renik, rejects the traditional claim that "the analyst addresses the patient's, rather than the analyst's own psychic reality" (Renik, 1996, p. 509) and also rejects as a pretension the claim "that the analyst's analytic activity does not consist essentially of communicating his or her personal judgments" (*ibid.*); Renik makes clear that these personal judgments are based not, as traditionally claimed, on "disinterested understanding"—which, he believes, accords the analyst "undeserved authority"—but on the analyst's personal values, beliefs, and goals.

This is a high price to pay for escaping the Grünbaum Syndrome. Indeed, it is not entirely clear in what ways contemporary psychoanalysis remains psychoanalysis when its essential structure and core assumptions have been relinquished. After all, the essence of psychoanalysis, and the reason for the selection of the very term psycho-analysis for the therapeutic process, lies in the claimed therapeutic benefit of analysing the mental contents in the patient's mind. It is, of course, true that there are some clinical situations in which the analyst does attempt to help the patient to take a new perspective, usefully reframe a problem, or construct a new meaning system, rather than discover existing meanings. But in these activities, psychoanalysis is not distinct from a variety of other influence processes. It is only in the claimed link between truth and cure that psychoanalysis makes a unique and profound potential contribution.

But if false interpretations can cure, then why should we care about the truth? The obvious response, and one that might be embraced by many patients, is that truth is valuable in its own right and it is unacceptable to purchase mental peace at the cost of living a lie. Despite such potential concerns, new-view theorists do not advocate providing informed consent to patients about what they are doing, but rather continue to interpret in a way that appears to be an attempt to discover what is in the patient's mind. That it would indeed be hard even for "new-view" analysts to work if they carried their philosophical positions into their clinical work is shown by the disjunction between the conceptual stance they take and the clinical material they present, in which they routinely make claims about what is the case regarding the patient's mental states.

Mitchell's response to the objection that it is unacceptable to ignore the truth is to argue further that there is no truth about mental contents to be discovered. According to Mitchell (1998), "there are clearly no discernible processes corresponding to the phrase "in the patient's mind" for either the patient or the analyst to be right or wrong about" (p. 16). Indeed, according to Mitchell (1998), there is no "preorganized" mind to which interpretations need tally or correspond. Rather, the analyst not only constructs a new meaning system for the patient but "interpretively constructs" the patient' mind itself. A social-constructivist twist is given to this position when Mitchell argues that the patient's mind is constituted by the analyst's "interpretive constructions" and by the patient–analyst interaction. According to this view, the analyst does not confront a pre-organized mind with a relatively stable structure and stable set of central dynamics. Rather, Mitchell proposes a "relational" conception of mind in which the patient's mind has no inherent individual character of its own but rather is indefinitely fluid and malleable, waiting to be shaped and organized by "each new intersubjective relationship".

In putting forward the relational constructivist account, contemporary analysts are reacting against the arrogance of some Freudian analysts who implicitly assume virtually infallible access to the truth about the patient's mind based on their theory. Many contemporary analysts reject the assumption of special authority regarding what is going on in the patient's mind and limit their claims to expertise in "meaning making, self-reflection and the organization of experience" (Mitchell, 1998, p. 2). They attempt to democratize the analytic situation by limiting their task to co-constructing new perspectives and narratives through negotiation with the patient. The rejection of the notion of a truth about the patient's mind allows rejection of the perceived arrogance of traditional analysts in prematurely claiming to know the truth and in confidently imposing their understanding on the client.

There is much to be admired in the new view's rebellion against genuine elements of arrogance in traditional psychoanalysis. However, the road to intellectual hell is paved with good political intentions. It is a bizarre feature of contemporary intellectual life that all sorts of relativistic doctrines expressing scepticism that there is a truth are proposed as ways of correcting what are seen as the arrogance and unrestrained uses of power that derive from an overly confident belief that one knows the truth. However, rather than encouraging respect for opponents' arguments and the humility that comes from a proper recognition of how difficult it is to discover the truth and how far we probably are from such knowledge, relativistic doctrines collapse argument into a form of power and potentially encourage unrestrained exercise of power. With respect to the psychoanalytic situation, what can be more arrogant than believing that one is constructing the patient's mind unrestrained by any truth? In maintaining that the patient's mind is "interpretively constructed", one risks violating the independence and integrity of the patient far more profoundly than the traditional purportedly arrogant view does.

There are a number of broader philosophical currents which, though unarticulated by new-view theorists, constitute a supporting base for their position. One such current is a combined anti-representationalism and anti-realism applied to the nature of mind. That is, just as anti-representationalists such as Richard Rorty argue against the idea that our theories about an independently existing external world are, in some sense, representations of that world, so similarly do new-view theorists argue against the idea that interpretations of another's inner world can be representations of or correspond to that inner world. Just as, according to Rorty (1991), theories are to be judged, not by their correspondence to an (unknowable) external reality, but rather by their pragmatic value in regard to a given task and for a particular community, so similarly new-view theorists argue that psychoanalytic interpretations are to be judged not by the degree to which they tally with what is real in the patient, but by their pragmatic value, coherence, and serviceability in regard to therapeutic and life task. Just as, according to Rorty, it makes little sense to talk about correspondence between our theories and the ultimately unknowable *ding-an-sich* of external reality, so similarly it makes little sense, according to new-view theorists, to talk about one's interpretations corresponding to or tallying with what is going on in the patient's mind.

There are two ways of construing the new view's claims about the lack of truth of claims about mental contents. The first is that there is simply nothing in the mind at all to label as contents. Sometimes Mitchell does seem to talk this way. Indeed, Mitchell sometimes takes this position about not only unconscious contents but also conscious contents. It may seem extreme to claim that there are no conscious contents except what is constructed, but this sort of claim is virtually necessitated by the new view's position on the unconscious. The reason is that, as we saw in the earlier discussion of Mischel's account of the nature of unconscious content, it is a widespread assumption across many accounts that unconscious contents are fixed relative to conscious contents. We are not going to spell out the objections to the claim that literally no contents of any kind exist in the mind, conscious or unconscious. We are, after all, directly aware of some of the contents of our perceptions, beliefs, desires, and other intentional states.

The second construal of the new view position on content is more subtle. Consistent with the conception of mind as fluid and shaped by each new social interaction, Mitchell (1998) and Stern (1999) propose that psychoanalytic interpretations shape and give language to vague, unformulated, and inchoate unformulated experiences and thereby *create* new contents and experiences out of some sort of primitive experience. As Mitchell puts it,

> to understand unconscious processes in one's mind or that of another is to use language in a fashion that actually creates new experience, something that was not there before. [Mitchell, 1998, p. 18].

This idea is more fully developed by Stern (1999) who observes that certain unformulated experiences prior to being reflected on and put into words, are more like "glimmers of meaning" (p. 92), "thoughts not yet thought, connections not yet made, memories that one does not have the resources or the willingness to construct" (p. 12). Stern and Mitchell are arguing here, perhaps justifiability, against the Freudian assumption that unconscious mental contents are generally clear and distinct representations waiting to be discovered and are fully formed "hidden realities" that except for being unconscious are just like conscious contents. A prototype of this view is the Freudian notion that once repression is lifted, the distinct unconscious wish that was repressed (e.g., an incestuous wish) emerges into consciousness unchanged and in no wise different from conscious wishes.

The idea, then, is that interpretations give shape and language to inchoate unformulated experiences, and that many mutually incompatible alternative such constructions are equally allowable.

In effect, Mitchell and Stern are arguing for the *indeterminacy* of unconscious mental contents.[2] If unconscious mental contents are indeterminate, it would appear to make little sense to ask that interpretations tally with what is (unconsciously) going on in the patient's mind. This requirement would make sense only if there were determinate unconscious contents (and processes) in the patient's mind with which interpretations could tally. But, we are told, it is the very interpretations themselves that shape and thereby create the hitherto inchoate and unformulated mental contents.

There are two ways of understanding this thesis about the inchoateness of unconscious mental states. The first is that it results from defence. In claiming the inchoateness of unconscious states, Stern, for example, emphasizes that the appropriate model for defence is not banishment from consciousness of clearly delineated and fully formed mental contents, that is, repression, but rather the motivated failure to further process or spell out vaguely experienced "glimpses of meaning". But this argument seems incoherent. The defensively motivated failure to process or spell out clearly implies that something is being defended against, that is, being kept from being fully and explicitly experienced. Hence, some interpretations will tally with what is being kept from being fully experienced and other interpretations will not or will to a lesser extent.

Consider some specific examples taken from Fingarette (1969), whose work has some affinities to the new view. They include a man's failure to spell out his recognition that he has been a failure in realizing a certain ambition, Hickey's inability to spell out his hatred of his wife in O'Neill's *The Iceman Cometh*, and Sartre's example of a woman's "bad faith" reluctance to spell out her engagement in flirtation. In each of these cases, what needs to be spelled out are determinate and identifiable mental contents: a sense of failure, unacknowledged hate, and unacknowledged flirtation. If, in each case, the individual's unformulated "glimmers of meaning" have not been spelled out for defensive reasons, the clear implication is that a determinate and identifiable mental content is being defended against—a sense of failure, hatred, and flirtation. Although, as Mitchell and Stern maintain, language and interpretation may well articulate and give shape to these defensively unformulated "glimmers of meaning", they will do so only if they tally with the determinate mental contents being defended against. If they do not tally with these determinate mental contents, one might more accurately say that they mis-shape unformulated experiences.

Second, Mitchell's claims about the indeterminacy of unconscious content depend not on the theory of defence but on a broader assertion that its unconscious mental processes are inherently inchoate. It may well be the case that a good deal of material interpreted in psychoanalytic treatment does not consist of deeply repressed wishes and ideas that emerge in their original form once repression is lifted, but rather of vaguely and fleetingly experienced thoughts, feelings, fantasies, and sensations that have not been spelled out. It may also be true that the classical view of unconscious mental contents as distinct, clear, and fully formed mental contents, no different from conscious contents save that they are unconscious, is wrong and that, as Mitchell and Stern maintain, unconscious mental contents are generally unformulated, fleeting, and unarticulated. However, even if interpretation consists in articulating what has remained unarticulated and spelling out what has remained unformulated rather than uncovering fully formed wishes and ideas, the question of whether and to what degree interpretations "tally with what is real" still remains central. For although language and interpretation may articulate and give shape to what had been unarticulated, something is being articulated, given shape, and spelled out. After all, when one spells out, there must be something that is spelled out. Another way to put this is to say that, even on this version of the new view, unconscious mental contents are not completely indeterminate, ready to be entirely shaped and determined by an indefinite set of interpretations. If this is so, it remains the case that interpretations are "answerable" to existing mental contents in the patient's mind, even if these mental contents are vague and unformulated. Mitchell here seems to run up against a kind of paradox: how can there be content, no matter how vague or inchoate, that is not determinate to the extent that it is just what it is?

Thus, one might say that at the heart of this version of the new view there is a confusion between vagueness of content and indeterminacy of content. This is a confusion that occurs in the philosophical literature as well. For example, Robert Van Gulick, using analogies to animals and infants, argues that there can be unconscious mental states that have content but are indeterminate:

> Searle focuses on examples of conscious human mental states such as seeing a car from a certain angle or wanting a glass of water, and in such cases there is indeed a high degree of self-awareness about the state's finely individuated intentional object. But states can have aspectual shape even when their content is far less determinate and the agent far less self-aware. . . . Not all intentional states need be so determinate . . . My desires and my self-aware intentional states in general can have a degree of specificity and determinateness that the desires of cats and small children cannot. Nor can the in-principle unconscious states posited by [certain theorists]. [Van Gulick, 1995, pp. 205–206]

Van Gulick argues here that not all conscious states need have fully determinate content (e.g., the conscious states of a cat or a small child need not), so unconscious mental states need not have fully determinate content, either. However, Van Gulick confuses indeterminacy with vagueness, as Searle notes in a rejoinder.

> There is also a confusion in Van Gulick about the determinacy of content. He thinks that because cats and small children cannot conceptualize in as fine grained a manner as we can that their intentional states are thereby indeterminate. He thinks in short that lack of specificity in fixing the conditions of satisfaction is the same as indeterminacy. But it is not. In the case of indeterminacy, there is simply no fact of the matter about what the intentional content is, in the case of lack of specificity there is just a large range of possible conditions of satisfaction within the fully determinate intentional content. If I want a red shirt there may be a range of possible shades of red that will satisfy me, but that does not prove that there is no fact of the matter about what my desire is, that my desire is indeterminate. Vagueness is not indeterminacy. [Searle, 1995, p. 228]

That is, even if it is not expressible in our natural language, and even if it is extremely vague and inchoate, there is still a truth about the content of a mental state that possesses intentional content, including those that occur in the minds of children and animals. This is what it means for the content to be real. Indeterminacy implies that incompatible spellings-out of the content are equally correct given all the facts; vagueness does not imply this. If what you want is a red shirt, it is incorrect to say as a spelling-out or interpretation of the content of your state that what you want is a shirt specifically of red shade R1. The point about indeterminacy is that two incompatible interpretations of a content are correct given all the possible facts, but in the case of the desire for a red shirt, it is incorrect to say that the desire's content is for this or that specific shade of red, even though each of the specific shades are outcomes that would satisfy the desire. Similarly, Mitchell is confused to think that there is no determinate content with which interpretations can tally just because the analyst may spell out these vague contents in specific ways.

The ultimate point here is that the notion that unconscious mental states are vague or linguistically unformulated or difficult to describe does not imply they are indeterminate and thus does not eliminate the possibility of addressing the question of veridicality of interpretations. Thus, the new view's claim that it need not be concerned with the truth because there is no truth about unconscious states due to their vagueness is incorrect. Nor does this approach really save psychoanalysis from the feared "Grünbaum Syndrome", for there is little left of the psychoanalytic enterprise if one adopts this vision. The new view appropriates the name of psychoanalysis without the substance. Indeed, one can say that the new view represents not an escape but a total capitulation to Grünbaum's critique, in that it responds by abandoning any claim that is the target of Grünbaum's argument. Grünbaum's critique was aimed at showing that psychoanalytic theory lacks evidential and epistemological credentials and thus cannot be considered to be supported by the evidence usually cited, thus should not be accepted, but it left open the in-principle possibility that confirmation could occur (indeed, this in-principle point is implied by Grünbaum's devastating critique of Popper's claim that psychoanalytic theory is unfalsifiable). The new view's defence of psychoanalysis takes away even this thin reed of hope by renouncing the possibility of confirmation, or even that psychoanalytic interpretations are the kinds of things that can be confirmed or disconfirmed. Surely, even aside from the unsoundness of the new view's arguments, this is a case where the new view's cure really is worse than the supposed disease—the "Grünbaum Syndrome"—it was meant to treat.

Notes

1. In alphabetical order.
2. Mitchell (1998) appears to argue also for the indeterminacy of conscious mental contents.

References

Crits-Christoph, P., Cooper, A., & Luborsky, L. (1988). The accuracy of therapist's interpretations and the outcome of dynamic psychotherapy. *Journal of Consulting and Clinical Psychology, 56:* 490–495.

Ellenberger, H. (1970). *The Discovery of the Unconscious.* New York: Basic Books.

Freud, S. (1914d). On the history of the psychoanalytic movement. *S.E., 14:* 2–66. London: Hogarth.

Freud, S. (1916–1917). Introductory lectures on psycho-analysis, Part 3. *S.E., 11:* 243–496. London: Hogarth.

Freud, S. (1950a). *The Origins of Psychoanalysis.* M. Bonaparte, A. Freud, & E. Kris (Eds.). London: Imago.

Fingarette, H. (1969). *Self-Deception.* Berkeley, CA: University of California Press.

Geha, R. E. (1984). On psychoanalytic history and the "real" story of fictitious lives. *International Forum of Psychoanalysis, 1:* 221–229.

Grünbaum, A. (1984). *The Foundations of Psychoanalysis: A Philosophical Critique.* Berkeley and Los Angeles, CA: University of California Press.

Grünbaum, A. (1993). *Validation in the Clinical Theory of Psychoanalysis: A Study in the Philosophy of Psychoanalysis.* Madison, CT: International Universities Press.

Janet, P. (1889). *L'Automatisme Psychologique.* Paris: Alcan.

Meehl, P. E. (1983). Subjectivity in psychoanalytic inference: The nagging persistence of Wilhelm Fliess's Achensee question. In: J. Earman (Ed.), *Minnesota Studies in the Philosophy of Science: Vol. X. Testing Scientific Theories* (pp. 349–411). Minneapolis: University of Minnesota Press.

Mischel, T. (1963). Psychology and explanation of human behavior. *Philosophy and Phenomenological Research, 23*: 578–594.

Mitchell, S. A. (1998). The analyst's knowledge and authority. *Psychoanalytic Quarterly, 67*: 1–31.

Renik, O. (1996). The perils of neutrality. *Psychoanalytic Quarterly, 65*: 495–517.

Rorty, R. (1991). *Objectivity, Relativism, and Truth: Philosophical Papers* (Volume 1). New York: Cambridge University Press.

Searle, J. R. (1995). Consciousness, the brain, and the connection principle: Reply. *Philosophy and Phenomenological Research, 55*: 217–232.

Spence, D. P. (1980). *Narrative Truth and Historical Truth: Meaning and Interpretation in Psychoanalysis*. New York: W. W. Norton.

Silberschatz, G., Fretter, P. B., & Curtis, J. T. (1986). How do interpretations influence the process of psychotherapy? *Journal of Consulting and Clinical Psychology, 54*(5): 646–652.

Stern, D. B. (1999). Unformulated experience: From familiar chaos to creative disorder. In: S. A. Mitchell & L. Aron (Eds.), *Relational Psychoanalysis: The Emergence of a Tradition* (pp. 74–107). Hillsdale, NJ: Analytic Press.

Van Gulick, R. (1995). Why the connection argument doesn't work. *Philosophy and Phenomenological Research, 55*: 201–208.

CHAPTER EIGHTEEN

The evasiveness of Freudian apologetic

Frank Cioffi

Introduction

T his paper examines some recent responses to attacks on the value of Freudian theory. The main defect of such defences is that when they take the form of the abandonment of much of classical Freudian theory and it is maintained that what is valuable is Freudian method (dream interpretation, free association etc.) it must be explained why a method that regularly led to conclusions that the apologist rejects should nevertheless be retained. If the defence takes the form of arguing for the value of the notion of unconscious motivation then Freud's particular use of this notion must be defended and not that which featured in humane discourse before Freud expounded his distinctive version of it. The argument that Freudian theory can only be appreciated when more loosely or figuratively construed is also addressed. Some suggestions are advanced as to the sources of our emotional attachment to Freud.

Who owns Freudian theory? The retreat to platitude and why it matters

The following sequence of rhetorical questions was advanced as grounds for ignoring a work critical of Freudian theory: "'Is it reasonable to assume that early childhood experiences affect adult personalities?' 'Does a mother's love really matter?' 'Is sex important?' 'Do people act without full awareness of their motivations?' The answer to all these questions seems obvious" (Coolidge, 1999). This retreat to platitude is a common resort of Freudian apologists. It matters because in producing such a bland account of Freud's discoveries it obscures the fact that, although many of Freud's more distinctive theses may have been abandoned, the method which authenticated these repudiated claims is still advanced as the sovereign means of determining the secret springs of action and thus the need to address this contradiction and its implications is evaded.

In his reply to a criticism of his defence of psychoanalysis Thomas Nagel argues that "A fundamental problem in making progress with this dispute is that there is no agreement over what should be regarded as Freud's distinctive contribution." (Nagel, 1994b, p. 56). This is at best confused and at worse disingenuous. For to what "dispute" is Nagel referring? There is a straightforward, uncontentious answer to the question as to "Freud's distinctive contribution". It consists of those claims on whose behalf it had been urged for almost a century, against persistent denials from a marginalized sceptical minority, that they had been subjected to disinterested investigation and had been deemed worthy of credence. Indeed so much so that dissent from them could be considered evidence of unconscious psychopathological interference with normal ratiocinative processes (Charles Brenner on the Oedipus complex in the *International Encyclopedia of Social Sciences* (1968) for example). Furthermore, the claims in dispute are those which achieved acceptance so general that they figured in standard works of reference as having the status of facts as incontestable as the world's highest mountain or its longest river (Cioffi, 1998, pp. 87–88).

Then a change in the social and political climate supervened. The current platitudinized content of Freudian theory arouses the suspicion that it is less the result of increased clinical experience than of market research. This is a Freudian, Marshall Edelson, look-ing nervously over his shoulder at a feminist constituency as he expounds Freud's psychoanalytic view of women:

> . . . what (Freud) put forward, he put forward explicitly as based on work with relatively few cases and needing to be checked and investigated further. [Edelson, 1990, p. xiii]

There is a touch of Orwell's Ministry of Truth in Edelson's remarks. Here is Freud's final view of feminine psychology:

> we shall not be very greatly surprised if a woman analyst who has not been sufficiently convinced of the intensity of her own wish for a penis also fails to attach proper importance to that factor in her patients. [Freud, 1940, 23: p. 197]

I can detect no hint of a "need for checking and investigating further" in this remark. (And by the way, if a woman analyst were insufficiently aware of her wish for a penis, would not the mecha-nism of projection ensure that she detected an even more intense wish for one in her patients rather than none at all?) Even more market-orientated than Edelson is a review of Crews' *Unauthorised Freud* (1998), which hails the contribution of gender studies to the exposure of the "phallocratic" source of Freud's view of feminine psychology (Bresnick, 1998, p. 11). This would matter less if defences of Freud were unequivocally revisionist but, alongside the blander and more plausible or ideologically congenial reformula-tions, are hints that the more distinctive and implausible claims have not been entirely abandoned. Thomas Nagel invokes among Freud's achievements "the extended reach of the mind" (Nagel, 1994b, p. 56), or, as Freud put it, "the power unconscious ideas have over the body", but he provides no examples though the Freudian tradition is prolific of them. Had Nagel instanced something like the symbolic significance of the Wolf Man's constipation or of Dora's pseudo-appendicitis, the argument would have gained in concreteness at the cost of a loss in credibility. On the other hand, if his reticence implies a retreat from the characteristic Freudian mind-over-matter extravagances to the more sustainable claim that a troubled state of mind can influence a patient's health, he must justify treating this as part of the legacy Freud bequeathed rather than that which he inherited. In *Anna Karenina* (Tolstoi, 1965), we find the following discussion of Kitty Scherbatsky's illness, a tuber-culous condition.

> "But of course you know that in these cases there is always some hidden moral and emotional factor," the family physician allowed himself to remark with a smile. "Yes, that goes without saying," replied the celebrated specialist. [Tolstoi, 1965, p. 133]

Is it plausible to maintain that Tolstoi's original readers must have been startled by the view expressed in this exchange and that it is thanks to Freud that it is has become acceptable?

Are Freud's apologists "furtive" and "glib"

Elaine Showalter complained of Frederick Crews' criticism of Freudian apologists that "he can't concede that they simply disagree with him or interpret the data in a different way . . . (they) are not just wrong but furtive or glib . . ." (Showalter, 1997). This raises issues that transcend the Freud controversy. When are we justified in passing from ratiocinative to ideological or affective grounds in accounting for blatantly unwarranted claims to know-ledge?

Noam Chomsky once observed that

> Presented with the claims of nineteenth century racist anthropol-ogy the rational person will ask two sorts of question: What is the scientific status of the claims? What social or ideological needs do they serve? The questions are logically independent but . . . if the scientific status is slight then it is particularly interesting to consider the climate of opinion within which the claim is taken seriously. [Chomsky, 1971]

In the case of Freudian apologetic are we not, *pace* Showalter, justi-fied in passing to Chomsky's second type of question? For example, isn't it fair to infer from the following extenuations of Freud's departures from veracity evidence not just of intellectual error but of an infatuation from which the writers were determined not to be dislodged?

When Moll's *The Sexual Life of the Child* was published in 1909, Freud accused him of plagiarizing his "Three essays on sexuality" published two years earlier. Sulloway reports inspecting Freud's own copy of Moll's 1897 *Libido Sexualis* and finding those passages in which Moll alluded to infantile sexuality underscored; and concludes that it was rather Moll who had anticipated Freud. But Sulloway was not content to leave it at that. "Freud's claim of priority had symbolic status . . . Freud's accusation of plagiarism against Albert Moll must be seen in this light" (Sulloway, 1979, p. 470).

It has been claimed that a memoir said to provide direct evidence of the correctness of Freud's psychology of female development, Hug-Hellmuth's *A Young Girl's Diary*, was a fabrication. How do apologists deal with this shabby episode? Forrester and Appignanesi quote Helene Deutsch's verdict on the fabrication charge:

> if this was indeed the case, Dr. Hug-Hellmuth had both psychological insight and literary talent . . . The book is so true psychologically that it has become a gem of psychoanalytic literature. [Forrester & Appignanesi, 1992]

Forrester and Appignanesi are not perturbed by the complacency of this and conclude that this "verdict is as good as any" (*ibid.*, 1992, p. 73). In taking this indulgent attitude towards fraud they are in elite company. Elizabeth Roudinesco's comments on the charge that the claims as to the treatment of Anna O propagated by Freud and his colleagues is an "invention" illustrate the same insouciance.

> The truth of the story lies in . . . its legend and refers to the way in which the psychoanalytic movement tells itself the initial fantasies about its birth. [Borch-Jacobsen, 1997, p. 12]

A colleague sent me a photocopy of a page from the philosopher Ian Hacking's book *Rewriting the Soul* which contained this passage:

> Freud had a passionate commitment to Truth, deep underlying truth, as a value. That ideological commitment is fully compatible with—may even demand—lying through one's teeth. [Hacking, 1995, p. 195]

The only appropriate response to these rationalizations for complicity in deception is that which Macaulay made to an overpartisan biographer of Sir Francis Bacon, who extenuated Bacon's financial corruption on the grounds that Bacon "owed it to mankind to advance his own interests." "We do not really know how to refute such arguments," wrote Macaulay, "but by stating them" (Macaulay, 1961, p. 316).

Still further grounds for the suspicion that apologists are "calculating, evasive, slippery or inept", (Showalter, 1997) rather than just mistaken, as Showalter maintains, is provided by the manner in which an analyst, Jean Schimek, deals with the fact that, as he himself puts it, "An examination of Freud's texts of 1896 suggests that the early sexual trauma was not based on the patients' recovered memories but was reconstructed by Freud . . ." This is Schimek's comment, "This is not a startling or damning conclusion" (Schimek, 1987). How could Schimek maintain that there was nothing "startling or damning" in the fact that Freud's imputation of early sexual traumas to his patients was not based on their memories but on his reconstructions when he consistently denied this every time he had occasion to relate how the seduction error led him to the Oedipus complex?

I should like to explain why the matter of the unreliability of Freud's account of how the erroneous seduction theory led to the discovery of the Oedipus complex has momentous bearings on our judgement as to the credibility of Freud's theory of infantile sexuality and of the infantile aetiology of the neuroses in general. His later accounts, in which he falsely imputes the seduction error to his credulity in accepting as genuine his patients' apparent recollections of episodes of sexual molestation, divert attention from the unreliability of his habitual mode of reconstructing infantile life, since this and not his credulity was what led him to the seduction error. His real grounds for inferring non-existent episodes of molestation were, as he said at the time, his sense of the neatness of the articulation between the putative seduction and the content of the patient's symptoms. It was this same, demonstrably fallible, intuitive sense of isomorphy on which he based his certainty that he had reconstructed the infantile fantasies that replaced the molestations in his aetiology of the neuroses. Yet, not only did this go unremarked for many decades in which Freud's self-serving retrospective account was endlessly repeated, but even after this was called to the attention of the Freudians they resorted to various obfuscatory devices to evade, if not the fact, then, like Schimek, the implications of the fact. (Allen Esterson, 1993, provides a lucid and comprehensive account of the seduction episode and its importance.)

I once advanced as an example of Freud's tendentiousness his invocation of the infantile theory of anal birth to explain why the Rat Man was troubled by an image of ravenous rats being introduced into his helpless father's rectum (Cioffi, 1983, pp. 14–16). My objection to those who found this a striking instance of the infantile determination of neurotic symptoms, via the transformative mechanisms discovered by Freud, was that the image of the rat torture was a straightforward reproduction of an account given by the Rat Man a day earlier. James Hopkins' response was to insist that Freud was not invoking the infantile anal theory to explain the content of the obsession but merely its obsessional character (Hopkins, 1983, pp. 4–5). This is what Freud actually wrote:

> the rat punishment was based on the influence of two infantile sexual theories, that babies come out of the anus and that men can have them as well as women; a technical rule enables us to replace rats going in with babies coming out. [Freud, 1909d, p. 72]

Doesn't this show Hopkins to have blatantly distorted what Freud maintained? Whether this was due to an exculpatory motive so powerful that Hopkins could not acknowledge how grotesquely feeble was Freud's argument even after his attention had been directed to it, or whether he was adopting Hacking's rationale and "lying through his teeth" because his "ideological commitment to truth demanded it" only he can say.

I suppose these are examples of what Showalter (1997) would describe as apologists innocently "interpreting the data differently". But those who exerted themselves in calling attention to the "data" that apologists insist on facilely "interpreting" in exculpatory ways may feel that it is not lack of charity which leads them to find such apologists "not just wrong but furtive or glib . . ." (Showalter, 1997).

I am reminded by comments like Showalter's of Arthur Miller's account of the impression made on him by Lillian Hellman's

Stalinist apologetic: "I could hear the wagons drawing up in a circle around the camp and the clanking of rationalisations being piled upon the barricades ..." (Miller, 1988, pp. 257–258). I think I can hear the "clanking of rationalisations" in Showalter's defence of Freud as in that of Nagel, Hacking, Schimek *et al.*, but how can I make them hear it? In any case an enhanced awareness of the nature of the dispute over the good faith or disinterestedness of Freud's apologists makes its longevity less surprising

Were only hagiographers "stunned" by Freud's untruthfulness?

An alternative apologetic stratagem to stonewalling was employed by Jonathan Lear (Lear, 1995, pp. 18–25) and others. It takes the form of spurious candour in agreeing with the damaging exegetical material Freud's critics have called attention to but ignoring its implications. Lear says of the damaging claims as to Freud's judgement and probity assembled by Crews, "any one still in the grip of hagiography is likely to be stunned" (Lear, 1996, p. 581). This remark of Lear's reminds me of an occasion many years ago when I was watching the unfolding of the Watergate scandal on television and was touched by the loyalty of Julie Nixon Eisenhower's spirited defence of her father. Day after day she would appear on morning television to denounce his accusers and to assure the American people that anyone who knew her father as well as she did would realize how unthinkable was the behaviour of which he was accused. And then the bombshell of the tapes! A few days later it was announced that Julie Nixon Eisenhower would appear on morning television to give her response to the now documented role her father played in the Watergate break-in. Her response was admirable in its poise and succinctness : "Big deal!" And this is how Lear responds to the revelation of the extent of Freud's disingenuousness: "Big deal!" Having endured years of obstruction and vilification those who attempted to replace the legend of Freud's superlative integrity with a less honeysuckle account are entitled to some display of annoyance when apologists like Jonathan Lear imply that they knew it all the time and wonder what the fuss is about.

Why does the manifest inadequacy of Freud's evidential warrant for his "discoveries" matter? Because if we fail to address the question—why were these baseless theses credited and institution-alized—we lose the opportunity to make a discovery about our-selves just as enlightening and chastening as any of those attributed to Freud: the discovery of how quickly the normal habits of truth-seeking and truth-telling may be sacrificed on the altar of social convention, ideological agendas, and personal expediency by even the most admirable and distinguished members of the intellectual community. Whether anything as grim as this moral must be embraced will only be known when the questions raised by Freud's critics have been more pertinaciously addressed; a vague and inde-terminate acknowledgement of past error such as that evinced by Nagel, Lear, Showalter *et al.* is insufficient.

The retreat from literality

Let us look at the retreat from literality in the light of some remarks of George Orwell on Christian apologetic. A Christian correspon-dent wrote to *Tribune* protesting against some sceptical remarks in an earlier issue that "even the most central doctrines of Christian religion don't have to be accepted in a literal sense". This drew the following response from Orwell:

> If you talk to a thoughtful Christian you often find yourself being laughed at for being so ignorant as to suppose that anyone ever took the doctrines of the church literally. These doctrines have, you are told, a quite other meaning which you are too crude to under-stand. [Orwell, 1970, p. 125]

Isn't a similar tactic to be found among Freudian apologists?

Consider some representative dealings with the topics of infan-tile sexuality and the Oedipus complex. "What after all," asks Jonathan Lear "is the Oedipus complex? That he killed his father and married his mother misses the point" (Lear, 1995, p. 24). What is the point then? Something to do with the significance of hidden meanings, thinks Lear. Not much to blush at there. Peter Rudnytsky links the Oedipus complex to Heidegger and reduces the notion of infantile incestuous craving to a "psychoanalytic version of the hermeneutic circle" (Rudnytsky, 1987, pp. 64–65). This is how Stuart Hampshire evades the imputation of paradox in the charge that though he doesn't "really believe in the substantive assertions" of Freudian theory he has "a great reverence" for the theory itself and stands by dream interpretation, free association, etc. After explaining that he does not "believe that the evidence supports the separate propositions which attribute neurosis to this or that feature of the Oedipus Complex . . ." he adds "but then I don't think that you ought to think of the Oedipus Complex in quite such a precise way" (Hampshire, 1983, p. 114). Like the Christian apologists Orwell complained of, Hampshire leaves us in a complete state of bewilderment as to just what it is he does believe. What does he think Freud discovered as to the erotic relation of male children to their mothers and its influence on their later lives? How can he cling to Freudian dream interpretation and yet reject what it is said to have revealed? Do not Orwell's remarks on allegorical Christian apologetic apply as neatly to Hampshire:

> for controversial purposes a sort of handy-pandy game, repeating the articles of the creed in exactly the same terms as his forefathers while defending himself from the charge of superstition by explaining that he is speaking in parables. [Orwell, 1970, p. 125]

Here is a less sophisticated mode of obfuscation than Hampshire's: an analyst recounts his effort to convince Sidney Hook that the Oedipus complex was a reality:

> I asked Hook if he had a son. He did. Was Hook's relationship with his son quite like Mrs. Hook's relation with him. No, the relationship between mother and son was different, more affectionate and less competitive Did Hook know any family where these were absent? No, said Hook. "That is an Oedipus complex" said I. He'd have to think about it, said Hook. Nobody had put it just that way to him. [Kafka, 1998, p. 331]

(What a nice guy Sidney Hook must have been!)

The philosopher Jerome Neu complains of the unfairness of imputing to Freud the claim that the male child has a desire to copulate with his mother. "The sexual relations desired in Oedipal contexts must be understood more broadly" (Neu, 1995, p. 147). How much more broadly? Neu evades the point that however vague the infant's incestuous wishes may be they must be something for which penile amputation would be an appropriate penalty. On several occasions Freud invoked Diderot's dialogue *Rameau's Nephew* to convey his conception of what the infant would do if he had the strength of a grown man: "wring his father's neck and lie with his mother" (Freud, 1916–1917, p. 338; 1931d, p. 251 ;1940, p. 192). This makes it disingenuous to protest, as Neu does, at the imputation of gross genital desires to the child.

Here is another example of how pervasive in our culture is the compulsion to place a construction on familiar Freudian theses that is more seemly and less an affront to plausibility. It is from a distinguished classical scholar, Hugh Lloyd-Jones,

> . . . when Freud says that an infant is in love with his mother he is using not ordinary language but a metalanguage. In the language of ordinary life his statement is absurd . . . [Lloyd-Jones, 1982, pp. 166–167]

Might not a more candid and profitable course, than the bowdlerization of Freud's discoveries, be that counselled by John Ruskin with respect to traditional myths in general?

> . . . it is of the highest importance that you should . . . not efface under the graceful explanation that your cultivated ingenuity may suggest, either an extraordinary event really having taken place or the unquestionable light which it will cast upon the character of the person by whom it was frankly believed. [Ruskin, 1911, p. 5]

When is the unconscious Freudian?

For almost a century the two ideas summing up Freud's monumental discoveries were "sex" and the "unconscious". At first it appears that only one of these survived into centenary celebrations. In fact, closer inspection reveals that neither of them did. Not only did "sex" cease to mean what Freud meant by "sex" but the "unconscious" ceased to mean what Freud meant by the "unconscious", (although in both cases the responsibility is partly Freud's). Nagel writes, "There is now substantive reason to believe in the unconscious and in psychoanalytic explanations which refer to it— reasons of a kind available to Freud" (Nagel, 1994a). Since this is just what is disputed, it is a matter of great moment just how psychoanalytic explanations that refer to the unconscious are to be identified and distinguished from non-psychoanalytic explanations that refer to the unconscious. What I think Freud's critics want to be persuaded of is that there are genuine instances of explanatory successes deploying those notions that are peculiar to Freud and distinguish him from his rivals and predecessors. Thomas Nagel clouds this contrast when he speaks of psychoanalysis as interpreting people by 'by making sense of their point of view.' This sounds more like Carl Rogers or Aaron Beck than Freud. Nagel's terms are just those in which Freud's rivals differentiated their position from his. Nagel has just not given this matter sufficient thought. A few edifying catchphrases like "understanding from within", "vast expansion of psychological insight", etc., are all he offers in the way of analysis. The effect of this is to draw Freud so close to the pre-Freudian humanistic unconscious that it obscures just what it is that Nagel thinks we owe him. Our sense of Nagel's evasiveness is also due to the remoteness of his characterization of Freudian interpretation as "using our own point of view as an imaginative resource" from those instances of Freud's interpretative practice which naturally come to mind. Is what Freud was doing when he decided that Dora wanted to fellate her father and that the Wolf Man wanted to be anally penetrated by his, was using his "own point of view as an imaginative resource?"

Those readers who never nursed any convictions as to the emancipatory power of analytic philosophy will be less dismayed by the obscurity and feebleness of Nagel's arguments on this point than I am. This obscurity may be partly tactical. One sense must be given to Freud's conception of the unconscious to render it genuinely innovatory but another to make it so ubiquitous as to be undeniable. The problem for apologists has been finding something that is both credible and distinctive. If apologists construe the unconscious as just our intermittent ignorance or misjudgment of our motivations without specifying those features thatconfer distinctiveness on Freud's theory of its operations and consequences, they must deal with the objection that this notion of the unconscious is part of pre-Freudian vernacular psychology.

It is the distinction of the Freudian Raymond Fancher (1973) to have persuaded Adolf Grünbaum that there is "some empirical

plausibility in the psychoanalytic theory of defence mechanisms",
e.g., "denial and rationalisation, reaction-formation, projection and
identification" (Grünbaum, 1986, p. 281). Anyone who consults the
pages (217–223) to which Grünbaum expresses his indebtedness
might feel that Grünbaum would not have had to learn of these
mechanisms from Fancher if he had read five good books. Had one
of these good books been *War And Peace*, Grünbaum would have
found the defence "mechanism" of "projection" in Tolstoi's account
of the reflections of the Governor of Moscow before instigating the
lynching of a pacifist who has been apprehended distributing anti-
war literature and is surrounded by a crowd of indignant patriots.

> "There they are—the mob, the dregs of the populace," he said to
> himself . . . "They want a victim" . . . And this idea came into his
> head precisely because he too wanted a scapegoat, an object for his
> wrath. [Tolstoi, 1957, p. 1053]

How much more do we know of this phenomenon when we
have described it as a "mechanism" and called it "projection"?
Might we not have in the so-called mechanisms of psychoanalysis
a scientization of folk psychology rather than an augmentation of
it? Had another of Grünbaum's good books been *Anna Karenina* he
would have found this illustration of what Fancher taught him to
call "denial".

> At first Anna sincerely believed that she was displeased with
> [Vronsky] for daring to pursue her; but . . . having gone to a party
> where she expected to meet him but to which he did not come she
> distinctly realised by the disappointment that overcame her, that
> she had been deceiving herself and that his pursuit was not only
> not distasteful to her, but was the whole interest of her life. [Tolstoi,
> 1965, p. 143]

Here is Nagel's "extended reach of the mind" being anachronis-
tically parodied by Charles Dickens before Freud inaugurated it. In
Great Expectations a character complains of the way in which her
concern for the welfare of a relative has produced "nervous jerkings" in her legs: ". . . nervous jerkings, however are nothing new
to me when I think with anxiety of those I love . . ." Another relative adds supportively: "It is well known that your family feelings

are gradually undermining you to the extent of making one of your legs shorter than the other."

I hope these examples explain why Freud's critics are unimpressed by Nagel's appeal to the ubiquity of "rudimentary Freudianism".

To how much attenuation is Nagel subjecting the Freudian unconscious that he may persuade himself that there is now "substantive reason to believe" in it? In Nagel's sole example a businessman's son was told by an analyst at a dinner party that the reason he fell asleep when listening to the stock market report was connected with his relation to his father. That very night, Nagel tells us, the businessman's son recalled promising his father many years before that he would regularly listen to the stock market report. Putting aside the natural doubts that arise from anecdotal demonstrations of this kind, we must ask, what kind of repression is it that can be overcome merely by the suggestion that it exists? If this is Freudian repression what need is there for analysts to overcome it?

The Freudian unconscious as a flight from disquieting self-revelation

There is, in addition to Freud's own ambiguity, a non-intellectual motive for remaining unclear as to the sense in which Freud's chastening revelations are unconscious. Might we not take comfort in Freud's strong and more distinctive sense of "unconscious"—"totally alien"—so as to avoid too vivid a reminiscence of the paltry egoism and perversity of so much of our ruminative lives? Freud's repression is a mechanism which may be triggered without our collusion or connivance rather than a mnemonic for the recurrent or continuous warding off of unpalatable truths of which we are obscurely aware.

The assumption that mental life, particularly that pertaining to erotic and dismally egoistic fantasizing, is deeply unconscious and alien is one which promises to spare us a lot of squirming and wriggling. What Freud is practising, with our collusion, is a species of exorcism. He took the sting out of our shameful perverse fantasizing through a variety of devices not least of which was the invention of an abstract distancing notation—deviant objects, aims, and sources replacing the concrete, all too vivid, furtive, and shameful life of erotic reverie, thus reducing it to a ghostly ballet of libidinal trends and processes "sportively bombinating" in the alien reaches of the id. An example may suggest how the notion of the unconscious makes our wayward sexuality more tolerable. Which of these admissions is more troubling?

"I have sexual fantasies about close family members."
"My analyst has convinced me that I have an unconscious incestuous interest in close family members."

Though belief in the Freudian unconscious may sometimes have led people to indict themselves for shameful thoughts and desires of which they were strictly unaware. it would even more readily permit them to absolve themselves of shameful thoughts and desires of which they were too disturbingly, if only intermittently, aware, by relegating them to a realm of which they knew nothing. Even so devoted a Freudian as Lionel Trilling could write:

> Psychoanalysis so far from advancing the cause of authenticity actually subverts it in a radical way through the dichotomy it institutes in the mental life, one of whose elements is confined to a mere objective existence, hypothetical into the bargain, for which the subject is not answerable. [Trilling, 1972, pp. 45–46]

Taking the sting out of sexuality

Showalter wrote in her review of Crews that he was helpless to explain why so many intelligent people will concede all of his criticisms and yet refuse to abandon their "general loyalty to Freud". Substitute the old Soviet Union for Freud in this remark and you may have a feeling of *déjà vu*. Andre Malraux once wrote, "just as the Inquisition does not detract from the fundamental dignity of Christianity so the Moscow trials do not detract from the fundamental dignity of communism" (Caute, 1973, p. 181). Could it be some such pattern of argument that underlies Showalter's odd remark? This naturally leads us to ask in what the "fundamental dignity" of psychoanalysis lies once the validity of the charges against it are acknowledged. Some find it in its authorization of their unhappiness: Freud confirms us in our conviction that we are allowed to be unhappy and self-dissatisfied. In fact given our situation it is a wonder we are not more continuously unhappy than we are. Several other sources of this non-negotiable loyalty suggest themselves. Some think that without Freud there would have been no psychotherapy and, of course, if those who are grateful for the help they have received from therapists are convinced that the profession was invented by Freud it is not surprising that they are willing to extenuate any deficiencies in his views or character that have been called to their attention. But Freud's role as "the authority for a new ease in enunciating the sexual fact" (Rieff, 1961, p. 163) is the most common candidate for the gratitude he inspires in so many. (Though Freud insisted repeatedly that his emphasis on sexuality was a source of resistance and disparagement, an early letter to his friend Wilhelm Fliess reveals his better knowledge: "The sexual business attracts people. They all go away impressed and convinced after exclaiming: 'No one has ever asked me that before'" (Masson, 1985, p. 57).

In his book *What Freud Really Said*, David Stafford Clark provides some suggestions as to how this effect, both liberating and tranquillizing, might come about. He quotes Freud breaking off his discussion of sexual deviations with the words "Enough of these horrors", and comments "these things become less horrible if we do what he asks and apply the fruits of the theory of infantile sexuality to their understanding" (Stafford-Clark, 1967, p. 121). An adult sucking a penis looks less depraved (even "innocent" as Freud says) when assimilated to an infant sucking a nipple. It is also Freud's resort to an abstract theoretical vocabulary in his accounts of sexual life that helps to take the sting out of our perversities. Nobody ever fidgeted and swallowed his saliva while reading about the cathexis of deviant aims and objects. Bruno Bettelheim once observed that

> One cannot help but be impressed with much of Freud's wisdom and ingenious selection of technical terms. It is so much easier for the therapist to deal in his mind and feelings with what are called anal experiences, and to talk about them, than it is to deal with what is called "shit". [Bettelheim, 1967, p. 217]

A distinguished novelist who had come to doubt the justification for many of Freud's assertions explains why he nevertheless remained grateful.

Freud reconciled me to much that was baffling in others and, more important, in myself; and if, with a personality as anomalous as my own, I have none the less contrived to have an almost continuously happy life along admittedly austerely narrow lines, I owe it largely to him. [King, 1975, p 105]

One must respect this testimony and just regret that his understandable reticence made it impossible for him to be more explicit as to just what aspect of Freud's writings it was that exerted this beneficent influence. Nevertheless, it is a pity that more of Freud's apologists are not as candid or self-aware as to the personal sources of their attachment and admiration.

Is the human condition hidden from us?

Lear holds that Freud's distinctive contribution to human understanding is the discovery that "'the human soul has depth". Apologists who resort to arguments like Lear's may feel that if they can mount some generic defence of an hermeneutics of human existence then the arguments for dismissing Freud have been met. Although the sentiments Lear imputes to Freud have as much relation to him as the leaders in the *Christian Science Monitor* to the teachings of Mary Baker Eddy I don't want to leave the impression that all that is wrong with Lear's higher hermeneutics of the human condition is that it is not Freud. It is certainly not Freud, whose hermeneutic system is a closed one, but it is not all right either. What grounds are there for believing that there are deep unconscious meanings on whose correct apprehension our felicity depends? Lear, Nagel, and those who, like them, want to replace our "sweating selves" by something more edifying, are suspiciously oblivious of the subliminal appeal of their insistence on "the enigmatic nature of human motivation" (Lear, 1995, p. 22). Why enigmatic? Why not transparently petty, base, and squalid with streaks of nobility and only occasional, anomalous, opacities? Maybe our "sweating selves" is what we mostly are; not much more than that.

Let me sum up. The main reason for judging Freud's apologists evasive is that their unforthcomingness as to how much of what Freud asserted they now reject enables them to avoid explaining how they can persist in extolling a method that had repeatedly ratified theses they now hold to be false.

Whence the "general loyalty" to Freud?
The sweets of evasiveness

We can't say that if Freud had not existed we would have had to invent him, because there are good grounds for suspecting that the familiar indefatigable truth-seeker and disinterested student of the human condition did not exist, and that we did invent him. Someone described the prevailing image of Freud as a mixture of Moses, Maigret, Obi-wan Kenobi, and the Ghost of Christmas Past. This may be too populist a conception for some admirers and these may prefer Jonathan Lear's Freud: "a deep explorer of the human condition, working in a tradition which goes back to Sophocles and which extends through Plato, Saint Augustine and Shakespeare to Proust and Nietzsche". This is highfalutin' stuff which we must somehow reconcile with the Freud who informed Jung at the end of a holiday, "Today I resumed my practice and saw my first batch of nuts again" (McGuire, 1974, p. 359). How did Freud's dealings with his "batch of nuts" extend "the explorations into the human condition" of Plato, Saint Augustine, Shakespeare *et al.* Is not Lear's effusion a product of the same culture that gave us the Kennedys of Camelot? The compulsion to produce celebratory comment, however fanciful, is also illustrated by Edith Kurzweil, an editor of the *Partisan Review*, who speaks in her book of an occasion when "Anna O, relieved of her illness, embraced Freud" (Kurzweil, 1989, pp. 62–63). It makes an engaging picture but nothing like it ever happened, since Anna O was not treated by Freud and never met him. He only heard her story second-hand from Breuer. In spite of this Kurzweil spins a heart-warming story in which Freud allowed Anna O to 'question him' and 'to tell him what she chose to'. Of course, the motivation of Kurzweil's fantasy is transparent and there is a point of view from which it no more matters that Anna O did not embrace a solicitously attentive Freud in therapeutic gratitude than that St Nicholas was not "chubby and plump, a right jolly old elf"—the point of view taken by Elisabeth Roudinesco. In a similar vein, another of Freud's admirers, the novelist,

D. M. Thomas, argued that though the primal scene in the Wolf Man case may never have happened it was "beautiful", which meant that it had "a different, deeper, kind of truth" (Thomas, 1982, p. 45).

Thomas Nagel's observation that Freud has had "an effect much deeper than can be captured by a set of particular hypotheses" (Nagel, 1994, p. 34), and Showalter's talk of "a general loyalty" to Freud, which is nevertheless compatible with acceptance of the objections that Frederick Crews (1995) brought to general notice, reminded me of my own relation to the Catholicism of my boyhood. Although I have been an unbeliever from early youth, I have never lost my attachment to its iconology: the Blessed Mother, the babe in the manger, the annunciation to the shepherds, the magi following the star, the pieta , "Noli me Tangere" etc., etc. And so I feel an inwardness with the indeterminate loyalty of Nagel, Showalter, Hampshire et al. to their obscurely attenuated Freudianism. I can only hope that eventually they will come to deal with their tenderness in a more candid way and so distinguish more firmly between nostalgia and conviction. However, if they choose not to it will be perfectly understandable. Recalcitrant Freudians who have abandoned the distinction between prosaic truth and falsehood, or retreat to some sublime subtext, are reminiscent of the man in one of Freud's jokes whose deafness was diagnosed as brandy-induced. Sure enough, when he stopped drinking brandy his hearing returned. When his physician caught him once again drinking brandy and remonstrated, he produced the quite reasonable justification that although abstention had cured his deafness nothing he had heard was as good as the brandy. So it is with the Freud-infatuated. Nothing they hear from Freud's critics, however subversive of his pretensions, is as good as Freud. I happily concede that I have had nothing to say about Freud as good as the brandy.

Summary

In what precedes I have given reasons for concluding that recent attempts to meet the more radical objections to Freudian theory illustrate a deep-seated partisanship and that the problem this sets us is where the source of this non-negotiable loyalty may lie. Although the phenomenon is no doubt overdetermined, it is suggested that one potent source is its naturalization of negative affect—e.g., guilt, anxiety, frustration, conflict; another lies in its promulgation of an image of our condition that replaces the burden of our disturbing peripheral awareness of our venality and lasciviousness by deeply hidden, profound, and esoteric enterprises. Of course, such theses as to the ulterior motivation of Freudian apologetic are, unlike the inadequacy of the apologetic itself, incapable of demonstration.

References

Bettelheim, B. (1967). *The Empty Fortress.* New York: The Free Press.

Borch-Jacobsen, M. (1996). *Remembering Anna O.* London: Routledge.

Brenner, C. (1968). Classical psychoanalysis. In: D. S. Sills (Ed.), *International Encyclopedia of Unified Science* (pp. 1–11). Macmillan.

Bresnick, A. (1998). Review of Crews' *Unauthorised Freud, Times Literary Supplement,* 30 October.

Caute, D. (1973). *The Fellow Travellers,* London: Weidenfeld & Nicolson.

Chomsky, N. (1971). Review of Skinner's *Freedom and Dignity. New York Review of Books,* 30 December.

Cioffi, F. (1983). Psychoapologetics. *London Review of Books,* 2–15 June.

Cioffi, F. (1998). *Freud and the Question of Pseudoscience.* Chicago: Open Court.

Coolidge, F. L. (1989). Review of *Freud and the Idea of a Pseudo-Science,* by Frank Cioffi. *Choice, 36*(7).

Crews, F. (1995) *The Memory Wars,* New York: New York Review.

Crews, F. (1998). *Unauthorised Freud ,* New York: Viking.

Edelson, M. (1989). *Psychoanalysis: a Theory in Crisis.* Chicago: University of Chicago Press.

Esterson, A. (1993). *Seductive Mirage: An Exploration of the Work of Sigmund Freud,* Chicago: Open Court.

Fancher, R. (1973). *Psychoanalytic Psychology,* London: W. W. Norton.

Forrester, J., & Appignanesi, L. (1992). *Freud's Women.* London: Weidenfeld and Nicolson.

Freud, S. (1909d). Notes upon a case of obsessional neuroses. *S.E., 10:* 155–318. London: Hogarth.

Freud, S. (1916–1917). Introductory lectures. *S.E., 17:* 9–496. London: Hogarth.

Freud, S. (1931). The expert opinion in the Halsmann case. *S.E., 21*. London: Hogarth.

Freud, S. (1940). An outline of psychoanalysis. *S.E., 23*. London: Hogarth.

Grünbaum, A. (1986). Author's response. *The Behavioural and Brain Sciences, 9*: 281.

Hacking, I. (1995). *Rewriting the Soul*. Princeton, NJ: Princeton University Press.

Hampshire, S. (1983). Notions of the unconscious mind. In: J. Miller (Ed.), *States of Mind* (pp. 100–115). London: British Broadcasting Corporation.

Hopkins, J. (1983). Psychoapologetics. *London Review of Books*. 5(12) July: 7–20.

Hug-Hellmuth, H. (1919). *A Study of the Mental Life of the Child* (also known as *A Young Girl's Diary*) Washington: Nervous and Mental Disease Publishing.

Kafka, E. (1998). Review of Fred Crews' (Ed.), *Unauthorised Freud*. *Psychoanalytic Quarterly, LXVIII(2)*: 333–334.

King, F. (1975). Francis King. In: F. Raphael (Ed.), *Bookmarks* (103–107). London: Jonathan Cape.

Kurzweil, E. (1989). *The Freudians: A Comparative Perspective*. New Haven, CT: Yale University Press.

Lear, J. (1995). The shrink is in. *New Republic*, 25 December: 18–25.

Lear, J. (1996). Review of Fred Crews', *The Memory Wars. Journal of the American Psychoanalytic Association, 44*(2): 580–587.

Lloyd-Jones, H. (1982). *Blood for the Ghosts*. London: Duckworth.

Macaulay, T. B. (1961). *Critical and Historical Essays, Volume Two*. London: J. M. Dent.

Masson, J. (1985). *The Complete Letters of Sigmund Freud to Wilhelm Fliess*. Cambridge, MA: The Belknap Press.

McGuire, W. (Ed.) (1974). *The Freud/Jung Letters*. London: Hogarth.

Miller, A. (1988). *Timebends*. London: Methuen.

Moll, A. (1897). *Untersuchengen uber die Libido sexualis*. Berlin: Fischer.

Moll, A. (1909). *Das Sexualebens des Kindes*. Berlin: H. Walther.

Nagel, T. (1994). Review of *The Mind and its Depths*, by Richard Wollheim. *New York Review of Books*. 12 May: 34–36.

Nagel, T. (1994). Review of *Freud and His Critics*, by Paul Robinson. *New York Review of Books*. 11 August: 56.

Neu, J. (1995). "Does the Professor talk to God?": Learning from Little Hans. *Philosophy, Psychiatry & Psychology, 2*(2):

Orwell, G. (1970). *The Collected Essays, Journalism and Letters of George Orwell 1943–5*, Volume 9. Harmondsworth: Penguin.

Rieff, P. (1961). *The Mind of the Moralist*. Garden City, New York: Doubleday.

Rudnytsky, P. (1987). *Freud and Oedipus*. New York: Columbia University Press.

Ruskin, J. (1911). *Queen of the Air*. London: George Allen & Unwin.

Schimek, J. (1987). Fact and fantasy in the seduction theory: an historical review. *Journal of the American Psychoanalytic Association*, 35: 937–965.

Showalter, E. (1997). Review of Fred Crews' *The Memory Wars*, The *Guardian*, 12 June.

Stafford-Clark, D. (1967). *What Freud Really Said*. London: Macdonald.

Sulloway, F. (1979). *Freud, Biologist of the Mind*. London: Andre Deutsch.

Thomas, D. M. (1982). Review of Karin Obholzer, *The Wolfman: Sixty Years On*. *Sunday Times* (London). 14 November.

Tolstoi, L. (1965) [1871]. *Anna Karenina*. Harmondsworth: Penguin.

Tolstoi, L. (1957). *War and Peace, Volume Two*. Harmondsworth: Penguin.

Trilling, L. (1972). *Sincerity and Authenticity*. London: Oxford University Press.

INDEX